INTERASIAN INTIMACIES ACROSS RACE, RELIGION, AND COLONIALISM

INTERASIAN INTIMACIES ACROSS RACE, RELIGION, AND COLONIALISM

Chie Ikeya

SOUTHEAST ASIA PROGRAM PUBLICATIONS
AN IMPRINT OF CORNELL UNIVERSITY PRESS
Ithaca and London

First published 2024 by Cornell University Press

Library of Congress Cataloging-in-Publication Data

Names: Ikeya, Chie, author.
Title: InterAsian intimacies across race, religion, and colonialism / Chie Ikeya.
Description: Ithaca : Southeast Asia Program Publications, an imprint of Cornell University Press, 2024. | Includes bibliographical references and index.
Identifiers: LCCN 2024010374 (print) | LCCN 2024010375 (ebook) | ISBN 9781501777134 (hardcover) | ISBN 9781501777141 (paperback) | ISBN 9781501777158 (pdf) | ISBN 9781501777165 (epub)
Subjects: LCSH: Intermarriage—Social aspects—Burma. | Conversion—Social aspects—Burma. | Intermarriage—Political aspects—Burma. | Conversion—Political aspects—Burma. | Belonging (Social psychology)—Burma—History. | Burma—Colonial influence—History.
Classification: LCC HQ1031 .I349 2024 (print) | LCC HQ1031 (ebook) | DDC 306.8409591—dc23/eng/20240320
LC record available at https://lccn.loc.gov/2024010374
LC ebook record available at https://lccn.loc.gov/2024010375

This book is dedicated to Auntie Rosie and Mio
and to the memory of Uncle Mohan (1916–2005)

Contents

PREFACE AND ACKNOWLEDGMENTS

I never met any of my grandparents. They passed away long before I was born. Or so I was told growing up. As it turned out, my maternal grandfather, Albert Maitland Hood, was alive and well when I was born. I even met him in the summer of 1984, when I visited Burma for the first time. To this day, it takes a photo of my grandfather sitting with my brother, taken at a restaurant in Rangoon that year, to assuage my incredulity. Did we really meet our grandfather? No one—not our mother, our father, nor our aunts, uncles, and cousins in Burma—had told us that he was our grandfather. He died before we returned to Burma in 1987. Only many years later would we find out the truth.

My grandfather left my grandmother, Daw Thein Yin, for another woman while she was pregnant with my mother. My mother's four older siblings had known their father growing up and lived a relatively comfortable life. My mother's experience of childhood, in contrast, had been both materially and emotionally austere. Abandoned by her husband and deprived of his financial support, my grandmother raised my mother all on her own, selling off all the land and jewelry that she possessed, piece by piece, over the next eighteen or so years. When she was hospitalized for complications due to diabetes, her eldest daughter, Phyllis, sold her own jewelry to pay for the hospital bills.

My grandfather would not even grant his first wife her dying wish. Though he had been cruel to her, she still had affections for him. She had forgiven him and, before she died, wanted to see him. He never came, my mother recalls bitterly.

My mother was nineteen years old and a student at Rangoon University when my grandmother died in her arms. I imagine that it broke my mother. And when she landed in the clinic of the renowned cardiologist Dr. Mohan in the early 1970s for heart palpitations, she turned to him and his wife, Dr. Hnin Yee, for emotional as much as physical healing. In them, she found a pair of surrogate parents. And when my family moved to Burma in 1987, they became my surrogate grandparents.

We would spend almost every weekend in the home of "Uncle Mohan" and "Auntie Rosie," as we called them. Whenever possible, I would cajole my parents into letting me spend the night with my favorite "elder sister," Ma Mona. Ma Mona standing in the kitchen and preparing my breakfast in the morning—it is one of my clearest and fondest childhood memories. I have another memory of my sleepovers at the Mohans': the entire family kneeling on the floor of Uncle Mohan and Aunt Rosie's bedroom, their hands clasped on the bed in prayer. This is how I often found them when I awoke in the morning and walked down the hallway in search of Ma Mona.

I had assumed at the time, and long after, that Auntie Rosie was the source of the family's Christian faith. It had not occurred to me that she was a Christian convert. It certainly never crossed my mind that she became Christian only after she married Uncle Mohan. In my childish mind, Christianity was the religion of the *bo* ("Europeans" or "Anglos" in Burmese), not of Indian people like Uncle Mohan, just as Buddhism was the religion of the Burmese. I knew that Auntie Rosie, like my mother, was of *bo* descent and presumed that she had been raised Christian.

My assumptions about Auntie Rosie's family genealogy and my conflation of religion, race, and nationality were upended when, in my late teens, I asked her for the first time about her *bo* heritage. She vaguely remembered that her ancestors went by the name of "De Vries." She thought that they might have been Dutch. But she did not become Christian until relatively recently. Her parents were Muslim, as were her siblings, except for those who had, like her, become Buddhist or Christian as adults. She had not only *bo* ancestors and Burmese ancestors but also Arab ones, she explained. I was utterly confused. And intrigued.

I was not the first to be so intrigued. Ma Mona recalls that she and her sister Ma May Htwe tried to learn about their lineage. "Don't be nosy" (*sat su de*), responded their maternal grandmother Daw Helen May, or Mummy Gyi ("Great Mummy"), as she was affectionately known. We will never know why she rebuffed her granddaughters' inquiry. Perhaps she thought her granddaughters had an overly inquisitive mind. Or perhaps it was the nature of the query that troubled Mummy Gyi. Were there personal memories or family secrets that she was unwilling to expose? Or was she discomfited by a query to which she had no straightforward answer?

Even the great matriarch could not have offered a straightforward answer to the deceptively simple question. For theirs was a dizzyingly heterogeneous family, at once ordinary and extraordinary in colonial and postcolonial Burma, as I discovered.

I cannot express in words how profoundly indebted I am—and this book is—to Auntie Rosie, Ma Mona, Ko Timmy, Ko Maung, and Ma Htwe. Their openness and generosity in sharing their memories, as well as their family library of photographs and memorabilia, have sustained my writing over many years. As only they know, they have been my refuge for as long as I can remember. I thank them for entrusting me to tell their family history and encouraging me to come to terms with my own messy family/history.

Teresa Hood, alias Daw Mya Kay Thee, and Ikeya Osamu, alias U San Min, have gifted me a lifetime of support and storytelling. Their stories—so lively, painful, and riotous—have taught me to recognize how remarkable are ordinary people and lives that make history but do not make entry into History. Suzy Lyon has inspired and sustained me in times of normalcy and crisis. Ikeya Hitoshi and Mayako did the heavy lifting of caring for our father when he was diagnosed with cancer in 2021 and then for our mother when she managed to leave Myanmar, ravaged by the military coup and the pandemic. I admire and appreciate the loving compassion and understanding of these family members.

Christian and Mio are my most constant critics and champions. *Gokurō samadesu.* Thank you for your indulgence and wonderfully abundant affection.

Daw Htay cared for Mio as though she was her own grandchild at a critical moment that made possible this book's birth. My dear friends and interlocutors—Wendy Fu, Asher Ghertner, Suzy Kim, Rick Lee, Preetha Mani, Aleena Pitisant, Wan Kiatkanid Pongpanich, Isaac Trapkus, and Wai Sann Thi—provided much needed wisdom, humor, and support while this book gestated. I could not have pulled this off without you.

Thank you to the many students, faculty, and staff who invited me to share my progress on the book, as well as colleagues and friends who participated in panels, symposia, workshops, and conversations. Special thanks to Christoph Emmrich, Chiara Formichi, Niklas Foxeus, Erik Harms, Seth Koven, Shobna Nijhawan, Thomas Patton, and Guo-Quan Seng. Parts of this book have been presented at Brown University, City University of Hong Kong, Columbia University, Cornell University, KITLV / Royal Netherlands Institute of Southeast Asian and Caribbean Studies, Kyoto University, MOMA, National University of Singapore, Northern Illinois University, Rutgers University–New Brunswick, University of Michigan, University of Toronto, Yale University, Stockholm University, and the Royal Swedish Academy of Letters. Various sections of chapters 2, 3, and 4 were published in earlier versions in the following journal and books and are reworked and reprinted with permission here: "Belonging across Religion, Race, and Nation in Burma-Myanmar," in *The Palgrave International*

Handbook of Mixed Racial and Ethnic Classification, edited by Zarine L. Rocha and Peter J. Aspinall (London: Palgrave Macmillan, 2020), 757–778; "Transcultural Intimacies in British Burma and the Straits Settlements: A History of Belonging, Difference, and Empire," in *Belonging Across the Bay of Bengal: Religious Rites, Colonial Migrations, National Rights*, edited by Michael Laffan (London: Bloomsbury, 2017), 117–138; "Colonial Intimacies in Comparative Perspective: Intermarriage, Law, and Cultural Difference in British Burma," special issue, *Journal of Colonialism and Colonial History* 14, no. 1 (Spring 2013). The feedback I received in these different contexts has been and remains invaluable.

Barbara Andaya, Temma Kaplan, Tamara Loos, and Bonnie Smith read iterations of this work at various stages. I thank them for their limitless generosity, unfaltering encouragement, and much more.

Dr. Hlaing Hlaing Gyi, the late Dr. Myo Myint, Daw San San May, Dr. Than Yin Mar, and U Thaw Kaung provided assistance with archival research in Myanmar and the United Kingdom, for which I am deeply grateful.

I owe thanks to many others, including students, colleagues, and friends from my days at the National University of Singapore, Center for Southeast Asian Studies at Kyoto University, and Rutgers University–New Brunswick, my institutional home since 2012: Jeremy Arnold, Shaun Armstead, Tuna Artun, Maitrii Aung-Thwin, Mia Bay, the late Rudy Bell, Allastair Bellany, Tiffany Berg, Dale M. Booth, Aurore Candier, Shikha Chakraborty, Sylvia Chan-Malik, Indrani Chatterjee, Betul Cihan, Paul Clemens, Barbara Cooper, Belinda Davis, Kayo Denda, Leah DeVun, Melissa Feinberg, Annie Isabel Fukushima, Nadia Guessous, Sumit Guha, Douglas Kammen, Paul Hanebrink, Hayami Yoko, Jackie and Masao Imamura, Allan Isaac, Jennifer Jones, Toby Jones, Vishal Kamath, Samantha Kelly, Eri Kitada, Kojima Takahiro, Kyozuka Maiko, Bo Bo Lansin, Matthew Leonaggeo, Oiyan Liu, Johan Mathew, Jim Masschaele, Matt Matsuda, Jennifer Mittlestadt, Maznah Binti Mohamad, Nakanishi Yoshi, Anjali Nerlekar, Nyi Nyi Kyaw, Juno Salazar Parreñas, Sara Perryman, John Phan, Catherine Raymond, Joanna Regulska, Anuja Rivera, Dawn Ruskai, Johan Saravanamuttu, Meheli Sen, Tansen Sen, Arlene Stein, Michelle Stephens, Julie Stephens, Suriani Suratman, Judith Surkis, Michelle Tan, Sarah Tobias, Cami Townsend, Mika Toyota, Alicia Turner, Peter Vail, Candace Walcott-Shepherd, Thongchai Winitchakul, Mabel Wong, Xun Liu, Reiko Yamagishi, Carla Yanni, and Faizah Zakaria. I cherish their wit, camaraderie, and mentorship. I am especially thankful to the faculty and students in the field of women's and gender history/studies at Rutgers University who have enriched this book in innumerable ways.

At Cornell University Press, Sarah E. M. Grossman has been an exemplary editor. Jacqulyn Teoh, Jennifer Savran Kelly, Michelle Scott, and the marketing team deserve special thanks for moving the production process forward. I deeply appreciated the engaged and generous comments by the two anonymous readers. They pushed me to both refine and amplify my arguments.

Finally, I thank the institutions that supported the research for this book in the form of grants and fellowships: the Center for Southeast Asian Studies at Kyoto University, Japan Foundation, National Endowment for the Humanities, National University of Singapore, and Rutgers University.

The imperfections of this book are all mine.

Note on Terms, Names, Transliteration, and Translation

Burmese is used to refer to the language or to a person or people in general of Burma or Myanmar, whereas Burman or Bamar is used to refer to the majority ethnic group in the country. I refer to the country as "Myanmar" for the post-1988 period and "Burma" for the pre-1988 period. There are no surnames in the country, and therefore Burmese names appear in their full form at every occurrence in the book. In the bibliography, Burmese names have been alphabetized by the first letter of the first syllable of the name. Where appropriate, honorifics such as "Daw" and "U" have been added to names, but these prefixes do not affect alphabetization nor appear in the bibliography. Occasionally, some Burmese language sources have both an English and Burmese title; in these cases, the original English title has been retained. In citing Burmese-language sources and transliterating Burmese text, I follow the Romanization system based on the BGN/PCGN 1970 agreement. The names of well-known Burmese people and places have been cited according to the most commonly used English spelling.

When writing Japanese names, I follow the Japanese practice of placing the surname first, followed by the given name. I transliterate Japanese-language words using the modified Hepburn system. The only exception is with widely recognized names like Tokyo and Osaka.

Any unattributed translations from Burmese and Japanese sources are my own.

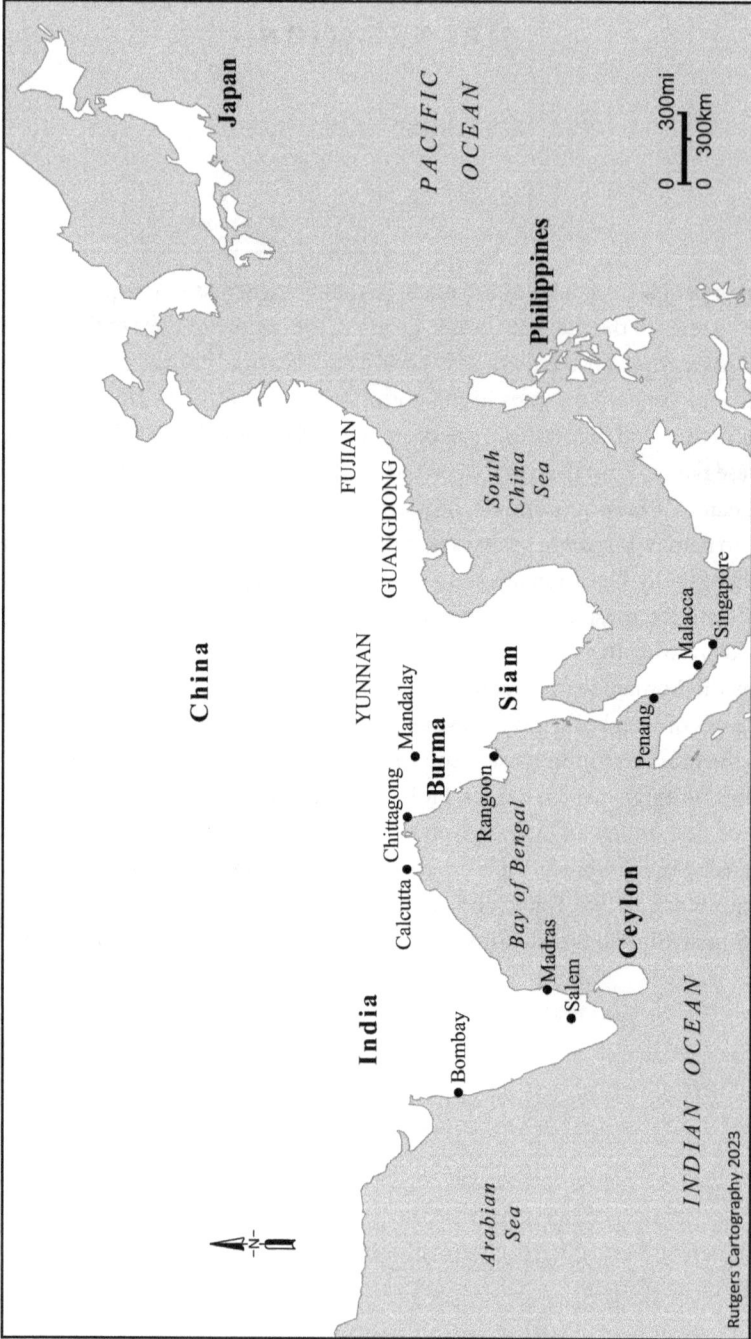

MAP 1. Asia, from the Arabian Sea to the Pacific Ocean.

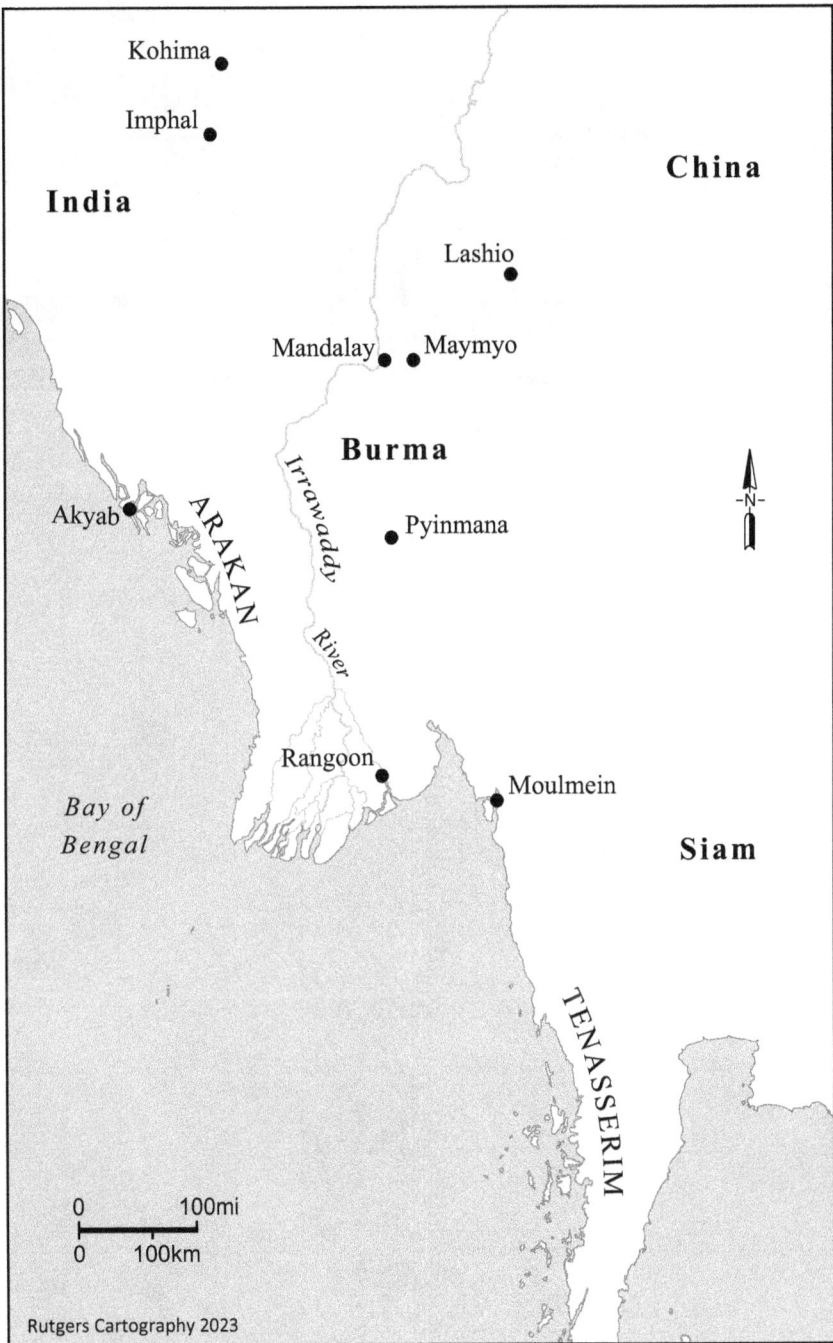

Map 2. Colonial Burma.

Introduction

When, in the late 1910s, Ahmed Meah returned to Rangoon from attending the Calcutta Medical College, his mother, Ma Galay, expected her youngest son to help her manage the thriving family property business as his four siblings had done and marry the nice Muslim woman she had chosen for him. Ahmed did neither. He opened his own medical practice and eloped with Helen May, the Baptist nurse with whom he worked. Ma Galay never imagined that her ordinarily obliging son would defy her to marry a Christian, let alone the orphaned child of an Anglo father and a Karen mother. Her late husband, a Persian merchant and a *syed*—a descendant of the Prophet through Fatimah—who had served Burma's last royal family, must be turning in his grave, she thought.

In truth, Ma Galay had more in common with Helen than she cared to admit, not least in her own mixed lineage and minority status as a Muslim Mon-Arab woman in a predominantly Buddhist Burman society. Nevertheless, and even though Helen converted to Islam, Ma Galay disowned Ahmed. Decades later, perhaps Helen considered doing the same to her daughter Rosie Hnin Yee when she married the Indian émigré and Christian convert Rajagopal Pondicherry Mohanarajan without the approval of her parents. But Helen did not. She of all people knew that their family descended from many generations of intermarriage and conversion. Rosie was following in the footsteps of her forebears.

Families with unruly ties and genealogies such as those of Ma Galay, Helen, and Rosie were prevalent in nineteenth- and twentieth-century Burma. Under British (1826–1942, 1945–1947) and Japanese (1942–1945) colonial rule, Burma became a destination for millions of people from other parts of Asia, from northwest India to Japan, turning the colonial capital Rangoon into one of the busiest ports for immigration in the world. They consisted of middling classes of professionals who worked for the government and private companies as clerks, accountants, doctors, and hospital assistants, as was the case for Helen's father, Alexander Joseph Defries. They were also traders like Ahmed's father, who belonged to a semiofficial merchant class that allied itself with the Burmese royal family or the British colonial administration—at times both— to act as the fiscal agents for the ruling, official class in return for patronage and concessions. Many among the fifteen million who left the Indian subcontinent for Burma between 1834 and 1930 were indentured "coolie" laborers who were employed in Burma's rice fields, mills, rubber plantations, factories, and docks.[1] During World War II, nearly three hundred thousand Japanese soldiers, imperial personnel, and conscripts from Japan's colonies landed on Burmese soil. By contrast, during the entire British colonial period for which we have census data (1872–1941), there were fewer than sixty thousand Europeans in Burma.[2]

These immense human movements included women like Mohanarajan's mother, Indalamar Padmavati Naidu, a young schoolteacher and widow who left Salem, India, for Rangoon with her nine children in search of a better life. For the first time in history, a steady stream of women from India, China, and Japan began migrating to Burma at the turn of the twentieth century. Historians have indeed maintained that this unprecedented rise in female migration from other parts of Asia sounded the death knell for intermarriage and assimilation in Southeast Asian societies. "When, around the turn of the century, female immigration took on significant proportions," explained a pioneering scholar of overseas Chinese communities in Southeast Asia, "an increasing number of immigrant men no longer found it necessary to bring culturally alien women into their homes."[3]

Yet colonial labor and employment policies ensured that migration to Burma remained a male preserve. Few migrants could afford to pay their own passage, and most incurred debt prior to arrival in their destination, from formal indenture to informal debt in the form of advances for expenses from recruitment agents, labor brokers, employers, or relatives. The price of migration was pronounced for women, whose wages were depressed on the presumption that female labor was of inferior productivity and quality.[4] Because women were ineligible for government employment (even though the policy of "sex disqualification," as it was known, had been abolished in the metropole), they had limited prospect for upward mobility in employment. These conditions discouraged women from migrating and male migrant workers from bringing their spouses and children. As a consequence, the proportion of women born in the Indian subcontinent to their male counterpart steadily decreased over the years, from 1:4 in 1881 to 1:6 in 1911, hovering at the low ratio in subsequent decades (table 0.1). The ratio of China-born women to men increased but not more than 1:3 (in 1921). The only migrant population that bucked this trend was the Japanese. Japan-born women in Burma outnumbered their male counterpart until the decennial government census of 1931.

Disproportionately male, Asian migrants forged intimate relationships with Burmese women within and outside the legally and formally recognized institution of marriage. Over the course of the twentieth century, these relationships became flashpoints for far-reaching legislative reforms and Buddhist revivalist, feminist, and nationalist campaigns despite continual insistence by British authorities that the Burmese held neither religious nor legal objections to intermarriage. Mohanarajan's arrival in Burma in the 1920s coincided with mounting questions in the judiciary, legislature, and popular press about whether to restrict the ability of Burmese women to intermarry or convert. By the time he was a student at Rangoon University, government and public opinion had reached a rare consensus: the intermarriage and conversion of Burmese women was an underlying cause of the major upheavals of the period, including the territorial and administrative separation of Burma from India in 1937 and the "anti-Indian riots" of 1938, the most spectacular incidence of communal violence in colonial Burma.

In a distinctly gendered dynamic, no attempts were made to govern the spousal or religious choice of Burmese men. Only in the case of Burmese women was intermarriage presumed to lead inexorably to conversion. Only in the case of Burmese women was intermarriage equated with treason. A Burmese woman, but not a Burmese man, who intermarried was considered an infidel and traitor who had betrayed her own religion, race, and nation. It has remained so ever since.

Combining archival research in Burmese, Japanese, and English sources with the family history of the Meah-Mohans, I explore how and why intermarriage and conversion turned into matters of imperial, national, and communal crisis that justified interdiction and violence. This is an unchronicled history that threatens prevailing paradigms that have structured understandings of intimacy under colonialism and how it ought to be studied. This book elucidates a history that has been obscured by the hegemony of *métissage* (or *metijaze*), the sexual and cultural mixing of Europeans and Indigenous peoples,

Table 0.1 Populations in Burma by Birthplace, 1881–1931

	BORN IN INDIA		BORN IN CHINA		BORN IN JAPAN		BORN IN ENGLAND (INCL. WALES AND SCOTLAND)		POPULATION IN BURMA	
	MALE	FEMALE	MALE	FEMALE	MALE	FEMALE	MALE	FEMALE	MALE	FEMALE
1881	146,883	35,865	10,449	865	5	6	4,415	324	1,991,005	1,745,766
1891	233,398	47,321	20,423	2,637	20	49	5,904	665	3,879,183	3,729,369
1901	354,061	61,892	38,063	5,265	24	76	4,876	563	5,282,408	5,081,205
1911	423,169	70,530	51,783	10,395	310	356	5,233	912	6,183,494	5,931,723
1921	486,799	85,953	76,301	26,043	223	226	4,498	2,606	6,735,518	6,433,588
1931	510,207	95,092	70,904	18,635	411	159	4,784	1,340	7,480,676	7,166,821

Source: Compiled from *Census of British Burma*, 1881, and *Census of India*, 1891–1931.

in narratives of colonial encounters that have delimited intimacy as necessarily involving white, European subjects. InterAsian intimacies have been far more pivotal to the historical developments that have defined the nineteenth and twentieth centuries—colonialism, migration, racism, religious revivalism, feminism, and nationalism—than acknowledged by scholarship. The book illuminates the expansive range of intimate transactions and transgressions generated by shifting imperial political economies that mobilized people across far-flung spaces and the kinds of government schemes and organized movements that sought to control them. In so doing, I join scholars who have called attention to the history of obfuscated affinities among variously enslaved, colonized, indentured, and racialized people—Indigenous, Black, and Asian—brought into proximity by concurrent and intersecting processes of transatlantic and transpacific slave trade, European liberalism, settler colonialism, and Asian labor migration to the Americas.[5]

As my formulation "interAsian intimacies" signals, however, the foci of the book are not transoceanic connections but transregional ones. The primary destination for Asian migration in the nineteenth and twentieth centuries was not the Americas but Southeast Asia, a region that fell under European and US colonial rule in a piecemeal fashion starting in the sixteenth century. This regional mobility of Asians has been the focus of much recent scholarship on transnational histories of Asia that investigates flows and exchanges of an intermediate scale, smaller, multidirectional, and more continuous than the kind that have been the subject of the global scale and the East-West axis of analysis.[6] *InterAsian Intimacies* stands in common cause with this emergent body of historical scholarship. But it shares neither its impulse to recuperate Asia as a cosmopolitan zone of connectivity nor its focus on the labor and capital of men at the expense of those of women.[7] Rather, I am concerned with comprehending how interAsian intimacies made religious and racial difference matter and understanding how women like Ma Galay, Helen May, and Rosie, who found themselves at the center of this unfolding process, remade their lives and lifeworld.

Though frequently interpreted as correlating with religious and racial tolerance or indexing assimilation, intermarriage and conversion were, instead, precisely how people in Burma came to know and care about what it meant to be—or not to be—*buddha batha bama amyo*, "the Burmese Buddhist kind." A distinctly twentieth-century nomenclature, it conjoined the term *buddha batha* (literally "the language of the Buddha"), which was itself a nineteenth-century addition to the Burmese lexicon, and the phrase *bama amyo*, meaning "Burman" or "Burmese lineage and race," to name and delineate a Burmese Buddhist community of people ostensibly united by common heritage.[8]

Wielded by those who self-identified as "the Burmese Buddhist kind" not only as a reference to the religious and racial majority population in the country but as a synonym for "natives," "sons of the soil," and "insiders," buddha batha bama amyo was as much an expression of "community" as of a form of knowledge and power.

The more legal, religious, and political authorities in Burma discussed the intermarriage and conversion of Burmese women, the more certain they became in their knowledge of what set the Burmese Buddhist apart from its constitutive others, the amyo gya ("other kinds"). This development, what I call "Burmese Buddhist exceptionalism," was undergirded by a logic of reduction and conflation. On the one hand, Buddhism, Islam, Hinduism, Confucianism, and so forth were reduced to a set of fundamentals: a Muslim man could unilaterally divorce his wife while a Buddhist man could not; a Buddhist widow could remarry while a Hindu one could not; Buddhist children were entitled to inheritance regardless of sex while Confucians followed the rule of primogeniture; all amyo gya, of whatever religion, observed patrilineal kinship structures while bilateral descent was the norm among the Burmese Buddhist; and the former practiced endogamy and proscribed marriage across caste, clan, and sect while the latter imposed neither religious nor legal prohibition on exogamy.

On the other hand, the debates on intermarriage and conversion collapsed and confused religious affiliation, sexual desires, patriarchal rights, and legal status in a process, which Judith Surkis has termed the "corporealization of law," that "wed together faith and family law, religion and sex."[9] Indian Muslim men were polygamous; Indian Hindu men were bigamous; Japanese and Chinese men alike had concubines, and for that matter, so did European men who kept mistresses. The difference was that the latter were committing adultery—a criminal act—whereas polygyny and concubinage were licensed by religious laws and customs among the Chinese, Indian, and Japanese. In fact, this was also the case among the Burmese Buddhist. By glossing over this inconvenient truth, Burmese Buddhist men were idealized as uniquely monogamous, companionate, and respectful of the conjugal rights of women while sexual and moral degeneracy were ascribed to the amyo gya. On this basis, Burmese Buddhist women were mandated to couple with Burmese Buddhist men and repudiate amyo gya husbands.

Importantly, it was interAsian intimacies, not the familiar religion, race, and gender coupling of European Christian men and Indigenous non-Christian women, that prompted lawsuits, legislative impasses, literary production, and media discourse. The most vociferous critics of intermarriage and conversion were not colonial authorities or European or Japanese expatriates but those who self-identified as buddha batha bama amyo. The amyo gya whom they most routinely accused of enticing young Burmese women to consent to sex, conversion, and concubinage under the cover of love were Indians, Chinese, and, during World War II and its immediate aftermath, the Japanese.

The persecution of the Rohingya, a minority Muslim ethnic group, as "Bengali terrorists" waging "love jihad," an alleged conspiracy to forcibly convert unsuspecting women to Islam through rape and duplicitous marriage, is only the most recent iteration of this alarmist imagination of the Burmese Buddhist as an exceptional community perennially imperiled by degenerate foreigners. It has, now as in the past, served to authorize eugenicist projects aimed at consigning Others to second-class status in Burma and controlling the sexual and reproductive conduct of women in Burma. Put differently, interAsian marriage and conversion were the grounds upon which the intimate frontiers of the Burmese nation—its innermost sanctum and its most penetrable borders—were constituted.

Burma is not an exception. Those whose intimate lives and selves have been deemed public concerns across Southeast Asia have been by and large Asian Others: Muslims in the case of Buddhist majority nations, such as Thailand, as in Burma; Indian or Arab Muslims (as opposed to Malay Muslims) in the case of majority Muslim nations, such as Malaysia and Indonesia; the Chinese across the board; and the native-born descendants, of mixed heritage and otherwise, of these variously othered peoples. The fear of the intimate exploitation and violation of presumptively vulnerable women by these Asian Others and through intermarriage and conversion has allowed governments and nationalists in the region to subject their minoritized populations to both mundane and exceptional forms of violence and to politicize the sexual and reproductive choices of women under the guise of protecting them from Asian Others. All the while, they declare themselves liberal, multicultural societies that, unlike neighboring countries in South Asia and East Asia, oppress neither their women nor their racial and religious minorities.

This book offers a new framework for rethinking how we chart the history of belonging and how it was defined and demarcated in the crucible of imperialist and nationalist formations. The advantage of interAsian intimacies as a paradigm is not limited to the recovery of occluded histories of intimacy. Like intersectionality, such an interpretation allows scholars to scrutinize the shifting articulations of different registers of power—religion, race, lineage, and nation—that may appear to be fixed, stable, and discrete and yet are historically encompassed by the polysemic referent "Asian." It calls into question the primacy of concepts and categories, such as creole, métis, and Eurasian, derived from histories of relationships centered on whiteness that haunt the scholarship on colonial intimacies. It challenges the scholar to unravel the Eurocentric bourgeois ideology of intimacy as sexual and romantic relationships in the "private" domain of the couple and to grasp the linkages and slippages between different forms of intimacy implied by the interwoven theories of intermarriage and conversion this book explores.

Métissage

The proliferation of studies of gender, intimacy, and colonialism began as a rejoinder by feminist historians to scholarship that wrote women out of the history of European empires.[10] As their work has shown, the putatively private sexual, affective, and reproductive relations of European men with Indigenous women and, subsequently, métis, creole, or Eurasian native-born women formed the backbone of racist, heteropatriarchal regimes of domination in imperial and national contexts.[11] According to what has become a standard interpretation, these women at first accrued wealth, prestige, and power in exchange for their intimate labor as brokers and companions who provided comforts of domesticity as well as access to markets, land, and networks of patronage to European men. This intimate infrastructure of early European colonial incursions followed an established pattern of "temporary marriages" in the case of southern Asia, especially its commercial centers, whereby an itinerant trader formed "a sexual relationship with a local woman who would act as his wife and commercial partner for as long as required."[12]

This ancien régime of intermarriage and conversion—and cultural amalgamations, creole accommodations, and hybrid identities—met its demise in the era of "high" or "new" imperialism (c. 1870–1914), when more than 80 percent of the world came under the control of a handful of European imperial powers. It was not just the borders and boundaries of colonial territories that were redrawn at this time but the line between the colonizer and the colonized and the rules that governed relations across this divide.

The so-called problem of métissage authorized colonial and metropolitan governments to engage in these adjustments. Colonial policies restricting European women from residing in the colonies were relaxed; white mistresses and their white children displaced native-born women and Eurasian children. Even as those formerly deemed beyond the pale of "whiteness" like Jews, southern Europeans, or the Japanese achieved recognition as racially white, European women in the metropole and colony forfeited their national and civil status as European upon marriage to a man of a colonized or subject race. The 1914 British Nationality and Status of Aliens Act exemplified the government attempt to restrict métissage among British women. It deprived British women who married an "alien" of their British nationality.[13] No such penalties were placed on British men.[14]

Even without such laws, British women were penalized for métissage. British officials, politicians, academics, and the press advised British women against marrying Asian or African men and demanded the enactment of anti-miscegenation laws similar to those in South Africa at the time. They censured British women in métissage as low-class and morally bereft and treated their children as social pariahs. Such women were understood to have abandoned their duty as the mothers of nations and, therefore, were unentitled to Britishness and citizenship.[15] Paradoxically, the women who took up the call to serve as moral guardians of the British race, family, and nation were vilified by colonial officials as not only "the true bearers of racist beliefs but also hard-line operatives"[16] who jealously policed contact between Europeans and colonized peoples. They were scapegoated for the racist intimate infrastructures of colonialism over which they had no control.

Meanwhile, Eurasians in the colonies were denied access to top-tier education, career opportunities, and membership in European-only churches and clubs, ensuring that that they had little choice but to form a class of second-order Europeans, perceived as inferior to "pure-bred" Europeans but superior to the native population. Not coincidentally, "Eurasian" was one of the rare categories of mixed or multiple affiliation used in the colonial census. It served as both a signifier and a reminder of the insurmountable difference between the ruler and the ruled. As children, Eurasians were removed from their native-born mothers and placed in orphanages for Eurasians or sent "back home" to the metropole to be raised in boarding schools and by their paternal relatives. High imperialism left in its wake broken families, mothers, and genealogies.[17]

Métissage did not erase so much as produce distinctions between colonizer and colonized. While construed as a threat to the colonial political and social order that endangered the religious, racial, and cultural integrity of presumptively primordial communities (e.g., European, white, Christian), métissage was the very phenomenon through which colonial and metropolitan governments improvised their tactics of domination and regulated the differential distribution of rights and responsibilities.

This narrative of the decline of métissage throughout European empires continues to be regarded as paradigmatic of the history of intermarriage and conversion under colonialism tout court, even in the context of Asia where métissage was numerically insignificant relative to interAsian intimacies. It is as though Asians were people without intimacy, except when they came into contact with European colonials and expatriates. This is a paradigm of colonial intercourse that unwittingly reproduces a possessive, imperialistic calculus of intimacy that constituted the bourgeois conjugal and domestic relations of the liberal individual as the only recognizable form of intimacy—and the property and privilege of Europeans—and ascribed to non-Europeans deficient or deviant forms of family, kinship, affect, and sexuality, thereby rationalizing their subordination.[18] The tenacity of this colonial division and distribution of intimacy is such that successive works that have aimed at comparative, connective analysis of the "imperial politics of intimacies" have covered the British, French, Dutch, Portuguese, Spanish, and US Empires but not the Japanese.[19]

The focus on European and US colonialisms to the exclusion of the Japanese Empire is reflective of a broader pattern in postcolonial studies. In the US and European academia, scholarship on the Japanese Empire has traditionally focused on its peculiarities as the only "non-Western" colonial power in the modern period. Put differently, Japanese colonialism has been analyzed primarily as an anomaly.[20] And if postcolonial scholars have ignored Japan, then scholars of Japan and its empire have marginalized the study of Japan's wartime imperial expansion to the borders of Burma and India, which entailed the most spectacular deployment of troops in Japanese history—an estimated over two million from Japan and another half million conscripts from other parts of Asia (mainly Taiwan and Korea).[21] Even as they have uncovered the history of migration, intermarriage, and collaboration in and beyond Japan's formal empire to include Pacific islands and North and South America, they have overlooked similar dynamics in the territory that Japan occupied during World War II.[22] This oversight has further diminished the history of interAsian intimacies and impeded the analysis of the effects of multiple colonizations on intermarriage and conversion.

The historiographical fixation with métissage is striking for yet another reason. If the Japanese Empire has been the orphan of postcolonial studies, the British Empire—and namely British India, the "jewel of the crown"—has been its star attraction, comprising the lion's share of theoretical and empirical studies of colonialism. Ironically, there are few subjects that have vexed historians of India more than Hindu-Muslim communalism, which, by all accounts, culminated in the bloody partition of India (into India and Pakistan) along religious lines in 1947 and its attendant phenomena of mass rape, abduction, and forced "recovery" of women on both sides of the geopolitical divide. As the scholarship on the history and legacy of the partition has revealed, the flashpoints for Hindu-Muslim communal agitation, throughout British colonial rule and long after the partition, were interfaith marriage and conversion, particularly of Hindu women of lower castes to Islam through seduction by the "lustful Muslim male."[23]

In other words, while scholars of European empires, not least the British Empire, have studied métissage as foundational to imperialism and racism, scholars of India have turned a critical eye to Hindu-Muslim intermarriage and conversion to explain the advent of Hindutva (the Hindu right) and nationalism. The problem is not just that historians of European empires have been remiss to place undue emphasis on métissage at the expense of the equally, if not more, significant question of Hindu-Muslim marriage and conversion in the context of British India nor that the two bodies of scholarship—one on empire, métissage, and race and the other on nation, religion, caste, and Hindu-Muslim marriage and conversion—remain siloed. The issue, more importantly, is that interAsian marriage and conversion have been analyzed primarily as a vortex of antagonism rather than sites of intimacy.

Mobile Men and Local Helpmates

Meanwhile, the emergent paradigm of "inter-Asia" within the field of Asian studies, once partitioned into hermetically sealed subregions of East, South, Southeast, and Central Asia, has turned the spotlight on previously neglected movements and interactions that trespassed or transpired at the interstices of these artificial subregional divides.[24] The main protagonists of histories produced in this vein are not European adventurers, traders, officials, and mercenaries but instead Asian men. Some are recognizable figures known for their globe-trotting intellectual and political peregrinations as well as their sympathies for pan-Asianist ideologies and movements: Okakura Tenshin, Rabindranath Tagore, and Sun Yat Sen to name a few.[25] Others are laboring classes of "coolie" men upon whose backs European empires flourished. In between these classes of Asian migrants were the so-called merchants without empire, also primarily from India and China but as well from the Arabian peninsula. As owners of business, land, and capital, their wealth and power placed them well above the majority of the Indigenous population. But they were neither formal agents of empire nor metropolitan subjects. Despite some legislative representation as minority communities, they were politically disenfranchised people with little institutionalized access to the colonial and metropolitan governments on which they relied for protection and patronage.

Despite, or perhaps due to, its attention to mobile Asian men and Asian interactions, this emergent transregional history has maintained a surprisingly conventional understanding of intermarriage and conversion that does not stray far from that of métissage. Conceptualizing Asia as an interlinked cosmopolitan universe of connections and circulations, Prasenjit Duara observed that prior to the advent of colonialism and nationalism, politics and states did not dominate identity formations and societies had "soft boundaries, where individual community difference (say, in diet or deities) would not prevent large-scale and un-self-conscious borrowing in other respects."[26] This is not a novel vision of Asia but one that has long held sway over specialists of Southeast Asia and the Indian Ocean. In their analyses, both geographies were crossroads of the world distinguished by their connectivity and conviviality; intermarriage, mixed births, conversion, and transgenderism were widespread practices that embodied the pluralistic practices and mentalities characteristic of the region and the readiness and fluidity with which state and society "localized" the foreign.[27] It was the intensifying contact with "foreign men"— from across the Indian Ocean and the South China Sea, from Europe, Arabia, and Asia—during the age of expanding European empires and capital that explained the demise of this "strong current of localization." The point is not that racism, religious fundamentalism, sexism, and homo- and transphobia were distinctly European Christian colonial afflictions, which is an argument about colonial rupture that has been made by scholars of the Americas before and after European colonization.[28] Rather, Asian migrants too hailed brides from their "homeland" with the goal of reproducing self-sustaining communities in the colony as soon as the mobility revolution of the nineteenth century shrunk the distance between their national or religious "homelands" and "host" societies.[29] For these men, no less than for European colonizers, intermarriage and conversion represented temporary institutions. They too disparaged "the bastardization of their culture and the distortion of family values, an explicit comment on the influence of local women," and applied pressure on the latter to adopt the social and cultural norms and behaviors of their migrant husbands.[30]

InterAsian history mirrors the history of métissage and its myopia in another respect: it is a narrative about traveling men and their Indigenous helpmate that tethers native and native-born women to an imagined existence of domesticity. Women seldom appear as brokers of contact and change. As a new generation of historians have shown, however, women from China, Japan, and India from the highest to the lowest strata of society crisscrossed Asia during the so-called age of mobility revolution, and not just as an underclass of "unwilling" coolie laborers, prostitutes, servants, and bondmaids, as so often presumed.[31]

The women who have entered the picture as local wives are identified as "nodal points" at which "valuables such as houses and lands, and values such as lineage identification" accumulate.[32] In a gendered division of labor, men are depicted as circulating across oceans and continents sowing seeds and spinning webs of exchange, debt, patronage, pilgrimage, and kinship, while women are relegated to the role of repository and reproducer, domesticating and nourishing what have been sown, spun, and propagated by men. Despite challenging scholars to think critically about the archives of mobility, interAsian history has continued to prioritize the empirically knowable world of men over the less easily recoverable and fathomable stories of female mobility, enterprise, empire building, and lineage making, such as those of Ma Galay and Helen May. In this respect, interAsian history has reinforced the tendency in histories of métissage to make mobility the property of colonizers and fix Indigenous women in both time and space as "the stationary object on whom intimacy is bestowed, visited, forced."[33]

InterAsian Intimacies challenges the one-dimensional figure of the local helpmate and reimagines her as a historical agent not only enmeshed in family and affective ties but also versed in political, economic, and social speculations and manipulations. At the same time, it unsettles assumptions about the insularity of foreign men and the cosmopolitanism of natives to interrogate the part that both groups played in the history of interAsian conflicts.

Stories and Sources

The narrative follows the arc of the family history of Rosie Hnin Yee and Pondicherry Mohanarajan (henceforth Auntie Rosie and Uncle Mohan, see fig. 0.1), beginning with the stories of Auntie Rosie's maternal and paternal grandparents, Di Di Diana Ogh and Alexander Joseph Defries, and Ma Galay and U Choe. Their experiences of intermarriage and conversion span the fall of the last Burmese monarchy, Burma's administrative and territorial incorporation into the British Empire, the Japanese occupation of and retreat from Burma during World War II, and the first half century of Burmese independence. What makes their life stories and perspectives so important however is not just the diachronic view of interAsian intimacies that they afford but also the fact that they are a family of amyo gya who have been marginalized and stigmatized as foreigners over many generations.

Admittedly, they belonged to a section of the elite. U Choe was a royal serviceman, and Ma Galay socialized with royalty; in the aftermath of his death, she built a lucrative real estate empire in Rangoon. Their descendants attended premier schools, not just in colonial Burma and India but in metropolitan London. Uncle Mohan, who came from humble beginnings, went on to become the first cardiology specialist in Burma and a personal physician to Khin May Than, the third and favorite wife of the socialist military dictator Ne Win. None

FIGURE 0.1. Auntie Rosie and Uncle Mohan in Maymyo. Photo taken c. 1969. Courtesy of Dr. Hnin Yee and Mona Han.

of this, however, minimizes the penalty of being amyo gya—Muslim, Christian, Indian, Arab, convert, and *kabya* (mixed).

The family stories that appear in this book were shared with me over the course of my lifetime, long before and after I began training as a historian, and in my relationship to the family as amyo, albeit what anthropologists and sociologists call a "fictive kin" who is not related by consanguinity, adoption, or marriage. Growing up in Burma, it was a weekly ritual to spend an evening and share a meal with Auntie Rosie, Uncle Mohan, and their children, relatives, and friends and listen to the grown-ups narrate legends of their ancestors—handed down to them by the matriarchs Di Di, Ma Galay, and Helen May, who outlived their husbands—and whisper their family secrets in the comfort and privacy of their home in Rangoon. Virtually every person who was party and privy to this storytelling was a woman.

This experience of homosocial, women-dictated creation of memory, meaning, and knowledge compelled me to grapple with the gap between the finished history of interAsian intimacies that have been chronicled in written records and government archives and the unfinished, living history told in families. It furthermore presented me with an unexpected personal confrontation with the problem of the archival and historiographical dispossession and disfiguration of women.

Generations of feminist scholars who have researched and written about the lives and histories of Black, Indigenous, enslaved, colonized, and indentured women have struggled with the formidable challenge of finding women in archives that systematically ignore them.[34] Organizations led exclusively by men, Christian churches and colonial governments have left behind archives structured around the patriarch in which women appear as appendages to men. Little more than their partial name tends to be ascertainable through legal, administrative, or ecclesiastical records of marriage and family. For example, birth and baptism registers list the "Surname" and "Quality, trade, or profession" of the father, not the mother, thus ensuring a gendered, structural asymmetry in the recovery of family histories and intimate pasts. In colonial contexts, moreover, native and non-European women in particular were deemed unworthy of record keeping; when they do appear in official archives, they often do so as slaves, coolies, prostitutes, concubines, and orphans.

Feminist scholars of the last quarter century have taught us to reconsider where and in whom history resides and to stretch the definition of archives and sources. They have also challenged us to reclaim archival material for contrary purposes to creatively disorder official accounts and dominant narratives.[35] In the absence of such endeavors, warns Insook Kwon, masculinist narratives, imperialist or nationalist, monopolize truth and sweep away colonized women's realities.[36]

What is at stake therefore is not simply the due diligence of a historian: scour archives, consider multiple sources, scales, and angles of history, and so on and so forth, though these are all requisite modes of doing history that I adopt here. Rather, it is the recasting of history so that we do not continue to banish women like Ma Galay, Helen May, and Auntie Rosie to a state of unknowability or leave them vulnerable to "readings and misreadings of whoever chooses to make assumptions about them, however hostile or insulting their preconceptions may be."[37] It is in this insurgent spirit and modality of historical inquiry that I have turned to intergenerational storytelling. For the same reason, the reader will find me engaging in imaginative interpretations throughout the book. I deploy these discipline-crossing, genre-bending techniques to remember what the archive has obscured and history has devalued. What follows is my attempt to reimagine what it means and takes to do history.

The first half of the book tacks back and forth between the life stories of Auntie Rosie's grandparents (chapter 1) and parents (chapter 3) and stories of mixed marriages, births, and families that appear in civil court records (chapters 2 and 4). Together, the four chapters illustrate how wives of migrant men crossed geopolitical, legal, and social boundaries to take charge of their fate and fortune and lead lives unconfined to the putatively feminine—and unchanging—domain of sex, domesticity, and reproduction.

British authorities continually ran up against relations that transgressed administrative classifications and legal jurisdictions and exposed the absurdities of government schemes to organize subjects into discrete religious and racial communities governable by their respective laws. They also found themselves trying—and tried by—lawsuits against Burmese women in such marriages and families, often initiated by their husbands and in-laws who contested the women's claims to conjugal rights, children, and inheritance. Allying with the plaintiffs, colonial jurists ruled that intermarriage and conversion obliged a Burmese Buddhist woman to relinquish her rights to property and become a legal subordinate of her Chinese, Hindu, or Muslim husband. They pitted minority rights against indigenous rights along gender lines—as Chinese, Hindu, and Muslim patriarchs' rights against Burmese Buddhist women's rights—to routinely undercut women's personhood and property and shore up patriarchal rights, all under the cover of protecting both the rights of religious minorities *and* women's capacity to consent to intermarriage and conversion. InterAsian intimacies thus became the grounds for elaborating and consolidating—not dismantling—colonial presumptions about divisions in "Oriental" religions, races, laws, and families and the imperial authorization of patriarchy.

The remaining chapters move out of the courtroom into the court of public opinion to explore how intermarriage and conversion of Buddhist women became the locus of political agitation, legislative activism, collective violence, and national shame and imperial nostalgia, while also viewing the upheavals of the 1930s, World War II, and the Japanese occupation (1942–1945) through the prism of Auntie Rosie and Uncle Mohan. In the decades leading up to World War II, chapters 5 and 6 show, those who self-identified as "protectors" of the buddha batha bama amyo ("Burmese Buddhist kind") launched a virulent legislative and press campaign aimed at restricting the ability of Burmese Buddhist women to intermarry or convert. They charged amyo gya ("other") men with seducing unsuspecting Burmese Buddhist women into fraudulent marriages and involuntary conversions and enjoined Burmese Buddhist men to regain control over their women, heritage, and territory. They imagined the Burmese Buddhist as an exceptional amyo ("kind") governed by enlightened norms that recognized women as autonomous rights-bearing individuals. The preservation and regeneration of this heritage required the emotional, sexual, and reproductive labor of Burmese Buddhist women, who were exhorted to couple with Burmese Buddhist men. Those who married amyo gya against this conjugal mandate were blamed for the degradation of the Burmese Buddhist amyo. A complex assemblage of claims, the idea of Burmese Buddhist exceptionalism combined the judicial discourse on Burmese Buddhist law with ideas of degeneration and heredity, and love and marriage rooted in the pseudoscience of eugenics that linked racial difference with sexual deviance and in popular understandings of the Buddhist doctrines of karma and merit.

Intermarriage and conversion proved no less politically charged during the Japanese occupation of Burma, when interAsian marriage and family were upheld as models of pan-Asian solidarity. Chapters 7 and 8 engage with memories of women as students, teachers, translators, informants, and wives of occupiers who have been depicted in Burmese narratives of antifascist, anticolonial resistance as traitors and shameless mistresses of the Japanese, and in wartime and postwar Japanese accounts of the occupation as temptresses. Characterizing women as willful accomplices, both Burmese and Japanese narratives deny women the benefit of political calculus and patriotism they grant to occupied men who collaborated with the Japanese. They also obscure how new dynamics of power and patronage were enacted and managed through everyday relations of intimacy between Japanese occupiers and colonized women and conceal the complicity of the Burmese political and intellectual elites in routinizing gender and sexual exploitation. As these chapters demonstrate, interAsian intimacies remained under the Japanese perilous sites through which distinctions between colonizer and colonized—and among the colonized—were reconstituted and made to matter.

Even as I track shifts in perceptions, practices, and experiences of intermarriage and conversion and their political and social ramifications, I stress the persistence of the politics and prose of intimacy across colonialisms. The history of interAsian intimacies is best understood as not one of colonial rupture but one of a cumulative regulation and institutionalization of marriage, family, identity, and the body politic by and across different patriarchal regimes of domination.

CHAPTER 1

Making Kin and Remaking Worlds

There are two extant documents that place Alexander Joseph Defries (1869–1908), Auntie Rosie's maternal grandfather, in Burma. The first is a register of his burial in a cemetery in Rangoon, the capital of British Burma, on 27 November 1908. Signed by the chaplain of the Anglican Rangoon Cathedral, it shows that Defries, an "assistant hospital steward," died of tuberculosis on 26 November 1908, aged thirty-nine.[1] The second record, and the only one that ties him to his wife and their children in Burma, is dated 7 October 1910, almost two years after his death (fig. 1.1). It indicates that on 28 September 1910, "Diana" baptized her three daughters with the name Defries at Christ Church in Mandalay.[2] Once the only church in Mandalay, it had come to be known as the city's "Burmese Church" after St. Mary's Church was established in 1902 as a Church of England specifically for the English and Europeans.[3] We can only approximate the ages of the three children—Helen May (b. 1900), Cecilia Elisabeth (b. 1903), and Juliet Gabriel (b. 1907)—for only the years of their births are entered into the baptismal record.

Two ecclesiastical records—neither of which were filed by Defries himself—represent the entire body of extant textual evidence linking Defries to Burma. Yet, based on these two pieces of documentation, and thanks to the vast troves of church registers spanning the entire globe that have been rendered readily searchable by digital genealogical research sites, we can trace his ancestors seven generations back to the seventeenth century and, as Auntie Rosie had

BAPTISMS Solemnized at *Christ Church, Mandalay* _____ of Europeans or Eurasians for the Quarter commencing from _____ the 1st day of
July 1910 to the 30ᵗʰ day of *September* 1910.

Serial No.	When Baptized.		Said to be Born.			Child's Christian name.	Sex.	Parent's Names.		Abode of parents.	Quality, trade, or profession of father.	Name of priest or minister by whom the ceremony was performed.
	Year.	Month. Day.	Year.	Month.	Day.			Christian.	Surname.			
1104.	1910	Sept. 26	1910	July	12	Marilyn Cynthia	daughter	William Cousins	Menezes	Magok	Trader	C. E. Garrad.
1105.	1910	Sept. 28	1909	–	–	Helen May	daughter	Alexander Joseph Diana	Defries	Mandalay	Steward	C. E. Garrad.
1106.	1910	Sept. 28	1905	–	–	Cecilia Elisabeth	daughter	Alexander Joseph Diana	Defries	Mandalay	Steward	C. E. Garrad.
1107.	1910	Sept. 28	1907	–	–	Juliet Gabriel	daughter	Alexander Joseph Diana	Defries	Mandalay	Steward	C. E. Garrad.

I, THE REVEREND *C. E. Garrad*, Minister ~~and Chaplain~~ of *Christ Church Mandalay* do hereby certify that the foregoing returns numbered 1104 to 1107 are true and faithful copies of all the entries in the Register of Baptisms relating to Europeans or Eurasians belonging to, and kept at the Church or Station of *Christ Church Mandalay* within the *District* in the Archdeaconry of _____ in the year of Our Lord, one thousand nine hundred and *ten* as therein entered and made between the first day of *July* and the *thirtieth* day of *September*, 1910.

STATION *Christ Church, Mandalay* } _____ (TRUE COPY) _____ WITNESS MY HAND _____ (₂) *C. E. Garrad*, '2 4 0

The *7ᵗʰ October* 1910. } _____ A. B. _____ Minister ~~and Chaplain~~ of *Christ Church Mandalay*

G. B. 1. B. F.—No. 418, Stock 3-5-1910—500.

FIGURE 1.1. Baptismal record of Helen May, Cecilia Elisabeth, and Juliet Gabriel, the children of Diana Di Di Ogh and Alexander Joseph Defries, 1910. Record of Baptisms at Christ Church, Mandalay, dated October 7, 1910. By permission of the British Library.

speculated, to the Netherlands. But Defries himself was one among the many seventh-generation Defries family members born and raised in the "Presidency town" of Madras, the capital of one of three major administrative units for British India: Madras, Bombay, and Bengal. The eldest of eight children of Albert Anthony Defries and Adriana Defries, who were first cousins, Alexander Joseph hailed from a Catholic merchant family that had once belonged to the Madras elite. According to the writer Fanny Emily Penny, a long-time Madras resident, "the De Fries family were of Dutch origin, and the name appears on a monument at Cochin dated 1670, put up to the memory of Gerrit Jansz de Vries, who was born at Oldenburg, and came out in the service of the Dutch East India Company."[4]

What the immense caches of ecclesiastical records shrouds in mystery, and what Penny's account of the "Dutch origin" of the De Fries family elides, are the lineages of the early female ancestors of the family. We know nothing about Gerrit de Vries's wife, if he had one, or about the mother of his children in Madras. The same holds true for his son Johannes De Fries. Likewise, we know next to nothing about the spouses of de Vries's grandson (Johannes De Fries Jr.) and great grandson (John De Fries), Francesca (?–1788) and Theodora (1728–1812). Not until the next generation do we start to have the maiden names of the women who married De Fries men. The lack of a name—or a complete name—is itself telling; it implies that the women were native women. The anonymity of the wife and mother in marriage and baptismal registers in colonial India, Durba Ghosh has shown, functioned as a code for her race and the illegitimacy of her relationship to her spouse and children. The presence of a European first name, such as "Francesca" and "Theodora," indicated that a native woman had been converted and renamed. Such common practices in recordkeeping simultaneously produced and erased the genealogies of local women.[5]

Given the nearly total absence of female European immigrants in Asia in the seventeenth and eighteenth centuries, the first few generations of the wives and mothers of the De Fries family in Madras were almost certainly born in Asia. The British and the Dutch East India Companies alike tolerated sexual and marital relations between its European employees and "Indian born" or "Indies born" women, in the parlance of the time, whether they be Asian or "Eurasian," a category reserved for the offspring of a European father and an Asian mother.[6] The British imagined that their sexual propriety set them apart from the libidinal Spanish and Portuguese Empires in which *mestizaje* (*miscigenação* in Portuguese), what the British termed "racial amalgamation," was endemic. Yet neither the East India Company (EIC) nor the British colonial administration enacted anti-miscegenation laws, and only officers of the company and then the Indian Civil Service (ICS) were officially discouraged from marrying native women. In practice, both encouraged their rank and file who could not afford the kind of upkeep a European wife supposedly required—a spacious private residence, servants, European food, and so on—on their salary to opt for what they construed to be an economical domestic arrangement: a mistress or maidservant who would perform a host of physical, sexual, and emotional labor for a fraction of the cost of maintaining a European wife. Asia-born women, they posited, demanded less and delivered more than Europe-born women, not least hearty offspring who thrived in the tropics. Such relationships, expected to be temporary and nonmatrimonial, were justified and naturalized as most conducive to the health, well-being, and budget of the single European servants of the Raj who may otherwise resort to "indecent" conduct (i.e., homosexual acts).

The directors of the EIC entitled every baptized child of a soldier enlisted in its army to a monetary gift of five rupees, acknowledging the ubiquity of intimate relations between its soldiers and women in India and their importance to company rule.[7] Such company regulations compelled European men to baptize and accept as their own the children they had with "Indian born" women. But they did not motivate the men to recognize as wife or mother (of their children) the women with whom they cohabited. While some EIC men did marry their "Indian born" companions, many more did not. These unwed women were consigned to the status of "concubines," housekeepers, or slaves, passed on from one European master to another even as their children were manumitted and claimed as legitimate heir by their European patriarchs.[8]

When company men did marry Asia-born women, they tended to be Eurasian women, who were sought after by European men of all nationalities as suitable wives and bearers of European Christian children.[9] These women were predominantly mestizas of Portuguese descent at first. As an imperial power, Portugal had encouraged the marriage of Portuguese men to "heathen" women throughout the Iberian empire on the basis that it not only helped achieve the important objective of Catholic proselytization but also produced interpreters and intermediaries indispensable to imperial expansion. As a result, by the time Gerrit Jansz de Vries set foot in India, a sizable Portuguese-speaking Catholic mestiza community had developed in Madras, lying less than ten kilometers to the north of San Thome, once the heart of a prosperous Portuguese settlement.

The fact that early generations of the De Fries in Madras were buried in Catholic cemeteries may be read as evidence of the family's mestiza matrilineage. Housed in the "Luz Church" (otherwise known as the Church of Our Lady of Light), one of the oldest Christian churches in Madras, are memorial tablets in English and Portuguese dedicated to John De Fries (1734–1796) and his mother, Francesca; wife, Theodora; and children. One historian even describes John De Fries as "a Portuguese born in Madras," rather than a Madras-born Dutch, whose partnership with the English free merchant Thomas Pelling "represented a union for business purposes between the English and the Portuguese community at Madras."[10] The two men founded one of the main mercantile firms in Madras, Pelling & De Fries, which served as a major exporter of Indian diamond to Europe and creditor to Portuguese and Armenian traders.

Correspondence between former officers of the British East India Company indicates that John De Fries was viewed as an important asset to British interests in India and served as a trusted adviser to powerful men in the company who prized "his local knowledge and long experience in business."[11] His sons Adrian, John (Jr.), Lewis, and Henry succeeded to his firm and cemented the stature of the De Fries family in Madras as prominent merchants, financiers, and property owners. The respect that the De Fries brothers commanded from the British was such that they were appointed to various committees set up by the Fort St. George governor and council. Adrian and John (Jr.) De Fries were among four Catholic "persons of property and fair character" appointed in 1789 as "Syndics," or lay trustees, as part of a British effort to curtail the influence of the French Capuchins among the Roman Catholics in Madras.[12]

If the eighteenth century was one of ascendancy for the De Fries, the nineteenth was one of decline. Over the course of the century, the patriarchs stop appearing on lists of municipal boards and committees; they no longer leave wills; and there are no more announcements of society weddings. The only paper trails left of later generations of the De Fries are ecclesiastical records that return their professions as steward, clerk, writer, station master, store warder, fitter, driver, and band master. None are addressed or titled "Esquire." By the time Auntie Rosie's grandfather Alexander Joseph was born, the De Fries had become a working-class "Anglo-Indian" family. Commonly understood to mean "country-born," the term Anglo-Indian distinguished Europeans and Eurasians who were born and lived in India from their expatriate counterparts whose permanent residence was in Britain.[13] They had fallen into obscurity, paralleling the rise and demise of the EIC (1757–1873).

Becoming Anglo-Indian, Karen, Baptist

The decline of the De Fries was not a unique tale. Throughout the nineteenth century as direct imperial rule by the British government replaced company rule, Catholic Eurasians such as the De Fries found themselves ostracized by Eurasians of British descent, who were predominantly Protestant. Perhaps it was the desire to be accepted into British Eurasian circles that prompted some members of the De Fries family to join St. Mary's Church, the oldest Anglican church in Madras. But most did not. Not even Albert and Adriana, Alexander Joseph's parents, who adopted the new Anglicized spelling of their surname: "Defries."

Anglo-Indians also lost many privileges they once enjoyed. Superior employment opportunities, such as the ICS, that offered the highest income, prestige, and chance for promotion were staffed by European men educated and recruited in Britain. Men of European descent educated in India were excluded from such careers and deemed fit only for subordinate levels of the public services and private European commercial sectors, particularly those connected with transportation, communication, and engineering, where they worked in a restricted managerial capacity. In the late nineteenth century, the colonial administration circumscribed even further its preferential treatment of Anglo-Indians in response to Indian nationalist demands for greater participation in state sectors. These obstacles to socioeconomic and career advancement resulted in the proletarianization of the majority of the 100,000 or so Eurasians and close to half of the 150,000 or so Europeans in India by the turn of the century. They were labeled "poor whites" or referred to euphemistically as "domiciled Europeans." Workhouses and homes for "vagrant" whites were created with the goal of segregating and disciplining poor Europeans, who threatened to tarnish the illusion of white racial superiority.[14]

If we are to believe a 120-page "Burma brochure" on Eurasians and Anglo-Indians published in Rangoon in 1910, the idea that Eurasians and Anglo-Indians were inferior Europeans affiliated with but subordinate to the ruling elites prevailed among these communities in Burma. Authored by R. E. Culley, who identified himself as "one of the community," the text was presented as a guide for the comprehensive reform—mental, spiritual, physical, social, political, and economic—of the Eurasian community in Burma. He conceded that "there is apparently some ground for justification of the prejudice entertained by Europeans against fraternizing with the Eurasian" and discussed at length the innumerable "defects" alleged to be characteristic of Eurasians, including idleness, intemperance, untruthfulness, rudeness, early marriage, and "broken or baby English." While lamenting that Eurasians had been "disowned" by "vain" Europeans, he hoped that by throwing light on what was "wrong or defective in the character of the Eurasian community," he could help the community "take active as well as effective steps to rectify what is amiss, or make good what is lacking."[15]

If Alexander Joseph Defries had hoped to escape the unenviable fate of Eurasians and Anglo-Indians in Madras by crossing the Bay of Bengal to the frontier colony of Burma, then he was probably disappointed. But we do not know what motivated him to move to Burma, when no one else in his extensive family appears to have made the journey. Or when he arrived in Burma, for that matter. What we do know is that Di Di Diana Ogh met him sometime before 1900, when their eldest daughter, Helen May, was born.

One of fourteen children of Shwe Maung Ogh, Di Di belonged to a large Karen family—a categorization Auntie Rosie was quick to correct. Actually, she explained, the Oghs were "not pure Karen." The prevailing theory among the Oghs is that they are also of Armenian or Portuguese descent. In the seventeenth century, Armenians established themselves in port cities, such as Syriam and Pegu, whence they brokered trade with Madras and competed and communed with other traveling mercantile groups, including the Portuguese.[16] It is not at all implausible that one or more of Di Di's ancestors hailed from these entrepôt communities or their descendants and that Di Di shared with Defries a mestiza lineage.

One of the main *lu myo*, or "kinds of people," in Burma, the Karen have come to be known for large-scale conversion to Christianity by American Baptist missionaries in the nineteenth century, although the majority of Karen to this day identify as Buddhist. Nevertheless, Christianity spread rapidly among the Karen after the arrival of Adoniram Judson, the founder of the American Baptist Mission (ABM) in Burma, in 1813, making the country the location of the United States' very first Protestant foreign mission. ABM envisioned the Karen as a special group, "a lost tribe whose oral traditions and customs had originated from Hebrew," in the words of the most well-known missionary among the Karen, Rev. Francis Mason. Within two decades of the first recorded Baptist conversion in Burma in 1819, ABM had gained 1,244 converts among Karens (compared to only 186 Burmans). By mid-nineteenth century, ABM claimed a Karen following of 7,750 strong (compared to 267 Burmans); by 1910, this number had increased to 54,799 (out of a total of 70,396 in Burma).[17] The Oghs were among these Karen converts who had joined the American Baptist church in large numbers in the second half of the nineteenth century.

One of the main reasons for the success of ABM among Karens, as opposed to the Burmans, was its enthusiastic support for literacy and education. It was the American Baptist missionary Jonathan Wade (1798–1872) who created the Sgaw and Pwo Karen scripts in the 1830s–1850s by adapting the Burmese script, thus turning Karen into a written language and promoting it as a medium of teaching and preaching. The establishment of the two-script system by ABM resulted in the conventional understanding of "Karen" as reference to a language or a people comprising two major subgroups, the Sgaw and Pwo.[18] ABM also educated Karen women who, the missionaries hoped, would help their husbands, children, and relatives remain or become upstanding Christians. It ran schools specifically for girls that provided instruction in nursing, midwifery, and the domestic sciences, in addition to reading and writing.

The impact of ABM education on the training of Karen women evangelists or on the expansion of the population of Karen converts is debatable.[19] Its effect on the professionalization of Karen women, however, is clear. Karen women came to be known as the most outstanding nurses in Burma.[20] They dominated nursing, the first and only profession aside from teaching open to educated women, European or Asian, in colonial Burma, where, as elsewhere in the British Empire, women were ineligible for government employment. Di Di was one such woman.

But Di Di belonged not just to the first generation of nurses trained in Burma. She must have been among the first women in Burma to be employed by the government, for she was a nurse at the General Hospital in Mandalay, where she met Alexander Joseph Defries, who worked as an assistant hospital steward. It is doubtful that Di Di would have easily given up the coveted position of a nurse in a government hospital, which might explain why she appears to have remained in Mandalay while Alexander Joseph left for Rangoon, where he died in 1908. Not long thereafter, Di Di gave birth to their youngest daughter, Emma. Emma does not appear on the record of the baptism of her elder daughters Helen May, Cecilia Elizabeth, and Juliet Gabriel at Christ Church in Mandalay in September 1910. Her exclusion was not an oversight; she was adopted during her infancy by an English couple who lived in Rangoon.

Auntie Rosie does not know why her aunt was given up for adoption. She imagines that her grandmother, widowed with four young daughters, must have had few choices. Di Di also decided to send her other daughters to Anglican orphanages that provided free education, room, and board to the "poor and destitute" children of European fathers and Burmese mothers whose fathers had either died or deserted them. Shortly after the baptism in September 1910, Di Di moved to Rangoon where she worked as a nurse for a Japanese doctor or dentist. There, she placed all her daughters in the care of others: Emma with the English couple, the Campbells, and the eldest three with the Bishop Strachan Home for Girls, one of two orphanages for Eurasian girls in Burma run by Christian missionaries and the only one under the management of the Anglican church.[21]

In British India (of which Burma was a province until 1937), as in other neighboring European colonies such as Indochina, a Eurasian child who lacked a European father due to death, abandonment, or neglect was considered orphaned, regardless of whether the child had a surviving mother or if the mother, as in the case of Di Di, remained in contact with the child.[22] Orphanages such as the Bishop Strachan Home for Girls and its brother institution the Diocesan Orphanage for European and Eurasian Boys at St. John's College were established with the belief that Eurasian children, in the words of their founder Dr. John E. Marks, "cannot be allowed to grow up as Burmese Buddhists."[23]

As with boarding schools, training homes, and correctional facilities established throughout European colonial empires, orphanages formed an imperial system of uprooting and institutionalizing Eurasian and Indigenous children with the goal of assimilating them. The wards of these institutions were baptized, given Christian names, compelled to learn the colonial language—whether it was English, French, or Dutch—and were forbidden from speaking vernacular languages. They followed a regimented program of basic education, Christian schooling, and hard labor and received harsh corporeal punishments for rebellious behavior.[24] Couching their coercive practices of assimilation in a language of benevolence, agents and supporters of child removal portrayed orphanages and homes as institutions for the redemption of mixed-race children who needed protection from their native families and cultural influences. "Left to their Burmese mothers, they could not speak English and were dressed either entirely or for the most part as natives and very poorly provided for," Dr. Marks wrote in his memoir as he recalled his motivation for starting the two Anglican diocesan orphanages in Rangoon. "To rescue them and give them Christian teaching and a good secular education," he explained, "seemed to be a work of charity as well as of necessity."[25]

Doris Sarah Easton, who moved from England to Mandalay in 1915 to become the first headmistress of St. Mary's School for Eurasian Girls, sympathized with her Eurasian students, who were scorned and ostracized by the English expatriates in the city. Yet she shared their condescension toward Eurasians, describing her Eurasian charges, for instance, as "very devoid of brains" in her diary. In December 1917, she wrote that her fiancé, Arthur Percy Morris, then headmaster of the Government School of Engineering in Insein, was "rather down" because a Eurasian headmaster had joined the school, and under his watch, the students had "got slack," having lost all the discipline that Morris had instilled in them.[26]

Orphanages for Eurasians had a reputation for villainizing native women in particular. The European and American missionary men and women who ran the orphanages resorted to Orientalist stereotypes of colonized women; their mixed-race children were the unfortunate consequences of their loose morals, not of the European or Eurasian fathers of the children. In other words, Eurasian children needed to be shielded as early as possible from the pernicious influences of their native mothers.[27] Nevertheless, many native women placed their children in the care of the very institutions that maligned them because they offered vocational training in such fields as nursing and teaching that prepared the charges for the limited occupations open to women at the time. Take, for example, the Eurasian Home for Destitute Boys in Rangoon, which served a relatively mixed student population in spite of its name: about half of the twenty-nine students who studied at the home as day pupils were female, as were an additional six boarders. Though the primary goal of the home was to cultivate "the Christian character" of the students, its course offerings included English-language instruction in reading, writing, arithmetic, geography, history, and grammar.[28] The combination of English-language instruction—what came to be known as Anglo-vernacular education—and female education, however rudimentary the curriculum may have been, represented a rare opportunity for the colonized population. Even as late as the 1870s, Buddhist monastic schools remained the main and, for most people in Burma, the only provider of education, and they offered neither English-language nor female instruction. As such, there were advantages to be gained from the British imperial order that penalized Eurasians as second-order Europeans.

Di Di's intentions and desires, her thoughts and feelings, are beyond our grasp. Try as we might, we cannot know them with any certainty. That said, I believe that she baptized her daughters Helen, Juliet, and Cecilia at the Anglican Christ Church in Mandalay with the objective of placing them in the sole Anglican orphanage for Eurasian girls in Burma. I imagine that Di Di made this decision on the basis that as boarders at the Anglican orphanage, her daughters would receive admission into the schools run by the Anglicans, such as St. Mary's School for Girls in Rangoon, reputed to be among the leading educational institutions in Burma at the time and the best school for girls.[29] Di Di was raised Baptist, and her late husband was Catholic. Yet she sent her daughters neither to, say, the Roman Catholic Mission St. Joseph's Convent in Mandalay nor the American Baptist Mission Eurasian Home for Girls in Moulmein. By placing her daughters in the care of an orphanage, Di Di capitalized on the promise and the potential of paternalistic imperial rhetoric to better the lot of her Eurasian children.

Becoming Muslim, Zerbadi, Sayyid

We know even less about Auntie Rosie's paternal grandfather, Shwe Kyeik Kat U Choe, than about Alexander Joseph Defries. While it is possible to mine the vast collection of ecclesiastical returns in the archives of the British India Office to map out the genealogy of ordinary European or Eurasian Christians like Alexander Joseph, no such accessible archive exists for a Muslim individual such as U Choe. To make matters worse, historic Muslim cemeteries in Mandalay were razed by the Burmese government during the 1990s to make space for a large-scale urban development program, destroying thousands of gravestones engraved with epitaphs and biographical information. So we must rely on family memory and local histories of Mandalay and, in particular, of the *pathi* communities in and near the erstwhile capital with which U Choe was affiliated.

Often glossed as "Muslim," the etymology of pathi remains unsettled. The most straightforward and, in my opinion, the most plausible possibility is that pathi originated in the Persian word *pārsī* for "Persian." But the most popular theory, found in the famous *Hobson-Jobson* dictionary of "Anglo-Indian words and phrases," is that pathi is a corruption of Farsi: the modern Persian language, which had become a regional lingua franca in the aftermath of its adoption in India, at the end of the sixteenth century, as the official language of the Mughal bureaucracy; as such, it means "Farsi speaker." A much less known theory is that pathi derived from the Tamil word *palli* for "mosque," thus referring to those who worship at the mosque.[30] The former theory highlights the role that Persianized elites played as transregional conduits of Islamic practices and institutions; the latter underscores the centrality to this process of the later but far larger group of Tamil migrants. Classified by the British colonial administration as a Tamil-speaking "Musalman tribe" and characteristically "migratory" people, "Tamil" merchants, financiers, and laborers constituted one of the principal migrant groups from southern India to British Burma.[31]

The term pathi was often combined with *kala*, meaning "Westerners" or those coming from beyond the western and northwestern limits of Burmese imperial authority, who were, therefore, presumed to be subjects of other sovereigns (or possibly people not under the rule of any sovereign). Historians of Burma, especially of the colonial and postcolonial period, have tended to translate kala as "Indian" or "Muslim." During the interwar period, and as we see in chapters 5 and 6, "Indian" indeed became the predominant meaning of the word; it took on a pejorative, racialized sense, used to characterize various "dark" or "brown races" of the Indian subcontinent and, to a lesser extent, those of the Arabian Peninsula. But for centuries and for most of its long history of usage, kala was a generic category with no such geographic or ethnolinguistic specificity.[32] Nineteenth-century British administrative documents—from the first Anglo-Burmese treaty (1826), signed in the wake of the First Anglo-Burmese War (1824–1826), to the 1891 government census of Burma, the first to be taken after the third and final Anglo-Burmese War (1885) and the British annexation of Upper Burma[33]—confirmed the use of kala as a reference to "every race of India proper, of Western Asia, and of Europe," in the words of Henry Yule, the secretary to the 1855 mission to Burma from the (British) government of India.[34]

This apparent conflation of "every race of India proper, of Western Asia, and of Europe" irked the British. Yule claimed that the Burmese "misapplied" kala to "the English and other Westerns who have come from India to Burma." Sir Albert Fytche, the chief commissioner of British Burma during 1867–1871, similarly explained that "the Burmese mixed up English and all Europeans with the natives of India in one common appellation of Kuláh or western foreigners" and that it was only after the First Anglo-Burmese War that the Burmese "learnt to distinguish the more prominent of the nations lying west of them."[35] Perhaps they were insulted that the very term referring to populations they considered inferior, such as Muslims and British colonial subjects in India, also applied to them. In all likelihood, the distinction between kala byu (white kala) and kala,[36] and the appearance of the word bo in the colonial period as the common parlance to denote the English or Europeans, was initiated or popularized by the British in an attempt to demarcate a clear boundary between themselves—the so-called more prominent of Western nations—and their subject peoples.

Yet the Burmese did distinguish among the kala, just not in the same racialized ways that the British deemed necessary. They used it in conjunction with such qualifiers as pathi to distinguish Farsi-speaking, mosque-going, or "Persian" kala like U Choe, from, say, English-speaking, churchgoing kala like Alexander Joseph Defries. And by the time Yule set foot in Amarapura, the capital of the Konbaung Empire at the time, there had developed a diverse pathi kala community (see fig. 1.2):

> Some families believe themselves to have been settled in Burma for five or six hundred years; other are descended from Mussulmans of India or Western Asia, whom chance or trade has brought hither as voluntary emigrants in later years; others from Mahomedans of Aracan, of Munnipoor, and perhaps of Kachár, forcibly deported by the Burmans during their inroads into those countries. But all having intermarried with the natives they are undistinguishable at sight from other Burmans, except those whose family migration is of late date, and who possess, it struck me, a very peculiar and distinct physiognomy.[37]

Yule had been informed by "a respectable Indian Mussulman" that there were some twenty thousand such families in the area. But he proposed an estimate of eight thousand to nine thousand as "a better guess at their numbers."[38]

According to family lore, U Choe was a distinguished pathi who supplied high-quality fabric to the royal court of King Mindon (r. 1852–1878). For his

FIGURE 1.2.   A mosque at Amarapura (1855). A photo by Linnaeus Tripe, an officer from the Madras Infantry and the official photographer for the British diplomatic mission to Burma in 1855, with a view looking toward the ornately embellished minaret of a mosque at Amarapura in Burma. Reference: Photo 61/1(52). By permission of the British Library.

service to the royal household, he was given the title Shwe Kyeik Kat (golden sequin). Auntie Rosie recalls her grandmother Ma Galay reminiscing about the days when she accompanied her husband to the palace, where he would roll out bales of cloth and carpet for the princesses to purchase, and she would play with the royal princesses. Judging by such family tales and by his title, he must have been a member of the Shwe Kyeik Kat royal service group under the Shwe Daik Wun (office of "gold store," king's personal treasury).[39]

U Choe also had a Muslim name: Mohiuddin (or Mohideen). The name was probably an Urdu rendition of the Arabic name Muhyi al-din (also Muhyi id-din) meaning "renewer" or "reviver" of Islam. It was during the burial proceedings of her parents and, subsequently, her sister Jenny (Muslim name Noor Jehan) that Auntie Rosie learned that they were sayyid: descendants of the Prophet through Fatima.[40] A green cloth cover was placed upon the coffins of her father and sister to signify their sayyid lineage. Though green is generally understood as the color of Islam—it is believed to have been the favorite color of the Prophet Muhammad and heaven is described in the Quran as a place where people wear garments of fine green silk—it has also functioned as a distinctive sign of the *sāda* (plural for sayyid). As nobility, their sartorial practices were regulated since the early periods of Islam, and one requirement was that they appear in green to ensure that they were recognizable to the public. Under some governments, such as the Ottoman, only sāda were permitted to wear green turbans.[41] Though Muslim, Auntie Rosie's mother, Helen, was denied this badge of distinction.

As with Defries, we do not know precisely when U Choe set foot in Burma—or from where, for that matter. That he was a speaker of Urdu, a Persianized form of the main North Indian vernacular that, along with Bengali and English, replaced Farsi as the bureaucratic language in the 1830s in India under the direction of the East India Company, might be taken as indication that he had spent a substantial amount of time in India prior to arrival in Burma. Neither the fact that he was pathi nor that he was sayyid helps us confirm, refine, or refute this speculation. Since the sixteenth century, Persianized merchants, scholars, literati, and artists had made inroads into the inner circles of royal households across polities around the Bay of Bengal as intermediaries who connected regional rulers to the mercantile network of the Indian Ocean. Such men may or may not have been of Persian descent, but they had adopted certain Islamic cultural forms and practices and knew Farsi.[42] The sixteenth century also marked the beginning of the Hadrami immigration from Hadramawt, in present-day Yemen, to the Indian Ocean littoral and the Malay Archipelago, which continued through the nineteenth century.[43] Arriving on Arab merchant ships plying between the ports of the Persian Gulf, Bay of Bengal, Strait of Malacca, and the Spice Islands (in the Moluccas), these "highly-mobile, mixed-blood, [and] polyglot" scholars and entrepreneurs made the Indian Ocean "the oyster in which they cultivated the pearls of wealth."[44] The Hadrami sāda stood out among them, achieving significant social and political influence based on their exceptional status as descendants of the Prophet Muhammad.

By the nineteenth century, Persianized and sayyid men from both near and far had woven themselves into the fabric of courtly life in Burma. They included the likes of the Bengali Muslim poet Arakan Abdul Hakim, a.k.a. Pay

Taloo, who served as Pagan Myo Wun (governor of Pagan) under King Bagyidaw (also known as Sagaing Min, r. 1819–1837); Sayyid Ahmed Abdul Rahman of Manipur, who was a royal interpreter under King Bagyidaw, King
Tharawaddy (also known as Shwebo Min, r. 1837–1846), and Pagan Min
(r. 1846–1853); Mullah Ibrahim, who moved from Surat in western India with
his brothers Hashim, Kasim, and Mohamed to supply silk, velvet, satin, and
other imported goods to the royal court and was appointed *akauk wun* (officer
of tax collection) by King Tharawaddy in return for his service; and Mohamed
Noor, a.k.a. Shwe Paw, who was tasked by King Mindon to build a lodge in
Mecca for hajj pilgrims from Burma, no doubt as a reward or in exchange for
his profitable export business of precious stones to Mecca from Mogoke,
known for its high-grade rubies.[45]

Through intermarriage, these men and their wives gave rise to settlements
of pathi who were described by the aforementioned emissary Yule as thoroughly assimilated. "They wear the Burman dress, speak the Burman language, and are Burmese in nearly all their habits," he noted, adding that "every
indigenous Mussulman" had two names, one Burmese and the other Muslim:
"As a son of Islam he is probably Abdul Kureem; but as a native of Burma,
and for all practical purposes, he is Moung-yo or Shwepo."[46]

As such naming practices reveal, the pathi in Burma fashioned themselves
as multiply affiliated people who occupied a distinct niche. Typically characterized as lowland agricultural polities, Burmese empires nevertheless depended on the import and export tariffs, precious metals, and luxury gifts
yielded by long-distance trade "to manipulate political patronage, embellish
the royal capital, and finance both domestic and mercenary armies."[47] The
pathi were critical to this transregional trade and represented what historians
of the overseas Chinese have termed bureaucratic capitalists: a semiofficial
merchant class that allies itself with princes and nobles to act as the fiscal agents
for the ruling, official class in return for royal patronage and concessions.[48]

Chinese, or *tayôk*, as they were called in Burmese, were also important bureaucratic capitalists in Burma. Hokkien and Cantonese merchants from the
southeastern Chinese provinces of Fujian and Guangdong plied the coasts of
Burma while Yunnanese silk, cotton, tea, and jade merchants helped broker
the overland caravan trade. By the eighteenth century, the *Yangwentun Xiao-
yin* (A little ballad of Yangwentun) served as a Yunnan–Burma travel and moral
guide for young men journeying from western Yunnan to Mandalay and its
surrounding area via Bhamo. The ballad reminded (the reader) to not abandon his attachment to his Chinese "homeland," to return home within "one
year or two, and at most three to four years," and to refrain from taking a Burmese wife. But Yunnanese traders, like their pathi kala counterparts, often

settled in Burma, married Burmese women (even if they also had Chinese wives), and had Yunnanese-Burmese children. And they became an increasingly influential commercial and social presence in and near the capital cities of Amarapura and Mandalay.[49]

The piecemeal British colonization of Burma in the nineteenth century made bureaucratic capitalists like U Choe—and marriages like his to Ma Galay— more, not less, vital to the political economy in Upper Burma. In the decades following the British annexation of Lower Burma in 1852, the colony developed a highly specialized single-product export economy focused on rice, eventually becoming the world's leading rice producer and exporter. The Konbaung administration in Upper Burma responded to this unprecedented commercialization of rice agriculture in British Lower Burma through economic diversification, exporting such items as cattle, teak timber, petroleum, jade, rubies, cotton, and silk textiles. Pathi and tayôk traders played an outsized role in this expanding external trade. The former group specialized in trade with the court. Its ties to merchants abroad and access to British companies and cheaper credit gave it the upper hand in the import-export trade.[50] Yunnanese, Hokkien, and Cantonese merchants focused on private trade, with the latter two groups moving from the coastal areas in Lower Burma into Upper Burma to take advantage of their familiarity with the English language and British commercial practices, as well as their connection with the South China Sea trading network.[51]

Meanwhile, European traders and firms struggled to establish themselves in Mandalay or elsewhere in Upper Burma. They could not compete against the multilingual pathi and tayôk with their knowledge of extensive regional trade networks as well as the royal household. Once annexed, Upper Burma, which, like Lower Burma, was governed as part of the British Raj, did promise opportunity to British subjects such as Defries from metropole and colony. But even the colonial government-related employment sector was not the exclusive domain of British men. The middling class of professionals who worked for the government and private companies, such as clerks, accountants, doctors, and hospital assistants, were more likely to be Bengali migrant men.[52]

In other words, Asian merchants were not only the most numerous but also the most powerful commercial brokers for much of the eighteenth and nineteenth centuries. Intermarriage and the social reproduction of intermediary communities were shared features of pathi and tayôk adventurer-traders within the mercantile world of Burma and southern Asia. The trade relations and networks that they forged were inseparable from the marriage and kinship relations they established.

Like these Asian intermediaries, and like Alexander Joseph Defries, U Choe married in Burma. Actually, he married two women who were sisters. His first marriage resulted in two children. Upon the death of his first wife, he married her younger sister, Ma Galay. She was fifteen years old when she married her erstwhile brother-in-law.

To Auntie Rosie's knowledge, Ma Galay, better known by her grandchildren by the Urdu term for paternal grandmother "Dadi," was a *zerbadi* of Mon and Arab descent. Zerbadi, which is probably a corruption of the Persian word *zīr-bād* meaning "below the wind," entered the Burma census for the first time in 1891 as a category of race referring to "the offspring of a Muhammadan native of India by a Burmese wife."[53] But the term did not always reference Muslim Indian patrilineage. John Nisbet, the Conservator of Forests in British Burma from 1895 until 1900, defined zerbadi as "the children of Indian and Burmese unions," as did his fellow British colonial officer R. Grant Brown.[54] The Burmese category pathi kala was not a reference specifically to Muslims from India, and as such, it seems likely that in common usage zerbadi had a more capacious meaning that included descendants of pathi kala born in Burma.

One might reasonably speculate that Ma Galay and her forebears hailed from Siam or the coastal towns stretching from the Gulf of Martaban down the Tenasserim littoral where Mon speakers were historically most populous and Arab merchant ships frequently stopped. Was she herself a sayyida? Sayyida are not known to have immigrated like their male counterparts. But she might have been born to a sayyid and a Mon woman, known as *muwallad*. This is quite possible in light of her marriage to U Choe who was a sayyid. And not because sayyid men were inclined to marry women within the sāda community but rather because a sayyida, unlike a sayyid, could not pass on her tie to the Prophet Muhammad if she married a man who was neither a sayyid or sharif (descendant of the Prophet through Hasan, the older son of Fatima).[55] The success of the diasporic sāda, which consisted of male immigrants for most of its history, depended not only on its prophetic genealogy but this rule of patrilineage.

We have no idea if the sāda in Burma in the nineteenth century observed such marriage and kinship prohibitions for there exists no scholarship on the subject. But it offers an explanation for why Ma Galay married U Choe after her elder sister passed away. More than just an example of a sororate marriage, that is, remarriage of a widower to his late wife's sister as a form of control over the property, labor, sexuality, and fertility of the widower, it might have served as a means to consolidate and perpetuate her sayyid lineage.

Feminist scholars have cautioned that kinship transactions in women by and between men, and even by women, are rarely beneficial for the women who are exchanged. The story of Ma Galay helps capture the complexities of such practices that treated women as objects of political and economic transaction.[56] She was young when she married U Choe. Aged only fifteen, she was already a mother of two children by her departed sister. To debate what choice or agency she had in the matter would be an exercise in absurdity. Her choices were overdetermined.

But U Choe was a known quantity. If Ma Galay was expected to marry a sayyid, then she may have preferred to marry one who was not just prosperous and well-connected but had also proved himself to be virile. Recall that U Choe already had two daughters from his previous marriage, whose ability to perpetuate their prophetic ancestry was encumbered by their gender; only marriage to a sayyid or a sharif would ensure that their sayyid status would be passed down to the next generation. If Ma Galay married U Choe and bore him sons, she would seal the patrilineal transmission of his pedigree—and perhaps also hers. Put differently, the marriage gave her a chance to become a sayyid maker. It may have been her marriage to U Choe and subsequent birth of sons with him that propelled her ascendancy as a powerful matriarch.

Ma Galay's life in Mandalay and as a wife is opaque to her descendants. In contrast, their memory of her as a widow in Rangoon is vivid. After U Choe passed away, Ma Galay relocated with her children to Rangoon, where she oversaw a lucrative business in financing and urban real estate. In addition, Ma Galay possessed considerable land in Syriam across the Bago River from Rangoon that she rented out, joining the small rank of landlords—an overwhelming percentage of whom were "nonresident" moneylenders and businessmen—who owned an increasing portion of land and properties in the Irrawaddy delta. This was a region that had transformed into the world's leading producer and exporter of rice (see map 2).

While pushing for the rapid expansion of the rice economy in its new colony, the British administration did little to regulate land tenure and tenancy, placing no restrictions on the transfer of agricultural land to nonagriculturalists. The increase in rice cultivation and the price of paddy, combined with the laissez-faire government practice, turned land into an attractive investment, fueled land grabbing, and precipitated mass expropriation of land from cultivators as well as an unsustainable hike in rent in the delta. Already by the early 1900s, almost one-fifth of the occupied land in the thirteen principal rice-growing districts of Lower Burma had passed into the hands of predominantly nonresident nonagriculturists. Within a decade, the number increased to nearly one-quarter and continued to increase thereafter.[57] As the annual report of the British administration for 1911–1912 emphasized, areas contiguous to Rangoon such as Syriam were particularly affected by this phenomenon. The report also pointed out that "a large portion of the non-resident owners were of non-Burman nationality and had thus no interest in their land or tenants save the extortion of as large an income as possible from them."[58]

The longtime ICS officer and scholar John S. Furnivall lamented that "the greatest achievement in the history of Burma"—that is, "the reclamation by Burmese enterprise of ten million acres of swamp and jungle"—ended tragically with "a picture of imposing Government offices and business houses in Rangoon, and gilded *chettyar* temples in Tanjore, while in the rice districts, the source of almost all this wealth, nearly half of the land is owned by foreigners, and a landless people can show little for their labour but their debts, and, for about half the year, most of them are unable to find work or wages."[59] The grievous agrarian conditions of Lower Burma would come to a head in the 1930s as the world descended into an economic depression. Burma would erupt in the largest peasant uprising in Burmese history—the Saya San Rebellion of 1930–1932—and in anti-Indian riots expressing widespread anger with the British administration's deregulation of land, as we explore in chapter 5.

For the privileged class of landlords such as Ma Galay, however, and for the time being, business was good. All but one of her five children lived off the rent they collected from the buildings and paddy fields they owned in Rangoon and Syriam. She paid for Ahmed, the youngest child and the only one to be formally educated, to attend the Calcutta Medical College, a premier medical school considered the birthplace of modern medical education in India. For leisure, the family sailed up and down the Irrawaddy River between Rangoon and Mandalay on the boat they owned, playing cards on the long journeys to and fro.

Would Furnivall have considered Ma Galay one of the "foreigners," as he put it, who had turned large populations of the Burmese into a landless, indebted people? Can we accurately apply to Ma Galay the administration's assessment of the nonagriculturalist, non-Burman absentee landlord as having "no interest in their land or tenants save the extortion of as large an income as possible from them"? Perhaps her tenants were not so badly off. Though a noncultivator and a "non-Burman," she had regular contact with her tenants over the years. Or so Auntie Rosie thinks. She remembers that every year, her grandmother's tenants brought paddy and produce from their land as either offerings, rent, or both.

At the same time, Ma Galay was a shrewd and exacting entrepreneur. For example, she gave out inheritance to all five of her children well before her death and demanded, from each of them, *no bo*. Literally "breast price" or "milk price," the Burmese phrase refers to the unrepayable debt children owe their mother for her embodied labor of pregnancy, birth, and nurturing. The notion of "milk debt" is not unique to Burma. It is a common cultural trope for filial duty found across Asia that establishes a mother's right to her children and a moral obligation for children to care and support their mother, especially in old age.[60] Ma Galay also made Ahmed pay her back the cost associated with his medical training in Calcutta. Significantly, Ahmed still had sufficient inheritance left to purchase multiple properties, including a lakefront estate in central Burma upon marriage, and defray the cost of educating his many children in Burma and England.

Such financial success must have required sharp business acumen on the part of Ma Galay. Her Arab connections may have given her a commercial edge; the turn of the twentieth century marked a shift in economic activities of Arabs in the region, a growing number of whom became providers of credit secured on urban property.[61] The land and properties she owned might also have been acquired with or by U Choe or by her affinal relatives. Such possibilities notwithstanding, that a young widow like her managed to thrive as a landlord remains remarkable in light of the predominance of men in the world of speculative land investment. Her competitors included the *chettiar* financiers from South India, the single most important moneylending community in Burma referenced by Furnivall in the above excerpt.[62] A powerful group that dominated networks of finance across the Bay of Bengal, the *chettiars* have become central characters in histories of commerce, capitalism, and colonialism in Burma and, more broadly, southern Asia. Ma Galay's life story serves as a useful and necessary reminder of the crucial role that women and their cunning and capital—not only migrant men and money—played in the far-reaching socioeconomic transformations of the nineteenth and twentieth centuries.

Reimagining the Local Wife

The scorned mistresses and orphaned children of European colonial masters are familiar figures in the history of métissage. They are central to the plot of George Orwell's first and semiautobiographical novel, *Burmese Days* (1934), arguably the most well-known English-language novel about colonial Burma. Himself an Anglo-Indian raised primarily in England, Orwell was born in India to an ICS officer and a French-English mother who had grown up in Moulmein. Orwell joined the imperial police service in Burma in 1921 and remained there until 1927. He drew on these personal and familial experiences in writing *Burmese Days*.

The novel follows the story of John Flory, a middle-aged English timber merchant living in a Burmese outpost, and his embattled attempt to escape his life of discontent: with his job, his relationship with his Burmese mistress

Ma Hla May, the local expatriate community, and British imperialism. An opportunity presents itself when a most eligible English bachelorette, Elizabeth Lackersteen, arrives in town. Flory recognizes that she is a "heartless" individual who shares none of his own sympathies for the natives and disaffections with the British. Yet Flory pursues Elizabeth, seeing marriage to her as his only salvation.

The two Eurasian characters in the novel, Francis and Samuel, are described as "thin and weedy and cringing," and generally lowly, groveling, and incapable creatures—not fully human but too human to treat as animals. Shunned by the European expatriates, they live off the charity of the Burmese. At the end of the novel, Francis and Samuel drag Ma Hla May out of a church where she has just accused Flory, in front of his European compatriots, including Elizabeth, of abandoning her "like a pariah dog" after their long and clandestine relationship. Described as "perhaps the first useful deed of their lives," Francis and Samuel redeem themselves by banishing the native mistress.[63] In the end, Ma Hla May personifies not only the native mistress but as well the native mother spurned by her own blood.

The life stories of Di Di and Ma Galay capture how misleading and demeaning is this image of "the Burmese mistress." Even if Defries had refused or hesitated to recognize Di Di as his wife and Helen May, Juliet, and Cecilia as his daughters, and even if he had abandoned Di Di and their children in Mandalay and left for Rangoon, there is little resemblance between the complex, spirited life of Di Di and the caricatured, abject character of Ma Hla May. Both Di Di and Ma Galay led intrepid lives unconfined to the putatively feminine domain of sex, domesticity, and reproduction, attaining a level of socioeconomic mobility that defied the odds. Such women call into question the scholarly emphasis to date on the large-scale transregional movements of men and challenge us to reconceive the pitiable historical figure of the "native wife" as a dynamic subject who moved in between and across multiple languages, lineages, and confessions.

The life stories of U Choe and Defries too unsettle how we have come to understand nineteenth-century changes in patterns of mobility. The single most outstanding aspect of migration in nineteenth-century Asia was the unprecedented mass migration of mostly young, laboring men from China and India who, historians have maintained, had no intention of settling in their destinations, unlike their predecessors. If migration during the age of sail slowed movement enough to give rise to settlement, intermarriage, conversion, and creolized societies, the age of steam made them obsolete and less appealing to migrant men. The premature deaths of Defries and U Choe make it impossible to know if they considered themselves sojourners and their respective marriage "temporary" with the expectation that they would eventually depart from Burma. The fact is that they both lived out their lives in Burma and formed enduring intimate relationships in the country.

Were their stories representative of the multitude of migrants from different echelons of society who set foot in Burma and married Burmese women? They were certainly not atypical, as revealed by stories of intermarriage and conversion that have entered the British colonial legal archive, to which we now turn.

CHAPTER 2

Mobility and Marital Assimilation

In a discussion of Asian migrants and intermarriage in nineteenth-century Burma, the name Chan Ma Phee (1848–1920) is likely to come up. Chan migrated from Fujian to Burma via the British island colony of Singapore to become the preeminent rice dealer among the Chinese in the 1890s and, like Ma Galay, a wealthy landlord and financier. His prosperity was such that in 1903, he substantially financed the expansion of the main Hokkien temple in Rangoon, known as the Foken Chinese Temple or the Kuanyin Temple complex, originally built in 1861. Chan had the means to arrange a marriage to a China-born, or *sinkeh* (*xinke*, literally "new guest" in Chinese), bride for himself. Instead, he married Aye Mya, a daughter of rice farmers in a suburb of Rangoon (fig. 2.1). They consecrated a shrine at the Shwedagon Pagoda, one of the most venerated Buddhist sites in Burma—a legacy that has kept the memory of the Sino-Burmese couple and their marriage alive.[1]

Readers of the section on "prominent Chinese" in *Twentieth Century Impressions of British Burma* (1910), in which Chan appears, would be correct to conclude that migrants like Chan who married Burmese were outnumbered by those who married Chinese women.[2] But published biographies of such men, as detailed as they might be, are both incomplete and deceptive. Take, for instance, Choa Chuan Ghiock. According to his obituary dated 25 January 1900 in the *Straits Times* (the main newspaper in the British Straits Settlements), the

FIGURE 2.1. Chan Ma Phee, dressed in Chinese formal wear consisting of surcoat with an embroidered badge and black hat with a finial, is pictured with his wife Aye Mya, wearing a white Burmese blouse and her hair coiled into the customary chignon known as *sadohn*. Source: Arnold Wright, *Twentieth Century Impressions of British Burma* (London: Lloyd's Greater Britain, 1910), 311. Courtesy of Cornell University Library.

sixty-three-year-old Malacca-born Choa had spent forty years in Rangoon, returning to Singapore only eight years prior to his death. Elsewhere, he is described as "one of the leading Chinese merchants in Rangoon," who, after long managing the Rangoon branch of the firm of Leack, Chin Seng & Co., retired in Singapore a rich man. What these brief accounts of Choa fail to mention is that throughout much of his adult life, he had maintained spouses and children in both Rangoon and Singapore. We know this because of a legal dispute among his grandchildren over his estate that had reached the Judicial Committee of the Privy Council in London, which served as the final court of appeal for the entire British Empire.

The record of the case reveals that Choa had left behind not only "a considerable amount of landed and house property" in Singapore and Rangoon but also in Singapore, a "Chinese wife," Choo Bin Lee, with whom he had three children; three additional children in Singapore from another "Chinese wife," Chee Koo Yiang, who had predeceased him; a "Burmese wife" and three children in Rangoon; and a "concubine" with whom he had a daughter, though it is unclear where.[3] That Choa maintained multiple marriages and families does not mean that he treated them equally. In his will, prepared during the last few years of his life, Choa left a house in Rangoon for his Burmese wife "for life and after her death for her son" and made over other houses to his daughters in Burma and their children after them. Yet he left the house in Rangoon in which he resided to his surviving Chinese wife and his sons by her, not to his Burmese wife or their Sino-Burmese children. His will divided up his residual estate among his sons by his Chinese wives in Singapore, excluding his Sino-Burmese son in Rangoon (and all his daughters).[4] Choa may have been closer to his Burmese wife and children—he did spend most of his adult life living in Rangoon—but his Chinese family received the greater share of his material belongings.

The marriages of the small minority of migrant men who struck gold in the colonies in the manner of Chan and Choa have become the stuff of family legends and public knowledge. They are also preponderant subjects of civil cases compiled and referenced as precedents by the British colonial administration. Most of the clients of the colonial civil courts in Burma were propertied people; they had assets to devolve and distribute and could afford legal expenses and court fees that added up as the lawsuit dragged on. But more than a few middling and working classes of migrant men and their stories of intermarriage and conversion have entered the colonial legal archive. Thus we know that when Karim Khan, an émigré from India who worked as a hospital assistant in Burma like Defries, died in Toungoo in 1907, he had been married to Ma Kye for some twenty-seven years and had four children.[5] An intriguing figure who complicates the static categorization of landowners in Burma by colonial authorities as majority foreign, absentee, nonagriculturalist, and moneylender and minority native, resident, and cultivator, Ma Kye was a Burmese paddy trader, financier, and landlord who let out her land to tenants. By her own admission, she had secured the seed money for her business from her husband as well as from a *chettiar*. With the money, she built a lucrative paddy-trading and moneylending business, which more than supplemented Karim's modest income as hospital assistant and from his private medical practice.

Their partnership allowed the couple to finance the costly medical training of Abdul Rahman Khan Laudie, Karim's son from another marriage. Ma Kye recalled that she spent about Rs. 20,000 on Abdul's education in Toungoo, Rangoon, and eventually England. To put this figure in perspective, the annual salary of British civil and army officers in colonial India ranged from Rs. 8,000 to Rs. 20,000.[6] This education enabled Abdul to pursue a successful career in the Indian Medical Service. Also thanks to her business, Karim and Ma Kye acquired sizable land holdings, considerable enough in 1914 to induce Abdul, by then a civil surgeon in Punjab, to sue Ma Kye for possession of the land.

The notion that due to the transient nature of their work, laboring classes of migrant men were even less likely than the likes of Chan, Choa, and Karim Khan to "settle" or intermarry also resists generalization in Burma, where colonial authorities remarked on the frequency of marriage between "Tamil cultivators" and Burmese women. Seniyappa Anamalay Pillay was one such migrant laborer who appeared in the Chief Court of Lower Burma in July 1906 to appeal a court decree that had awarded the estate of his deceased wife Ma Me to one of her brothers, Po La. Pillay's testimony was recorded as follows:

> The appellant when asked his description said that he was born in Madras, and that he was by race Sudra. Later on in his evidence he said he was from birth a paraiah. He asserted that Ma Me was his wife, and that he and she had married 16 or 17 years previously. There was no ceremony but they agreed to live together, and did so until she died. They had no children. She used to cook food for him, and he used to eat with her. All along he used to go to the Hindu Temple, but he used to go with her to the Pagoda and to *Pongyi Kyaung* [monastery]. He said they used to light candles at the Pagoda and worship there. He professed to know some Burmese prayers.[7]

Despite "evidence that the two were regarded as man and wife," Po La had successfully argued that Pillay was not his late sister's legal husband for she was Buddhist and he was Hindu. As Chief Justice Fox, a longtime government advocate and civil servant in Burma, explained, "a Hindu of one of the castes recognized by the Hindu faith cannot lawfully marry anyone who does not belong to the caste to which he or she belongs."[8] The question of the validity of intercaste marriage according to Hindu law and the legal entitlements of the children of intercaste union constituted a major jurisprudential debate in British India. There, the colonial courts, after spending much time and energy adjudicating the issue, had determined that caste-endogamous marriage was de jure the norm and the rule.

Nevertheless, Fox found in Pillay's account of his life with Ma Me sufficient proof of "permanent alliance." His assertion that Ma Me used to cook for him must not have been lost on the judge, who would have been familiar with Orientalist scholarship that described casteism as the defining feature of Hindu society and the mundane activities of cooking and eating as gatekeeping exercises that established social distance among Hindus of different castes. Fox decided the case in Pillay's favor, citing the prevalence of marriage between Burmese women and "Tamils of the lower orders" such as Pillay, who did not, Fox reasoned, "consider themselves bound by a rule of Hindu law."[9]

The colonial legal archive bears witness not just to partnerships that endured and prospered but as well to migrant men who left behind their wives and families in Burma to try their luck in another colony or return to their natal families elsewhere. The transcripts of another lawsuit that reached the Privy Council tell in unusual detail the story of one such case.

Hailing from Calcutta, the brothers Abdul Hadee and Hadjee Hoosain Bindaneem were merchants in Rangoon by the middle of the nineteenth century. Having had a less than prosperous career, though, Abdul Hadee returned to Calcutta a poor man sometime before his death in March 1886. Though he had no property to speak of, he apparently left a will in which he left everything to his (much wealthier) brother, noting, however, that he had a child in Burma and wished that his brother should give him "something." Hadjee Hoosain, on the other hand, made quite a fortune in Rangoon, though he had no children prior to his death there in February 1890. Having thus died without an heir, a search began for Abdul Hadee's son in Burma to hand over to him a handsome estate. Thanks to the efforts of "some enterprising gentlemen at Calcutta," it was soon discovered that Abdul Hadee had married a Burmese woman by the name of Ma Thai and had indeed had a son, Abdul Razack, a.k.a. Maung Hpay.[10]

Through Ma Thai's testimony, we know that her marriage to Abdul Hadee, which took place sometime around 1854, was first proposed by her sister in Rangoon. Mah Thai was a young divorcée living with her parents in her native village about a half day's journey from Rangoon, where Abdul Hadee came to meet her. Recounting their first encounter, Ma Thai recalled that she asked him if he would live together with and look after her for a long time, to which he replied that he would. Abdul Hadee then visited her several more times before their marriage. On the day of the marriage, Ma Thai was placed "in an inner room" and was asked by someone in the outer room if she loved him and consented to the marriage. Mah Thai's description of her marriage was recorded as follows: "My husband said something which I did not understand. Abdul Hadee said he would marry me according to Kala custom.

I agreed. . . . I said he would have to give dower according to custom among Kalas. I did not understand; but it was said it must be according to Kala custom, and so I said he must give dower according to Kala custom."[11]

Ma Thai then moved to Rangoon to live with Abdul Hadee after what must have been an Islamic marriage. She never met his brother Hadjee Hoosain or any of his relatives and did not know why they did not come to see her. She also remembered that she "worshipped as he did" while they lived together, repeating prayers "in some kala language" that she did not understand but that her husband did not allow her to go to the mosque with him. She knew both that there was a mosque in Rangoon and "that wives of Moguls go to the mosque" but did not know why Abdul Hadee refused to take her along when she expressed her desire to do so.[12]

About a year and a half later, Ma Thai returned to her mother's home to give birth. Upon their son's birth, she sent a message to Abdul Hadee, who replied that he was too busy to come but sent money for expenses and a message to her parents to look after her. He went to see her only twice thereafter: first, about six months after the birth of their child, when Abdul Hadee gave their son a Muslim name, Abdul Razack. He wrote the name on a piece of paper, which Ma Thai had copied on a palm leaf for fear it might be lost. Abdul Hadee returned six months later, hoping to take his wife and son with him to Rangoon. Yet Ma Thai refused. She never heard from her husband again, although he continued to reside in Rangoon for the next twenty years or so. In the words of Lord Macnaghten, who delivered the judgment for the Privy Council:

> He was at that time apparently in prosperous circumstances, but he made no provision for her or for the child. . . . Mah Thai was very badly off, but she never applied to her alleged husband for assistance, nor did she make any attempt to see him, though she knew where he lived, and he had, she said, been kind to her while they cohabited together, and she liked her life with him. At the end of two years, or four years as she says in one place, she married a Burman by whom she had seven children.[13]

Abdul Razack was raised by Ma Thai's parents, who gave him the Burmese name Maung Hpay, and lived the life of "an ordinary Burmese peasant," that is, until he was "discovered" by his paternal relatives at the age of thirty-five.

Based on these stories about intermarriage from the colonial legal archive, it would seem that kinships formed in Burma by migrant men remained strictly localized; their wives and children were tied to Burma (or another locale or colony), while the men were at liberty to come and go. Yet Burmese women achieved a measure of mobility through their marriage to migrant men, as even the case of Ma Thai shows. The move to the bustling, cosmopolitan capital Rangoon from her natal village, though insignificant in terms of physical distance, must have felt like a major leap to Ma Thai.

Marriage likewise required Ngwe Bwint, another young divorcée who married a Muslim migrant from India, to traverse different lineages, languages, religions, and geographic locations. In the 1880s, she met and married Rahim Rasool Khan, who had moved from western India to run a small retail business in cloth in a remote village in Lower Burma. Ngwe Bwint converted to Islam. Rahim Rasool, who came to be known by his Burmese name Po Sin, gave her infant son from her previous marriage, Ngwe Ya, a Muslim name, Azam, raising him as his own. When Ngwe Ya was about eleven years old, Rahim Rasool sent him to the village of Atodra in Surat District, where his parents lived. Ngwe Ya was schooled there, becoming fluent in Gujerati, Urdu, and Arabic, and converted to Islam. Perhaps to oversee her son's upbringing, or perhaps to provide similar educational opportunities for her daughters, Ngwe Bwint moved to Atodra with her daughters in tow shortly after her son's departure from Burma.[14]

There is more to their story, to which I return momentarily. Before doing so, I want to consider the implications of these stories of interAsian intimacy for our understanding of intermarriage and conversion in the nineteenth century, long regarded as a watershed moment. There is every indication that intermarriage and conversion prevailed among Asians during the period in question, even among the wealthiest migrants who could afford wives in/from the "homeland" and even among the laboring and putatively transient classes of men. Stories of their intimate relationships in Burma, both fleeting and lasting, make untenable the dichotomous conceptual division of migrants into sojourners and settlers in the first place. While some, like Abdul Hadee, abandoned their Burmese wives, others forged lifelong ties that cannot be dismissed as temporary arrangements. They established marriages and families in Burma even as they participated in a transregional web of commerce, conversion, and kinship. Importantly, so did Burmese women.

Such intimate relationships were not illicit. Nor were the children of such intermarriages considered illegitimate. Not only did migrant men legally recognize their children with Burmese wives, but their relatives also went to great lengths to honor and transmit their family's legacies, as evinced by the story of Abdul Razack, a.k.a. Maung Hpay. Even Choa Chuan Ghiock, who allotted far less of his estate to his Sino-Burmese children than to his sons by his "Chinese" wife, acknowledged his familial ties to the former and their entitlement, albeit graduated, to inheritance and succession. These were patterns in interAsian intimacies that survived well into the twentieth century, long after the British completed its colonial expansion into Upper Burma and interAsian migration peaked numerically, right up until the exodus of the British on the eve of World War II, as we see in chapters 3 and 4.

The very same stories, however, suggest that the prevalence of intermarriage and conversion should not be taken as evidence of their general social acceptance. After all, Choa did privilege his "Chinese" family over his Burmese wife and children in his will. The testimony by Ma Thai also raises the possibility that her husband, by refusing to introduce her to his family or take her to the mosque, had kept their marriage hidden from his kin. The story of Ngwe Bwint, Rahim Rasool, and Ngwe Ya also offers a glimpse into the proscriptions and penalties that accompanied intermarriage and conversion in Burma.

Margins of Acceptability

After Ngwe Ya completed his studies in Atodra, Rahim Rasool expected his multilingual, India-educated son to help him with his business, just as Ma Galay did. Unlike Ahmed, Ngwe Ya did just that upon his return to Burma. But like Ahmed, he promptly married against the wishes of his parents. It is unclear what infuriated Rahim Rasool: that the woman Ngwe Ya married was a servant in his (Rahim Rasool's) employ; that she was a widow, two years older than his son, who already had two children from a former relationship; that she was Buddhist and did not convert to Islam upon marriage to his son; or that Ngwe Ya could not be persuaded to give up his Buddhist wife and return to India with his mother, who had come rushing to intervene. If we are to believe the allegations made against Ngwe Ya by his relatives, Ngwe Ya not only failed to convert his wife but had himself undergone conversion—or rather, reversion—to Buddhism upon marriage. Though Rahim Rasool never severed his ties with Ngwe Ya, he took calculated measures to disinherit the man he once considered his son. He requested the local district court to declare that Ngwe Ya was not his son and excluded the latter from his will entirely.

Ngwe Ya had clearly crossed a line. But what line had he transgressed? For the purposes of the legal battle over Rahim Rasool's estate, the plaintiff, Ngwe Ya, and the defendants, Rahim Rasool's second wife and his daughters with Ngwe Bwint, debated the nature of his trespass as a matter of religion, defending and disavowing affective and material family ties on this basis. Ngwe Ya testified to the authenticity of his conversion and biography as a devoted Muslim son and therefore a legitimate and deserving heir. The defendants asserted that Ngwe Ya had willfully abandoned his Muslim family and identity.

But if the issue indeed was Ngwe Ya's alleged apostasy or failure to convert his wife to Islam, then how did Rahim Rasool interpret this behavior: as evidence of deficient piety, filiality, or manliness? Perhaps all of the above.

In another story of familial strife involving adoption, intermarriage, and conversion, a zerbadi woman married a pathi kala to the objection of her adoptive Bamar parents. According to the court record, Ma Ye, "a Burmese lady of considerable fortune," and her husband, Ko On, adopted in 1858 the two zerbadi daughters of her cousin Ma Ku and Ebrahim Cassim Chayanglia.[15] Ma Ye had a close relationship to the two girls and their mother from long before the adoption, serving as a protege of sorts for Ma Ku, who was in financial straits and whose husband was an absent husband and father. Ma Ku worked for Ma Ye at one point and gave birth to her younger daughter, Me Gale, under Ma Ye's roof. These circumstances, plus the fact that Ma Ye and Ko On were childless, resulted in the adoption of Ma Ku's daughters, who were named heirs to the estate of the wealthy couple. What the court record does not tell us is if there were other motives behind the adoption. Perhaps it was just a charitable act by an affluent matriarch intent on helping her struggling relative. Though perhaps the adoption, Ma Ye hoped, would bring Ma Ku back into the fold and ensure that her zerbadi daughters grew up Buddhist.

We do know that the girls were raised Buddhist and that Ma Ye objected to Me Gale's elopement with Ismail Lotia and conversion to Islam when she was eighteen years old. The marriage suggests that Me Gale was not dissociated from the pathi kala community in Moulmein, to which her father belonged, as a result of her adoption by a Bamar couple. And against the disapproval of her adoptive mother, Me Gale married a pathi kala just as her birth mother had. In time Ma Ye condoned the marriage and accepted Ismail as her son-in-law, giving him employment and renting a house for the couple and their three children. When Ismail passed away in 1884, Me Gale and her three children moved back in with Ma Ye and Ko On.

Both stories convey anxiety over intermarriage and conversion, even among people who were themselves party to such relationships, raising the questions of what they signified to the persons directly affected by the intimate relationships, and how it was perceived by the broader society. These are difficult questions to answer not least because of the scarcity of historical sources that would allow us to do so from the perspective of the individuals in the relationships.

Nevertheless, historians have interpreted them as evidence of the negative impact of intensified diasporic interactions on intermarriage and the pluralistic sensibilities, creole practices, and hybrid identities associated with it. According to this line of explanation, Rahim Rasool's disapproval of the marriage of Ngwe Ya to a Buddhist woman who failed to convert to Islam; the marriage of Me Gale to Ismail Lotia; and the division of inheritance arranged by the aforementioned bigamous Choa Chuan Ghiock prior to his death, which subordinated his Burmese wife and Sino-Burmese children to his "Chinese" family in Singapore, all signified a development from within migrant populations that became less amenable to "localization" and less accepting of intermarriage. Some historians attribute the preference for endogamous marriage over intermarriage to a growing insularity or concern with purity among migrants.[16] Others interpret the shift as a strategy of kinship organization by migrants seeking to build ties with major political and economic players, less and less of whom came from Indigenous populations as European colonial expansion and consolidation proceeded.[17] Both explanatory frameworks emphasize, like the historical narrative of métissage, the increased population of women in the colonies who shared the languages, lineages, and ritual activities of migrant men, either because they were themselves migrants from the "homeland," daughters of intermarriages, or, like Rahim Rasool's daughter, had been sent "home" for education. Both presume that native attitudes toward migrants and intermarriage remained more or less accommodating or that any changes they may have undergone were immaterial.

The notion that Burmese society is by tradition accepting of intermarriage and conversion has represented a prominent feature and ingrained assumption of European discourse on Burma. For centuries, British adventurers, envoys, and colonial officers narrated with fascination what they portrayed as the Burmese openness to intermarriage. In the popular travelogue *A New Account of the East Indies* (1727), the Scottish merchant captain Alexander Hamilton described Burmese women as "very fond of marrying with Europeans" and "obedient and obliging wives" who became indispensable commercial partners to their husbands.[18] Writing in the 1790s, Michael Symes, the British embassy to the court of Ava, also made frequent references to the liberality with which the Burmese encouraged men "of whatever climate or complexion" to marry Burmese women "and consider themselves as natives of the country":

> They are sensible that the strength of an empire consists in its population; and that a prince is great and powerful, more from the number of his subjects, than from the extent of his territory: hence the politic indulgence that the Birman government grants to every sect freely to exercise its religious rites: they tolerate alike the Pagan and the Jew, the Mussulman or Christian, the disciples of Confucius, or the worshippers of fire; the children of whom, born of a Birman woman, equally become subjects of the state, and are entitled to the same protection and privileges, as if they had sprung from a line of Birman ancestry.[19]

Like Hamilton, Symes emphasized that Burmese women were known to be faithful wives of foreigners, even those who "come to pass a temporary residence amongst them."[20] Written approximately a century later, the travelogue of Colonel Fitz William Thomas Pollok, who served in the British imperial army, differed only slightly from those of Symes in its description of Burmese women and their relations with foreign men: "Burmese women and girls are free to visit European families; a bevy of girls will not hesitate to visit even a bachelor, just to show themselves off and their ornaments, and perhaps to attract an admirer, for these little women have no objection to accept a *kala* (a foreigner) as a husband according to their laws and customs—and very good wives they make, too."[21] As Pollok's contemporary and aforementioned Conservator of Forests John Nisbet explained, such unions were "not degrading" to a Burmese woman, "and after its dissolution she frequently marrie[d] well, without a taint of immorality besmirching her reputation on account of such previous union."[22]

An 1875 divorce trial in the Special Court of Lower Burma offers another late nineteenth-century account of how intermarriage—between Muslim migrants and Burmese women in this case—were regarded, though from the perspective of the two most powerful colonial jurists in British Burma: the judicial commissioner and the recorder. The former had jurisdiction over the territory outside Rangoon and the latter over Rangoon and all criminal cases in any part of Burma where the accused were European subjects. The judicial commissioner and the recorder occasionally convened the Special Court of Lower Burma, which, until 1900, was the court of appeal for Rangoon and Moulmein, the two most important cities in Lower Burma. On this occasion, Judges Wilkinson (recorder) and Quinton (judicial commissioner) came together in May 1875 to review an application for divorce by Mi Shwe Ywet from her husband, Kumal Sheriff. The characterization by the two judges of marriages between "Mahomedans from other countries" and Burmese women is worth quoting at length:

> In a country like this, where a large number of Mahomedans from other countries have taken up their residence, and in very many cases their permanent abode, and where the natives have no race prejudices against alliances with foreigners, and whose religion offers no impediment to such, we find these mixed marriages everywhere existing among them, which have been duly celebrated according to Mahomedan rites; the wife having previously renounced her own religion and embraced that of her husband. Such an alliance is not regarded by either party as one of a temporary character, or in any way partaking of concubinage such as the

liaisons that at one time prevailed here between Europeans and the women of the country, but as a formal and a binding marriage. It only requires a short experience of this country to know that these marriages are regarded amongst the Mahomedan community as being of as binding a character, and as conferring on the wife as honorable a position in the family, as if she had been of Mahomedan descent; for she holds the same position as the husband's other wife does if he happens to have another. The offspring likewise of these marriages are brought up in the Mahomedan faith, and are acknowledged by their father as his legitimate children, and, at his death, share in his property as such.[23]

The opinion of the judges confirmed the widespread practice of intermarriage as a "binding" and "honorable" institution. On the other hand, it challenged the view of intermarriage, held by contemporary British observers like Yule (the envoy to Amarapura), as an effective, often comprehensive means of assimilating migrant men. The judges emphasized, instead, how intermarriage served to "convert the Burmese wife" who "renounced her own religion and embraced that of her husband." Ironically, Mi Shwe Ywet had appealed for a divorce on the basis that she "never was anything else than a Buddhist, though to enable her husband to marry her she did profess Mahomedanism."[24] She testified that she and Kumal had also been married by Burmese customs, the latter having asked the permission of her parents to marry her and provided bride price. The judges even acknowledged that they doubted that conversion in "all cases, or even in many," was "the result of conviction of the truth of the religion embraced." The point is that intermarriage, according to the judges, was common in Burma, not because it served an assimilative function but because the Burmese had neither "race prejudices" nor "religious impediments" against it.

The assessment of Muslim-Buddhist intermarriages by the judges were challenged by the census report of 1911. In his discussion of "Burmese marriage customs," the superintendent of the census, C. Morgan Webb, stated that "the prohibited degrees of marriage among the Burmese are few," and "marriage restrictions, so fundamental in a country where caste prohibitions are supreme, are of comparative unimportance where caste is almost unknown." He described marriage in Burma as a "purely secular" affair, nothing more than "a civil contract dissolvable by either party practically at will." He also claimed however that "the country opinion is strongly held with regard to the admixture of the Indian and Burmese races" while "the fusion of Chinese and Burmese strains is generally considered to be a most advantageous racial combination" that "improved the indigenous racial stock."[25] The report thus confirmed the idea that there were no "religious impediments" but contradicted the notion that there were no "racial prejudices."

These British discourses about intermarriage, spread across centuries, were unevenly sexist, Orientalist, and racist. The accounts by Hamilton, Symes, Pollok, and Nisbet othered intermarriage in Burma as beyond the pale of Christian, Anglo-Saxon ideas and ideals of marriage premised on the separation into opposite and oppositional realms emotional, sexual attachments and material, economic exchange. They exoticized and eroticized Burmese women as desiring carnal knowledge of foreign men—a familiar trope of the native female in Anglo-European narratives about colonial adventures and conquests. In their fantastical narrations, Burmese women beckoned penetration by "men of whatever climate or complexion."[26] Such discourses of intermarriage in Burma closely mirrored European fetishization of the institution of the "harem." European men and women were desperate to know the very institution they condemned as the inner sanctum of Oriental sexual excess.[27]

The commentaries on intermarriage by Judges Wilkinson and Quinton and the census superintendent Webb were devoid of such Orientalist tropes. Still, they served to reproduce colonial difference. For one, they represented intermarriage as something that colonial subjects, not imperial agents, did (or imperial agents *no longer* did, according to Judges Wilkinson and Quinton). Webb additionally perceived marriage in Burma as bereft of the sacrality of the Christian institution of marriage—a "purely secular affair" as he put it—and, as such, easy to enter and easy to exit. The "secular" and "contractual" nature of marriage practices among the Burmese, not the sexuality of Burmese women, accounted for the prevalence of intermarriage in Burma.

While described as "the country opinion," Webb's assessment of the "admixture" of Chinese, Indian, and Burmese races also betrayed a eugenicist belief that a scientific process of racial mixing, sterilization, and segregation could produce more desirable human breeds and ultimately eliminate inferior, less desirable ones. The pseudoscience of race and eugenics had been on the ascendancy among scientists, policymakers, and administrators in Britain and its empire.[28] The likes of Webb endorsed "the Chinese-Burmese admixture" as a form of positive eugenics, that is, of cultivating superior human traits and regenerating the Burmese race. But they disapproved "the admixture of the Indian and Burmese races" as productive of "a degraded and demoralized race," in the words of G. F. Arnold, the financial and revenue secretary to the government of Burma in 1908.[29]

Neither Webb nor Arnold explained the logic behind this disparate assessment, which may have struck them as self-evident. According to the decennial census of 1881 for British Burma, the first that tried "to obtain information concerning the persons of mixed race," there were three classes of mixed races: "the crosses between the indigenous races or those which, though not indigenous, are cognate with those that are"; "the crosses between indigenous and Indian races"; and "the crosses between the indigenous or Indian and the European races."[30] The so-called Chinese-Burmese admixture belonged to the second category, crosses between cognate races, while the "Indo-Burman" represented a crossing of putatively unrelated races. By implication, even more dangerous was the third category of mixed races: those that crossed the so-called white and yellow or brown races.

Despite its discrepancies, this colonial discourse on intermarriage in Burma was surprisingly consistent in some key respects. It portrayed intermarriage as a prevalent and sanctioned practice against which there were neither religious nor legal objections. It emphasized the permanent nature of intermarriage, insisting that it was binding, if not always abiding, and that the woman party to the relationship was regarded as a legitimate wife. It did not question the authenticity and validity of intermarriage. And there was agreement on the transformative power and potential of intermarriage that were manifested in the putative assimilation of migrant men, conversion of Burmese women, and the racial regeneration and degeneration of the Burmese.

What is significant about these claims about intermarriage in Burma is not their veracity but what they reveal about the mentality of the men making the claims. Yet the consistency with which they were rehearsed turned the British colonial discourse on the Burmese tradition of intermarriage into received wisdom that even historians have treated as a close approximation—if not an unmediated reflection—of the historical reality.[31] It is not at all clear however that Burmese society placed "no impediments" to intermarriage or that there were no social and legal consequences for intermarrying and converting.

Burmese Buddhist Law of Marriage

The opinion among British colonial officials that there were no "race prejudices" or "religious impediments" against intermarriage among the Burmese stemmed from their understanding of "Burmese Buddhist law," to which they also referred as "Burmese Buddhist customary law." Their understanding of this law, in turn, was based on their interpretation of a small group of the indigenous *dhammasat* ("treatise on dhamma" or "instructions of dhamma") texts available in English translation. Extant in thousands of palm-leaf and paper manuscript versions, they were widely circulating legal texts that outlined rules related to matters such as inheritance, marriage, contract, theft, and assault and

prescribed methods of dispute settlement. They existed alongside other cor-
puses of law that might be described as "Burmese Buddhist" that sometimes
overlapped and conflicted: namely, the *vinaya*, or monastic law, whose jurisdiction was limited to the sangha (monastic community), and *rajasat*, or royal law,
enacted by kings and ministers.[32] Upon colonization of Burma, the British
identified the *dhammasat* genre of legal literature as the basis of "Buddhist law"
that would govern disputes concerning "succession, inheritance, marriage or
caste, or any religious usage or institution" among Buddhists in the colony.

Legal reforms represented a cornerstone of the self-professedly liberal British Empire, whose stated mission was to replace the tyrannical "rule of men"
with the just and equitable "rule of law."[33] British imperial governance was
supposed to protect the rights of autonomous individuals from being infringed
upon by the rights of the family or community or suppressed by despotic mon-
archs. It would guarantee the liberty of individuals, most notably the individual right to private property, thus paving the way for a capitalist economic
system of market freedom and equality. Whereas the "rule of law" was to prevail in the so-called public sphere of money, market, and politics, the very
first governor general of India, Warren Hastings, decided against establishing
a standard body of territorial civil law that applied to all imperial subjects. Presented as a concession to the laws of the colonized, he exempted from imperial intervention the so-called personal realm of marriage and family. He
mandated that the family and religious affairs of the subjects of the British
Raj should be governed by their "personal laws," formulated as laws that applied only to members of particular religious community.[34] Under this legal
dispensation, the civil courts administered the "Burmese Buddhist law" in cases
where the parties were Buddhist, "Muhammadan law" in cases where the parties were Muslim, "Hindu law" where the parties were Hindu, and "Chinese
customary law" where the parties were Chinese.

The tensions and deceptions that marked the process of codifying "Hindu
law" and "Muhammadan law" were mirrored by the British administrative cu-
ration of "Burmese Buddhist law." British legal authorities recognized that
actual social practices often diverged from the dictates of textual law and exhibited important regional and local variations. Yet they sidestepped the variety of written law and the plurality of interpretations held by Burmese jurists
and scholars. According to the aforementioned ICS officer and scholar Furnivall, the practice of referring disputes for arbitration to the local *thugyi* (village headman) had declined significantly by the 1890s, and decisions by a *thugyi*,
even when ratified by a Burmese judge, were set aside by the judicial commissioner as contrary to Burmese law, signifying the displacement of custom
by "the rule of law."[35]

Having chosen the *dhammasat* texts as the foundational sources of law in Burma, they engaged narrowly with this legal corpus. They relied on the *Manu kyay dhammasat*, the only example available to them in English translation, as representative of "Burmese Buddhist law" when in fact it was "a never very popular, late eighteenth-century compendium."[36] Imperial deference to local laws, in the British Raj as in other contemporary European colonies, not only concealed significant areas of ignorance and uncertainty among colonial authorities in their knowledge of various "personal laws" but also masked the high degree to which ostensibly local laws were products of the colonial administration.[37]

An exemplary artifact of this process of colonial knowledge appropriation was *A Digest of the Burmese Buddhist Law concerning Inheritance and Marriage; being a collection of texts from thirty-six Dhammathats, composed and arranged under the supervision of the Hon'ble U Gaung, C.S.I. ex-Kinwun Mingyi* (1899).[38] Translated into English in 1909, it formed the basis on which the British made authoritative statements about "Burmese Buddhist" marriage laws. A perusal of this urtext reveals a resounding silence on the subject of intermarriage and conversion, at least as the British would have recognized them: as marriage between spouses of different race or religion and change in one's religious identification. Accordingly, British colonial authorities claimed with confidence that "the prohibited degrees of marriage among the Burmese are few."[39]

Yet the language of the *dhammasat* leaves no doubt that individuals in matrimony were expected to uphold and propagate the *thathana* (Pali: *sasana*), or the teachings of the Buddha. The *Ketuja dhammasat*, for instance, instructs a wife to abandon and separate from her husband if he "does not follow *sīla* (in Buddhism, virtue, morality, or right conduct) and has no shame in doing unmeritorious acts," while the *Manu kyay dhammasat* lists, among the eight kinds of husbands a wife may vituperate, "a husband who neither knows nor venerates the Three Gems [Buddha, dharma, sangha]." Similarly, a "good wife," according to the *Vinicchayarāsi dhammasat*, was enjoined to revere and venerate not only her parents and parents-in-law but also monks.[40] Just as elite representatives of such religions as Christianity, Islam, and Judaism defended their religion as the only true religion, so too did monks and ministers in Burma see the teaching of the Buddha as the only truly right—and therefore superior—view. Thus, an 1872 text compiled by an interior minister at the courts of Mindon and Thibaw that provided a brief survey of Christianity, Islam, and Hinduism warned that "those people who stay outside of thathana have not destroyed the wrong views even if they venerate Myanma (i.e., Burman) monks, listen to Myanma sermons, observe uposatha days, make donations, and build monasteries and rest houses."[41] Evidently, there were people with "wrong views" who were "passing" as followers of the Buddha, raising concerns about the state of the preservation and propagation of the thathana.

Such designations of "falling outside of the thathana" or "having wrong views," Alexey Kirichenko points out, were not only religious; they "were as often applied to members of other ethnic groups, both indigenous and foreign."[42] The sangha itself was divided and hierarchized on the basis of lu myo—for example, Burman, Mon, Shan, Manipuri, Northern Thai—in the seventeenth and eighteenth centuries, and the Burman monastic group held monopoly over appointments to the monastic hierarchy developed by the crown.

The penultimate king of Burma, Mindon, like his contemporary Siamese counterpart King Mongkut, is remembered as "an enlightened monarch" whose reign oversaw modernist reforms. Historians have highlighted how Mindon, known as an exceptionally devout patron of the thathana, gifted land and teak for the construction of mosques in Mandalay for his pathi subjects, and sponsored a lodge, or waqf house, in Mecca to facilitate their pilgrimage or hajj.[43] He welcomed migrant men from near and far even to high ministerial posts and the inner circles of the royal family. Rather than promulgate new laws to govern the marriage and family of such individuals, he left untouched an 1807 royal order, or *amein daw*, that granted pathi kala and *ponna* (Brahmin)[44] leaders the authority to adjudicate matters concerning their respective communities.[45] This echoed the practice of the Mughal administration in India, which left non-Muslim communities to administer their own laws to their own members through their own specialists.[46] Only on the eve of the British annexation of Upper Burma did King Thibaw form a "department of joint court" for the purpose of hearing cases concerning the "pathi, tayôk, and kala lu myo gya residing in Mandalay."[47]

Konbaung kings such as Mindon liked to idealize themselves not as the leader of a particular community but as *cakkavatti*—world conqueror who preserved the thathana and prepared the world for the coming of the next buddha—who ruled over a diverse population, akin to the contemporaneous Mughal, Qing, and Ottoman Empires. They patronized and protected people of linguistic, confessional, and ritual heterogeneity, some of whom were originally clients or dependents of another sovereign patron, who swore allegiance to the Burmese king. As though to instantiate this political vision and boast about the vast and heterogenous domain under its rule, the royal administration compiled lists of 101 categories of more or less discrete lu myo who supposedly inhabited the Burmese *naing ngan daw*, the country or sphere of influence under the Burmese sovereign.[48] This type of patron-client political dispensation was also premised, Victor Lieberman argues, on a conception of political legitimacy in which "authority derived from the power and charisma of the patron, and because each of his clients was tied to him by separate personal bonds, there was no need for a common identity among followers."[49] Shared rituals, language, literature, music, arts, dress, diet, and so on—whether we call this "culture" or "ethnicity"—neither determined nor guaranteed allegiance and political solidarity.

But Mindon, as with his predecessors, forbade his pathi subjects from engaging in activities and behaviors that openly or directly contravened the thathana, such as the slaughter of animals, which the pathi in the country might have viewed as an important ritual of Eid. Mindon may have treated his pathi subjects with tolerance or even benevolence. But he also expected them to uphold, at least publicly, the supremacy of the thathana. Indeed, the eighteenth and nineteenth centuries represented a period of integration and assimilation for Burma as elsewhere in Asia and Europe, which experienced the expansion of metropolitan cultures and a domination of a "core ethnicity" that claimed a privileged relationship to religious truth.[50] Even as royal clienteles remained multiethnic, Lieberman notes, "by 1770 Burmese completely dominated the court, and to local people and foreign visitors alike the empire had become identified, indeed synonymous, with its northern core ethnicity."[51]

Lieberman cautions against equating the ascendancy of "Burman ethnicity and Theravada orthodoxy" under the Konbaung administration with the formation of a dominant, supralocal subjectivity. He argues instead that the instrumental appropriation of practices and habits associated with the political center served as visible emblems of loyalty, especially during periods of conflict and crisis—warfare, famine—that yoked the welfare of heterogeneous local communities to that of the political center.[52] Even so, government attempts "to make culture and political authority congruent," said to be uncharacteristic of "pre-nationalist" Asia, had gained ground in Burma long before the era of nationalism.[53]

Placed in this context of growing Burman and Buddhist hegemony in the centuries leading up to British colonialism, the absence of legal and religious interdictions on marriage among people of different lu myo takes on significances that colonial officers and historians alike have overlooked. The context also recasts the family disputes over Ngwe Ya's marriage to a Buddhist woman and alleged reversion to Buddhism, and Me Gale's elopement with Ismail and conversion to Islam. The lack of prohibitions against intermarriage (of certain kinds) is best understood as indicative not of a culture of pluralism and tolerance but rather of a modality of social control that brought "outsiders" or "strangers" into a web of personal and political bonds of patronage and obligation, subjecting them to existing structures of hierarchy. What the British envoy Symes described as the custom of encouraging migrant men to "marry

Birman wives, and consider themselves as natives of the country" is better analyzed as a process of subjecting migrants and those who putatively held "the
wrong view" to the rule of the Konbaung administration and the teachings
of the Buddha.

This explains why the Konbaung government did not prohibit migrant men
from marrying native women but barred them from relocating with their wife
and children—a regulation that was a recurrent matter of dispute between the
government and the British colonial administration in their early dealings.[54]
Such rules and regulations were not, as scholarship on Burma has tended to
emphasize, merely measures intended to secure wealth in people, the fiscal
foundation of the administration.[55] Burmese kingdoms were long plagued by
the battle against runaways and rebels who switched patron rulers, became
monks, or sold themselves into slavery to reduce their service and tax obligations and otherwise evade government attempts to manage their lives.[56] According to this interpretation, royal orders and *pyat sa* (legal decisions)
regulating intermarriage among people who belonged to different categories
of commoners—each owing different kinds of services and taxes to the king
and his local representatives or to monasteries and private patrons—were motivated by fiscal priorities. Their overriding objective was to limit mobility
between service and tax groups that undermined service and tax extraction.[57]
Yet Konbaung kings measured their success by their ability not only to control wealth in people but also to propagate the thathana. It was one thing for
subjects of the British Empire to enter into Burmese territory, marry Burmese
women, and "consider themselves as natives of the country," as Symes put it.
For them to leave with their Burmese wives and children and convert them
into subjects of another sovereign or to "the wrong view" was quite another
matter. The same concern prompted rulers in neighboring Siam to go so far
as to issue a law condemning Mon and Thai subjects who gave their daughters
to English, Dutch, Javanese, and Malay men, making them liable to a range
of punishments, from confiscation of property to execution.[58]

Compliance and Defiance

From the vantage point of the social and political elites and authorities in Konbaung Burma, intermarriage was not just a sign but also a technique of subjection, expected to make loyal, productive subjects out of migrants. To be sure,
the pathi, kala, and tayôk of Upper Burma spoke Burmese and wore Burmese
dress even as they composed in other languages, had non-Burmese names, and
worshipped at the mosque, as one British colonial authority after another ob-

served. Such practices of simultaneous multiple affiliations, however, were created in a milieu that assumed the predominance of the Bamar and the thathana. This was an assumption and ideology that many migrants accommodated and exploited; the social dynamic that anthropologists have conceptualized as "situational ethnicity," wherein a person emphasizes or deemphasizes particular cultural, ethnic, or other communal affiliations and allegiances depending on the context (i.e., different ethnicities for different situations), is well-documented in Burma. At the same time, there were Karens, Chins, and other migrants in Upper Burma who, even as subjects of the Burmese king, refused to accept the supremacy of the Bamar and the thathana.[59]

It is striking that both of Aunti Rosie's grandmothers, the Karen Baptist Di Di and the Muslim zerbadi Ma Galay, married men who shared their batha. In their eyes, the act of marrying a pathi or Christian migrant may have signified an intimate act of disobedience in the tradition of James Scott's "everyday forms of resistance": quiet, subtle, and mundane forms of defiance of efforts at social control and subjection by Buddhists and the Bamar.[60] The same explanation might be applied to the decision by Me Gale to marry a pathi kala like her father against the wishes of her Buddhist adoptive parents or, for that matter, the insistence by Rahim Rasool and Ngwe Bwint that their son Ngwe Ya marry a fellow Muslim, convert or otherwise. If so, then endogamy and conversion (to Islam or Christianity) were attempts to put marriage into the service of minority communities.

There is yet another possibility. Perhaps Me Gale did not see her marriage to Ismail as an act of dissidence or betrayal of her adoptive parents or as a shift in her allegiance from Buddhism to Islam and from the Bamar to the pathi kala. Ngwe Ya too may not have predicted that his marriage to a Buddhist woman would result in the accusation by his family that he had left the Muslim fold. And if he did not prevail upon his wife to convert to Islam, as his relatives charged during the trial, even at the risk of disinheritance by his family and even as he remained himself Muslim, then perhaps we ought to understand Ngwe Ya's actions as a form of noncompliance with either the social pressure of the majority Buddhist to embrace the thathana or his family's expectations of endogamy and conversion.

These family dramas bring into sharp focus both female agency in conversion (of themselves or their family and relations) and the challenges posed to family relations by intermarriage and conversion. Both have been marginalized by the historiographic preoccupation with the readiness of states and societies in Southeast Asia to accept and accommodate migrants. Tellingly, a study that specifically examines the difficulties faced by Indigenous—and predominantly Muslim—women who married Chinese migrants in the Dutch

East Indies does not once raise the question of conversion or religion.[61] This reflects the prevailing popularity of the idea that Chinese migrants in Southeast Asia became Muslim or Christian only and nominally for the purpose of marrying Muslim Malay and Christian Filipina women.[62]

In keeping with the growing consensus in the voluminous literature on conversion, this utilitarian explanation of conversion challenges the once common assumption that conversion entailed a complete and irreversible obliteration of preexisting convictions and social ties. Incidentally, migrant men were hardly exceptional in converting for pragmatic reasons. The aforementioned story in which Mi Shwe Ywet filed for divorce from her Muslim husband, claiming that she professed to be Muslim in order to consecrate their marriage even as she remained Buddhist, is just one among many such cases that populate the colonial legal archive, as we see in chapter 3. Still, such legal narratives do not tell us what repercussions, if any, this very expectation that Mi Shwe Ywet "profess" to be Muslim had on the marriage itself or her social and familial relations.

In addition, the abundance of such examples of "pragmatic" conversions, as Barbara Andaya warns, should not lead us to underestimate female perceptions of conversion as a way of advancing their spiritual ambition and reputation or, I would add, to dismiss the meaning and effect of conversion via intermarriage upon migrant men.[63] As the stories of family conflicts explored above reveal, conversion in the context of intermarriage was not a mere formality, a symbolic identification with no real consequence. Ngwe Bwint, as far as we know, shared her husband's expectation that their son marry a Muslim woman. The refusal by Ngwe Ya's wife to convert to Islam and, possibly, his "reversion" to Buddhism under her influence resulted in his disinheritance. In her testimony, Ma Thai confessed to have had little understanding of the "kala customs" of marriage ceremony, as she put it, that she underwent to wed Abdul Hadee. Yet she also expressed interest in learning about them and in going to the mosque. Even in cases of intermarriage without conversion—or none that the British colonial civil court recognized as conversion—such as that of Seniyappa and Ma Me, who remained Hindu and Buddhist, respectively, their long marital life crossed religious conventions and communities. Ma Me accompanied her spouse to the Hindu temple, and Seniyappa went with her to the pagoda to worship. Intermarriage and conversion were not simple matters in Burma prior to the twentieth century. These intimate acts were already imbued with potent social, spiritual, and political implications. For both British and Burmese governments, and migrants and natives, intermarriage and conversion represented powerful institutions of transformation and transgression.

CHAPTER 3

Religion, Race, and Personal Law

In 1905, two zerbadi women filed in the Chief Court of Upper Burma an appeal against a decision by the District Court of Mandalay that "Muslim law," not "Burmese Buddhist law," should apply to Burmese Muslims insofar as inheritance and succession were concerned.[1] The zerbadi women claimed that there was "abundant evidence that outside the Courts the Zerbadis [sic] voluntarily and habitually applied the Buddhist law in cases of inheritances."[2] As evidence, the appellants called over a dozen witnesses. Mullah Ismail, the son of the zerbadi merchant and *akauk wun* (tax collector) Mullah Ibrahim mentioned in chapter 1, testified that prior to and immediately after the British annexation of Upper Burma in 1886, the zerbadi settled questions of inheritance according to the laws applicable to Buddhists; Aga Javad, identified as a longtime "Persian" resident of Mandalay, stated that in the forty years that he lived in Burma, he had not once heard of a zerbadi requesting the application of Muslim law; Mahomed Isaak, an elderly zerbadi and honorary magistrate of Mandalay, explained that Muslim zerbadi did not strictly follow the Buddhist law, though they were guided by it, and in general chose to deal with matters of inheritance without going to the courts; Maung Hla, a fifty-year-old zerbadi lawyer, affirmed that cases involving zerbadi were not decided according to Muslim law; as did Cho Gyi, a sixty-two-year-old woman and one of only two women witnesses, who claimed that "in the King's time Zerbadis divided their inheritance according to Buddhist law," clarifying that property acquired during marriage was the joint property of husband and wife.[3]

The testimonies of these witnesses indicated the prevalence among elite, propertied zerbadi of a practice known among legal scholars as "forum shopping": of choosing, in a plural legal system, a body of law or forum of dispute resolution that is most likely to deliver a favorable outcome.[4] The presiding British judges refused to acknowledge that Burmese Muslims submitted themselves to Buddhist law of their own volition, however. They were willing to concede that most zerbadi had Burmese names, spoke Burmese, and dressed in Burmese style. One even declared that he was persuaded that there existed "from time immemorial a custom having the force of law, by which questions of inheritance and succession affecting the Zerbadis [sic] of Mandalay have been decided by Buddhist law."[5] But the judges would not countenance the assertion that this custom reflected the will of the zerbadi subjects. They dismissed the appeal by reasoning that Burmese Buddhist law had been "forced on the Zerbadis [sic] by a despotic monarchy" that refused to permit the application of any other law.

The British authorities were clearly affronted by the testimonies that contradicted the imperial narrative of Oriental despotism and British liberalism. Burma's colonization was, as discussed in the previous chapter, justified on the basis that the British were the true bearers of justice replacing a "despotic monarchy" with the just and equitable "rule of law" that liberated the subject population from the absolutist "rule of men." The insistence by the zerbadi litigants and witnesses that Burmese kings had already put into place a "rule of law" that did not interfere with the personal affairs of the zerbadi could have only rubbed the British jurists the wrong way. Ironically, zerbadi satisfaction with the jurisdiction of "Burmese Buddhist law," expressed during the trial, was once shared by British subjects in Burma. One of the earliest Anglo-Burmese treaties (1826) recognized the authority of the Burmese monarch to administer justice to British nationals and natives of India. It resulted in few complaints, and British subjects acknowledged that Burmese magistrates "usually respected the 'standards of civilised nations' and often favoured them over the locals, especially for civil matters such as debt, inheritance, and litigation."[6] Some British officers had even described Burmese Buddhist law, admiringly, as "enlightened."[7]

The British judges found equally inconceivable the notion that Muslims would genuinely desire the application of "Buddhist law." According to them, a Muslim was a Muslim because the person followed Muslim law; a Hindu was a Hindu because the person adhered to Hindu law; and so on. In the words of one English Orientalist scholar, jurist, and authority on law in British India:

"Little or no change has taken place in the religious opinions of the natives since the days of Hastings and Jones: the Hindu still venerates the Institutes [of Manu] that have served to regulate the conduct of his forefathers for upwards to twenty centuries; and the Muhammadan looks with undiminished respect on the precepts of the Koran."[8] British colonial legal reforms in India were shot through with such Orientalist assumptions about colonial subjects as people who "rigidly and ritualistically followed their own law in all matters of social custom, religious duty, and commercial transaction."[9] Only by oppression would a Muslim make use of Buddhist law. The British judges cast themselves in the role of objective experts rescuing oppressed Muslim subjects who were unable to discern their own oppression. They thus rationalized their paternalistic refusal to grant the weight of truth to the testimonies by the zerbadi appellants. In doing so, the judge enshrined a colonial jurisdictional imperative: Buddhist law applied only to members of the Buddhist community (and only to their familial and religious affairs); Muslims could not have recourse to Buddhist law, just as Buddhists were precluded from the application of Muslim law. The British formulation of "personal law" and its orderly implementation depended on a simple and stable classification of legal status, to each of which one and only one "personal law" could be uniformly and inexorably applied. The judge ignored a fact laid out in plain sight. The adherence to the Muslim law of inheritance, however widespread it may have been among Burmese Muslims at the time, did not preclude a practice among the same group of following the Buddhist law of inheritance.

Scheming Like a Colonial State

Masquerading as immutable reality, the "inconceivability" of Muslims exercising the Buddhist law of inheritance was a legal conjecture that reflected the logic of colonial governance. Armed with such technologies as the census, maps, and cadastral surveys, and experts such as Oriental philologists, Indologists, and anthropologists, the British administration in Burma, as elsewhere, set about studying its new possession to govern it.[10] The territory was surveyed, demarcated, and mapped out into geographical areas ascribed with topographical and ethnographical features. Its population was partitioned into discrete, delimited racial and religious groups that were governable by their respective religious law.

The decennial census report of 1891, the first to be taken after the incorporation of Upper Burma into British Burma, is a model specimen of this process of colonial bureaucratic learning and knowledge production. Maps of the province were accompanied by a detailed discussion of the natural division of the colony into low-lying river basins and alluvial plains (of Arakan, Tenasserim, the Irrawaddy delta, the Chindwin valley, etc.). According to the report, the physical environment of these fertile lowlands—grassy, swampy, forested, and temperate—manifested itself "somewhat strangely and yet very markedly in the difference between the complexion and physique of the dwellers of the delta and of the drier and hotter districts of the upper province." People of the southern half of Burma were allegedly "fairer and stouter" than those farther north. Nevertheless, the report indicated, the Burmans in general "resemble[d] the mountaineers of the Himalayas," spoke a language similar to Tibetan, and thus "belong[ed] to the same stock."[11]

People of Burma who descended from an "impure" or different "stock" included the Arakanese, who were said to "approximate more closely to Hindu and Musalman customs in secluding their women" and to be "cleverer and more persevering than the Burmese generally." Shans were described as "Sinitic": light in complexion and characterized by "a Chinese type of face," namely, almond-shaped eyes. And owing to their habitat—"a mountainous region [where] the necessaries of life are not so easily obtained as in the fertile deltas of the Irrawaddy"—they were a "thrifty," "independent," and "restless" people. The "better class" among them also exhibited, the report added, "a cleanliness and comfort not found among Burmans of the same rank." Birthplace, physical traits, and language were thus construed as indicative of the race of the inhabitants of the province, who were divided into major racial categories that mirrored the precolonial categories of lu myo: Burman (or Burmese), Talaing, Shan, Karen, Karenni, Chin, Kachin, Arakanese, and so on. In addition, the report identified five main categories of "immigrant" races: Chinese, Hindu castes, Mahomedan tribes (or "Musalman tribes"), Eurasians, and European nationalities (see table 3.1).[12]

As this pattern of racial differentiation suggests, the British administration relied on the category of religion, which they employed from the very first colonial census that included the province of Burma, to aggregate their subjects into separate categories of immigrant versus Indigenous populations. The census of 1881 had already declared that the Burmese were "all Buddhists."[13] The 1891 census repeated the determination that Buddhism was the prevailing religion in the colony, "not only of the Burmans, but of their kindred races." The report claimed, "Its tolerance agrees with their easy-going good nature," elaborating that the "tolerant" nature of Buddhism had enabled it to incorporate *nat* worship (animistic worship), the "creed of the people before the introduction of Buddhism." The "tolerant" nature of Buddhism, combined with what the report described as the Burman "faculty of assimilating and

Table 3.1   "Chief Nationalities" Enumerated in Lower Burma in 1872 and 1891

NATIONALITY	1872	1891
Burmese	1,583,801	2,682,879
Arakanese	331,448	354,599
Chaungthas	9,634	3,492
Yabeins	5,436	2,197
Chins	51,117	60,383
Daingnets	3,548	1,910
Mros	7,875	15,666
Kwemis	18,969	14,200
Kathès	1,845	1,775
Talaings	181,602	466,324
Karens	331,255	531,756
Karennis	451	1,696
Taungthus	24,923	2,732
Shans	36,029	107,506
Chinese	12,109	34,462
Hindu castes	35,230	142,522
Mahomedan tribes	95,683	206,890
European nationalities	5,154	8,702
Eurasians	4,023	6,296
Others	7,016	12,640
Total	**2,747,148**	**4,658,627**

Source: H. L. Eales, *Census of 1891, Imperial Series (Burma Report)*, Volume IX (Rangoon, Burma: Government Printing, 1892), 193.

absorbing the lesser tribes and nationalities with which they are brought into contact," had allowed the Burmese race to propagate, "absorbing the wild hill tribes, and even some of the Indian settlers."[14]

The report also emphasized, however, that "exotic" religions were making inroads among the Burmese; alongside "the Europeanizing force of the British rulers on the one hand, and the admixture of foreign Chinese and Indian blood on the other," this development had apparently given rise to fears in the province that the Burmese race would gradually disappear if it did not cling to its religion and faculty of assimilation. According to the report, two "exotic" religions in particular had gained ground: Christianity and Islam. The former, it stated, was no longer "merely the religion of temporary settlers" and had "almost become the national religion of the Karens." There was also noticeable increase in the number of people who returned themselves as "Mahomedan." The report attributed this increase to "the influx of Chittagonian and Indian coolies, who every year in gradually increasing numbers flock down to work at the rice-mills in Akyab and Rangoon"—Chittagonian being a catch-all phrase used by the British to refer to people from the Chittagong division in Lower Bengal, bordering Arakan. It acknowledged however that the zerbadi were becoming "a recognizable portion of the inhabitants of Burma." Unlike Islam and Christianity, Hinduism remained thoroughly "exotic," the report concluded, and "show[ed] no signs of becoming a part of the religious life of the settled as opposed to the temporary inhabitants of the soil." As if to explain this failure of Hinduism to take root in the country, the report pointed out that Hindus did not "take to cultivating the soil for themselves," and the few that did "very often become Burmanized and adopt Burman names, and no longer remain Hindus in the strict sense of the term."[15]

The category of "Chinese" should have thrown a wrench into this scheme to separate the population of Burma racially and religiously into indigenes and foreigners. Europeans were homogeneously identified as Christians. Indians were conflated with "Hindu castes" and "Mahomedan tribes." But the Chinese were "nearly evenly divided between Buddhism and Nat-worship," the census report stated, wasting no time to explain: "This is due to the fact that the Burmese enumerators refused to accept the Taoist [sic] Chinaman as a true Buddhist, and the return is a striking commentary on those writers who would class all Chinamen as Buddhists."[16] The report thus immediately squashed the conclusion suggested by the census returns: that the Chinese, though an "immigrant" race, shared the two religions that the British most closely associated with Burma. According to the report, those Chinese who were classified as *nat* worshippers were in fact Daoists. And those who identified as Buddhist were not Buddhist in the sense that the Burmese were Buddhist. Their brand of Buddhism had Daoist inflections that rendered it inauthentic in the eyes of the Burmese. The Chinese were foreign in race and religion after all.

This interpellation of Chinese Buddhist as Daoist or syncretized Buddhists posed a problem for the judicature that it could not resolve for decades to come: what "personal law" should apply to the Chinese in Burma.[17] But it kept intact the administrative tethering of race, religion, and origin (immigrant vs. Indigenous). In this equation, religion, race, and origin status were co-constitutive. Religion mapped neatly onto race (and vice versa), and origin was made legible through religion and/or race. It made descriptions such as "Burmese Buddhist" or "Indian Hindu" appear tautological, while others such as "Hindu Burmese" or "Christian Burmese" were made to seem anomalous and questionable. It naturalized the division of the population in Burma into the category of either immigrants or natives and into the major "stocks" of Burmese, other "Asians" (i.e., Indian and Chinese), and European.[18] It naturalized, too, the colonial political ideology of communalism that attributed to colonized subjects immutable, irreconcilable religious differences that purportedly served as the founding and organizing principles of community. Like despotism and tribalism, communalism was an essentialist concept "reserved for the analysis of social and political conflicts in the 'backward' parts of the colonial and post-colonial world." It captured, allegedly, the inherent incapacity of primitive societies (in Asia, Africa, and the Middle East) to overcome their religious bigotries to become modern, rational, secular nations like those in Europe and the United States.[19] Yet another possible reason British jurists balked at the insistence by Muslim zebardi litigants and witnesses that they willingly turned to "Buddhist law": because the testimony controverted the colonial idiom of communalism that constituted colonized populations as individuals and collectives governed by religious fanaticism.

Such classification schemes primed the colony for efficient, economical white minority rule. To this end, the peoples and terrains of the colony were constituted as standard types and quantifiable aggregates. Divided and subdivided along racial and religious lines, the colony's population was assigned different productive potential, economic roles, and capitation taxes. The colonial government cataloged a variety of racial and religious minority groups—for example, Christian Karen, zerbadi, and Hindu—that, the British alleged, required protection (from the majority Burmese and Buddhists). The rhetoric of the judges who decided the 1905 case against the zerbadi appellants echoed this self-image of the British imperialists. It was their putative responsibility to save and free minorities like the zerbadi who had been oppressed by Burmese Buddhist society. The partitioning of the colony into ever smaller populations of minorities justified British colonial rule also by ensuring that no racial group achieved majority status; it thereby further consolidated British minority rule.[20]

Colonial attempts at schematization were not intended to capture the complex reality of the colony or to affirm the plurality of different human individuals and collectivities they named, mapped, and counted. In this respect, the heteronormative logic of the census operation is revealing. In contradistinction to the variety of racial, religious, linguistic, occupational, and other categories that appeared in the census over the years, only two categories of sex were ever used: male and female. Civil condition was similarly classified using a binary (single vs. married), and the latter condition only applied to heterosexual marriages. And the basic unit of enumeration in the census, the household, could be headed only by men, or so it appears. Though census instructions made no such stipulations, the sample registers appended in census reports show that only adult men, as the head of household, were questioned by census takers.

Only their responses—not those of their wives or other adult members of the household—required accounting.[21] Presented as an objective, scientific process of surveying and reporting, bureaucratic learning was a simultaneously constitutive and regulatory process that constructed the very social identities and structures that it framed as preexisting and awaiting discovery.

In colonial times, as in precolonial times, political-economic considerations underwrote government attempts to classify, control, and manipulate society. But while the patronage model of politics under the Konbaung administration condoned overlapping, nested batha and lu myo affiliations, the colonial regime of white minority rule made bounded, exclusionary classifications imperative. The classifying mind of European colonial governments throughout Southeast Asia, as Benedict Anderson argued, rejected "multiple, politically 'transvestite,' blurred, or changing identifications."[22] An individual could claim to belong to one and only one racial, religious, and gender category.

The judiciary, separated from the executive branch of the colonial administration in Burma only in 1906, operated in a similar vein. British jurists might have imagined themselves enlightened, liberal sovereigns whose rule was not only just but also tolerant of religious and legal difference. In practice, they rejected the intricacies of actual lives and practices that either challenged the orthopraxy presumed in codified personal laws or defied the colonial ordering of society, as in the court case brought by zerbadi appellants. The administration was not about to let the Muslim zerbadi cross the line that they had drawn between Buddhists and Muslims.

The Curious Exception of the Zerbadi

As the category of zerbadi itself suggests, however, the British were open to recognizing certain kinds of mixed identifications. We have already seen in chapter 1 that Eurasians had become a target of government surveillance and discipline in British India. The zerbadi, which became a subgroup of the new umbrella category "Indo-Burman races" in 1921, was the only other nomenclature of mixed or multiple racial identification included in the colonial census from 1911 onward. While the colonial administration in Burma noted in the census of 1872 that the growing numbers of "the Indo-Burman and Chino-Burman" were worthy of attention, the decennial census of 1881 was the first "to obtain information concerning the persons of mixed race."[23] Its first attempt returned sixteen different "principal mixed races of Burma," whose total population came to 230,484 (table 3.2).[24] But the next census (of 1891) counted only five "mixed Asiatic races"—Shan-Burmese, Kamu-Karen, Shan-Chinese,

Table 3.2 "Principal Mixed Races of Burma," 1881

Burman-Chin	1,554
Burman-Chinese	4,886
Burman-Karen	713
Burman-Shan	24,309
Burman-Talaing	177,939
Burman-Toungthoo	1,076
Talaing-Shan	9,517
Chin-Karen	989
Shan-Chinese	1,213
Shan-Karen	1,323
Toungthoo-Karen	2,486
Hindustani-Burman	8,968
English-Burman	703
Total Indigenous and allied mixed races	230,484
Total Indo-Burman races	10,620
Total European-Burman races	762

Source: F. S. Copleston, *Report on the Census of British Burma, taken on the 17th February 1881, Part I, Report* (Rangoon: Government Press, 1881), 71.

Manipuri (Ponna), and Zerbadi—in addition to Eurasian.[25] The number of categories of mixed races steadily dwindled over the next several decades. By 1901, only three were included—Chinese-Shan, Zerbadi, and Eurasian—and by 1911, only Zerbadi and Anglo-Indian, which replaced Eurasian, remained.[26] What motivated the administration to recognize the zerbadi, a numerically negligible category of mixed race at a count of merely twenty-four when it first entered the census, while ignoring or eliminating others? (See table 3.3.)

Why, furthermore, did the administration employ the term "Indo-Burman," as with zerbadi, only to refer to "the offspring of a Muhammadan native of India by a Burmese wife"?[27] The children of non-Muslim Indian men (or women) and Burmese women (or men) were never enumerated. The administration was inclined to highlight "the considerable amount of inter-marriage between Indian Muslims and females of the indigenous races of the province," while downplaying the frequency of Indian Hindu-Burmese marriages.[28] Yet the number of male Hindu immigrants from India far exceeded that of their Muslim counterpart, and the sex ratio among Hindu and Muslim immigrant populations was comparably skewed (tables 3.4 and 3.5). And for many decades, the British acknowledged that the marriage of "surplus Hindu males" to Burmese women contributed to the sharp increase in the Hindu population in the colony. They also conceded that they faced "extreme difficulty" in forming an

Table 3.3   Zerbadi, Indo-Burman, and Eurasian Populations of Burma, 1891–1931

YEAR	ZERBADI	INDO-BURMAN (INCL. ZERBADI)	EURASIANS
1891	24	N/A	7,022
1901	20,423	N/A	8,449
1911	59,729	N/A	11,106
1921	94,316	125,262	16,688
1931	122,705	182,166	19,200

Source: Compiled from *Census of India*, 1891, 1901, and 1931.

Table 3.4   Sex Ratios of Muslims and Hindus, 1901–1911

	MUSLIMS IN BURMA			HINDUS IN BURMA		
	MALE	FEMALE	DISPARITY	MALE	FEMALE	DISPARITY
1901	220,099	119,347	100,752	236,930	48,544	188,386
1911	271,428	149,349	122,079	306,700	75,588	231,112

Source: Government of India, *Census of India, 1911, IX, Burma, Part I, Report* (Rangoon: Office of the Superintendent, Government Printing and Stationery, 1912), 95–96.

Table 3.5   Sex Ratios of Immigrants from India (nearest whole thousands), 1921

RELIGION	PERSONS	MALE	FEMALE	FEMALE PER 100 MALE
Hindus and animists	392	330	62	19
Sikhs, Aryas, and Brahmos	5	4	1	23
Muslims	163	146	17	12
Others	12	7	5	76
Total	**573**	**487**	**86**	**18**

Source: Government of India, *Census of India, 1921, X, Burma, Part I, Report* (Rangoon: Office of the Superintendent, Government Printing and Stationery, 1923), 90–91.

estimate of this population. "Most of the children of such unions are brought up as Burmans and as members of the Buddhist religion," the report of the census of 1911 insisted, but added:

> A small minority are brought up strictly as Hindus in the full sense of the term, fulfilling the three requirements necessary to constitute a true member of the Hindu community, namely, membership of a recognised Hindu caste, acknowledgement of the supremacy of the Brahmans, and veneration of the cow. But intermediate between these two classes of persons born of mixed Hindu and Burmese marriages, there is a large and indefinite number of persons who can only be defined by the contradictory term, "Casteless Hindus."[29]

The report recorded the population of this group of "casteless Hindus" of mixed parentage "who have not been brought up as Buddhists, nor as strict Hindus, but have adopted generally Hindu modes of life" as 99,707 strong, up by more than 40,000 since the previous census in 1901.[30] Significantly, the report considered it a major factor in the increase by over 100,000 of the Hindu population in Burma between 1901 and 1911.

The British did not enumerate the Sino-Burmese population in Burma either, not after 1901, the last census that included the category of "Chinese-Shan"; and by 1891, the census had dropped the category of "Burman-Chinese," which returned a far higher population than the former in the census of 1881 (table 3.1). The colonial census reports repeatedly emphasized that the Chinese population "amalgamate with the Burmans far more readily than do the Natives of India."[31] The report for 1911 claimed, "The extreme disparity in the numbers of the sexes is accompanied by a large degree of intermarriage between the surplus Chinese males and the women of the Burmese race," emphasizing that Chinese men were "markedly favored suitors" among "the women of all the races in the province."[32] If we are to believe the census reports, the Sino-Burmese population in Burma must have been considerable. Yet the colonial administration decided not to continue classifying or quantifying it. The reason for this, according to the report for 1891, was that any attempt to enumerate the Sino-Burmese would have been "very ineffectual" because they were "very jealous of being considered true Chinamen, and, as they dress and consider themselves as apart from the natives of the country."[33]

Far from idiosyncratic, colonial governments across Southeast Asia counted select "racial combinations" and enforced legally defined racial divides between Europeans (and Eurasians), "foreign Orientals," and natives.[34] The category "Sino-Malay" never entered the census in British Malaya and the Straits Settlements. And neither did Malay vernacular terms, such as *anak awak*, that referred to the children of Siamese or Burmese fathers and Chinese or Baba (Straits-born Chinese) mothers.[35] In these British colonies and protectorates, the only classifications available for people of multiple or mixed racial identification were "Eurasian" and *Jawi Peranakan*, the Malay equivalent of zerbadi. As with the term zerbadi, the British administration employed Jawi Peranakan only to refer to the descendants of Indian Muslim fathers and Malay Muslim mothers. Yet, in their dictionary, published in 1894, the British colonial officers Hugh Clifford and Frank Swettenham defined Jawi Peranakan as "the name given by Malays to the offspring of a Malay and a native of India."[36] In this instance, Islam was not an explicit part of the equation. Some thirty-six years later, though, C. A. Vlieland, the author of the 1931 census of British Malaya, remarked that while Europeans regarded the cognate Jawi Pekan as meaning "a mixture of Indian and Malay blood," Malays "frequently applied [the term] to an Indian who has in fact no Malayan blood in his veins, but is a Muhammadan who has settled and married in Malaya."[37] The category Jawi Peranakan was omitted altogether from the census by the twentieth century.

Similarly, in the Philippines, the legal category of the "Chinese mestizo" (*mestizo de sangley*)—created by the Spanish in 1760 to refer mainly to children of intermarriages between *sangley* (a term later changed to *chino*) fathers and *indio* (native) mothers—was abolished in the late 1880s.[38] With the notable exception of one census in South Sumatra that classified Arabs of mixed descent as "Arabieren (Peranakans)," there was no intermediary category whatsoever in the Dutch East Indies.[39] While in French Indochina, the colonial administration used the Vietnamese term *Minh huong* to refer to the Sino-Vietnamese.[40]

In British Burma, however, the colonial administration also generated little data on cross-category marriages and births among the "indigenous racial groups." Major categories such as "Shan-Burmese" disappeared after the 1891 census without explanation, although frequent references were made to "hybrid" Indigenous races.[41] Census statements on "the extreme instability of racial distinctions" in Burma reveal not only that intermarriage among those described as Indigenous races were frequent but also that the census takers struggled to determine the race of the children of such unions, let alone measure the size of such populations. "Race in Burma," the 1911 census report claimed, "is not a fixed definite phenomenon capable of presentation in a set of tabular statements." It noted, with disquiet, that race in Burma "is vague and indeterminate, and in a stage of constant fluctuation," and that racial identification "changed and transformed, separated and amalgamated, and members transfer[red] themselves from one to another with the greatest facility." The tabulation of Indigenous races was "a presentation of a momentary phase of racial distribution" that did "not necessarily represent a distribution of the population into separate and mutually exclusive racial groups."[42]

In 1921, language was made the primary basis of classification of races of Burma (and only of Indigenous races), providing some "scientific basis" for what was at best a pseudoscientific endeavor. Predictably, it in no way solved the problem of indeterminacy that continued to trouble the census takers, who complained: "Some of the races or tribes in Burma change their language almost as often as they change their clothes."[43] Such admissions belied the exacting terminologies and tabulations of difference that filled the voluminous pages of colonial censuses. "There is no reason to believe that figures of Hindus and Muslims are not correct," the 1931 census confidently stated before adding the following explanation without a hint of irony: "The ordinary Burmese enumerator is not distinguished for his linguistic ability but he often knows sufficient Hindustani to be able to ask an Indian whether he is a *Hinduwalla* or a *Musalaman*; in other cases the services of an interpreter or a friend who knows Hindustani might be called in. In many cases it is possible to tell a man's religion from his appearance."[44] Colonial taxonomies and enumerations, derived from such self-assured yet dubious procedures, masked the coercive, ascriptive operation of the census. Race and religion alike were imposed references.

The aversion of colonial administrations toward in-between categories makes the British official recognition of the zerbadi/Indo-Burman all the more intriguing. This special interest in the zerbadi/Indo-Burman no doubt reflected the extent to which the British had naturalized Buddhism in Burma and alienated Islam. As other scholars have shown, the British discovery of Burma and Buddhism occurred concurrently and via their previous experience in India.[45] The moment of the British colonization of Burma coincided with unprecedented scholarly and popular interest in Buddhism among the British. Though Buddhism originated in India, it was rendered coterminous with Burma, representing not only the religion of the majority population but a natural match—a "tolerant" religion for a "tolerant" people among whom "caste was almost unknown," as observed in the censuses. The colonial gaze naturalized and indigenized Buddhism in Burma.

The forging of "Hinduism," "Buddhism," and "Islam" via the British colonial administrative process of governing India and Burma as colonies also resulted in the construction of Islam as a foreign and aggressive religion. Hinduism was supposedly the indigenous religion of India and the foundation of Indian civilization. In India as in Burma, Islam and Muslims were "foreign elements."[46] And the 1891 census, which claimed Hinduism to be the most persistently "exotic" religion in Burma, characterized the children of Hindu fathers and native women as more assimilable than the zerbadi because the former "usually adopt the religion of the mother" while the latter "usually became Muslims."

Exemplifying this Orientalist construction of Islam, the government abolished the category of "Burmese Muslim," of whom there were 6,872 according to the 1891 census, from the decennial census of 1901. In effect, the British excised "Burmese Muslim" from colonial administrative taxonomy. Many of the individuals who had previously returned their "religion" and/or "race" as "Burmese Muslim" were compelled to identify as zerbadi, which probably accounted for the sudden increase in the zerbadi population from a mere 24 to 20,423 within a decade (table 3.3). At the stroke of a pen, the British administration rendered Islam essentially foreign to Burma while characterizing Buddhism as thoroughly Burmese. What's more, it turned Indian patrilineage into an intrinsic characteristic of Burmese Muslims and made illegible communities who considered themselves native Muslims with no ties—patrilineal or matrilineal—to India.[47]

This alienation of Islam, as well as Hinduism, as a foreign religion occurred hand in hand with the othering of Indians as foreigners. The 1919 edition of *The Annual Register*, a popular British annual "review of public events at home and abroad," reminded the reader that "in race, in culture, and in religion, the affinities of Burma are with Siam and China, not with India," and rejected the idea of the continued administrative linking of Burma to India: "The political and administrative union of Hindustan and Burma was reasonable and convenient, so long as both were being governed from above by an irresponsible British autocracy. It would become most undesirable, if not quite impracticable, after the introduction of effective democratic elements, since the union would then involve the domination of Burma by an alien India."[48] At roughly the same time, and in anticipation of the 1921 government census, Arakanese Buddhists from Akyab in Arakan, which had by then been ruled as a British colony for almost a century, asked to be distinguished from the *yakaing kala* (Arakanese kala) so that the latter did not appear in the "Arakanese" racial category.[49] And so it was: appearing as a subgroup of Indo-Burmans in the 1931 census was the category of "Arakan Mahomedans" defined as "the descendants of Arakanese women who have married Chittagonian Muslims."[50]

Just as the category Eurasians symbolized the imperial presumption that colonial difference and the racial inferiority of the colonized peoples could never be overcome, the zerbadi/Indo-Burman category signaled the belief among the British that the radical difference of Islam could never be assimilated in a society that they had essentialized as Buddhist. The zerbadi/Indo-Burmans were a people forever alien in "Buddhist Burma."

Belonging beyond Categories: The New Burmas

The idea that Islam was intrinsically alien in Burma would have offended Ma Galay and U Choe, as well as their youngest child, Ahmed, and his wife, Helen May, the eldest daughter of Di Di and Defries.

Sometime in the late 1910s, Ahmed had returned from attending the Calcutta Medical College with not only a medical degree but also a new last name: Meah. His corresponding last name in Burmese was Mya. Auntie Rosie does not know why he chose to register for medical school under this name rather than Mohideen (or Mohiuddin). Ahmed might have selected Meah as an alternative spelling of Mir, a titular nomenclature of the sayyid according to the 1901 census of India.[51] But if that had been the case, it seems peculiar that his children grew up unaware of his sayyid lineage. Another possible explanation is that Meah derived from *miah sahib*: an honorific that some men among the English-educated Muslim middle class of barristers, civil servants, college teachers, and doctors in Bengal at the turn of the twentieth century used to refer to themselves.[52] If so, then Ahmed was emphasizing his identification with this emergent community of Muslim professionals rather than his connection to the sāda.

Ma Galay had expected that upon his return home with the status-enhancing medical degree, Ahmed would help her manage the thriving family business like his four siblings. She had also chosen a suitable Muslim bride—perhaps a sayyida—for Ahmed to marry. But Ahmed did neither. He started his own medical practice in Rangoon and eloped with Helen, who worked at his clinic.

Following in the footsteps of her mother, Helen had become a nurse, though it is unclear what role Di Di, who had passed away when her daughters were still teenagers, played in Helen's career path. Nursing was not just one of the few professions open to women but a well-established one among Karen women in Burma (as discussed in chapter 1). Nurses were also in high demand.[53] It is not hard to imagine that Helen, who must have had to support herself and her sisters upon leaving the orphanage, found nursing a practical and practicable profession. She probably received training as a nurse at the Rangoon General Hospital, which offered two-year training courses for "indigenous women" (as opposed to three-year courses for European and Anglo-Indian women), or at the Lady Dufferin Hospital, which trained hundreds of women in nursing and midwifery.[54]

When Helen met Ahmed, she was engaged to her first cousin and fellow Baptist Freddie. Aware that Ma Galay would not approve their relationship, Helen and Ahmed decided to run off to Mandalay to marry and start a new life. Fatigued from the travel, Ahmed suggested that they disembark at Pyinmana, located halfway between Mandalay and Rangoon and situated on the Rangoon–Mandalay main railway line, for a brief respite. They never proceeded to Mandalay, marrying in Pyinmana instead. This is how Auntie Rosie recounts her parents' marriage. Her eldest daughter, Mona, heard a different story. Ahmed was equivocal about their courtship, not only because Helen was already engaged but also due to the disparaging views of his friends for whom Helen was not good enough: a ward of orphanages for Eurasians and "poor whites," she was beneath someone of Ahmed's pedigree and affluence. In his characteristically nonconfrontational style, Ahmed ran away to Mandalay rather than break off or commit to his relationship with Helen. In her typically confrontational style, Helen followed him. She kicked open the door to his apartment, grabbed him, and went in search in the middle of the night for a Muslim authority to officiate the marriage ceremony. Helen converted to Islam, and the couple signed a Muslim nuptial contract (*nikah*). In recounting this story to her grandchildren, Helen made one thing clear: she ran off with Ahmed, not the other way around.

News of the marriage shocked Dadi, who disowned Ahmed. Estranged from his family, Ahmed decided not to return to Rangoon. He and Helen settled down in Pyinmana, a place to which they had no prior connections. Using what was left of his inheritance, Ahmed bought a hilltop estate, consisting of three mansions and a view of Shan Kan (Lake Shan). Ahmed and Helen established the only medical clinic in town, the New Burma Medical Hall, after which the couple and their children came to be known locally as the "New Burmas."[55]

Was it the prospect of starting anew that inspired the couple to make Pyinmana their home? Compared to Rangoon, Pyinmana was a quiet, rustic town. Pyinmana was included for the first time in the British government census of 1891, which listed the population of the town as only 12,926.[56] At the time of annexation, most of the houses in the town, covering an area of about one square mile, "were surrounded by thick groves of plantains and other fruit trees" and "a dense belt of sugarcane and other high crops, through which it was difficult even for an elephant to make its way." The town had "a fine municipal bazaar," a courthouse, an American Baptist station, a hospital that could accommodate three dozen patients—though no residing government-appointed doctors—and a dispensary.[57]

Pyinmana, however, was also a relatively prosperous and cosmopolitan town, located in one of the most valuable teak-producing areas in Burma. The lessee of the teak forests in the Pyinmana District (covering an area of 6,000 square miles) was none other than the Bombay Burmah Trading Corporation, the British-owned timber and trading firm fined in 1885 by King Thibaw of illegally exporting logs to avoid paying export duty owed to the Burmese state, which led to the Third Anglo-Burmese War and the annexation of Upper Burma. Even by official counting, Pyinmana was home to a large number of Muslims, Hindus, and Chinese, who together represented about a quarter of the total population by 1911.[58] The Muslim community in particular appears to have been well-established, if the lack of gender disparity among its population or the existence of a number of "Mahomedan" schools—six out of ten "lay" or nonmission schools in Pyinmana—is any indication.[59]

Pyinmana experienced an agrocommercial boom right around the time Ahmed and Helen moved there. Regarded by some as one of the most promising agricultural areas in all of Burma, it became the site of the Pyinmana School of Agriculture, founded in 1923 by the American Baptist Reverend Brayton Case. A son of missionary parents, Case was born and raised in Burma.[60] He set up the school along the Hampton-Tuskegee idea of industrial education on two hundred acres of land granted by the British government, which also underwrote the operating costs of the school. The Hampton-Tuskegee model of education was developed after the US Civil War with the ideological program of "uplifting" African Americans, that is, to provide a "practical, industrial education" that taught the moral and manual skills deemed necessary for former slaves to become self-supporting in the impoverished South.[61] Evangelicals such as Case viewed this style of "scientific" agricultural education as a way to "produce Christian men to whom the people of Burma will look and say, 'I wish I could be a man like that. I wish my son could do what he can. I wish I had a God that blessed his people like that.'"[62] Pyinmana also emerged as the headquarters for all the large trading and moneylending firms operating in central Burma to the south of Mandalay.[63] Consequently, its population increased by almost tenfold between the time of the first census and 1931: from 12,926 to 111,003.[64]

As Pyinmana grew, so did the New Burma clan, as Ahmed and Helen had eleven children in quick succession. Pictured in the studio photo on the cover of this book are the eldest daughter and son, Kitty Khatiza Khin Sein (b. 1922), standing beside her aunt Cecilia, and Hardy Hardie Ne Win (b. 1924), sitting on his mother's lap. Everyone is dressed stylishly for the studio photo. Ahmed has on a sport coat and a tie and Helen and Cecilia wear white Burmese blouse and silk *longyi* (sarong-like ankle skirt) and have their hair coiled into the customary chignon known as *sadohn*. Both children don a pair of black Mary Jane shoes with white socks, but Kitty sports a wool winter coat over a dress and a bonnet, while Hardy is fitted out in an embroidered velvet jacket over a pair of shorts and a gold-brocaded velvet *kufi* (Islamic prayer cap).

Seven other children lived to adulthood: Angela Aisha Khin Nyunt Yee (b. 1927), Jenny Noor Jehan Khin Set Yee (b. 1929), Rose Razia Hnin Yee (b. 1931), Trevor Rafi Pe Win (b. 1934), Duncan Shaffi Kyaw Win (b. 1935), Raymond Ali Jan Zaw Wynn (b. 1937), and Helen Fatima May Wynn (b. 1939) (see fig. 3.1). The New Burmas also included Helen's sisters Cecilia and Juliet. Helen had taken them out of boarding schools upon her marriage and put them through medical school—no small feat considering the miniscule number of women who attended the Government Medical School at Rangoon in the 1920s. Last but not least, the New Burmas included cooks, nannies, and servants, many of

FIGURE 3.1. Auntie Rosie with her sister Jenny and their parents, Helen May Defries and Ahmed Mya Meah. The photo was taken in a studio in Rangoon in the 1950s in celebration of Rosie's medical degree from Rangoon University and Jenny's master's degree in philosophy from Yale University. Courtesy of Dr. Hnin Yee and Mona Han.

them lifelong caregivers for the family. Helen and Ahmed spent the entire day at the clinic only to return home in the evenings. Neither performed household chores; neither went near the kitchen. Helen made only one exception. For Eid, she would make *shai mai*: also known as *sayviah* or *sevyian*, the sweet vermicelli served with fried cashews, coconut shreds, raisins, and milk was—and still is— the signature dish cooked for the holiday marking the end of Ramadan (the ninth month of the Islamic lunar year) and the breaking of the fast in Burma.

Still, the labor of childrearing fell on the shoulders of women. Those who raised the brood of New Burmas—Daw Kha, Zainab, Daw Than, and, eventually, the eldest child, Kitty—were all women. And let us not forget the Catholic nuns. Once the children were old enough to start boarding school, about four years old, they were rarely home. Though their father was a son of a sayyid and their mother a Muslim convert, Auntie Rosie and her siblings were placed in the charge of the Italian or Irish sisters who ran the Catholic convents they attended.

Catholic nuns in Burma, as elsewhere, were known for their strict discipline and corporal punishments. As boarders, parents were only able to see their children over holidays. While Christian boarding schools and orphanages differed in their goals and ambitions, they shared the belief that native and Eurasian children should be raised in a purely Christian environment, removed from the influence of their natal families and communities; the institutions of the boarding school and orphanage were to function as the surrogate family for the children.[65] Symbolically, all children who attended mission schools were deprived of their given Burmese names (if they had one) by the Irish nuns who insisted on giving their students Anglo-Christian names that they could pronounce and remember.

A product of the Christian boarding school herself, Helen was well aware of the demands placed on the boarders and their families. Nevertheless, boarding was often the only way her children could attend the Catholic schools in such major cities as Rangoon and Mandalay that represented premier institutions for primary and secondary school education in Burma. Over the course of the nineteenth century, mission schools—run by Barnabite Roman Catholic missionaries, American Baptist missionaries, and the Anglican missionary group the Society for the Propagation of the Gospel—had gained a monopoly over Anglo-vernacular and English education. They dominated secondary and tertiary education and had cornered the market for female education as well. All of this was accomplished with the support of the colonial administration, which relied on the mission schools it aided via grants for the provision of English as well as secondary education, and the training of local English-speaking clerks and interpreters for the colonial administration and European trading firms.[66]

Helen, as with her mother and sisters, was a beneficiary of the zealous efforts by missionaries to Christianize and civilize the natives. If her example is any indication, missionary efforts to instill Christian and Eurocentric conceptions of piety and feminine virtue in native women met with limited success. Helen converted to Islam and showed no interest in the art of homemaking or housekeeping. Hardly exceptional, she was representative of the many colonized men and women who repurposed their experience of Christian education in ways that the missionary teachers never intended. As more and more Burmese parents were able to afford to place their children in boarding schools, the number of boarding facilities in Burma increased from 132 in 1905 to 472 in in 1921.[67] These parents joined a growing cohort of colonial subjects the world over who, regardless of their religious affiliations, were enrolling their children in mission schools to take advantage of the promise of upward social mobility through education.

Pyinmana did have an Anglo-vernacular school and a mission school, which Auntie Rosie and her sister Jenny attended briefly. As a rule, however, Helen and Ahmed placed all of their children in Catholic mission schools away from home as boarders. Still, they had reservations. For a time, Helen placed Pusu, Jenny, Rosie, and Cecilia's two sons (Reggie and Sunny) in the care of friends—a Burmese pastor and his wife, who had recently moved from Pyinmana to Toungoo—so that the children could attend St. Joseph's Convent School in the city without boarding. The children were then placed as boarders for many years in St. John's Convent in Rangoon, one of the most successful privately managed schools in the eyes of the government. Yet, again, Helen took the children out of boarding. Shortly before the outbreak of World War II, Helen entrusted them in the care of a Karen aunt who resided in Rangoon.

Interestingly, the children never lived with their paternal grandmother, Ma Galay, although she also lived in Rangoon. Long before Auntie Rosie began attending St. John's, her parents and Ma Galay had reconciled. Her eldest sibling, Kitty, "practically grew up under the wings of Dadi," recalls Kitty's daughter Ma Kathy. The grandmother taught Kitty how to gamble! Apparently, Kitty was Ma Galay's favorite grandchild, whom she loved to indulge. Constantly overruled by Ma Galay in her attempts to discipline Kitty, Helen perhaps decided to limit her visits to Rangoon to the holidays, when she would travel with the children to stay with Ma Galay.

We can only surmise the motivations behind Helen's actions. However, one thing is certain: she was determined to keep her children as close to each other and to their kin as she could manage without compromising their education.

Auntie Rosie fondly remembers the few times each year that she returned home. Even now, she lights up when recalling the joy of reuniting with her elder siblings, who had likewise returned home for the holidays, and the excitement of meeting new additions to the family. "There was a new baby every time we returned to Pyinmana for the holidays," she told me. Sometimes, the baby was her sibling; sometimes, a niece or nephew whom Helen and Cissie helped deliver. The children also delighted in the break from the daily routines of the Catholic convent and its austere culinary options. A scrumptious assort-

ment of food awaited them at home: their favorites included common Burmese dishes, such as *kyet a mit hin* (chicken liver and gizzard curry), *ga zun ywe
kyaw* (stir-fried morning glory), and *pe hin* (lentil soup). Other staples at the
table were *ngapi ye* (fermented fish or shrimp sauce / paste) served with *to zeya*
(raw / boiled dipping vegetables), *chin ye hin* (tangy soup), and rice: these were
dishes that Helen required for herself at every meal.

A set of dishes were specially prepared also for Ahmed, who was on "the
Hay diet." For as long as Auntie Rosie could remember, her father was on the
diet developed by the American physician William Howard Hay in the 1920s
that prohibited the combined consumption of certain groups of food—namely,
starches and proteins—during the same meal. Ahmed was a creature of habit.
Every day he would eat toast, six egg yolks, vegetable stew, chapati or bread,
salad, and flan for dessert. He did not eat meat, though in his eighties he ate
one ounce of minced lamb in the form of a cutlet. He never ate rice. The cooks
for the family catered to these eclectic dietary needs and wishes, in addition
to preparing everything halal.

As is obvious from the names of the children or the typical meal of the New
Burmas, theirs was a bewilderingly heterogeneous family. Muslims, Christians,
and Buddhists; zerbadi, Karens, Burmans, and Eurasians; and Burmese, Urdu,
and English speakers all lived together as one unit. Everyone ate halal, the men
in the family went to the mosque for Eid, and Ahmed and Helen recited Muslim prayers. The children, however, were not taught Muslim prayers. They
learned, instead, to recite Christian and Buddhist prayers from their aunt Cissie and the longtime servant affectionately called A May Than, or "Mother
Than." The New Burmas were a polyglot family, moving fluidly between different batha: language and religion. As the colonial census pointed out, people
in Burma were known to "change their language almost as often as they change
their clothes." Many, like the New Burmas, were multilingual and availed
themselves of different languages. "Religion" was clearly viewed as existing
or functioning in a similar way. Like language, it was formative of one's per-
ception and experience of the world. And as with language, one could identify and express oneself through different religious idioms.

This versatility in batha, however, was too much for Helen's liking at times.
As the only general medical practitioner in town, Ahmed welcomed visits by
traveling *pongyis* (Buddhist monks) who stopped by his home for medical con-
sultations. These visits, which turned into philosophical ruminations on Buddhist scriptures, irritated Helen. "Why are you talking everyday *anicca*
[impermanence], *dukkha* [suffering], and *anattā* [nonself]?" she would chastise
Ahmed.[68] She even complained directly to the *pongyis*, letting them know that

she had little tolerance for what she perceived, probably correctly, as their attempt to propagate the buddha batha.

Though both Ahmed and Helen were practicing Muslims, Helen was the more devout of the two. She was the only member of the family who observed the daily fast during Ramadan. In her old age, Helen hired a teacher to instruct her in reciting the Quran in both Arabic and Urdu. She also began covering her head during prayer, though she never wore a veil of any sort in public. Adhering to the doctrinally conservative view that the visitation of graves by women is prohibited by Islam, Helen refused to go to the cemetery where Ahmed and their daughter Jenny were buried.[69] Memories of Helen among her descendants thus paint a portrait of a self-consciously pious Muslim convert, albeit one that does not resemble the stereotypical image of the devout Muslim woman for whom the metonym is the veil. It is a portrait that troubles once again the idea that conversion in the context of intermarriage is purely pragmatic. Like other women converts we encountered in chapter 1 who demonstrated curiosity and conviction in the batha of their spouses, her conversion to Islam was more than just a means to an end. Did Helen feel pressure to model herself after the women in Ahmed's family who, by all accounts, were "very religious"? In contrast, the Meahs have described none of Ma Galay's sons as particularly religious. Perhaps Helen wanted to prove to Ma Galay, her sister-in-law, or to herself that she was a worthy wife and daughter-in-law, befitting a sayyid, despite her humble background and her status as a convert. Or to ensure that her descendants were not denied the prestige and status that came with being sayyid—that is, if they ever chose, unlike their father, to accentuate their prophetic lineage.

Yet neither Helen nor Ahmed raised the children to identify exclusively—even principally—as Muslim, according to Auntie Rosie. Their personal experiences as well as shared family histories of migration, intermarriage, and conversion may have inclined Ahmed and Helen to nurture pluralistic sensibilities in their children rather than accept the colonialist model of family and community—that is, as seeded and determined by putatively impenetrable religious boundaries. Or is it possible that Helen and Ahmed feared that overt performances of Muslimness might create problems for their children? As discussed above, the British had singled out the zerbadi and Muslims in general as "foreigners" in Burma. This may have been the reason the children were known by their Anglo-Christian names instead of their Muslim names. Such an interpretation, however, is not consonant with Auntie Rosie's memories of Pyinmana. The local community never made her family feel like outsiders, she says. The residents of Pyinmana referred to her parents as "Mummy-gyi" (grandmother) and "Papa-gyi" (grandfather): terms of endearment and kinship. Auntie Rosie recounted many poignant stories that evoked the affection with which her parents were regarded in Pyinmana, but one stood out. Ahmed had gone to Rangoon for medical treatment, accompanied by Helen. Unbeknownst to the couple, word had spread in Pyinmana that Helen was returning with his body (i.e., his corpse). They arrived at the train station in Pyinmana, both in good health, to find that a large crowd of the town's people had gathered to pay their respect.

There is no denying that the New Burmas were an extraordinary family. But as the following chapter shows, they were neither unusual nor unfamiliar relations in colonial Burma. Rather, they were quite typical of the many marriages and families that straddled administrative categories and legal boundaries, as court records of domestic disputes attest. The prevalence of such personal relations never moved the British administrators to revise their classification schemes or to acknowledge the problems immanent in their strategy of governance. Instead, colonial authorities persisted in enforcing the bureaucratic illogic and illusion of a religiously and racially segregated colonial society, rendering common forms of intimacy and subjectivity illicit. Their insistence on the validity of colonial schemes also entailed the fabrication of another powerful unreality: a Burmese woman who married a "foreigner" came into the fold of her husband, adopting his religious and legal status, while immigrant men (and their locally born sons), even those who were culturally assimilated, retained their own religious and legal personhood. On the basis of this fantasy and alibi, colonial officials rationalized their consolidation of a patriarchal legal regime of alienation.

CHAPTER 4

The Alienable Rights of Women

In 1905, R. K. Muduliar, alias Maung Maung, had his right to his father's estate contested by his cousin W. R. Vanoogopaul.[1] According to the latter, Maung Maung was an illegitimate child who descended from two generations of illicit unions between Hindu men and Burmese women. Maung Maung's maternal grandmother, Thu Za, Vanoogopaul pointed out, was "Burmese Buddhist," not Hindu. The legal principle recognized by the British that there was no such thing as "Hindu by conversion" meant that Ma Gun, Thu Za's daughter with her Hindu husband Narainsawmy Naidoo, was neither a legitimate child nor a Hindu. Maung Maung, the son of Ma Gun and "an orthodox Hindu" named W. V. Ramasawmy Mudaliar, was likewise illegitimate and not Hindu. Vanoogopaul, it would seem, had a watertight case.

However, the presiding judges reasoned that Thu Za, though Buddhist at the time of her marriage to Narainsawmy, was regarded as Hindu and brought up all her children as Hindus and married them to Hindus "according to Hindu rites."[2] The judges declared lawful the marriage between Thu Za and Narainsawmy and validated the Hindu status of Thu Za, Ma Gun, and Maung Maung.

A decade and a half later In August 1921, the Privy Council heard two consolidated appeals concerning the estate of a wealthy Indo-Burmese merchant Ohn Ghine (1858–1911).[3] A respected member of Rangoon's elite circles, he had led an illustrious life, not least as an elected member of the Rangoon Municipality, an honorary magistrate, recipient of the Companion of the Order of the Indian Empire and the title of Ahmudan gaung tazeik ya min (Recipient of the Medal of Honor for Good Service). He had even represented the province of Burma at the coronations of King Edward VII and Queen Alexandra in 1902.

Ohn Ghine had died in 1911 during a visit to England, leaving behind a will appointing his wife, Ma Yait, and daughter, Ma Noo, as trustees. One of his sons, Chit Maung, contested the validity of the will on the basis that his father was Hindu and, as such, did not have absolute testamentary power. Actually, the will was also invalid under the so-called Burmese Buddhist law. On the basis that the concept of a will was nowhere to be found in the *dhammasat* according to which inheritance among Buddhists in Burma was strictly intestate, the British colonial administration categorically disallowed wills for the Burmese Buddhist. The notion that Buddhists in Burma were prohibited from disposing of their property and disinheriting rightful heirs by will was hardly established fact. The colonial administration debated on multiple occasions (1881, 1888, 1904, and 1917) the question of whether testamentary power should be conferred on Buddhists. Notwithstanding historical evidence of testamentary alienation of estates by Buddhists, each judicial debate determined that Buddhists in Burma had no capacity to make a will. This made Burmese Buddhists the only "religious community" denied the power to testate because Chinese Buddhists, on the account of a "Chinese custom" of testamentary power, had been granted an exception to this ruling—a point to which I return later in the section.[4]

Had Hindu law been applied to Ohn Ghine's estate, as Chit Maung requested, then Ma Yait and Ma Noo would have been entitled only to maintenance and only until their (re)marriage, with the estate passing to his sons for administration. Under Burmese Buddhist law, on the other hand, Ohn Ghine's estate would have been divided among the surviving wife and children. The issue to be decided therefore was the religious status of Ohn Ghine.

It is worth noting that when questioned in 1907 and in his capacity as a municipal commissioner of Rangoon by the Royal Commission upon Decentralization in India, Ohn Ghine had self-identified as a "Hindu-Buddhist" native of Burma.[5] And in theory, the "personal law" of an individual was determined confessionally—that is, by the person's professed religious affiliation. Predictably, colonial jurists discounted this hyphenated religious identity and went about figuring out Ohn Ghine's one and only true religion.

All parties involved agreed that Ohn Ghine was "as much Burmese as Indian by blood, and in dress, language and manner of life he was more Burmese than Indian." He came from an Indo-Burmese family whose members professed to be Hindus and yet also "worshipped at the pagoda, fed the pon-gyis [monks] and observed Buddhist fasts and festivals." As Viscount Haldane remarked, Judge Robinson, who first tried the case, had been "right in think-ing that Ohn Ghine observed to a certain extent the rites and ceremonies of the Hindu religion, but that he also observed and followed the Buddhist reli-gion to a great extent and was far from being an orthodox Hindu."[6]

No one considered Ohn Ghine "an orthodox Hindu." But was he Hindu enough to warrant the application of Hindu law to his estate? If not, could he be considered a Buddhist instead? The lawyer for Ma Yait portrayed Ohn Ghine as Buddhist, emphasizing that he had sent his sons to a monastic school for Buddhist instruction and took a leading role in supporting several notable Bud-dhist projects. Ohn Ghine had been an active member of the Maha Bodhi Society, founded in 1891 for the promotion and propagation of Buddhism in India and beyond, and the Rangoon-based International Buddhist Society, founded by Britain's first Buddhist monk, Ananda Metteyya (1872–1923).[7] In 1900, he sent a letter to the governor of Madras on behalf of his "Buddhist Co-religionists," requesting the return of certain Buddhist relics held at the Madras Museum to be placed in a shrine that he was building in Rangoon. The following year, he gave an address on behalf of the Buddhist community in Rangoon to the viceroy, Lord Curzon, and traveled with fellow Burmese pilgrims to the temple of the Sacred Tooth Relic in Kandy, Lanka (Ceylon). As recently as 1907, he had written to one of his sons in England admonish-ing him to "daily think of the Buddha." Three years later, his son Chit Maung married "a Burmese girl, according to Burmese custom"—a fact that Justice Twomey declared "a serious lapse from rectitude for a Hindu," though he ex-plained away this "serious lapse" as typical of "the general laxity" of marriage customs among the Hindu Indo-Burmese, attributing to the group the laxity the British had come to associate with Burmese marriage laws and customs.[8]

The evidence presented by Ma Yait failed to convince the judges that Ohn Ghine was Buddhist. His "liberality to Buddhist monks and his liking for Bud-dhist prayers and practices," as the judges put it, did not amount to a "clear renunciation" of the Hindu faith.[9] They merely confirmed the conventional wisdom among British colonial officers that Hindu immigrants in Burma, to quote from the census report of 1891, "very often become Burmanized and adopt Burman names, and no longer remain Hindus in the strict sense of the term."[10] The judges underscored Ohn Ghine's support of the Hindu temple in Rangoon, for which he served as one of the trustees, as well as the fact that Ma Yait herself chose to observe Hindu rites at her father's cremation, though she also invited Buddhist monks. From the perspective of the judges, Ohn Ghine had "seriously lapsed" not only as a Hindu but also as a Buddhist, for he had not sponsored the temporary ordination (*shin byu*) of his sons as monks. The British considered this rite of passage, in which a son enters the monastery as a novice, as synonymous with Burmese Buddhism and "by far the most important event in any Burman's life."[11] In determining whether individuals should be subject to Burmese Buddhist law, British judges invariably asked the question of whether they had performed the *shin byu* of their son(s). Ohn Ghine had not.

Still, the Privy Council determined that Ohn Ghine could not be regarded as Hindu because his "Hindu-ness" was so divergent from "pure" Hinduism as to render him non-Hindu.[12] Refusing to declare the late Ohn Ghine a Buddhist, the council decided to apply to his estate the Indian Succession Act (of 1865). The so-called rule of justice, equity, and good conscience, this was an act that a colonial court could deploy when it determined that there was no other law that could be applied to a particular case (more on the Indian Succession Act to follow).

Unlawful Conceptions

As these cases about Hindu-Buddhist marriages and conversions demonstrate, the civil courts had to answer for the confusion created by the colonial system of personal law: What was the status of marriages and births that transgressed religious categories and legal jurisdictions? This judicial uncertainty had made intermarriage and mixed births susceptible to two types of interconnected legal challenges: the legality of the marriage and the legitimacy of the birth(s); and the personal law to be used to govern the affairs and property of the individuals, spouses, or families in question.

Colonial jurists maneuvered around these legal questions rather than offer straightforward answers. They accepted the conversion of Buddhist women to Hinduism to make way for lawful Hindu-Buddhist marriages, contravening their own position on the impossibility of "Hindu conversion," as in the case of Mudaliar. Still, there were many cases where the court dismissed outright the legal validity of relationships that the litigants claimed were matrimonial. In 1906, when Shwe Me was sued by her Hindu husband, Doramoswami, the two had lived together for sixteen years and had six children. But Doramoswami argued in court that because she was not Hindu, she was not his lawful wife, unlike his wife in India. He successfully denied her any right to his property.[13]

In 1914, Ma Myit similarly found her marriage to Rathna Pillay declared unlawful, though in her case, the lawsuit had been filed not by her husband but by a firm seeking to confiscate a mortgaged property owned jointly by her and Rathna. The district court ruled that although Ma Myit and Rathna "did not live in wedlock," they should nevertheless be treated as a lawfully married couple because "they considered themselves partners in life as well as business, as in the case of a Burmese family." Unmarried the couple may be in the eyes of Hindu law, but according to Burmese Buddhist customary practice, the district court argued, Ma Myit and Rathna were wife and husband, and the latter could legally mortgage their joint property without Ma Myit's consent. The Chief Court of Lower Burma disagreed, rejecting the notion that the couple should be regarded as "a Burmese Buddhist husband and wife." It insisted that Rathna was not Buddhist and that more than cohabitation was required for him and Ma Myit to be lawfully married. "The tie of marriage did not exist between them," Justice Hartnoll declared: "They could separate at will and there was no binding contract between them. They did not enjoy the advantages of marriage nor were they bound by the obligations of marriage."[14] To Ma Myit's relief, the judgment enabled her to retain control of her property.

The predicament of the legality of intermarriage was by no means confined to Hindu-Buddhist relationships. Thu Kha nearly suffered the same fate as Shwe Me in 1915 when her Chinese husband, who had deserted her and their two children, claimed that she was not his wife but merely a mistress.[15] Saw Maung Gyi had refused to pay maintenance and hoped that declaring Thu Kha a mistress would relieve him of his financial obligation as husband and father. Fortunately for Thu Kha, Saw Maung Gyi's own witnesses, including his relatives, recognized the two as man and wife. Chit May had less considerate relatives. Upon the death of her zerbadi husband, her mother-in-law attempted to take possession of her late husband's estate on the basis that Chit May was never a lawful wife and her children were illegitimate. The presiding judge ruled in Chit May's favor, citing the strong evidence of her conversion to Islam as well as "cohabitation and repute" in the case.[16]

As the case of Chit May suggests, cohabitation and repute, which were sometimes deemed sufficient criteria for establishing the legality of Sino-Burmese and Hindu-Buddhist marriages, were not adequate proof of marriage between a Muslim and a Burmese. If the reader will recall, Judges Wilkinson and Quinton, who decided the 1875 Muslim-Burmese divorce case discussed in chapter 2, emphasized that such marriages were "binding" and "honorable" so long as they had been celebrated according to Muslim rites *and* the wife had "renounced her own religion and embraced that of her husband."[17] Recall also that Mi Shwe Ywet, the Burmese wife in the case, maintained that she "never was anything else than a Buddhist." But the judges ignored her confession, granting her request for divorce because she had apostasized. According to the British judges, formal conversion to Islam was requisite to a lawful marriage between a Muslim groom and a Buddhist bride; and the bride was Muslim for all intents and purposes unless and until she formally renounced Islam. What she really thought or felt about Buddhism or Islam was immaterial. British judicial authorities time and again refused to question the Muslim status of a woman who, they acknowledged, had converted only to marry a Muslim man, "whilst at heart she remain[ed] the whole time a Buddhist."[18]

The legal obsession with conversion presented both a challenge and an opportunity for the spouses in Muslim-Buddhist marriages. Many Burmese women took advantage of the apostasy provision to annul their marriage, like Mi Shwe Ywet.[19] The conversion requirement proved to be advantageous in a different manner in the case of Ma Pu. In 1892, her Muslim husband Mouna Maung Gale sued her lover Nga Pale for adultery. Mouna Maung Gale characterized Ma Pu as an observant Muslim whom he had married by offering money to the mosque and giving matrimonial consent in the presence of witnesses. No one denied that Ma Pu had an amorous affair with Nga Pale. Yet Ma Pu averred that she never converted to Islam and was therefore never married to Mouna Maung Gale. To the district magistrate who adjudicated the case, that Ma Pu and Mouna Maung Gale "lived together as man and wife" was beyond dispute. Much to his chagrin, however, the judge conceded that her relationship to Nga Pale could not be considered adulterous because she had never converted to Islam.[20]

Judicial conflicts and contradictions over the legal status of mixed marriages and births served as strategies for evading marital commitments and liabilities and contesting property ownership and devolution. Consequently, many women and men in Burma, having lived and raised children together over an extended period with their partners of a different batha, suddenly found their status as wife or husband challenged by the very individual they had considered their spouse or by the relatives they had cared for as in-laws.

When colonial jurists were asked to adjudicate only the question of the religious status of individuals whose legal jurisdiction was ambiguous, as in the case of Ohn Ghine, the Indian Succession Act provided one logical decision. The judges concluded that Ohn Ghine was too assimilated to qualify for the application of Hindu law but not enough to be deemed Burmese Buddhist. They thus released Ohn Ghine from the grips of personal law.

Yet colonial jurists rarely invoked the Indian Succession Act. Never defined with any precision, the law referred to presumptively universal notions of "justice, equity, and good conscience" as understood by British jurists. It created a loophole in the system of personal law through which British judges could apply the rule, if not the technicalities, of English common law: judge-made law based heavily on judicial precedent, adopted in the United States and many other colonies.[21] That they resorted to it only infrequently might have signaled their fear that the judicature would be seen as sidestepping its own rules to interfere in the personal affairs of the colonized. Colonial jurists did not refrain from making legal incursions into the personal domain, however. They did so using the legal principle of coverture: the idea that a wife was covered by the legal identity of her husband for the duration of the marriage, and her person, property, and labor were subject to his ownership.

Covert Rule of Coverture

Throughout the half century following the annexation of Upper Burma, British judges characterized the zerbadi and Muslim communities in Burma as "imbued with Burmese ideas" and "under the influence of Burmese customs,"[22] and the Sino-Burmese as conforming "more or less to Burman Buddhist practices in subscribing to religious works and festivals."[23] The chief justice who ruled in a landmark Sino-Burmese inheritance case asserted that "it must not be lost sight of that Chinamen have come and settled in Burma in growing numbers since the first occupation of the country," and "more than any other race they have inter-married and joined in the social and religious life of the people of the country."[24] But the alacrity with which British legal experts generalized Burmese influences on Chinese and Indian immigrants and their descendants contrasted with their refusal to allow Chinese, Hindu, Muslim, Sino-Burmese, and Indo-Burmese subjects to have recourse to Burmese Buddhist law. In not a single case discussed above did British judges allow this to happen. They would sooner overturn decisions by district courts—most likely presided over by Burmese judges—than allow the application of Burmese Buddhist law to the personal affairs of these subjects, as in the aforementioned case concerning the joint property of Ma Myit and Rathna Pillay.

Conversely, British jurists routinely subjected Buddhist women and their property to the personal laws of their husbands. The story of Ma Myit, as told by her children who were suing each other for inheritance, offers an illustrative example. Ma Myit had married Sit Shan around 1881 and had five children. Sit Shan also had a Chinese wife, Kyi Ya, with whom he had two children. Upon his death in 1902, his estate was divided "in accordance with Chinese customary law," leaving the three sons equal share and the widows and four daughters nothing. After Ma Myit passed away, her daughter Ma Sein decided to sue her brothers for a share in the estate of her father on the grounds that her mother was "Burmese Buddhist" and, as such, was entitled to a portion of her father's estate, which, in turn, would devolve to all five of her children.

The court ruled that Sit Shan's estate had been partitioned lawfully, not because "the Chinese Customary Law should apply to the estate of every Burmese woman who was married to a Chinaman" but because Ma Myit had "adopt[ed] her husband's form of religion, becoming, to all intents and purpose, a Chinese Buddhist." What convinced the two judges that Ma Myit had become Chinese Buddhist?

> She mourned for him for the period of three years prescribed by Chinese custom, and she put her children, as well as herself, into the mourning dress which is customary among Chinese and not among Burmese. She did not marry again, the second marriage of widows, though permitted, being regarded as disreputable by the Chinese. She sent both her sons to China to be educated. She married one of her two daughters to a Chinaman and she refused her consent to appellant's [Ma Sein's] marrying a Burman. When she died, she was buried in the Chinese cemetery in a grave of Chinese pattern and with the usual Chinese monument.[25]

"It is true that her burial in the Chinese cemetery may not have been due to any wish she had herself expressed," Judge Heald acknowledged but added that "it seems to me to show that she was regarded by the Chinese community at Pyapon as one of themselves." He concluded that it was "natural that Chinamen who are Buddhists, living in Burma, should to some extent, observe the religious usage of their Burmese Buddhist neighbours and much more natural that their Burmese wives should do so." There was no doubt in his mind that both Sit Shan and Ma Myit observed Burmese and Chinese customs. But he also had no doubt that Ma Myit "regarded herself as a Chinese Buddhist and attached herself to the Chinese community, to which her husband and her sons and the son-in-law, with whom she lived, admittedly belonged."[26]

That Ma Myit sent her sons to China, forbade one daughter from marrying a Burmese man and married another (Pan Nyun) to a Chinese man, and adorned mourning dress, an atypical practice in Burma, is indeed indicative of her effort to "Sinicize" herself and her family. But we cannot know whether, and to what extent, she "regarded herself as a Chinese Buddhist," as the judges asserted. It is not difficult to see that Ma Myit had good reason to make overt gestures of "Sinicization": she was not Sit Shan's only wife, and the other wife was Chinese. Ma Myit might have reckoned that public performance of a "Chinese" version of herself might be the most effective strategy of buttressing her status in the family and winning a greater share of its fortune—for her children, if not for herself—when the question of inheritance and succession arose. She, like Kyi Ya, was excluded from Sit Shan's estate, as were her daughters. But her two sons did inherit alongside the son by Kyi Ya. This is an important detail.

Recall the case of Choa Chuan Ghiock, discussed in chapter 2, who had wives and children in both Rangoon and Singapore. He left much of his estate to his sons by his Chinese wives in Singapore, excluding from his will not only all his daughters but also his Sino-Burmese son in Rangoon. If not for Ma Myit's efforts at Sinicization, her sons too might have been precluded from inheritance on account of her Burmeseness.

Such calculations seemed to have fallen beyond the purview of Justices Heald and Lentaigne, who assumed that Ma Myit's subjectivity had been transformed through her marriage to Sit Shan. Perhaps they could not relate to the precarious position in which wives of polygynous men like Ma Myit found themselves. Perhaps they were also reluctant to apprehend women as resourceful and strategizing (legal) agents. Most certainly they were governed by and governing with the doctrine of coverture—well and alive in Britain until the 1880s—that denied married women a separate legal existence from their husbands.[27] In English common law, marriage was premised on the idea that the conjugal couple was a unitary entity whose sole representative (economic, political, and legal) was the husband. The wife could neither own nor dispose of property; she could not earn money, contract a debt, or sue or be sued; she could not choose her own place of residence. In short, she was obligated to obey her husband. Propertied widows were deprived of control over family wealth; they received allowance paid from the interest on the deceased's estate while fiscal agency was invested in the hands of sons. This pattern of property distribution and devolution ensured that subsequent marriages that the widow might contract would not diminish the principal of the estate. Colonial authorities transposed this legal doctrine of women's dependent status and legal incapacity to India under the cover of honoring Hindu and Muslim laws, as they limited the propertied rights of women.[28]

The British judges' gendered presumptions about marriage, religious agency, and legal subjectivity were also evident in the way they explained the source of Burmese influences on Chinese and Indian men. According to them, it was "natural" that these men gravitated toward the customs of the country in which they had settled. They discounted the influence that the Burmese (or Sino/Indo-Burmese) wives and relatives of the migrant men and their descendants exercised over family dynamics, rituals, and resources.

Exemplary of this pattern was a case presided over by Justice Fox involving the adoption of a Burmese child by a Sino-Burmese couple. The plaintiff, Yu Lwai, claimed that he was the only lawfully adopted child of and heir to the deceased couple Wun Pain Wain (also spelled Wun Pein Hein) and Ma Phee, who also happened to be his uncle and aunt. As it turned out, however, the couple had adopted a Burmese girl, Ma Yin, in 1896, a full decade before they adopted Yu Lwai in 1906.

Justice Fox found extraordinary the decision by Wun Pain Wain to adopt a Burmese girl who belonged neither to the Chinese or Sino-Burmese community nor to his extended family. Wun Pain Wain was the son of a Chinese father and a Burmese mother and was "brought up to follow Chinese customs," Justice Fox emphasized; and both his wives, Ma Phee and Ma Pwa, were Sino-Burmese.[29] "If Wun Pain Wain was strongly imbued with traditions and feelings of his father's race," he pondered, "one would certainly have expected him to have adopted the plaintiff who is the second son of his elder brother." He continued: "It is remarkable however that his first adoption was of a girl, and that it was clothed with a prominent characteristic of one form of adoption amongst Burmese, namely, a declaration that the child should have rights of inheritance. This points to Wun Pain Wain not being so strongly imbued with the necessity of having a son as the ordinary childrenless [sic] Chinese married man is said to be." Justice Fox was puzzled by the names of Ma Yin's parents, which, as registered in municipal records, seemed "purely Burmese." "It is remarkable," he noted once again, "that one who held himself out as a Chinaman should adopt the child of pure Burmese parents." He never raised the possibility that Ma Phee, not Wun Pain Wain, may have been responsible for the decision to adopt a girl—and a Burmese one—and make her heir. Or perhaps Ma Po, his Burmese mother who was alive at the time of Ma Yin's adoption, had a say in the choice of the adoptee. Justice Fox concluded, rather, that "Wun Pain Wain had leanings towards the Customs of the country in which he was born and bred."[30]

The repeated pronouncements on the Buddhist or Burmese "leanings" of Chinese, Hindu, Muslim, Sino-Burmese, and Indo-Burmese men—such as visits to pagodas, donations to monasteries, *shin byu* of male relatives, and adoption of a daughter—made plain what the British jurists would not acknowledge: Burmese women shaped the lives and legacies of mixed marriages and families in palpable ways that challenged the ossified colonial image of the presumptively patriarchal Oriental family. One final story about adoption and inheritance lets us unpack just how flawed were such colonial beliefs about women and Oriental families.

In 1919, Lim Gaik Kin, better known as Margaret Lim, married Chan Chor Pine, the middle son of the wealthy Chinese merchant Chan Ma Phee, mentioned in chapter 2. Margaret's Sino-Burmese father, Lim Chin Tsong, was arguably the only Chinese businessman in Burma at the time more successful than Chan Ma Phee. An agent of the Burmah Oil Company who turned shipping magnate, Lim Chin Tsong was an influential member of the Committee of the Kheng Hock Keong (Rangoon Hokkien Association), a government-recognized advisory board, and the only appointed Chinese member in the Legislative Council from 1909 until 1922. Only a year before Margaret's marriage to Chor Pine, he had arranged the marriage of his son Lim Kar Gim to Khoo Shwe Lin of the most powerful Hokkien-Malay "Khoo" family in Penang. In Rangoon, too, and through the marriage of his eldest daughter, he united the two most prominent and affluent Hokkien-Burmese merchant families in Rangoon.

When Chor Pine died in 1933, he and Margaret were childless. Just eleven days after his death, Margaret adopted, on behalf of her deceased husband, Chan Cheng Leong—better known as Georgie Chor Khine—who was the younger son of her brother-in-law, Chan Chor Khine. She appointed him the sole heir to the estate of her late husband. "Such an adoption is said to be highly desirable, if not imperative," the presiding judge observed, "for a Chinaman who dies without male issue in order that the ancient and traditional rites of ancestral worship might continue to be performed in the family of the deceased."[31]

Were the endogamous marriage of Margaret and Chor Pine and the posthumous adoption of Georgie Chor Khine cultural imperatives? Perhaps. But it is just as likely that the main objective of the marriage was the consolidation of the businesses, wealth, and social status of two powerful Sino-Burmese families. That the adoption too was not the result of some ancient Chinese custom is suggested by the records of the lawsuit over Margaret's estate. According to her younger sister Iris, Margaret adopted Georgie "under duress" by her brother-in-law Chor Khine.[32] Chor Khine was not someone who could be dismissed. He had succeeded Ma Phee, becoming the head of the Chan family and business. He had also become the representative of the Hokkien community in Rangoon, nominated by the Committee of the Kheng Hock Keong as its representative on the Legislative Council (1928–1932). If Chor Khine insisted that Margaret adopt his son Georgie, chances were, she had little choice. She could not prevail upon her natal family to intervene because the Lim family, once a powerhouse, was in dire straits. Her father had filed for bankruptcy in the 1920s. While evading debt collectors, he was found dead in his home, prompting suspicions of suicide.[33]

As it also turned out, Chor Khine had hastily and clandestinely executed another adoption on the same day that Margaret registered Georgie as her late husband's adopted son: an adoption by Georgie, who was himself childless, of his nephew Chan Eu Ghee. In so doing, Chor Khine ensured that his deceased brother's wealth remained within the Chan family and out of the reaches of the Lim family.

But not for long. In 1936, just three years after the adoption, Georgie signed a release registering that he no longer was an adopted son of Chor Pine—and never of Margaret—and waived "all claims to the assets, moveables and immoveables forming the estate of Chan Chor Pine in favour of the Releasee (Margaret Chor Pine)."[34] Why? Georgie had sold off Burmah Oil Company (BOC) shares belonging to the estate of Chor Pine without Margaret's approval. In protest, she revoked the adoption. If leaving a male heir to oversee ancestral worship was the overriding concern, why was the adoption revoked, and why was no other male Chan family member adopted in lieu of Georgie? And why was Margaret not concerned with having an heir herself? She never adopted Georgie, as the initial adoption document and Georgie's subsequent declaration of release made clear.

This legal tussle suggests something of the financial, familial, and communal authority and influence that Margaret wielded. A childless widow only five years older than Georgie, Margaret somehow managed to compel him to void the adoption and install her as the sole administrator of her late husband's estate despite the fact that he was, as the legally appointed son and sole heir, fully within his rights to do what he did with the BOC shares. The measures that Chan Chor Khine took to limit Margaret's ability to access and control her late husband's estate likewise attest to his respect for her wit and power.

It is possible that Margaret just got lucky. Chan Chor Khine was no longer alive in 1936; he had shot himself in 1934. And perhaps the Chan family took mercy upon her and her natal family, who had fallen from grace. But I think it is more likely that Margaret navigated the gendered protocols of law and family successfully to secure her propertied rights and privileges as a widow.

The Colonial Alibi

Historical scholarship on family law, slave law, and plural legal jurisdiction over the last three decades has revealed that the basic function of law, whether in colonial or metropolitan contexts, is to configure complex social hierarchies while masking its operation as a means for calibrating political and economic prerogatives.[35] In the United States, for example, miscegenation laws, purportedly about the unnaturalness of interracial marriage and the protection of white women, were intended to secure the propertied, patriarchal rights of white men and to defend white supremacy against challenges by Native Americans, African Americans, and Asian Americans.[36]

The British in Burma, too, created a legal labyrinth that obscured how their regulation of interAsian intimacies shored up patriarchal rights to property and family and undercut women's rights even as they claimed to protect the autonomy of individuals from family and community. Against evidence to the contrary, the colonial rulers determined that intermarriage entailed outmarriage for Burmese Buddhist women who were presumed to have married out of their own religion and law and into the patriarchal religions, families, and communities of their spouses. Allying with subjects who asked to exempt their family and property from the jurisdiction of Buddhist law, they pitted minority rights against indigenous rights along gender lines—as Chinese, Muslim, and Hindu patriarchs' rights against Burmese Buddhist women's rights—to alienate women of their property and personhood. The colonial alibi for this patriarchal alliance and consolidation were the Burmese Buddhist women themselves whom the British jurists typecast as consenting partners and willing agents in their own alienation—alienation in the legal meaning of the transfer of property and the social sense of estrangement. Colonial legal experts camouflaged their authorization of patriarchy as the imperial protection of the rights of religious minorities *and* of women's capacity to consent to intermarriage and conversion.

Feminist historians have examined the many ways in which the colonial, chivalric ideology of "white men saving brown women from brown men" legitimized European imperialism.[37] The plight and suffering of native women and girls at the hands of their own men and their patriarchal "tradition"—the private manifestation of Oriental despotism—was at the front and center of colonial representations of the Orient as Other; while the "uncivilized" custom of polygamy was reported to be the norm among all Oriental races and religions, Hindus were distinguished by child marriage and sati (widow immolation) and Muslims by the institutions of *pardahnasin* (a woman who observed seclusion and lacked the ability to act as her own economic agent) and *talaq* ("repudiation," or the unilateral male right to divorce).[38] Paradoxically, and reflecting the Janus-faced nature of imperial assimilation, these othered practices that represented the ostensible targets of European civilizing missions were exempted from imperial legal intervention. Oriental despots were to be eliminated in the so-called public realm of politics and the economy. In the so-called private domain of marriage and family, however, Oriental patriarchs would be allowed limited power and autonomy. The colonial judiciary dismissed diverse family structures, marriage practices, and competing interpretations of law to strengthen the legal basis for heteronormative, male-dominated family regimes and weaken the claims of women to inheritance as daughters, wives, and widows—all under the guise of respecting local traditions in religious and family matters.[39]

Interestingly, the British took exception with the Burmese. Burmese Buddhist laws and customs, British officials praised, were free of the social evils common among other Oriental societies. For example, the judicial commissioner and legal scholar John Jardine, while granting that Burmese Buddhist law recognized the husband as "the lord of his household" and of his wife, marveled at the Burmese wife's "wonderful facilities for terminating the marriage whenever she so desires." He rendered incomparable this "liberty . . . conceded in so full a measure to the married woman," unlike *patria potestas* (the Roman law of "paternal power" over daughter and wife) and "unknown to the Hindu law."[40] Also writing in the late nineteenth century, another British officer in Burma proclaimed: "Marriage does not confer upon a husband any power over his wife's property, either what she brings with her, what she earns, or what she inherits subsequently; it all remains her own, as does his remain his own." He added that women in Burma had always had "freedom from sacerdotal dogma, from secular law," and that "in no material points, hardly even in minor points, does the law discriminate against women."[41]

Writing a decade later, another colonial officer observed that the reason it was often said that "the women do most of the hard work of the country" was "not because they are the slaves of their husbands" but rather because "they occupy a position of independence and responsibility." He echoed his predecessor's views:

> Not only do sons and daughters inherit equally from their parents, but a married woman has an absolute right to dispose as she pleases of property acquired or inherited by her either before or after marriage. She is usually a partner in her husband's business, and as such has just as much right to sign for the firm as he; but she may have a business of her own, with the proceeds of which he cannot interfere. Even in matters in which she has no part, she is usually consulted before an important step is taken.[42]

Yet another British officer wrote in his "handbook" on Burma that whereas a Japanese wife "treats her husband as an idol," the Burmese wife treats her husband "as a comrade" and "is far ahead of her lord in the matter of business capacity by the way in which she rules the household without outwardly seeming to exercise any authority."[43] The British thus held up the Burmese Buddhist woman as the rights-bearing autonomous individual idealized by the British political discourse of liberalism. In so doing, British officers neglected the nonexistence of women's rights over their own body. The *dhammasat* did not recognize marital rape. As wives, women had no right to withhold consent from their husbands.

That a woman possessed ownership over anything but her own body reveals not only the myopic nature of the British discourse of Burmese Buddhist law but also something about the function of law, property, and gender in Buddhist societies. As the work of D. Christian Lammerts has suggested, autonomous control over property brought into and acquired during marriage enabled women to materially support the sangha.[44] Women who had no sons, biological or adopted, or surrogate kinsman (or kinsmen) to *shin byu* could still perform the meritorious deed of donating property to the sangha and contributing to the propagation of the teachings of the Buddha. Far from confirming gender equality or the liberty of women, this legal-property regime was predicated on the incapacity and dependency of the female person.

But the British admiration for Burmese Buddhist law was overwhelming. So much so that they conveniently excused the fact that polygyny remained legal under Burmese Buddhist law by characterizing it as a form of marriage that no longer had social sanction. As a judge on the Chief Court of Lower Burma put it: "It is not forbidden to a Burman Buddhist to have two wives at the same time; but it is universally conceded that the leading principle of Buddhism is rather monogamy than polygamy, that polygamy is rare and that it is considered disrespectable."[45]

When British judges had the choice of applying this "liberal" Burmese Buddhist law to subjects who straddled religious and racial categories, they refused. And when they had the opportunity to apply it as the personal law of Burmese Buddhist women with "non-Buddhist" or "Chinese Buddhist" partners, they resisted. In rhetoric, they abhorred what they took to be the subjugation of women under Oriental laws and praised what they regarded as the incomparable independence of Burmese wives. In practice, they refrained from constraining the patriarch's right to put his house in order. Far from "saving brown women from brown men," white liberal imperialists allied with brown men who appealed to the colonial state for immunity from Buddhist law to circumvent the established legal capacity and independence of Burmese women. Some men convinced the colonial jurists to, furthermore, transfer their female kin out of the jurisdiction of Buddhist law into that of Chinese, Hindu, or Muslim law against the wishes of the women. Akin to Arab mercantile elites in the Straits Settlements who weaponized personal laws against their spouses to protect their businesses and property, such individuals abetted the colonial state in the consolidation of colonial jurisdiction and displacement of indigenous forms of power and authority.[46] This patriarchal alliance between British imperialists and their colonial subjects created a legal enclosure that systematically alienated Burmese women.

When brown men challenged, rather than abetted, this alliance, colonial jurists blocked them from having recourse to Buddhist law. It was virtually impossible for subjects with Hindu, Muslim, or Chinese agnatic kin to escape their patrilineal personal status through religious conversion or intermarriage. Personal laws were nominally based on religious affiliation but were practically determined by ties of patrilineal filiation. In this sense, and as Judith Surkis observes in her study of Muslim law and personal status in French Algeria, religious personal status was *"jus sanguinis* with a religious name"—except in the case of the Burmese Buddhist, who could alter their personal status through conversion and intermarriage.[47] As we have seen, colonial jurists subjected Burmese Buddhist women, on the account of their intermarriage and conversion, to the jurisdiction of their Hindu, Muslim, Indo-Burmese, Sino-Burmese, or Chinese spouses. When the Burmese Buddhist wife failed to prove conversion, jurists declared legally null and void the marriage, depriving the wife of legal claims to the estate of her husband and children.

In other words, colonial judicial experts protected a patriarch's rights to property and family. They curtailed the women's marital and property rights by routinely moving Burmese Buddhist women out of what they had codified as a bilateral family-property regime and into the jurisdiction of what they essentialized as patrilineal family-property regimes (i.e., Chinese, Hindu, and Muslim laws). This setup channeled property and family along gender-religion-race divisions, away from Burmese Buddhist women toward men of foreign status. Colonial law and its arbiters facilitated the very process that the Konbaung administration legally prohibited: the removal of property, including wife and children, by immigrant subjects and other sovereign powers. The case of Burma provides a uniquely vivid illustration of the penchant of colonial jurists for licensing patriarchal legal-family-property regimes and undermining what they themselves hailed as the exceptional rights of Burmese women—all the while proclaiming themselves to be defenders of the rights-bearing autonomous individual.

Colonial jurists were neither uniformly nor unfailingly determined to observe this scheme. The roundabout ways in which they dealt with the challenges of personal law, passing judgments that contravened judicial norms, may have signified their willingness to—and colonial law's ability to—accommodate the particularities of individual cases. In fact, recent scholarship on colonial law, in British India in particular, has tended to emphasize its malleability, if also its violence and unjustness.[48] What gave law its power as a technology of governance, according to this body of work, was the flexible framework of plural legal jurisdiction and its contestation by colonial subjects. The lack of clarity over the criteria for determining what kinds of marriage and family qualified as "modern" fueled, rather than deter, efforts at marriage and family reforms, such as the outlawing of polygamy and the legislation of age of consent in the nineteenth and twentieth centuries. The inconsistencies of colonial judicial rulings may also speak to the anxieties the jurists had about what, in their mind, amounted to a complete overhaul in the legal personhood of a woman when she was removed from the jurisdiction of Burmese Buddhist law: from a self-possessed, autonomous, propertied individual to an incapacitated dependent. This might have haunted colonial authorities who imagined themselves to be liberal, paternalistic rulers.

There were also occasions where colonial jurists were unable to obstruct the will of Chinese, Hindu, and Muslim men who had arranged to transmit property to their wives or daughters, even adopting daughters instead of sons with the intention of making them heir to their estate. Such cases baffled the jurists, as we have seen. We have also seen that colonial jurists were willing to declare many an intermarriage unlawful, as a corollary effect of which the Burmese Buddhist wife retained her own personhood and property. Such rulings, however, came at a price. Colonial law would let Burmese Buddhist women hold on to their property or their marriage, but not both; it would recognize either their religious belonging or their matrimonial tie, but not both. From this vantage point, there was little ambiguity or flexibility in colonial law and justice.

Propertied women like Auntie Rosie's grandmother Ma Galay may have discerned the changing realities of laws governing property and family. Muslim women, like Burmese Buddhist women, had rights to inherit and control their own property according to Islamic law—rights that the British chiseled away under their covert implementation of coverture. A court case about a young zerbadi widow of an elite Muslim man in Mandalay, like Ma Galay, suggests that women like them apprehended this legal enclosure.

E Khin was sixteen years old when she wed Haji Po Tha, a wealthy Mandalay zerbadi nearly four times her age, around 1913. He was twice married, widowed, and childless. Few Muslims in Mandalay rivaled Po Tha in wealth. He had set up a *waqf* (Muslim family trust, as explained in chapter 2), consisting of land and properties, that provided for two mosques and a madrasa. Upon the death of his second wife, he must have become a most eligible widower given that he had no children. Whoever he married next stood to inherit a considerable fortune upon his death, which could happen relatively soon given his age. His death, in turn, would make his surviving wife a most eligible widow, which is likely what happened to E Khin when Po Tha died in 1919. She was no older than twenty-three years old when she became the main heir to his enormous estate, valued at more than Rs. 100,000, worth approximately 1,500,000 pounds sterling in 1919.[49] Regardless of the economic situation of

E Khin's family, or who initiated or brokered the marriage, material considerations must have factored into the decision-making process.

Once married and widowed, E Khin fought to hold on to her late husband's estate. He had intended to formally set up another waqf, in addition to the one he had established prior to their marriage. He had informed E Khin, as well as his friends and religious and legal advisers of his intentions, though he died before he got around to drawing up a deed for the second waqf. E Khin not only refuted the existence of a second waqf but also contested the validity of the first. When ordered by the courts to produce the original deed, as well as the account books, for the first waqf, which, apparently, Po Tha had left in her possession, she refused. In the eyes of the judges, E Khin "prevaricated a great deal."[50] Maybe she felt that the waqfs deprived her unfairly of her late husband's estate. Perhaps Po Tha had promised her that he would revoke or reduce the waqf he had founded before their marriage. Perhaps she was incredulous that the courts were willing to contemplate the existence of a second waqf for which there was neither written documentation nor deed, based on the oral testimony of "really respectable men," as the judges put it, and against her testimony.[51] Is it possible that E Khin was "prevaricating" because the legal system seemed to her to be unjust?

Knowledge of such experiences in the hands of colluding colonial jurists and "really respectable men" may have prompted Ma Galay to apportion her estate and disburse inheritance to her children well before her death. In the face of an increasingly patriarchal legal system that penalized women with intimate ties extending beyond the boundaries of the Burmese Buddhist, Ma Galay perhaps decided to govern her family affairs outside of the courtroom as much as possible.

The subjective effects of such colonial machinations are harder to gauge. One could reasonably speculate that the litigants could not have been unaffected by the legal arguments and judgments about their personal status and relationships. They may have developed new understandings of what it meant to be Buddhist, Hindu, Muslim, Sino-Burmese, or zerbadi; what separated a Burmese wife from a Chinese wife; and whether marriage between a Buddhist and a Hindu or a Muslim were respectable or desirable. At the same time, it is presumptive to conclude that their social imaginaries were transformed by government regulations of peoples, relationships, and properties along and across its categories of rule. We must also concede that we cannot determine with any degree of precision or certainty the impact of legal adjudications on the thoughts and feelings of the litigants because court transcripts end where the legal proceedings end. They give us only an incomplete and fragmentary picture of marital discords and family disputes and how or whether they were resolved.

It also bears remembering that litigants did not seek the help of civil courts in defining their subjectivities. Legal decisions about property hinged on legal definitions of the personal status of the litigants, that is, their religious, racial, and gender status. The litigants, however, never tasked the courts with deciding their identity. Scholars such as Lauren Benton have emphasized the centrality of cultural identities to jurisdictional politics and the efforts by litigants "to draw jurisdictional lines in ways that were consistent with their own images of group distinctions."[52] My analysis shows on the contrary that "group distinctions" and "cultural identities" were rarely the primary concern of those who waged courtroom battles over the question of legal jurisdiction. Law was an instrument for possessing and alienating property and family, which were the primary reasons people made use of the colonial civil courts. Some sought to reclaim their runaway or adulterous spouses; others tried to formally sever marital and familial ties. At the heart of these cases also lay property. The restitution of conjugal rights compelled a delinquent husband or father to pay maintenance; legal repudiation of a spouse or a child dispossessed the individuals of inheritance and succession. Such court battles were fights over feelings and relationships that had been affronted and hurt but ones that only people with property to keep, gain, or lose could afford to wage.

The selective, class-specific nature of civil court cases makes the courtroom stories of interAsian intimacies all the more revealing of how illusional were colonial constructions of social identities and relations. Colonial jurists frequently commented on the "orthodoxy" of upper-caste, upper-class Hindus and Chinese, which they contradistinguished with the permissiveness of marital, sexual, and familial relations among the "lower orders." This was to be expected: the elite everywhere have historically legitimized and secured their prerogatives by upholding gendered, ritualized, and culturally encoded rules of conduct. Acts of impropriety risked the loss of entitlements, as exemplified by the allegorical figure of the European woman who, by bedding or wedding non-European men, forfeited her membership in the ruling class of Europeans.

Similarly, the many propertied, privileged Asian elites we encounter in the court records had much at stake in their observance and performance of piety and propriety. Yet few of them confirmed colonial definitions of who or what constituted a Chinese, Hindu, Muslim, and Burmese Buddhist. The complexity and multiplicity of their selves and families confounded the colonial jurists. Like the New Burmas, they were a living testament to the disjuncture between classification schemes and lived experiences, between the legal impossibility and the irrefutable reality of belonging across religion, race, and law.

Intimate Trespasses

Civil court cases are, by nature, about disaffection. Embittered battles over marriage, fidelity, and inheritance by wayward husbands, repudiated wives, disobedient children, and conniving relatives—these are the stuff of courtroom dramas. Colonial rule of personal law was, by design, about alienation: of women's property and personhood and of immigrants and their spouses and descendants from Burmese society. I have tried to lift the veil of these legal plots. The people we encounter in the court records defended and dissolved material and non-material attachments against colonial interdictions. Classified as belonging to mutually exclusive identities and communities, they nevertheless assembled knotty marriages and families, and personalities and religiosities that colonial jurists struggled to untangle. As we have seen, these intimate trespassers not only offended colonial authorities. They also scandalized their loved ones. But the frequency of such objections was matched by the regularity with which people who, having initially reacted with displeasure, came around to accepting the transgressions. Bonds and bounds of social belonging were thicker and stickier than the colonial order permitted.

The legal archive of interAsian intimacies shows that kabya (mixed) families like the New Burmas remained unexceptional in colonial Burma. It attests to the "colonial contrivances designed to keep 'their' natives separate and distinct from 'foreign Orientals'" but not to their success.[53] The stories told in the preceding pages expose the legal fiction of the unassimilable foreigner and his obliging native wife for what it was: a colonial alibi. As we see in the following chapters, this colonial alibi turned anticolonial alibi. Burmese Buddhist politicians, lawmakers, and activists weaponized, in the 1920s and 1930s, the colonial legal transformation of intermarriage into outmarriage. They turned the Burmese Buddhist wife and convert of an amyo gya (Other) into a symbol of the subordination of the Burmese and attempted to mount legal prohibitions against intermarriage and conversion. They proclaimed themselves to be critics of British imperialists and champions of the Burmese Buddhist community. Yet they too galvanized bureaucratic learning and caring about interracial, interreligious, and interjural marriages and births. The elite Burmese Buddhist men and women who led the campaigns to regulate intermarriage and conversion were themselves legislators, lawyers, and their wives and children. They were among the coterie of Burmese with a front-row seat to the machinations of the colonial legal institution and its reality. They understood that the management of marriage and family was key to British imperial rule. And they grasped the potential of marriage and family reforms to restructure colonial relations of power.

CHAPTER 5

Burmese Buddhist Exceptionalism

> In intimate social intercourse, the determining factors
> are intermarriage, interdining, and the visiting
> together of temples and churches. These factors are
> absent in the social intercourse of Burmans with
> Indians, while they are present in that of Burmans
> with Europeans and Anglo-Indians. A Burman is
> seldom admitted into a mosque or a Hindu temple,
> and much less to an Indian religious function, while all
> pagodas and Buddhist religious functions are open to
> all the nationalities of the world.
>
> —Taw Sein Ko, "Burmans and Indians" (1913)

"In social matters, it is true, that Burmans and
Indians are wide apart," was what the Cambridge-educated civil servant and
Orientalist Taw Sein Ko had to say when asked by the Royal Commission on
Public Services in India (1913) to comment on the "impression that Burmans
have a prejudice against Indians."[1] According to him, the Burmese perceived
Indians to be an unsociable kind who shunned gracious attempts by the Burmese Buddhist to create relationships of exchange, reciprocity, and conviviality through offerings of food ("interdining"), women ("intermarriage"), and
rituals ("religious functions").

Himself a Sino-Burmese, his assessment of the state of Burmese-Indian "social intercourse" was likely informed by his unfavorable opinion about Indians. It is no secret that he described the Chinese as more tolerant than
"Mohammedans and Hindus."[2] The son of a Hokkien merchant and a Shan
princess, he climbed up the ranks of the ICS to become an influential political
intermediary and translator between the British, Burmese, and the Chinese.
He no doubt saw himself as an epitome of the compatibility of the Chinese
and the Burmese and the success of Sino-Burmese relations.

Yet his opinion about Indians in Burma was not uncommon at the time. It
became more prevalent in the subsequent decade, as indicated by the speeches
Mohandas K. Gandhi gave during his two-week visit to Burma in 1929.[3] In one,
he admonished migrant Indians for failing to share the lot of the Burmese and

urged that they check their "habit" of "causing harm" to their hosts.[4] In a confidential report on Burma presented at the All India Congress Committee on 27 March 1929, Gandhi explained that there was, "in the growing national consciousness, resentment against Indians carrying on intercourse with Burmese women without any formal marriage."[5] And in a letter addressed to "Gujaratis Resident in Burma," written after his return to India, he again brought up the issue of marriage among Burmese women and Indian men:

> My feeling is that the Indians have been taking advantage of the innocence of these simple women. The educated people of Burma do not approve of the conduct of the Indians with regard to their women. It would not pain them if Indians married Burmese girls with proper ceremony, but I could see they intensely dislike those who merely indulge in their sexual urge. Indians ought to keep their conduct in this matter above board.[6]

Such complaints about "the conduct of the Indians with regard to [Burmese] women" circulated widely in the 1920s amid a geopolitical campaign for the administrative separation of Burma from India. In one typical example published in *Thuriya Magazine* (The Sun Magazine), a pioneering Burmese-language magazine that was known for its criticisms of the British administration, a cartoon demeaned an assorted group of male foreigners—a Muslim Indian wearing a fez, a Sikh Indian wearing a turban, and two Chinese wearing the queue, among others—as mosquitoes sucking the blood out of "Mother Burma" under the watchful eyes of the British colonial master hovering above them (fig. 5.1).[7]

Memorandums pleading for separation flooded the newspapers in the wake of a visit by the Indian Statutory Commission in January 1929 to assess the possibility of constitutional reforms.[8] They denounced the suffering of "the sons of the soil" in the face of the unchecked tide of "an innumerable number of the poorer Indians, of an alien faith, or a foreign race."[9] Cheap Indian labor, they complained, had displaced Burmese labor, while Indian financiers came to Burma only to "return to their homes carrying away with them large sums of money."[10] One memorandum likened Burma to "a milch cow" that was being milked dry by "a clever Indian milkman" and warned that the continued connection of Burma with India—"what with their very meagre and frugal style of living," "their low standard of civilization in matters of social life and ideals and outlook so opposed to those of the Burmese people," and "their caste system so repugnant to the Burmese people"—could only mean "ruin and starvation to the Burmese people."[11]

What Taw Sein Ko neglected to point out, and what Gandhi failed to recognize, was that amyo gya (Others) in general, not only Indians, were accused of abusing the hospitality of the Burmese. Thus, in their frequent expression of

FIGURE 5.1. "Mother Burma": a cartoon in *Thuriya Magazine*, September 1926. Source: *Thuriya Magazine*, September 1926, 100.

discontent with the amyo gya, the popular magazine *Myanmar Alin* (The Light of Burma) spared not one category of amyo gya from criticism. Also, while confirming Taw Sein Ko's claim about the widening chasm between Burmese and Indians, these publications disagreed on one crucial point. The problem was not that there was no intermarriage between these groups—there was too much of it, in fact—but that sexual intimacy did not translate into social intimacy.

An editorial published in February 1912 with the English title "National Deterioration" and the Burmese subtitle "The deterioration of the Burmese" expounded on these concerns. The foreigners of today were an ungracious group that prevailed upon the Burmese to abandon their own amyo by adopting the dress and habits of outsiders, it complained. It lamented, furthermore, that the marriage of Burmese women to these "foreign guests" no longer helped assimilate the men because the children were absorbed into the amyo of the father rather than the amyo of the mother. "Burma welcomes the arrival of foreign men, giving them ready access to Burmese women who marry English men, Chinese men, and Indian men," but, it protested, "the reverse is not the case."[12] "Burmese men are not granted the same degree of mobility—they are not admitted into other countries—and have no access to foreign women. As such, people of other religion, race, and nationality can propagate their kind through intermarriage while Burmese men are denied the opportunity to similarly regenerate our own kind through intermarriage."[13] In sum, the Burmese amyo was degenerating due to the arrival of unassimilable "foreign guests" who jealously guarded their patrilineage.

Boycott Foreign Husbands!

The countless commentaries on the amyo gya in Burma published at the time followed a similar script that culminated in the condemnation of the inequitable taking of "our women" by alien men. Amyo gya were not satisfied with dispossessing the Burmese of their land, natural resources, and businesses; they also took possession of Burmese women while denying Burmese men access to "their women." Amyo gya men thereby robbed the Burmese of the means of economic production and social reproduction. Under foreign occupation and incursion, the Burmese deteriorated not only into precarious proletariats— "groveling squatters in our own country,"[14] as one article put it—but also into a castrated amyo whose women became the property of amyo gya patriarchs.

The outcry over the amyo gya spilled out into the streets as the pioneering women's organizations of the country made "the problem of intermarriage" their cause célèbre. The opening salvo was fired on 11 July 1921 during a demonstration against the imprisonment of U Ottama (1879–1939). The first pongyi to be jailed by the British, the Arakanese monk was the most famous member of the General Council of Burmese Associations (GCBA, f. 1911), the largest political organization in British Burma. He was also a protégé of the Young Men's Buddhist Association (YMBA, f. 1908), an organization formed by England-educated Burmese civil servants who were outspoken critics of the Christian missionary-dominated system of government education, holding it accountable for "Burman decay," namely, the diminished knowledge of the teachings of the Buddha (thathana) and "pride of race" among the Burmese. Upon his return to Burma in 1918 from a long stint in India, where he forged a close relationship with Gandhi and the Indian National Congress, and a global tour that included stops in China, the United States, Egypt, and Japan, he emerged as a conduit for elite urban-centered sociopolitical formations such as the YMBA and the GCBA to connect with rural audiences. He came to be known as the "Gandhi of Burma" for mobilizing mass support for non-violent anticolonial boycotts of imported products that were inspired by Gandhi's swadeshi (Indigenous goods) movement in India.

Though memorialized as one of Burma's earliest national martyrs, what Ottama preached about, mainly, was the deterioration of the Burmese Buddhist amyo under British colonial rule.[15] "Out of taxes paid by Buddhists," he argued, in calling for the boycott of government taxes, "missionaries of an alien religion are being paid and fed and provided for while the monk is being deprived of his natural living."[16] He exhorted young pongyi to leave their monasteries to defend the thathana against the threat of British colonialism. The young monastic followers of Ottama, in turn, propelled the rapid growth of village-level wunthanu athin (religion and lineage protection societies) and their women-led, sister associations, wunthanu konmaryi athin (young women's religion and lineage protection societies).[17]

In fact, Ottama arguably had more in common with contemporaneous Buddhist and Hindu ideologues such as Anagarika Dharmapala (1864–1933) and Bal Gangadhar Tilak (1856–1920) than Burmese nationalists.[18] We know that he was in contact with Tilak, who was imprisoned at the Central Jail in Mandalay from 1908 until 1914 as a political prisoner in exile, and likely also crossed paths with Dharmapala, who visited Burma on many occasions. The former valorized the "Hindu past" in India and deplored the material and spiritual devastation of Hindus under non-Hindu "foreign" rulers (i.e., Muslims and the British), while the latter, the man most closely associated with Buddhist revivalism and nationalism in Lanka, was preoccupied with the state of Buddhist dispensation under colonial rule.[19]

And like his Buddhist and Hindu contemporaries, Ottama instrumentalized the vernacular press to propagate his messages, which resulted in his arrest in 1921 on the charge of inciting "disaffection": the British colonial parlance for sedition. His offense? He had published a letter addressed to the then lieutenant governor of Burma, Reginald Craddock, in Thuriya, his favorite medium of publication run by the YMBA and GCBA founder and ally Ba Pe. Entitled "Craddock, go home!," the letter attacked what Ottama and many other politicians in the country perceived as a miserly proposal for constitutional reform by Craddock, one under which all power continued to reside with the office of the governor.

His imprisonment by the British administration triggered public protests attended by not only young pongyi but also his large following among women. According to one estimate, provided by a lawyer from Pyinmana to the British authorities, around forty thousand women had come together at one point to decry the trial of Ottama.[20] It might have been at this precise gathering of women in support of Ottama, or perhaps at another. Either way, members of *wunthanu konmaryi athin* began appealing to Burmese Buddhist women to quit marrying amyo gya.

Two other women's organizations mounted similar calls to boycott amyo gya husbands: the Young Women's Buddhist Association (YWBA) and the Burmese Women's Association (BWA). Like the *wunthanu konmaryi athin*, they were formed as the women's organs of the YMBA and the GCBA, respectively, and formulated their mission as the preservation of the Burmese Buddhist amyo. They pleaded with Burmese Buddhist women to boycott amyo gya husbands, framing the conjugal boycott as an integral strategy in the broader campaign of noncooperation with the British. One of the first organized actions of the members of these women's associations was to condemn the use of imported clothes and textiles and to wear blouses made of *pinni* (light brown, homespun cotton) and *longyi* with local *yaw* designs originating in the western hill tracts of Burma.[21] The conjugal boycott of amyo gya men reinforced such embodied acts of resistance.

In addition, the BWA, whose three-hundred-some members had extensive personal and professional ties to Burmese lawmakers serving in the legislature, demanded legislative action on intermarriage. They appealed, in the name of the Burmese Buddhist amyo, for legal reforms that would prevent a Burmese Buddhist woman from forfeiting her spousal and property rights through her marriage to an amyo gya.

These women-organized agitations intensely politicized the female body as the embodiment of self-determination. In a sharp historical reversal, the body of the lay Buddhist female displaced the male body of the monk—who must renounce all carnal temptations, especially food, alcohol, and sex—as the primary focus of disciplinary control and asceticism. Inspired by the Gandhian swaraj (self-rule) movement and its emphasis on renunciatory bodily practice such as celibacy, vegetarianism, fasting, and the wearing of khadi (homespun cloth), women emerged as the primary target of this method of achieving self-government in Burma as in India.[22] Gandhi had in fact urged his women followers to renounce marriage altogether and devote themselves to the swaraj cause. "Religion and lineage protection societies" in Burma too envisioned the virgin bodies of Burmese women, untouched by foreign goods and men, as the bastion of Burmese sovereignty.

Unsurprisingly, when the all-male Legislative Council finally debated, in 1927, a proposal for marriage reform, it was a motion for the "Application of *Dhammathats* to Marriages between Burmese Women and Foreigners." Po Hla, the councilman behind the motion, explained the need for the reform as follows:

When a woman of Burma marries a foreigner and the marriage is contracted under the Burma Buddhist *Dhammathats*, the marriage is not valid. The marriage has to be contracted under the laws of their husbands who are foreigners. The women of Burma are therefore in a peculiar position quite different from their sisters of other countries. And this is a grievance not only to the women who marry foreigners but also to their children begotten by such union. For example, if a Chinaman marries a Burmese Buddhist woman and if he dies one day his wife has no right to his estate, although many children may have been born[,] because she is a woman. The sons only are entitled to the estate. If there are daughters, they also have no claim. Why? Because the Chinese Customary Law is applied.[23]

U Pu, the next Burmese councilman to speak, reassured his peers that the proponents of the motion had "no desire [for] the foreigners to leave the country." "Let those who come here without their partners marry the women of our country but let the *Dhammathats* prevail," he pleaded, adding:

A Hindu must be born a Hindu. Conversion will not mend matters. The marriage of a Hindu man with our Burmese woman is not valid although there may be a dozen issues. This is how we suffer. Again a Burmese woman must be a Mahomedan convert when she marries a Mahomedan. After her conversion to Mahomedanism, her husband can claim the liberty of marrying as many as four wives. In case the husband desires to divorce a Burmese wife, he has to pronounce the *talak* three times and thereupon she has to run away from the house.[24]

Councilman Kya Gaing declared that many Burmese lawyers like himself frequently encountered such cases of "legal disability" when Burmese women discovered, upon the death of their foreign husbands, that their children were illegitimate and that they had "forfeited the rights which their sisters, who married in their own religion, enjoy."[25] One councilman after another stressed that this was a far cry from the precolonial days when the *dhammasat* governed the marital affairs of all Burmese subjects. They agreed that the situation had reached a tipping point, threatening the "extinction" of the Burmese nation. "Besides taking our country and our property (they) take our sisters," U Pu decried, pointing out that fighting over constitutional changes would prove futile if the Burmese nation was to "become half-caste by gradual extinction."[26]

The lone Burmese councilman to oppose the motion, Kyaw Dun, did so not because he disagreed with these characterizations of intermarriage but rather out of his conviction that the legislature ought to prevent the practice altogether rather than pass resolutions that "amount[ed] to encouraging Burmese girls to marry foreigners." He inveighed against such marriages, proclaiming that there was no greater mistake than "for a woman to choose a wrong husband and flout her own religion."[27]

Many of the concerns that the Burmese legislators raised were legal conundrums to which British jurists were quite sensitive, as shown in chapter 4. Because the councilmen were themselves lawyers with knowledge of the ambiguities and conflicts internal to the colonial system of personal law, they framed their grievances about intermarriage as a problem of "legal disability" for the Burmese Buddhist wives and their children. Yet, and as councilman Tun Win expounded, the point was "to protect the Burmese women and children begotten by marriage with foreigners, *and* [emphasis added] also to preserve the Burmese nation and the Buddhist religion."[28]

The solution that the Burmese legislators urged was correspondingly legalistic: a more extensive application of Buddhist law that would supersede the personal laws of amyo gya. This would restore to Burmese women their rights to family and property of which they had been robbed through a patriarchal alliance among amyo gya men. While the proposed solution challenged the judicial edifice of British colonial rule, the justifications for the solution summoned staple Orientalist tropes of marriage and family: propensity for polygyny and unilateral repudiation (*talaq*) by Muslim husbands, preference for sons among the Chinese, and aversion to polygyny among the Burmese. It also reinforced the British characterization of intermarriage as the outmarriage of the Burmese wife, thereby reifying the legal fiction that underpinned the colonial legal system: that the subject population in Burma was made up of discrete and irreconcilable religious and racial communities. The coming together of these disparate communities necessitated the degeneration of the Burmese Buddhist amyo.

The assertion that intermarriage was leading to the "extinction" of the Burmese Buddhist amyo also appropriated the pseudoscience of eugenics that viewed reproduction and conjugal sexuality as important public—and national—concerns. In the first decades of the twentieth century, eugenics emerged globally as a scientific pursuit as heated debates over degeneracy and population decline took place.[29] At the International Eugenics Congresses in 1912, 1921, and 1932, eugenics experts claimed that there were biological explanations to social disparities and that a selective breeding of the finest human traits would improve "the human race." Influenced by eugenics, campaigns to uplift the working class out of poverty and emancipate women from involuntary motherhood and social inequity expanded. Emancipatory movements—whether emancipation of women, proletariats, or nations—across the world engaged racist theories of evolution and progress that tied biology to the so-cial and the political.[30]

Perhaps the Burmese legislators found inspiration in the aggressive rhetoric against "half-castes" and "racial amalgamation" that the British used to de-nounce the sexual relations of British women and non-British men. Certainly, they deployed that very same rhetoric in their condemnations of intermarriage in Burma. At the same time, they introduced novel elements to an otherwise familiar cocktail of colonial imageries. Councilmen alleged that the very men who wore Burmese dress, professed to be Hindu and Buddhist, and married Burmese women objected to the marriage of their daughters to a Burmese Buddhist. "So it is the case with Chinamen," Tun Win complained:

> When a Chinaman takes a Burmese girl we do not object. We are toler-ant people. But when a Burman boy happens to take one of the Chi-nese girls begotten by the Burmese lady, then they raise a hue and cry, and the boy is taken to Court. As a lawyer I have defended many cases of kidnapping. The girl may have attained the age of 16 or more, but the Chinese father will press his prosecution for kidnapping. And a Ma-homedan too is the same.[31]

Though formulated as a critique of the possessiveness of foreign men, the common refrain that Burmese men were denied access to "their" women while foreign men took "our sisters" was about Burmese men's envious desire to possess women. While attempting to legislate against marriage between amyo gya men and Burmese women, the councilmen saw no irony in the fact that one of several wives of a fellow legislator, the Arakanese Paw Tun, was an American, Sarah Elizabeth Jewett. Paw Tun was unscathed, as was the cele-brated Arakanese barrister and legal expert Chan Toon (1867–1904), who re-turned to Burma from London with an Irish wife, Mabel Mary Agnes Cosgrove. If we are to trust Cosgrove's memoir of their marriage, published as a novel the year after the death of her husband, England-educated Burmese men like Chan Toon and the English expatriate community alike viewed the marriage of a white woman to a native, even a rich and decorated one like Chan Toon, as an honor and "a triumph" for the latter. In retrospect, Cosgrove had little doubt that Chan Toon, in marrying her, "had been far-seeing[,] and calculat-ing on many advantages to accrue"; for him, the marriage was a way "to mix on terms of equality with the English people" and "a step so far in advance of anything hitherto"—even his scholarly and professional achievements.[32]

This characterization of Chan Toon by Cosgrove may have been exagger-ated. She made no secret of her resentment toward him and what she portrayed as a wretched and abusive marriage. But the fact is that Burmese councilmen attempted to impose legal constraints on "marriages between Burmese women and foreigners" but not on those between Burmese men and foreigners. It confirms that they sought to reconstitute—not reject—the sexual double standard of European empires that promised white men unhampered access to the bodies and properties of women of subject races while systematically denying colonized men (and white women) the same privileges. From their perspective, the vitality of the Burmese Buddhist amyo was intertwined with the virility of Burmese Buddhist men.

While mounted in the name of saving Burmese Buddhist women and their rights to family and property, the motion to bring intermarriage into the jurisdiction of Burmese Buddhist law was an attempt at Burmese Buddhist remasculinization and regeneration. Besides proposing to bring marriage, family, and property under the authority of the male-dominated government, the Burmese legislators sought to police the sexual and moral conduct of Burmese women. As such, it is not ironic that their critique of colonial law turned out to be anything but empowering for the women. In the narratives of the legislators, the Burmese wife of a foreigner was not just an obliging wife (as characterized by British jurists). She was an unsuspecting "girl" who was duped into a fraudulent marriage, too young to understand the "great mistake" she made in choosing "a wrong husband" and "flouting her own religion." Burmese legislators ascribed to the women an incapacity to think for themselves and laid the grounds for denying Burmese women the right to consent to intermarriage and conversion.

Bargaining with Patriarchy

What priorities drove women's organizations that proclaimed to champion Burmese women to ally with politicians who, in the name of the Buddhist Burmese amyo, sought to restrict the ability of women to control their intimate lives? The speeches of early women organizers and leaders in Burma have not been recorded for posterity to my knowledge. In general, the political activism of women in Burma has been deemed unworthy of documentation in government archives and chronicles of the nation. How the women envisioned their role and purpose as *wunthanu* agents has been assigned little historical value. What has mattered is the simple fact that they rallied behind their men and amyo. However, the speeches of one prominent member of the BWA who was known and beloved by the British and the Burmese political elites for her advocacy of Burmese women's rights have survived. Her name was Mya Sein (1904–1988), and she emerged as the face of the international campaign against intermarriage among Burmese Buddhist women.

Often referred to as "Miss May Oung" by the British, Mya Sein was the daughter of a well-known Arakanese couple, Thein Mya and May Oung. The latter was a famous attorney, judge, and ICS officer who, as home member on the Legislative Council (1924–1926), held one of the highest government positions open to Burmese people in British Burma. He was a founding member and president of the YMBA and a vociferous Buddhist revivalist. To him, to be a Burman was to be Buddhist, and the "lack of national feeling" that plagued the Burmese would be remedied only by a return to the teachings of the Buddha.[33] Though regarded by some scholars as personifying the "dawn of nationalism in Burma,"[34] May Oung's invocation of "national feeling" should not lead us to underestimate the thoroughly transnational scope and orientation of his sociopolitical affiliations and activities, like those of Ottama and, for that matter, his aunt Mya May. Mya May was a patron of the International Buddhist Society who financed and accompanied Buddhist missions to England, France, and Germany. She also sponsored and participated in a range of local efforts to revive Buddhism, beginning with the establishment of the Empress Victoria Buddhist Boys' and Girls' Schools in Burma, appointing May Oung the headmaster of the former.[35] Their shared conviction in the urgency of reviving the thathana played no small part in Mya May's arrangement of the marriage of her niece Thein Mya and May Oung.

Mya Sein followed in her father's footsteps. She earned a master's degree from St. Hugh's College, Oxford University, in 1927 and a diploma in education in 1928. She returned to Burma to become a superintendent of a girls' high school and a leading figure in several women's organizations, serving as the secretary of the BWA.

In 1931, Mya Sein was presented with two opportunities to expound on her views on the international stage. The first, taking place in January in Lahore, was the All-Asian Women's Conference. Organized by leading feminists in India, it gathered thirty-five delegates and over one hundred visitors from across Asia to "promote the consciousness of unity among women of Asia" and "take stock of the qualities of Oriental civilization so as to preserve them for national and world service," among other objectives.[36] The second, the Burma Round Table Conference (27 November 1931–12 January 1932) in London, represented the culmination of a series of commissions and conferences that were convened by the British government to assess constitutional reforms in India and Burma. The conclusion reached at the first Round Table Conference (12 November 1930–19 January 1931) was that Burma, like India, would be given a greater degree of self-government under revised constitutional structures and, in addition, would gain separation from India. In the aftermath of this conclusion, a separate Round Table Conference for Burma was called, with twenty-six delegates from Burma in attendance, for the purpose of deliberating the outlines of a constitution for a self-governing Burma separated from India.

What distinguished these two conferences was not just the nature of the occasions and the publicity that the latter generated but also their timing. The conferences occurred shortly after the world plunged into the catastrophic economic crisis known as the Great Depression (1929–1939), catapulting an unprecedented number of Burmese people into lives of unemployment, poverty, and indebtedness.[37] It precipitated the largest peasant uprising in Burmese history, aimed at the expulsion of the British, that lasted for two years starting in December 1930 and left nearly 1,700 dead.[38] In urban areas, labor strikes and race riots ensued. What the colonial administration called the anti-Indian riots of 1930—and, later, "the first anti-Indian riots"—began as a scuffle between the 2,000 some Indian migrant dockworkers who were on a strike for a wage increase and the group of Burmese laborers who had been brought in as strike breakers; it left at least 120 people, mostly Indian, dead.[39] This was followed by the anti-Chinese riots of January 1931: an altercation between a Cantonese noodle hawker and a Burmese customer turned into a weeklong rampage in Rangoon and nearby towns that forced Chinese residents to flee Rangoon.[40]

Amid this turmoil, the Dobama Asi Ayone ("We Burmese" or "Our Burmans" Association), modeled after the Irish nationalist Sinn Féin Party ("We Ourselves" or "Ourselves Alone" Party in Irish), published a manifesto inciting "self-respecting" Burmese people to be "unruly" (maik). Founded in 1930, Dobama Asi Ayone represented a new generation of young, urban, left-leaning intellectuals and activists who titled themselves thakin (master) to symbolize their goal of returning Burma to its rightful masters, the Burmese. From its inception, the group discouraged kabya Burmese from identifying as a foreign people and "pure" (sin sit) Burmese from admiring the foreign.[41] The manifesto, however, carried a decidedly adversarial, anti-Indian message. It repeatedly invoked "the Indian foreign guests who insulted the Burmese masters of the house," referring to the Indian dockworkers who fought with the Burmese strikebreakers in the 1930 riots. It claimed, with sarcasm, that the Burmese should be grateful toward Indians because "their insulting us made us discern with clarity our abjection." "Don't hate the Indians," the manifesto urged, advocating that what was needed was for the Burmese "to love one another more."[42] This was no endorsement of nonviolence. Instead, the manifesto issued a clarion call to the Burmese to stop being gracious and obliging and start disobeying and rebelling. "It is time to get offensive. It is time to be truly *maik*. Let us be *maik*."[43]

Such was the backdrop against which Mya Sein spoke as a representative of Burma, which may explain her bullish comments at the All-Asian Women's Conference. Throughout the conference, its organizers and attendees referenced Burmese and other "Buddhist" women (namely, Sri Lankan) as exceptional Asian women, unencumbered by "Oriental defects" and far ahead of not only other women of Asia but also of the "Occident." The adulation for Burmese women was to be expected. The organizers of the conference had long lauded Burmese women as the Oriental model of womanhood to be emulated. In her capacity as the joint secretary of the Women's Indian Association and the editor of the association's monthly journal, *Woman's Duty (Stri Dharma)*, the Irish theosophist-feminist Margaret Cousins (1878–1954) described Burmese women as "possibly the freest women in the East, taken all around," unfettered by either "caste system, purdah nor early marriage."[44] She praised Burma as a country that had "long given to her daughters social equality and liberty."[45] The Hindi writer, editor, and political activist Rameshwari Nehru (1886–1966), who was a fellow organizer of the conference, published numerous accounts of Burmese women in the Hindi monthly *Women's Mirror (Stri Darpan)*, which she edited, describing the Burmese wife as "a true friend and companion of her husband."[46]

Feminists such as Cousins and Nehru did not blindly appropriate colonial constructions of Burmese women discussed in the previous chapter. They drew on self-images of Burmese Buddhist womanhood crafted and circulated by women like Mya Sein's great aunt Mya May. A 1903 essay titled "The Women of Burma" that she contributed to the inaugural issue of the quarterly journal *Buddhism*, the official publication of the International Buddhist Society, offers an early example. In it, she wrote that it was because of the teachings of the Buddha that "unlike other Oriental women," the Burmese woman "is free and happy."[47] It was the reason "that in all the details of life—in the holding of property, in trade, in marriage, in divorce, in right to the children she has borne—she is everywhere regarded, not as the subordinate, the chattel and the slave of man, but as his loved co-worker, his dear companion in the work and play of life." "There are but few Burmese women, even in the villages," she added, "who are unable to read and write."[48]

Her comment about female education betrays the conceit of such congratulatory images of Burmese women. When she founded the Empress Victoria Buddhist Girls' School in 1897, it was the only Buddhist school for girls in Rangoon, serving a student population of sixty.[49] According to the government census of 1901, only 4.4 percent of the Buddhist female population in Burma were literate compared with 41 percent of the corresponding male population. After a decade, this figure only increased to 6 percent.[50] Mya May could not have been unaware of the deficiency of female education in much of Burma.

The Burmese delegates to the All-Asian Women's Conference perpetuated such misleading portrayals of Burmese women. Mya Shwe, the first to speak and an educator like Mya Sein, informed the attendees that Burmese women possessed rights equal to men and "mostly led lives economically independent of their husbands."[51] During the session titled "Motherhood, Polygamy and Traffic in Women," she claimed that "the public opinion" was so strongly against polygamy in Burma that there were "very few cases where a man really has the courage to marry more than one wife." And she told the audience that the last Burmese monarch had only one wife, "who evidently ruled him well."[52] Both assertions were deceptive: women in Burma continued to sue their Buddhist husbands in court for keeping additional wives or cohabiting with other women, and the last king of Burma, Thibaw, had multiple wives.[53]

Mya Sein, the Burmese delegate who had the most speaking time, also downplayed challenges confronting women in Burma. Medical care for women and children was inadequate, she acknowledged, but insisted that they did not suffer from "civilizational defects" apparent in other parts of Asia.[54] "The Burmese Buddhist woman," she observed, "is a joint owner of property with her husband" and is "virtually the head of the family and sometimes its sole support."[55] Yet, she stressed, "if a Burmese Buddhist woman married a Mahommedan, Hindu, or a Christian, she loses her rights, such as joint ownership of property, preferential right to inherit, divorce." Emphasizing that mixed marriages had placed Burmese women "in a highly disadvantageous position," she concluded that if women of different religions held equal rights, then "we would not need to pass any rules to protect the women of any one country."[56] Far from finding common cause, Mya Sein disparaged her "Oriental sisters" whose subordinate status to men enabled the degradation of Burmese women. If only amyo gya women were more like Burmese Buddhist women, then there would be no need for legislations "to protect" women in Burma. "Oriental sisters," like their male counterparts, were a liability for Burmese Buddhist women.

Mya Sein was more circumspect in her comments at the Burma Round Table Conference, which she kept brief, perhaps on account of that fact that her attendance as the only woman delegate had been contested right up until the eve of the conference. The British administration in Burma had proposed that the more senior Mya May, not Mya Sein, be the lone woman delegate in her capacity as the vice president of the BWA. However, Mya May insisted that Mya Sein accompany her to participate in the conference as a delegate. When her wishes were rebutted, she threatened to organize a boycott of the conference by the entire Burmese delegation. Only on the eve of the conference did the male Burmese delegates, who included friends of the late May Oung (who had passed away in 1926), request that Mya Sein be permitted to participate in the conference as their only woman delegate.[57] She was a token presence.

In her speech, Mya Sein stressed that women in Burma held "from time immemorial" a high social, economic, and political position: "We inherit equally with our brothers, and we have rights to our own property. Marriage in Burma is a civil contract, and I think that in no other country in the world do a man and his wife live in such equal partnership as in Burma."[58] In an interview with London's *Daily Herald* immediately after the roundtable conference, published under the title "The Land of Happy Marriage," Mya Sein elaborated on her argument about the equality of marital relations in Burma (fig. 5.2). Less than a month later, the interview was reproduced in toto in Burmese in *Thuriya* under a different title: "Burmese Women and Marriage" ("Myanmar amyo thami mya hnit ein daung hmu").[59] She described marriage in Burma as "a perfect partnership" based on "absolute equality," "common consent," "joint earning," and "joint inheritance," resulting in "no feelings of sex superiority or jealousy." "Another factor that helps to promote matrimonial happiness," she pointed out, was that under the Buddhist law, wills were not valid: "For example, should a wife, who has property of her own, die before her husband he inherits as a matter of course, and the same law prevails should the husband be the one to die first." Acknowledging that even Burma was "not a matrimonial utopia," Mya Sein added that when marital complications arose, a husband and wife could "obtain a divorce in the same way as they married—by mutual consent." She was quick to insist, however, that divorce was a rarity in Burma because there were "so many contented married couples for the reasons I have explained."[60]

Mya Sein thus equated marriage in Burma with the modern companionate marriage ideal, premised on individual consent, desire, and satisfaction rather than duty, obligation, and a procreative mandate. She next asserted that the "perfect equality upon which our happy partnerships are based" reflected the broader culture of sex equality in the country. "The Burmese woman has no inferiority complex, because there is no sex exclusion," she proclaimed and continued: "We are responsible for our own actions and therefore, when married, we are not just someone's husband or someone's wife." She reassured the reader that this individuality and independence of Burmese women did not make them "less home-loving," just ideal companions.[61]

Mya Sein, like her aunt Mya May, constructed a mythical figure of the Burmese Buddhist woman, presumed to be happier and freer than "any other Oriental woman." In her hands, Burmese Buddhist women were no longer

The Land of HAPPY MARRIAGE

No Wedding Rings.. and DIVORCE IF-YOU-PLEASE

"Marriage in our country is a perfect partnership because it is founded upon absolute equality."

by
Daw Mya Sein
(May Oung)
The only Woman Delegate to the Burma Round Table Conference

"IN no country in the world do man and wife live in such equality as in Burma."

When I made this remark in a speech at the Burma Round Table Meeting the other day, I had no idea it would so surprise people. Yet it is the truth.

Marriage in our country is a perfect partnership because, like all perfect partnerships, it is founded upon absolute equality.

In the first place marriage is a Civil Contract, an arrangement entered into on the grounds of common consent. By this I mean to say that

because a man and woman discover that they love one another, or because they believe that they are suited to one another, they agree to live together—to set up a new household.

There is a good deal of importance attaching to the phrase of "setting up a household." In old Burma a tax was levied upon every household, as being one particular unit. So the start of another home meant the commencement of a new unit of taxation, and the affair had a State importance as well as a personal one.

In Burma everything is shared in this marriage partnership. There are joint earnings and perhaps a joint inheritance. I mean to say that if a Burman receives an inheritance after marriage he shares it with his wife, or vice versa, as the case may be. A legacy or property, however, held before marriage remains the sole property of the individual. We have always had the equivalent to your Married Woman's Property Act. Business transactions entered into by married people are done in their joint names. If a house is purchased or a mortgage arranged, husband and wife must both sign the agreement.

Share Alike

Husband and wife keep no secrets from one another; but, of course, it would not be a perfect partnership if they did.

These conditions strengthen the ties of home life and the woman's place in the home as wife and mother. At times of agricultural crisis, wives often supplement the family income by referring into some kind of trading. Perhaps they have a little shop, or it may be they sell among their friends.

But whenever necessary the wife may be depended upon to help the family purse, for she feels that when the occasion arises it is just as fair and important for her to earn money as for her husband.

Naturally in these circumstances a

wife is more or less bound to know the extent of her husband's earnings. I am quite convinced that this equality in marriage leads to better understanding in every way. There are no feelings of sex superiority or jealousy. Everything shared—that is the whole idea. Business, troubles, joys, success, and happiness.

Another factor that helps to promote matrimonial happiness is that a Burman Buddhist is prevented by his religion from making a will. He cannot make his own arrangements to operate after death. There are definite laws of inheritance.

For example, should a wife, who has property of her own, die before her husband he inherits as a matter of course, and the same law prevails should the husband be the one to die first. After the death of parents the children automatically inherit, and other relatives and so on.

Divorce Not Common

I do not say there are never any complications, I know they do sometimes occur. Even Burma, where marriages are usually so happy, is not a matrimonial Utopia.

What happens if a husband and wife do quarrel? Well, they can obtain a divorce in the same way as they get married—by mutual consent.

If it is definitely clear that the divorce is the fault of one of the contracting parties, then that one must suffer, by receiving less property when the partnership is dissolved. But I do not think that there is any inequality in this, because the same would be the case in a business partnership, would it not?

Divorce is not common among

our people. There are so many contented married couples for the reasons I have explained. Also, although divorce is so easy, it is really a matter of public opinion.

The Burmese woman has no inferiority complex, because there is no sex seclusion. The absolute equality with man that she enjoys gives her a perfect knowledge of life and an ability to go unhampered into the world and earn her living if the case demands it.

Yet this does not make her less home-loving. The home is on a bigger scale with us than in England. We live in much larger families. Cousins, aunts and other relatives may form part of a household. This gives the mother time for outside work because her home duties are shared.

No Rings

Even outside the partnership of marriage there is complete equality. No difference of treatment is meted out to girls and boys. On Feast days we all go to the Pagoda. Women and girls share in the festival just as much as the men.

Burmese marriage is based on the same idea as that which governs us from birth. We women are all individuals having our own special personality. What we earn, what we own is ours. We are responsible for our own actions and therefore, when married, we are not just someone's husband or someone's wife. We are ourselves.

We do not wear wedding rings, so you cannot tell at a glance in Burma whether a woman is married any more than in your country you can tell the same about a man.

We Burmese women would consider that if we had to wear a wedding ring it would destroy that ideal of perfect equality upon which our happy partnerships are based.

In an interview.

Says Mr. Peppercorn..

I Would Rather Walk

SOME friends of mine took me out in their car for the day the other Sunday. It's a small car and there were nine of us. They didn't like to leave the dog at home, as he'd have been lonely, so he came as well.

I might have been all right if the rain had kept off. The forecast said we might expect some rain and, by gum, they were right. I like to be sociable, but when they asked me if I was doing anything next Sunday, I told them I had arranged to go walking; and so I had—on my lonesome, if only the missus has worn off.

FIGURE 5.2. "The Land of Happy Marriage": Mya Sein's interview with the *Daily Herald*. Source: *Daily Herald*, 7 December 1931, 8. By permission of the *Daily Herald*.

real women with real problems such as illiteracy and marital unhappiness. They were an icon of the Burmese Buddhist amyo. In so doing, Mya Sein sacralized the conflation of Burmese women with Buddhism. The reason the Burmese woman was such a rare specimen of the female sex, one that knew no "inferiority complex" nor "sex exclusion," was Buddhism, she posited. All women of Burma, regardless of their batha, had benefitted from the unparalleled liberty and equality made possible by the operation of Burmese Buddhist law. Without this sacred gift, a Burmese woman was a secondary sex condemned to a life of inferiority and subordination. Equally sacrosanct was the duty of Burmese women to safeguard this heritage and its transmission to future generations of Burmese women—that is, through marriage to fellow Burmese Buddhist men and abstinence from intermarriage and conversion.

It is possible to read Mya Sein's speech as a geopolitical strategy intended to appeal to the British imperialist ideology of saving native women from Oriental patriarchal oppression. I have myself suggested this line of interpretation in the past, arguing that Burmese nationalists justified their demand for self-rule on the basis that Burmese women needed to be saved from foreign men.[62] The refusal by the British government to grant Burma constitutional independence, even as it characterized the colony as essentially incompatible with India, turned the intermarriage and conversion of Burmese Buddhist women into a metonym for the colonial subjugation of Burma as an appendage of British India. The iconized Burmese Buddhist woman allowed the imagination of India as contiguous to Burma but civilizationally distant and, indeed, opposite, and thus requiring separation.

There were good reasons for thinking that the British might be receptive to this alarmist discourse. The British themselves held up the Burmese woman as the rights-bearing autonomous individual idealized by the British political discourse of liberalism. Whether or not the British helped the Burmese to save their women and their propertied rights from Indian patriarchs was a test of Britain's (and the British Empire's) stated commitment to liberalism and the protection of individual rights.

I no longer find this reading satisfactory. Mya Sein was not simply challenging the British to honor their purported liberal imperial mission. Like her privileged Burmese Buddhist kinsmen who populated the legislature and political parties, Mya Sein reiterated the notion that "the high status" of Burmese women was in danger of destruction by intermarriage and conversion to push a conservative agenda: the centralization of power in the hands of the Burmese Buddhist amyo just as Burma inched closer to achieving some measure of self-governance. What Mya Sein championed was not the egalitarian "caste-less" society that British colonial officers imagined Burma to be but a social hierarchy premised on religious Others. And in the name of protecting women, she proclaimed the Burmese Buddhist reproductive coupling the only legitimate object of desire for Burmese women. This was the price Burmese women would have to pay to defend their legal rights to family and property against the patriarchal rights of minorities.

Such tethering of the interests of women to those of community and nation in colonial contexts have rarely empowered women.[63] At the same time, feminist scholarship on women in right-wing movements such as Hindutva and the Ku Klux Klan has shown that women—even colonized women, even "anti-feminist" women—have empowered themselves as daughters, wives, and mothers of the nation, leveraging these positions to bargain with patriarchal authorities.[64] In other words, we should not presume that women like Mya Sein were passive followers of chauvinistic projects, as British colonial officials were known to do.

A case in point was the 1927 demonstration by members of the BWA in support of women's right to vote and to stand for parliamentary elections. It was co-organized by three BWA members: Mya Sein, Sarah Elizabeth Jewett (the aforementioned American wife of the councilman Paw Tun), and San Youn (1887–1950), popularly known as "Independent Daw San" after her *Independent Weekly*.[65] On the morning of 3 February 1927, the three women led more than a hundred women on to the premises of the Rangoon Municipal Hall and the Legislative Council to show support for a proposal to abolish "the sex-disqualification clause" that prohibited women from running for parliamentary posts. According to Mya Sein, the women demonstrators were all aware that the British construed any attempt by Burmese women to be elected to the council as nationalist. But she insisted that the demonstrators objected to the sex-disqualification clause primarily as feminists.[66] What prompted the demonstration was the concurrent struggle in England and India by women to remove sex disqualification on voting and attaining legislative posts and, more immediately, the appointment earlier in the year of Dr. Muthulaksmi Reddi (1886–1968) to the Madras Legislative Council as the first councilwoman in British India.[67]

The British may have dismissed Burmese women agitators as pawns of their men. But a considerable number of Burmese councilmen must have been convinced that the women would not simply do their bidding if elected to the legislature—enough to produce a coalition of otherwise ideologically opposed councilmen who voted against the motion, defeating it 46 to 31.[68] The fact that San Youn was among those shepherding the demonstration, as well as the agenda of the BWA, might have contributed to this belief. She had founded the *Independent Weekly* just two years prior to the demonstration, right after her second and abusive marriage ended in divorce. The name of the paper, San Youn explained, was inspired by the Irish nationalist paper the *Irish Independent* and signified her desire for Burma's freedom as well as her "determination to never return to the shackled life of a salaried worker or a married woman."[69] This rejection of colonization, wage labor, and matrimony as analogous forms of exploitation and oppression presented a stinging critique of marriage. Mirroring her quest for independence, San Youn singlehandedly ran the paper, not only authoring the editorials, headline news, and all its various columns but also managing the day-to-day operations of the press.

San Youn and Mya Sein collaborated as leaders of the BWA. Their activism centered similarly on Burmese Buddhist women. In fact, San Youn made her literary debut with a prize-winning semiautobiographical story, published under the pseudonym "a Burmese Buddhist woman" (*buddha batha myanmar ma*). Entitled "Khin Aye Kyi" after its Burmese Buddhist heroine, the short story chronicled Khin Aye Kyi's life of unwavering devotion to the teaching of Burmese language and literature, the propagation of the thathana, and the education of women.[70] Like Mya Sein, she failed to publicly reckon with the discriminations immanent in her privileges as a "a Burmese Buddhist woman" and her championing of women as defenders of amyo, batha, and thathana. However, San Youn took a much less sanguine stance than Mya Sein on the state of women in Burma, arguing that female education was a matter of liberating and advancing the Burmese nation. Significantly, and as I have shown elsewhere, from the moment she stepped onto the public stage with the publication of "Khin Aye Kyi," San Youn urged the people of Burma to trust their women.[71] Her message was consistent and resolute: do not deny Burmese Buddhist girls and women the opportunity for education out of fear that government and mission schools would turn them into Christians or degenerate Buddhists; if given the chance, Burmese Buddhist women will prove, like Khin Aye Kyi and herself (who had graduated from a mission school), that they are more than capable of serving as the backbone of the Burmese Buddhist amyo. Her message to and about Burmese Buddhist women diverged markedly from that of the Burmese councilmen.

Through their collaboration with each other and with fellow *wunthanu* men, women like San Youn, Mya Sein, and Mya May sought to inscribe their own agenda onto visions of the Burmese Buddhist amyo. That they referred to Burmese Buddhist women as not only possessing legal rights to property but also heads of household is revealing. After all, the "head of household," presumed by the British to be the father or husband, was the paradigmatic rights-bearing, property-owning, political individual. The idealization of Burmese Buddhist women as rights-bearing, property-owning "heads of household" was an attempt to guarantee for the women the right to be recognized as enfranchised individuals whose voice and vote counted. Such women were rewriting the script of Burmese Buddhist exceptionalism, refusing to allow it to be monopolized by men.

Their activism also made possible an unprecedented public discussion of "women's rights" as such. The legislative debate over the application of Burmese Buddhist law to marriages between Burmese women and foreigners resulted in the drafting, in the same year, of the so-called Buddhist Marriage and Divorce Bill (1927): a uniform set of laws that would govern marriage and divorce among all Buddhists in the whole of Burma. The bill spelled out the conditions under which marriage, divorce, and division of joint property could be legally effected among Buddhists. The direct result of the conjugal boycott campaign, therefore, was a piece of legislation that would, when enacted, regulate marriage not between a Buddhist woman and a non-Buddhist man but among Buddhists. It enumerated the rights of Buddhist women—to divorce, property ownership, inheritance, and succession—married to Buddhists, not to "foreigners."

The bill introduced a number of unprecedented provisions for legally effecting marriage and divorce. It outlawed polygamy and recognized monogamy as the rule among Buddhists in Burma for the first time. "This," the bill reasoned, "in view of the fact that polygamy is distinctly in disfavour [sic] and very rarely practiced, is not in reality a serious departure from the present law."[72] Yet, back in 1882, the British judge and legal scholar—and, at the time, the judicial commissioner of British Burma—John Jardine declared in one of his authoritative circulars to judges and magistrates that polygamy was condoned "by the Dhammathat as well as by established custom of Buddhists in British Burma."[73] While he subsequently, in 1914, described the Burmese as having become a "monogamous race,"[74] a survey of case law across the first few decades of the twentieth century indicates that polygyny was neither rare nor even discouraged among the Burmese.[75] And in all of these cases, the presiding judges upheld the idea "that the Buddhist Law recognized polygamy and that a Buddhist might marry at the same time two or more women all of whom have the status of a wife and not that of a concubine."[76]

The bill also recognized adultery and cruelty as grounds for divorce despite conceding that "the dhammathats are most nebulous about what matrimonial faults would entail divorce."[77] These provisions were sufficiently interventionist to beget a backlash from self-described Buddhist authorities. Within months of the drafting of the bill, the president of the Rangoon-based Burma Buddhist Mission sent a letter to the secretary to the government of Burma protesting the bill as a ploy to impose on Burma the Christian ideology and practice of monogamy, "a sugar-coated pill in Christianity prepared for the Buddhists to swallow," as he put it.[78] The bill did not become law. And it would take more than a decade for it to be debated again in the legislature.

As the quote above objecting to the Buddhist Marriage and Divorce Bill as "a sugar-coated pill in Christianity" suggests, women leaders and organizers like San Youn and Mya Sein walked a tightrope. Burmese Buddhist exceptionalism gave them an opportunity to bargain with patriarchal authorities, both British and Burmese, to advance social reforms that would have otherwise gained little traction, such as female education, franchise, and political representation; protection of women's spousal rights; and domestic violence. Doing so made them susceptible to denigration by the British as pawns of Burmese men and denunciations by the Burmese Buddhist as stooges of Christian invaders and other amyo gya. On account of their gender, the women could never shake off the suspicion that their decisions were unduly influenced by others. The double bind of continually reaffirming, on the one hand, their allegiance to Burmese men and amyo and, on the other, their credibility as advocates of social and political change for women, no doubt strained and constrained their ability to forge solidarities with amyo gya women activists as the example of the All-Asian Women's Conference illustrates. Their promotion of the ideology of Burmese Buddhist exceptionalism made them bona fide nationalists, but it cursed their collaboration with amyo gya women.

CHAPTER 6

The Conditions of Belonging

The Burma Round Table Conference concluded with a demand by His Majesty's government that a general election be held as soon as possible to determine if "the desire of the people of Burma is that the government of their country should be separated from that of India."[1] Held in late 1932, anti-separation candidates won the election handily, taking the majority of seats in the legislature and advancing a resolution for Burma to be federated with India albeit with the unreserved right to secede. Refusing to grant the right to separate later, the British instructed the legislature in Burma to separate now or never. In its true paternalistic fashion, the British government divorced Burma from India upon deciding at the end of 1933 that the Burmese desired it. Never mind that both the popular electorate in Burma and the anti-separation councilmen (and lone councilwoman) they elected to the legislature voted against separation from India.

The results of the election, therefore, turned out to be inconsequential. However, the British ultimatum—separate or remain forever attached—set in motion a full-throttle political campaign for and against separation. In the legislature itself, the separation question became inseparable from the inter-marriage question. The pro-separation faction of the GCBA, led by Ba Pe, recycled well-worn charges against amyo gya of seducing and mistreating Burmese women. One homed in on marriages between Burmese women and *chettiar* men as he expounded on "the deplorable position of Burmese women marrying non-Buddhists." The women, Ba Than claimed, were left "worthless" when their *chettiar* husbands abandoned them to return to India or for wives they subsequently brought from India. Even if they were not deserted by their husbands, he noted, "what is left after they die is taken away by their relatives from India."[2]

Councilman Kya Gaing, a separatist known for his acerbic tongue, directed at Councilwoman Hnin Mya his comments on marriages between Burmese women and "Chittagonians," who comprised the largest group of Bengalis in colonial Burma and, as such, were a much-maligned category of migrants.[3] The first woman elected to the legislature, Hnin Mya was an anti-separatist who followed in the footsteps of her more famous brother Chit Hlaing. A celebrated lawyer, erstwhile president of the GCBA, close associate of Ottama, and member of the Indian National Congress, he briefly presided over the Legislative Council as its president in 1932. Like her brother, Hnin Mya argued that federating with India was the surest path to independence from British colonial rule, one that would avoid the economic catastrophe that would ravage Burma were it to separate from India. In her speech during the final debate on the separation question, she reminded her peers that India is "a country of much preeminence in this world, and it is the place where Lord Buddha attained his Buddhahood and Nirvana."[4]

Kya Gaing responded that had Hnin Mya "been observant," she would have noticed that her very own neighborhood in Moulmein had become overrun by "bamboo shanties inhabited by Burmese women with Chittagonian husbands."[5] Why had these marriages become so popular? Because, Kya Gaing claimed, the men were reliable breadwinners who provided the income the "youthful maidens" required. He recounted one case of an arranged marriage between a recent Chittagonian émigré and a "beautiful girl." According to Kya Gaing, the man approached Hnin Mya's neighbor, who was herself married to an Indian man, offering her fifty rupees to arrange the marriage. The woman agreed to prevail on the "girl," motivated less by the monetary incentive than by her shame. "She was ashamed to think that she was the only one who is the wife of an Indian," explained Kya Gaing, "and so if the whole village married other Indians there would be no need for her to be shameful." She tempted the "girl" with a *longyi* given by the suitor, impressed upon her the importance of heeding the advice of an elder, and spelled out why she should accept the match: "Look at your brother-in-law, Nga Ni; he used to beat his wife when he comes home while he cannot earn anything. As for your sister, as money is scarce she cannot get anything and now all are in trouble. Now look at me. My husband used to get up early and find employment and then bring back the earning. See I have got gold bangles and a *longyi*. I am saying this because

I love you. So better do as myself." Having witnessed firsthand her sister's abusive marriage, the "girl" consented, and the elder woman received her matchmaking fees. Kya Gaing decried that without separation, such marriages would soon overwhelm Burma.[6]

Narratives by both Ba Than and Kya Gaing cast doubt on the legitimacy of the Indian-Burmese marriage, the sincerity of the Indian husband, and the intelligence of the Burmese wife. In the former, the Burmese wife was expendable, easily displaced by the "real" wife from the homeland and the relatives of the husband. In the latter, naive Burmese "girls" were baited into marriages with conniving men by the prospect of material benefits and by the ruses of Burmese women, themselves victims of seduction, who kept the cycle of humiliation turning by recruiting other women into the same fate. Tellingly, when Ba Maw, a leading anti-separation councilman, asked why nothing was said about the English and the Chinese, Ba Pe retorted that he had "not come across instances where the Chinese had gone against us politically" and that "those of the Chinese who are born and brought up here are like brothers to us."[7] Indians were perpetual strangers, incapable of true intimacy.

Pro-separatist lawmakers like Ba Pe, Ba Than, and Kya Gaing were prone to castigating Hindus and, especially, Muslims as the nemesis of the Burmese Buddhist amyo. They fixated on Muslim Indians and conversion, polygyny, and repudiation as symbols of the religious zeal, patriarchal privilege, and libidinal excess of Indian men and the abject powerlessness of Indian women. Such invective was a thinly disguised warning to all "alien" groups that the colonial administration had partitioned into minority voting blocs deserving political representation. As Ba Pe put it, the Chinese had not "gone against the Burmese politically."

Legislators also deluged the press with fiery denunciations of intermarriage. For example, *Thuriya*, owned by Ba Pe, ran daily opinion pieces entitled "The Suffering of Burmese Women Married to Others."[8] Against this background of renewed wrangling over the separation question, the vernacular print media became fertile grounds for sentimental, moralizing tales of intermarriage and conversion.

Degeneracy of the Heart

Published on the front page of the *Mandalay Thuriya* (The Mandalay sun), the sister paper of *Thuriya*, "Defend Our Amyo and Lineage" warned of the disastrous consequences of *varṇa saṅkara*.[9] A concept that appears in the Hindu *dharmaśāstras*, it means "the mixing of the *varnas*" and is often translated as "caste confusion" or "caste pollution." The article was written in the form of a *nissaya*: an interphrasal translation of a Pali text followed by a more elaborate vernacular gloss by the translator. Found in many parts of Southeast Asia, *nissaya* often function more as commentarial texts than as simple translations of Pali source texts, allowing the author to give edifying sermons on Buddhist teachings.[10] In this instance, the two-stanza Pali verse that the author translated was an excerpt from the Nītimañjarī (c. 1494 CE), a collection of versified moral maxims, written in Sanskrit and accompanied by a commentary that cited from the Hindu Vedic scriptures.[11] The Pali verse with which the article opened, therefore, was itself a translation from Sanskrit into Pali. Few readers would have discerned this fact because the author, Shwe Mann Thi, did not explain the origins of the Pali verses.

It is also unlikely that the author of the article in the *Mandalay Thuriya* was one "Shwe Mann Thi." That must have been the nom de plume used by the famous scholar monk and writer Ledi Pandita U Maung Gyi (1878–1939), whose Pali and Burmese translation of the Nītimañjarī was published posthumously in 1956, with a foreword dated 3 September 1920.[12] Not coincidentally, the Pali translation of the verses from the Nītimañjarī quoted at the beginning of the 1932 *Mandalay Thuriya* article match verbatim those in the 1956 publication.[13] Just as importantly, Ledi Pandita U Maung Gyi regularly employed the *nissaya* style in writing the popular "young ladies" column in the monthly *Dagon Magazine* (1920–1948), the first illustrated magazine in the country, for which he served as the editor.[14] *Nissaya* was a writing technique and "women" a subject he had helped popularize in the vernacular popular press.

The author began by observing that according to the *pa tan* (*paṭṭhāna* in Pali), or the canonical Buddhist treatise that examines the law of cause and effect, women are the root of causal relations. "If a Burmese woman marries a man of other amyo," he explained, "then the amyo of her children and grandchildren has been ruined." He lamented that there were "countless cases of women who mix with others," corrupting the Burmese amyo. "The more women desire to marry men of other religion and lineage," he warned, "the graver the damage to the amyo and the *dhamma*."[15]

He instructed the "good men" of Burma that it was their duty to deter "the evil custom" among foreigners of converting their Burmese Buddhist wives. It was also the duty of good Burmese men and elders "to guide and discipline young Burmese women to only marry our men whose intentions towards our women are kind and honorable, not driven by their obsession with wealth and riches." The author next did what few other critics of intermarriage did at the time, directly reprimanding Burmese women who married foreigners:

Women, too, should not be so short-sighted as to think that all is well if, in this lifetime, they can enjoy a life of riches. Such women will never escape the cycle of birth and rebirth and their children and grandchildren will also be polluted and lost forever. So, the entire (Burmese) amyo should abstain from marrying foreigners. Like learning to avoid poison that kills immediately, like steering clear of poisonous snakes, let us keep away [from *varṇa saṅkara*].[16]

Conspicuously, Shwe Mann Thi did not bring up the often-cited issue of "legal disability." Instead, he dwelled on the importance of right intentions and compassion as the foundation of marriage. Marriages of opportunism based on ignorance, greed, and—on the part of the amyo gya husband—zealotry, *varṇa saṅkara* was a product of ill intentions and, as such, destined to reproduce harm: the breeding of polluted offspring and the degeneration of the teachings and laws of the Buddha.

The author conveyed these messages using basic Buddhist cosmological ideas that would have been readily comprehensible to the Burmese readership. That desire is the root cause of the cycle of rebirth and suffering and that unwholesome volition results in the rebirth into lower statuses are both ubiquitous precepts among Buddhists in Burma. If marriages between Burmese Buddhist women and foreigners were outcomes of wrong motivations, as the author claimed, then the marriages were bound to cause more suffering. Seeded by demeritorious deeds, the descendants of intermarriage were poisoned fruits fated to be born into lives of misery.

This discussion of *varṇa saṅkara*, while underwritten by the Buddhist notion of karma and suffering, shared much in common with the eugenic, hereditarian view of degeneracy. Both associated immorality with othered races and religions, as well as the poor, and construed them as peoples in whom inhered undesirable characteristics, such as greed, malevolence, dishonesty, and delusion. Both claimed that degenerates passed on immoral tendencies to their descendants. In many ways, Shwe Mann Thi characterized *varṇa saṅkara* in the same way that miscegenation was defined and treated. His plea to "protect the amyo and lineage of the Burmese people" from the ravages of intermarriage smacked of European colonial and white supremacist cries to protect the honor of white women—whom they stereotyped as victims of lascivious "black," "brown," and "yellow" men—and hence the purity and virility of the white race. Yet it was not inferior genes but rather ill will that made intermarriage ruinous. Foreign men, the author insinuated, never married Burmese women with the right intentions. Their descendants inherited the moral failings of their parents.

His notions of *varṇa saṅkara* were also modernist. Like Mya Sein's speeches and interviews, "Defend Our Amyo and Lineage" drew heavily on an emergent liberal discourse of modern marriage. One of the most influential intellectuals behind this development in Burma was a close friend and former disciple of Ledi Pandita U Maung Gyi, P. Moe Nin (1883–1940). A Catholic convert and apostate, journalist, educator, and sexologist, Moe Nin is venerated as one of the founding fathers of modern Burmese literature and considered the most prolific writer of the colonial period. His numerous "treatises on love and matrimonial affairs" were authored with the professed goal of freeing sex and love from "irrational" customs and legitimizing a new model of intimacy and family: one that revolved around the heterosexual couple and privileged the husband-wife bond over that of the parent-child, and emotion, choice, and individualism over social obligation.[17] Echoing modernist debates about the conjugal family globally, Moe Nin idealized "the companionate love marriage," forged between two autonomous, equal individuals of the opposite sex, as the epitome of liberty and social progress.[18] He contrasted it to the presumptively traditional arranged marriage—with or without the consent of the individuals getting married—in which personal desire was subordinated to family's demands.

It is within this novel formulation of love and marriage that relationships of Burmese women to foreigners were disparaged. Casual unions inspired by base motives and brokered by unscrupulous relatives and go-betweens, they were the antithesis of true love and modern marriage. Intermarriage became a powerful trope that more than enabled the Burmese Buddhist to constitute themselves as an exceptional amyo distinguished and bound by lineage, religion, and a pure heart. Akin to what scholars have described as "dogma-line racism," "cultural racism," or "emotional nationalism," this logic configured difference according to sentiment and cast the amyo gya as predisposed toward malicious, treacherous, and overzealous behavior.[19]

Pathologizing the amyo gya in this manner—that is, as people with degenerate hearts—allowed the promotion of avowedly liberal expressions and alignments of desire while setting clear limits to them. In his corpus on love and marriage, Moe Nin set out to liberate individuals from an oppressive class-based hierarchy and morality that policed love between the rich and the poor, and the elite and the underprivileged. Excluded from this vision of intimate emancipation, however, were those who loved and married across religion and race (or within sex/gender). The modern ideology of love marriage in 1930s Burma empowered individual choice and the heterosexual conjugal couple as the foundation of the family. But it simultaneously subjected both the individual and the couple to the eugenicist expectation that Burmese Buddhist women make Burmese Buddhist men and the propagation of the Burmese Buddhist amyo the object of their devotion.

A well-known literary artifact exemplifying this curtailment of modern love and marriage was authored by the Marxist writer and Dobama Asi Ayone member Thein Pe Myint (1914–1978). Published in 1933, "Khin Myo Chit" is an archetypical tale of the coming of age of the male protagonist: a woman dies for her man, and the man learns to renounce his attachment to her to give his life to his community and country. The title, which is a feminine Burmese name that literally translates as "friend [who] loves [her] kind," alludes to the heroine of the short story, Khin Htway, a Burmese Muslim schoolteacher. She agonizes over her relationship with Htein Lwin, a young Burmese Buddhist anticolonial revolutionary. Their love for one another, she is convinced, calls into question Htein Lwin's loyalty to Burmese Buddhists and undermines his nationalist credentials. She resolves to end their relationship and rebuffs Htein Lwin's endeavor to see her. The decision wreaks havoc on her body, which wastes away under the unbearable weight of a broken heart. In her dying words, Khin Htway implores Htein Lwin to be strong if he loves her—to not succumb to grief as she will—and carry through with his struggle to deliver Burma from colonial rule. For him to see Burma a free and prosperous country, she says, would make her suffering worthwhile.[20]

Unlike Shwe Mann Thi and councilmen such as Kya Gaing and Ba Than, who placed in the hands of "good Burmese men and elders" the charge of saving Burmese women and, thus, the Burmese amyo from deterioration, Thein Pe Myint, like San Youn in "Khin Aye Kyi," portrayed young Burmese women as the true gatekeepers of the Burmese Buddhist community. It is the female protagonist Khin Htway who demonstrates true love and right intentions. Significantly, she was Bamar: a religious Other (batha gya) but not a racial Other (lu myo gya). The patriotic female Khin Htway had to be Burmese, for the amyo gya were incapable of true love. Only a Bamar Muslim woman understood that she was a crippling burden on a Burmese Buddhist man.

"Khin Myo Chit" imputed to Khin Htway a parasitic existence and an innate degeneracy. She lives off her host (Htein Lwin) without whom she cannot survive. Htein Lwin, in contrast, can finally thrive without Khin Htway, who is presumed to be incapable of reinvigorating the community of Burmese Buddhists. The story implied that true love and happiness for Htein Lwin resides in a relationship with a Burmese Buddhist woman who can be his helpmate and nurture future Burmese Buddhists. It left only one choice for a Burmese Muslim woman who loved a Burmese Buddhist: self-abnegation. This was a cruel romanticization and absolution of the eugenicist logic of Burmese Buddhist exceptionalism that construed Burmese Muslims as a threat to the health of the body politic, whose reproductive bodies needed to be controlled. By depicting Khin Htway's death as enlightened, willful suicide, the story insinuated that Burmese Muslim women like Khin Htway accepted their conditional belonging in the Burmese body politic—as bodies requiring containment.

This fantasy of Burmese Buddhist exceptionalism as a partnership between the selfless *myo chit* woman and the remasculinized *myo chit* man was typical of the younger generation of writers and activists like Thein Pe Myint. The lawyer Ba Bwa, in an article entitled "Are we going to neglect the women?" published in the popular monthly youth magazine *Kyi Pwa Ye* (Progress magazine), went so far as to proclaim young, educated women the only group capable of dealing with "the oppression and debasement" of Burmese women.[21]

Ba Bwa predictably attributed the state of Burmese women to their relations with lu myo gya, who, he claimed, had humiliated the country, coming and going as they liked, taking Burmese women as they liked. Like so many critics of intermarriage before him, he maintained that most women "sadly fell into the hands of lu myo gya" out of desperation, not out of *mettā* (loving-kindness) and *cetana* (generosity). The majority were destitute, prostitutes, or victims of immoral matchmakers. "Some Burmese women are bought off their parents and guardians by lu myo gya for a mere 25 to 50 rupees," he elaborated.[22] He bemoaned that no laws had been promulgated to protect these wretched women, no organization had been established to advocate on their behalf, and no outspoken critics of this deplorable state of affairs had emerged, in a complete dismissal of the fact that women's organizations were among the first to take up this role. In a slight to the older generation of Burmese lawmakers as well as women reformers, he blamed the old guard for failing Burmese women and called on the rising group of university-educated women to take the lead, in cooperation with youth organizations, to better the lot of Burmese women. Yet, even as he assigned to women the important role of national leaders, Ba Bwa spoke on behalf of Burmese women.

The "Indian's Mistress"

The suffering Burmese Buddhist wife of amyo gya, the ostensible subject of national concern, was spoken for and spoken about by anybody but herself. In this respect, the sensationalist legislative debates about her were strikingly like those that had taken place across colonial Asia around the same time. From British India to Japanese Taiwan, social reformers campaigned for and legislators deliberated intervening in or outlawing such "customs" as child marriage, widow immolation, and female infanticide. In response, politicians and reli-

gious authorities of mostly middle- or upper-class backgrounds evoked the imminent extinction of their putatively ancient communities to sanctify their
authority over women and to limit government interventions into communal
affairs.[23] Yet the suffering wives and widows themselves were consulted neither by the government nor even the reformists for their opinion.

So it was in Burma too. Not one woman was brought into the legislature
to speak about her experience or views of intermarriage. All the while, the
male-dominated legislature—and all male until 1929 when Hnin Mya was
elected—raised a hue and cry over the suffering of Burmese women married
to amyo gya. Not one of the countless articles that were putatively based on
firsthand knowledge of the women examined the concerns of the women on
their own terms. Such was the case of "An Indian's Mistress" ("Kala gadaw"),
an account about one Burmese wife of an Indian man.

Penned by the student activist, writer, and education reformer Po Kyar
(1891–1942), the article purports to be a reportage based on the author's unexpected encounter with a childhood friend, May Mya, on his way to the port
city of Sittwe in western Burma.[24] On board the boat to Sittwe, he meets a
couple he takes to be Indian. The husband, who is fluent in Burmese, explains
that he moved from India to Burma nine years ago. Po Kyar soon discovers to
his surprise that the wife of the Indian man, whom he mistook to also be Indian, is a Burmese convert to Islam and a native of his hometown with whom
he had gone to school.

Upon learning that her Muslim husband is a halal butcher, Po Kyar asks
May Mya if she herself also slaughters animals, an activity regarded as a demeritorious act that contravened the teachings of the Buddha. Seen through
his eyes, May Mya is an unrepentant convert and *kala gadaw*. She explains to
Po Kyar that in the hopes of bettering their lot, Burmese women, even those
already married to Burmese men, were flocking to Indian Muslim men. The
revelation confirms Po Kyar's worst fear: women like May Mya were not so
much wives as "mistresses" who prostituted not only their bodies but their beliefs for material benefits. "This is what it has come to," Po Kyar remarks,
horrified by what has become of his childhood friend.[25] He returns to Rangoon convinced that May Mya has transformed beyond recognition—she is
no longer recognizably Burmese—and beyond salvation. But the story takes
a proverbial turn when May Mya arrives at his doorstep: battered, disheveled,
and beseeching redemption.

Such narratives objectified the Burmese Muslim woman as a suffering captive who needed to be saved, turning her into an object of pity and redemption.
The kala gadaw embodied the deleterious effects of Burma's attachment to India under British colonial rule, beckoning rescue and "reversion" to Buddhism.

Such narratives also evoked the imminent danger to Burmese Buddhist women posed by the forced marriage, so to speak, of Burma to India and the urgency of securing a divorce.

As we have seen in the previous chapters, civil court records from colonial Burma were littered with women whose words and actions belie the caricature of the suffering kala gadaw: women who refused to relinquish control over the properties and businesses they jointly owned with their husbands; women who convinced or compelled their amyo gya husbands and kabya children to observe Buddhist rituals; women who "Burmanized," as it were, their amyo gya husbands even as they themselves assimilated the dietary, sumptuary, and childrearing practices of their partners; women who "reverted" to Buddhism to get out of marriages and families they found onerous; and women who had lovers and abandoned their amyo gya husbands. These women were not the gullible, meek victims they were imagined to be.

Though we have already examined a large sample of court narratives of intermarriage and conversion, it is worth revisiting the legal archive here to look at a marriage dispute that involved a young kala gadaw and had all the trademarks of the stereotyped Indian-Burmese marriage. Ma Enda (alias Mi Nafizunissa) was barely fifteen years old when she married Bodi Rahiman in 1909, who was ten years her senior. During their brief marriage of sixteen months, Bodi abused Ma Enda emotionally and physically; he then abandoned her, leaving her in the care of her mother. Ma Enda had had enough, and she pronounced *talaq* three times in a gesture of repudiation and ended their marriage. He promptly sued for the restitution of his conjugal rights.

Despite her youth, Ma Enda had obtained a prenuptial contract, perhaps at the counsel of her mother to whom she was close. The written agreement, signed by Bodi, provided that he "should not use any indecent, reproachful or abusive language" to Ma Enda nor "assault or pain her in other ways."[26] It furthermore stipulated that Bodi live with Ma Enda at her father's house for three years and, subsequently, at a place of her choice. It continued: "If I violate anyone [sic] of the aforementioned terms, then she will have full power to leave me forever, to give three *talaks* [sic] (irrevocable divorce) to herself and to take a second husband; I delegate my authority of divorce to her; at that time or afterward whenever she will take another husband, I shall have no claim upon her."[27] Bodi breached all three of the conditions laid out in the contract. The record of the trial shows that Ma Enda's mother frequently complained of Bodi's abusive behavior to Jumigrudin, a *moulvi* and a relative of her son-in-law, and that Bodi admitted to Jumigrudin that he had struck his wife. On the actual occasion of the divorce, immediately following a physical assault by Bodi, Ma Enda's mother sent for Jumigrudin and assembled a group of elders at her house so that her daughter could formally and in the witness of elders and the *moulvi* accuse Bodi of ill-treatment and exercise "the triple *talak* [*sic*]."[28]

Cases such as this no doubt informed the views of those who chronicled rising cases of the suffering kala gadaw. Yet, in depicting the women as naive "girls" in need of rescue, they concealed what was in fact a far more complex reality: while women like Ma Enda were indeed ill-treated by their husbands, they were also resourceful and assertive. They refused to acquiesce in their own victimization and protested inside and outside of the courtroom, even if their protestations fell on the deaf ears of the male local, community, and government authorities.

In the face of such women who turned out to be more enterprising than either the colonial masters or the Burmese lawmakers described them to be— or their husbands and partners wished them to be—Burmese Buddhist politicians, reformers, and intellectuals, like the British jurists we encountered in chapter 4, refused to acknowledge the women's cognizance and agency. The kala gadaw, as with other spouses of amyo gya men, were caricatured as helpless victims who married and converted against their will and against their better judgment. To concede that such women confronted the challenges posed by their intimate relations, including problems of misogyny and domestic violence, would have contradicted the key tenets of Burmese Buddhist exceptionalism: that the intermarriage and conversion of Burmese Buddhist women ineluctably robbed the women of their rights, individuality, and independence and, hence, that Burmese Buddhist women needed to be saved.

Separation and Conditional Inclusion

On 26 July 1938, approximately fifteen months after Burma separated from India, a mass meeting of some ten thousand attendees took place at the Shwedagon Pagoda, occasioned by the republication of *Dispute between a Moulvi and a Yogi* (*Moulvi yogi aw wada sadan*). First printed in 1931, the book was written by a school master, Shwe Pyi, as a refutation of a pamphlet containing "passages highly offensive to Islam" that had been published by a man who had had an argument with Moulvi Hassan Shah of Mingala Mosque in Mandalay. When reprinted in 1938, it was denounced by major news outlets as an "insult to Buddhism" and by the British administration as "deplorable."[29]

The meeting at the Shwedagon Pagoda had been organized by the General Council of the Thathana Mamaka Young Sanghas Association, a political firebrand even among the many conservative organizations of *pongyi* that had sprung up in the country. On the day before the meeting, *Thuriya* published in the name of a member of the Thathana Mamaka Association an article that the Riot Inquiry Committee, tasked by the governor of Burma with conducting an enquiry into the meeting and its aftermath, described as "a general attack, over the name of U Paduma, upon all foreigners in Burma." An English translation of the opening passage of the article was included in the final report of the committee:

> It has been known to the world that Burma is a Buddhist country. Peoples professing other religions come to Burma the country of the Buddhist without hindrance, and as they have been eating the flesh and sucking the life-blood of the Burmese, the whole of the Burmese nation not being able to bear, has raised a cry and clamoured [sic] many years since, and they are aware of it. But they without paying any heed insulted the Burmese Buddhist by seducing Burmese Buddhist women to become their wives, causing dissension in order to create such communities as *Dobama Muslim—We Burmese Muslim*.[30]

The tone of the meeting itself, according to the final report, "developed in a crescendo of vituperation and abuse against Muslims in general," with one *pongyi* after another giving violent speeches that "dwelt upon the Burmese-Muslim marriage question."[31] The resolutions passed at the meeting called on the government to immediately punish Shwe Pyi and enforce the Buddhist Women's Special Marriage and Succession Bill. An iteration of the legislative proposal debated in 1927, the bill mandated that the Burmese Buddhist law apply to all questions relating to marriage, divorce, succession, inheritance, and the ownership of property of "a woman belonging to any of the indigenous races of Burma, who professes the Buddhist faith," regardless of the religious status of her spouse.[32] The protesters in attendance warned that government failure to act would result in steps taken "to treat the Muslims as enemy No. 1 who insult the Buddhist community and their religion and to bring about the extermination of the Muslims and the extinction of their religion and language."[33]

Those gathered for the meeting then descended from the platforms of Shwedagon Pagoda, shouting, "Kala, kala, assault them, assault them!" "Flaming torch, flaming torch, burn, burn!" "Burmese women who marry kala, are husbands so scarce in Burma?"[34] They marched to Rangoon's main market, Soortee Bara Bazaar, and attacked those they identified as kala. The armed assaults and the looting spread throughout Burma, extending into September 1938.

The quantitative data produced by the Riot Inquiry Committee indicated that the Burmese were mostly on the offensive, and the victims of the riots were disproportionately Muslim: 139 Muslims, 25 Hindus, and 17 Burmese

were killed; 512 Muslims, 199 Hindus, and 145 Burmese were injured.[35] However, the rioters did not spare Hindus, "Tamil Christians," "Bengali Buddhist,"
and zerbadi, or Chinese, Anglo-Indian, European, and Japanese persons and
properties.[36] According to the president of the Burma British Association at
the time, the rioters "exhorted Burmans to get rid of the aliens."[37]

While the British administration described the riots as "anti-Indian," the Burmese adopted their own name for the event: *kala-bama taik pwe* (Indo-Burman
conflict). The expression was the title of a popular pamphlet that had sold 75,000
copies within two months of its publication immediately after the riots. The
pamphlet was written by Thein Pe Myint, whom we met above.[38] He had authored a satirical novel called *The Modern Monk* (*Tet pon gyi*) just one year prior
that had outraged the sangha.[39] Then came *Indo-Burman Conflict*, which saved
his reputation as a rising political writer and leader. Presented as a clear-eyed
analysis of the causes of the "Indo-Burman conflict," the pamphlet placed the
blame squarely at the feet of its victims. Thein Pe Myint lamented that the Indian migrants of today, unlike those of olden days, considered Burma their colony and grazing ground and denigrated as mere mistresses the Burmese women
with whom they became intimate, even after the women had abandoned Buddhism. "The Indians never take into consideration the interests of the Burmese,"
he repeatedly noted.[40] As might be expected of a Marxist, Thein Pe Myint distinguished between "capitalist" Indians and "poor ordinary Indians," pointing out
that the average Indian who came to Burma was not the real enemy of the
Burmese people. Nevertheless, he argued, it was reasonable that the Burmese
had come to resent all Indians. The 1938 riots represented the logical culmination of long-suppressed, righteous indignation with the behavior of Indians.[41]

The Riot Inquiry Committee confirmed Thein Pe Myint's description of
Burmese "resentment" against Indians in general and their relationships with
Burmese women specifically. "It became evident to us that one of the major
sources of anxiety in the minds of a great number of Burmans was the question of the marriage of their womenfolk with foreigners in general and with
Indians in particular," its interim report read.[42] However, and despite acknowledging that intermarriage was a "social problem" about which the Burmese
felt strongly, the committee concluded in its final report that intermarriage,
as with Shwe Pyi's book, was not the underlying cause of the riots. It was
merely fodder exploited by Burmese politicians, *pongyi*, and the press.[43] One
of the many passages in which the committee laid out its charge against the
press is worth quoting in its entirety:

We have in the interim volume of the Report shown the extent to which
an immature and irresponsible vernacular press in Burma has, in our

opinion, contributed to the creation, before and after the separation of India from Burma, of a communal problem between Indians and Burmans which was wholly foreign to the history of the country and to the traditional tolerance of the Burman character. We think that a wanton wedge of prejudice was, for political ends, driven between the two peoples living side by side in Burma—without any thought either of the real interests of Burma itself, of the contribution India has in the past made to the creation of modern Burma or to the future peace and prosperity of the country in which both Burmans and Indians will live as British subjects. This insane propaganda against Indians was allowed to go on. And, though we both sympathize and approve of a spirit of healthy nationalism as a sign of progress, we must condemn the deliberate and unnecessary destruction of the good relations between Indians and Burmans in Burma for which we think this press has been largely responsible.[44]

Propaganda by the press, politicians, and *pongyi*: it whipped Burmese people into a communal frenzy uncharacteristic of the "traditional tolerance of the Burman character."

The determination by the Riot Inquiry Committee that neither Shwe Pyi's book nor intermarriage were the real cause of the riots did not absolve Mahomed Hashim Patail, who financed the reprinting of the book in 1936, and his Burmese wife (and Muslim convert) from incrimination. The committee found the contents of *Dispute between a Moulvi and a Yogi* altogether uninspired and took interest in how it came to the attention of the public. Who was it that retrieved this pedestrian work from obscurity and shepherded it into republication? The unlikely culprit was M. H. Patail and his wife, or so the committee conjectured. M. H. Patail had obtained several dozen copies of the book in Mandalay and, having been "so taken" with the book, distributed them among his friends and relations in Rangoon. But M. H. Patail, who could not read Burmese, maintained that he never knew the contents of the book. "That is manifestly absurd and we cannot believe it," the committee objected on the basis that his Burmese wife did read Burmese and "most probably read" the book.[45] The committee thus insinuated that it was she who translated for M. H. Patail the substance of the book. Did she confirm this hypothesis? Did she encourage Patail to reprint the book? The committee, which appears to have interviewed every other person of interest, did not obtain a statement from her. It never even named her in the final report, which refers to her as "the Burmese lady" or "the Burmese-speaking wife" of M. H. Patail. By neglecting to hear her side of the story, the committee coded into their report the presumptive consent and culpability of the Burmese wife. The committee committed the very offense it accused Burmese politicians, monks, and the press of perpetrating: scapegoating the Indian and his Burmese wife. What's more, the British liberal imperialists used—yet again—the Burmese wife as their alibi for allying with their minority subjects and, furthermore, calling into question the capacity of the Burmese Buddhist to self-govern immediately after it attained a modicum of administrative independence from British India.

As the 1938 riots suggest, the separation of Burma from India in 1937 had done little to put to rest the acrimony over intermarriage and conversion. On the one-year anniversary of the riots, *Kyi Pwa Ye* ran an article entitled "One *amyo thami*'s lecture," with a subtitle "Bewarned those who give daughters to foreigners in marriage." It was authored notably and putatively by a woman who called herself "the mother of Burmese *amyo thami*."[46] The Burmese word *amyo thami* is an interesting locution that became popular only in the early decades of the twentieth century.[47] It is used commonly today as a polite term for a woman or a wife (just like its male counterpart *amyo tha* is used to mean "man" or "husband"). Etymologically, however, the term is a compound of amyo and *thami* (daughter) and literally means "amyo's daughter." As such, it is more accurately translated as "kinswoman," "womenfolk," or "fellow countrywoman." It does more than reference kinship ties or ancestry; it draws a boundary between an in- and out-group.

The author asked her fellow *amyo thami*—if the article was indeed written by an *amyo thami*—to quit marrying men of other religions and races, whether Indian, Chinese, or European, because the *amyo thami* can either destroy or propagate "our amyo, batha, and thathana."[48] She claimed that while many Burmese women entered into such marriages, one never came across Burmese men married to women of other batha and lu myo. She found this situation deeply embarrassing: Indian, Chinese, and English women protected their race and religion by abstaining from intermarriage while Burmese women ruined their amyo and batha, producing children who were "impure" Burmese.

The author then recounted a story of impoverished villagers who were propositioned by an Indian government clerk for their young daughter in marriage. The daughter, who was working as a servant at the time, protested, declaring that she would rather be a slave to a Burmese Buddhist master than marry a man of another religion and race. Seeing that her parents were ready to give her away in marriage to the Indian clerk to escape poverty, she asked her employer to intervene. The employer urged her parents to ask the Indian proposer if he would become Buddhist upon marrying their daughter. They did, only to be told flatly by the Indian suitor that he would not; he added that their daughter would have to worship the *kho da* (god) of Islam, as he did.[49]

Upon hearing this, the employer admonished the parents: "Do you see how faithful Indians are to their religion? You, on the other hand, are not at all attached to yours. If your daughter marries an Indian, not only will your religion but also your grandchildren will be ruined. Such marriages produce impure breeds and bottom feeders."[50] In conclusion, the author reiterated that Indian, Chinese, and English women safeguarded their religion and race by shunning intermarriage. She exhorted Burmese women to follow suit: "Do not allow your batha and amyo to be destroyed." She signed off with a prayer: "May Burmese *amyo thami* be freed from the grasps of racial and religious others."[51]

The kala gadaw thus remained an object of public feelings and opinions in the postseparation period. Discussions about intermarriage and conversion in the vernacular press did, however, make a pivot to the so-called problem of the Burmese who were not *sin sit* (pure, genuine). This subtle discursive shift entailed a sharpened focus on the kabya, in general, and on the zerbadi in particular.

Exemplifying this affective redirection was *The Problem of the Mixed* (*Kabya pyatthana*), also published the year after the 1938 riots. Arguably the most extensive vernacular polemic against the kabya, the 158-page book was authored by Pu Galay, an editor for Kyi pwa ye (Progress) Press. U Hla (1910–1982), who had cofounded the press with his wife and fellow writer Daw Amar (1915–2008), had commissioned Pu Galay to write the book.[52] "Some kabya treat Burma as not their own, as though they do not belong, which results in a real loss for the country," wrote U Hla in his foreword to the book by way of explaining the need for its publication.[53] By "some kabya," he had in mind the zerbadi or, as Pu Galay put it, kabya descending from Burmese women and Indian Muslim men. The gender-race-religion pairing of Burmese Buddhist women and Indian Muslim men reinforced the patrilineal definition of zerbadi and Indo-Burman adopted by the colonial administration. One of the most revered kings in Burmese history, Kyansittha (r. 1084–1112), who also happened to be a son of an Indian princess, was therefore not zerbadi because he was the son of a Burmese father, according to Pu Galay. Indeed, he wrote approvingly of such marriages between Burmese men and Indian princesses while ignoring the royal gifting of Burmese princesses to Indian men.[54]

U Hla defended the focus of the book by explaining that it was "impossible to cover all aspects of the kabya problem in one book" and that he intended it as volume 1 of what would become a two-volume tome.[55] The second volume never materialized.

In his opening passages, Pu Galay conceded that "a person who is not mixed is truly rare" and that all human beings were kabya in one way or another.

What he, like U Hla, found unnerving was that the zerbadi was Burmese in neither *thwe* (blood) nor *seik* (heart). "It's worse to be kabya in heart than to be kabya in body," he declared, insisting that "every person who lives and dies in Burma ought to share one blood, one heart, with Burmese people."[56] The remainder of the book chronicled the reputedly corrupt *seik* of the zerbadi. It painted an unflattering picture of the early history of zerbadis: as fugitives of the Mughal Empire and criminals executed for their transgression of the royal order by King Alaungpaya (r. 1752–1760) prohibiting cattle slaughter. Unworthy subjects they were, but Burmese kings bestowed upon them royal titles out of benevolence, stressed Pu Galay.

The British colonialists then arrived, Pu Galay continued, bringing with them "hordes" of Indians and upending the historically harmonious relations between zerbadi, kabya, and the Burmese.[57] His description of this more recent and populous group of zerbadis emphasized their kinship and affinity with the Burmese: they dressed like the Burmese, they went by Burmese names, and they spoke Burmese. He detailed, with express sympathy, the struggle of the zerbadi to make Burmese, not Urdu, the language of instruction in Islamic schools in the country. "Burmese Muslims are Burmese countrymen, born to people of the Burmese race and in the land of Burma," he asserted and blamed Indian Muslims for what he portrayed as the underdevelopment of the Burmese Muslim, that is, their lack of competence in either Burmese or English because of the dominance of Urdu in the madrasas.[58]

Pu Galay did not otherwise demonstrate compassion for his subject. The rest of the book elaborated on the chasm between the "pure and genuine" Burmese and the Burmese Muslims. The list of accusations against the latter ran long: they coerced Burmese women into conversion; they married multiple women and repudiated them; by agitating for constitutional representation, they had played right into the hands of the British, serving as pawns in the colonial game of divide and conquer; they had forsaken their own Burmese people to side with the British, only to find that they had alienated themselves as a community that was "neither Indian nor Burmese."[59]

The book ended with one last example of the so-called kabya problem: the failed attempts to legislate marriages between Burmese women and foreigners until 1939, when a bill governing the marriage of Buddhist women in Burma to non-Buddhist men was finally approved. The Buddhist Women's Special Marriage and Succession Act was scheduled to come into force in April 1940. The act was reproduced in full in the book as its final chapter.

The act required a Buddhist woman who intended to marry a non-Buddhist man to file a notice of intent with the registrar, usually a village headman or a magistrate, fourteen days in advance of the marriage—a procedure intended to allow any person with objections to the marriage to file a complaint with the registrar. It additionally instructed the registrar to publicize the intent to marry "by affixing a copy thereof at some conspicuous place in his office" and notify the parent or guardian, in cases where one of the parties were under twenty years of age and the (ex?) husband "if the woman had already married a man."[60] There was only one member of parliament who voted against this act, Pu Galay observed: the zerbadi barrister and councilman Mirza Mohamed Rafi.[61] A native of Burma who had campaigned against separation from India, he was, to Pu Galay, living proof that the zerbadi, though Burmese in body, suffered from a seditious heart. Their inclusion in the Burmese body politic demanded constant vigilance.

In the aftermath of the separation of Burma from India, proponents of Burmese Buddhist exceptionalism targeted with ever more precision those they constituted as "impure" Burmese and enemies within. Their objective was not the exclusion of these constituencies from Burma but their conditional inclusion as internal others and second-class Burmese.

The Entangled History of Colonialism, Communalism, and Nationalism

The 1938 riots did not constitute an aberration so much as a spectacular manifestation of the public outrage over intermarriage and conversion that characterized Burma in the decades leading up to World War II. Burma was not unique in this regard. In India, Hindu-Muslim violence resulted from panic over Hindu women, especially widows of lower castes, who were imagined to be satiating their sexual urges with Muslim men as prostitutes, mistresses, wives, and converts and, thus, allowing "violent and virile" Muslims to use Hindu wombs to produce Muslim progeny.[62] In French Indochina, intermarriage between Indian or Chinese men and Vietnamese women drew strong objections that the women were little more than concubines for the men.[63] Halfway across the world in North America, Asian migrants became targets of race riots, accused of endangering white, working-class manhood and white racial purity by preying upon unsuspecting white women and men. By 1931, twenty-one of the fifty states in the United States had enacted anti-miscegenation laws prohibiting the marriage of Chinese, Japanese, Korean, Filipino, Malay, and South Asian men with white women.[64] In these disparate contexts, transgressive sex and marriage stoked anxieties about "alien" Asian men that normalized the surveillance, deportation, and lynching of the othered men and inaugurated social and political campaigns, as well as legal reforms, in the name of "protecting" women.

The panic over intermarriage and conversion in Burma likewise elicited and rationalized the regulation of interAsian intimacies and women's bodies. Fantasies of the suffering Burmese wife of an amyo gya also played a pivotal role in the imagination of the Burmese Buddhist amyo: a community governed by exceptionally just laws and liberal sensibilities, and, therefore, worthy of preservation and protection from conversion, miscegenation, and degeneration. Much existing scholarship on nationalism has underscored the ongoing affective investment that is required in making a political community. As Naoki Sakai has argued, feelings, not ideas, constitute the nation.[65] The feelings of belonging to a particular imagined community, furthermore, are often cultivated by gendered, sexualized imaginations of injury by foreigners and intruders. As I have shown, the Burmese wife of an amyo gya served as a potent object of emotions that generated moving feelings of indignation, rage, and pity and stirred people toward or against each other.

An analysis of the ideological and affective work performed by the so-called intermarriage problem illuminates the embodied, intersectional nature of the co-constitution of self and Other in the making of nations.[66] At the same time, it unsettles established historical interpretations that reduce the violent developments of the 1930s, specifically, and the intellectual production and sociopolitical activism of the interwar period, generally, to a story about nationalism. One explanatory model, exemplified by the passage from the final report of the Riot Inquiry Committee cited above, construes the riots as the interruption of nationalism: in a blatant act of political opportunism, politicians, *pongyi*, and the press exploited the question of intermarriage and conversion to drive "a wedge of prejudice" between Indians and Burmese, giving rise to a "communal problem" that was "wholly foreign to the history of the country and to the traditional tolerance of the Burman character." The Burmese, who had developed "a spirit of healthy nationalism," were orchestrated into collective violence by politicians, monks, and the press. The incipient nationalism of the Burmese was thus derailed.

This was a colonial argument that conveniently justified continued British colonization at the precise moment that Burma took a step toward self-rule in the form of constitutional separation from India. The 1938 riots served as evidence that the Burmese, despite their "tolerance," had yet to learn to handle religious differences as a modern, rational, and secular nation should. Writing decades later, the ICS officer and scholar Furnivall put a different spin on this argument in his theorization of colonial Burmese society as a "plural society." By "plural society," he meant an ethnically and socioeconomically segregated society made up of atomized communities—namely, European, Indian, Chinese, and Burmese—that "had nothing in common but the economic motive, the desire for material advantage."[67] This fractious society was held together only by dint of British colonial rule. In making this argument, Furnivall indicted British colonialism; the problem of communalism was not a natural outgrowth of primordial allegiances but a monstrous creation of British colonial policies that made society in British Burma incapable of nationalism. These narratives share with each other and with subsequent theories of nationalism, including those by the political theorist Benedict Anderson, an oppositional conceptualization of nationalism and communalism: nationalism is a progressive form of collective belonging while communalism is regressive.[68]

This view is shared by scholars who explain mass mobilizations in interwar Burma through the optic of religious revivalism and cultural nationalism. According to them, the awakening of *myo chit seik* (love and devotion for one's amyo) launched the Burmese into defensive action. The so-called problem of intermarriage was the most grotesque evidence of British colonial tactics of domination: intermarriage, once a symbol of the tolerance and pluralism of Burmese society, had been transmogrified into an instrument of a covert warfare of conversion and dispossession under the auspices of plural legal jurisdiction. Burmese nationalists campaigned for the Buddhist Women's Special Marriage and Succession Bill and the boycott of intermarriage altogether to counteract the colonial deformation of marriage under colonialism. Religion, law, and marriage were sites of colonial incursion, and they became sites of anticolonial resistance.

These narratives of the triumphant or floundering march of nationalism instill a misleading Manichean opposition between communalism and nationalism, on the one hand, and colonialism and nationalism, on the other.[69] They obscure the intertwinement of these presumptively adversarial formations and ignore the logic of Burmese Buddhist exceptionalism undergirding the political agitation, legislative activism, and collective violence around intermarriage and conversion in interwar Burma. As I have shown in the previous chapters, the colonial ordering of Burma into discrete and irreconcilable religious, racial, and legal communities was an administrative sleight of hand. In reality, the longings and belongings of colonized subjects traversed communal divides in prolific ways. The ideology of Burmese Buddhist exceptionalism hailed Burmese Buddhists to not only disavow but also to lay waste to these real, unimagined intimacies on the basis that the Burmese Buddhist amyo constituted an endangered progressive force whose survival hung in the balance.

In an important study of Chinese feminism, Tani E. Barlow has demonstrated how founding national feminists in China as elsewhere during the 1920s and 1930s "engaged international biosocial, evolutionary, and revolutionary thinking both as nationalists and despite nationalism."[70] In it, she calls attention to the unfinished work of explicating the conceptual roots of modern projects of emancipation in "cryptoscientific arguments about racial difference and race improvement."[71] In interwar Burma, too, expressly progressive social and political movements—nationalist, feminist, and Marxist—collided with social-scientific explanations for the well-being of a community, society, or nation that tied biology to the social and the political.

I have often been asked if the ascendancy of militant Burmese Buddhist nationalism in the 1920s and 1930s was not a tragic yet also logical corollary of British colonialism. Communal difference and violence, like the anti-Indian riots of 1930 and 1938, were endemic to imperialist, capitalist modes of accumulation, to be sure. They helped ensure that immigrants and minorities led perilous lives, perpetually at the mercy of the colonial masters who ruled under the pretense of a just, benevolent, and representative government. The British secured not only ready access to migrant labor, expertise, and capital that lubricated the colonial economy but also compliance and allegiance from those they rendered aliens and minorities. The British had a vested interest in routinizing conflicts that would deter intercommunal alliances.[72]

Yet communalism cannot be explained away as a colonial strategy of domination. The theories of Burmese Buddhist exceptionalism that emerged in interwar Burma were all forged in the crucible of colonial transformations. But they were ideas and practices put into play by Burmese Buddhists who professed to be the apotheosis of tolerance and benevolence.

The Labor of Remembering Violence

The reader might be wondering about the conspicuous absence of the New Burmas from this chapter. That I have waited until this late juncture to address this absence may reflect the difficulty with which I have grappled in deciding how to discuss the family's memories of interwar Burma.

When I decided to embark upon this study, the question of how a family shaped by multiple generations of intermarriage and conversion such as the New Burmas experienced and remembered the violence of the interwar period was foremost on my mind. I prepared myself for what I presumed was a certain eventuality of stories of pain and loss. But such stories never materialized. The New Burmas do not recall being subjects of aggression in Pyinmana during the period or any other. They maintain that they came out of the 1938 riots unscathed, though we know that recurrent attacks on the zerbadi population in the town occurred, including an incident in which armed *pongyis* took revenge on behalf of a young monk who had been assaulted by zerbadis by attacking the houses of zerbadi residents.[73]

Ma Galay, the New Burmas, and their friends and relatives could not have been unaffected by the violence aimed directly at kabya, zerbadi, and batha gya people just like them. Did they fear for their lives and livelihood? Did Ma Galay's business suffer? What I found equally perplexing was the memory void left by Auntie Rosie's future husband, Pondicherry Mohanarajan, who came of age in interwar Burma. How is it possible that he had so little to say about the anti-Indian violence of the period?

In some ways, there is nothing astonishing about this. For as long as I knew him, Dr. Mohan, as he was referred to, was a man of few words. He rarely talked about himself. It was not until the eve of his passing in February 2005, and occasioned by a visit by his niece from afar, that he recounted to his daughters Mona and May his childhood. As Mona recalls, her father disclosed more about his early life in one evening than he had in his entire life. She had her theories of why this had been the case. Shame, especially on behalf of his children who were stigmatized for being kala kabya, was one likely reason. Perhaps he believed that his ties to India could one day jeopardize his status as a citizen of the country.

He may also have been embarrassed of his humble beginnings. His father, a school headmaster in Salem, India, died young, leaving behind a widow and nine children. Unable to make ends meet on her income as a schoolteacher, his mother, Indalamar Padmavati Naidu, set sail, sometime before 1921, to Rangoon with her children to join her brother. The family crammed into a small apartment in downtown Rangoon, and Indalamar found work teaching at the Reddiar School in East Rangoon. Founded by the wealthy businessman Raja Ramanathan Reddiar, it was one of three schools run by and meant for Hindus.[74] But before long, tragedy struck the family again. First, Indalamar succumbed to heart disease. When a heart attack finally took her after a long hospitalization, leaving her older children to raise the little ones, Mohan was only six years old. Then, his oldest sister passed away, leaving her son Henry, then aged five, without a mother or a father.

Uncle Mohan's recollection of his life as an orphan is reminiscent of the archetypical rags-to-riches story of self-helping immigrants. Everyone worked hard and scraped together every penny. Seena, the oldest brother, found work with the Burma Forest Department to support the family, and Purushotham started a bookstore, Standard Literature Co. The younger siblings had their own household duties. Every morning, Mohan awoke before sunrise and before the others and took the one shilling left on the counter to buy milk and coffee beans. He ground the beans using a mortar and pestle and prepared coffee for the older siblings before beginning the long trek to school on foot because he could not afford the bus fare. Neither could he afford to buy lunch. His only sustenance during the day was the single *be a gyaw* (yellow split pea fritter) that he bought with a penny on his way home from school.

Uncle Mohan's life story is as punctuated by the theme of self-reliance as it is shot through with the grace of others. Perhaps because he had been orphaned, perhaps because his mother had worked for the school, or perhaps because he was studious, Uncle Mohan received a scholarship to attend Reddiar. By the time he graduated from Reddiar, he was convinced that medicine was his calling. He dreamed of finding a cure for ailments of the heart—the kind that tormented and took away his mother and sister. But his family lacked the means to support further studies. Seena had in fact told him that he needed to find a job and should not expect to continue studying. Uncle Mohan resisted. He asked for a meeting with the dean of Rangoon University and persuaded him to grant him a scholarship for two years of intermediate studies. His sister Champi sold the only item of substantial monetary value in her possession—gold bangles intended as her dowry—so he could purchase books. When he finished his intermediate studies, the dean of the Medical College awarded him yet another scholarship.

This bare-bones outline of Uncle Mohan's youth was framed by the unanticipated generosities and opportunities that enabled a lowly immigrant orphan to become Burma's first and foremost cardiologist. Missing from it were references to the discriminations and terrors people like him and his family endured. It is hard not to respond with skepticism to his memory of coming of age in interwar Rangoon. Uncle Mohan was fourteen years old during the uprisings and riots of 1930–1931 and a twenty-two-year-old fourth-year medical student at Rangoon University, just one year shy of obtaining his medical degree (MBBS), at the time of the 1938 riots. As such, he witnessed the anti-Indian riots and saw how Burmese Buddhist exceptionalism mobilized the urban youth and shaped student politics.

One famous example was the University Boycott of 1936 in which between six hundred and eight hundred university students went on a strike to denounce what they believed to be a continued non-Burmese control of higher education that systematically prohibited the access of Burmese students to modern education. Uncle Mohan personified just what the boycotters were protesting: the preference given to the non-Burmese in higher education. At the same time, one of the main organizers and leaders of the boycott was M. A. Raschid (1912–1978), a zerbadi university student a few years Uncle Mohan's senior.[75] An active member of the Rangoon University Muslim Students Association, Raschid was elected the first general secretary of the Rangoon University Students' Union (RUSU), founded in 1931. A close friend of student leaders U Nu and Aung San, who would later become, respectively, the first democratically elected prime minister of Burma and a nationalist martyr, Raschid replaced U Nu as the president of RUSU in 1936. In the aftermath of the boycott, Raschid was elected to serve as the first student representative on the Rangoon University's University Council, formed as part of the deal reached by the university and the student protesters. Also in 1936, Raschid cofounded with Aung San the All Burma Students Union, intended as an umbrella organization that would unite the entire student population—university, high school, and middle school—in Burma, and was elected its first president.[76]

Raschid's successful student political career might have been cause for optimism. Yet Uncle Mohan also saw the hostile disputes that erupted over whether Raschid deserved to be at the helm of student organization and mobilization. When Raschid ran for the presidency of RUSU in 1932, he faced backlash from peers who objected to having two consecutive "kala" presidents, the first, Kyaw Khin, having been a Rakhine Muslim. It was Aung San who apparently kept in check the dissenters who sought to discredit Raschid.[77] Even a popular, bona fide *myo chit* like Raschid needed his powerful Burmese Buddhist ally to come to his defense. The fate of Raschid might have reminded Uncle Mohan, if he needed any reminding, that he, like Raschid, was a stranger within and that even Raschid could not escape the stereotyped expectation of the model minority: to know his place—beneath the Burmese Buddhist, that is—and to be compliant and unthreatening.

But Uncle Mohan did not dwell on such pasts. Do such lapses in memory speak to the routinization of violence in interwar Burma? Patricia Hill Collins points out that the routinized nature of violent micro-interactions in the form of "words, ideas and images conveyed through the media, curricula and everyday social practices" legitimize and make invisible violence against less powerful groups, so much so that people "have difficulty in identifying routinized violence as violence at all."[78] Both Uncle Mohan and the New Burmas may have escaped extreme acts of violence. But they could not have avoided mundane exercises of power, not least their subjection to the degrading epithets and images of the kala, kabya, and zerbadi. Such everyday forms of violence, as systematic and damaging as they were, may have become normalized.

Another possibility is that the anti-amyo gya sentiment evident in the media and in legislative politics did not reflect life on the ground. This seems to have been the opinion of P. D. Patel, a longtime lawyer and Rangoon resident who wrote a ten-page memorandum to the Indian Statutory Commission (discussed in chapter 5) offering his unsolicited input on the separation of Burma from India.

The England-educated Parsi lawyer had arrived in Rangoon in 1908 when he was thirty-three years of age.[79] Patel had lived in Insein, a predominantly Karen suburb of Rangoon, with his "native born" wife and children. He did not furnish further details of his wife or children. It is possible that she, too, was Parsi, though it seems more likely that she was Karen, given his "adoption" (his word) of Insein, a Karen stronghold, as his hometown: a district he represented as president of the Insein Municipal Committee (1912–1925). He had apparently also served as the secretary of the Rangoon Trades Association for twelve years (1913–1925).

Patel described himself as an Indian native who had made Burma his home. He expected to be buried in the country, and he was (in 1961, in the Parsi burial ground).[80] "I have always maintained friendship with the people of the country and to the best of my ability I have always helped them," he averred.[81] Yet, and as the memorandum indicated, he had serious grievances against "the Burmans." He claimed to be a "victim of intrigue on part of certain Burmans," as a result of which he was removed from the position of president of the Insein Municipal Committee in December 1925, after more than a decade of service.[82] He feared that the interests of the minority communities, such as Indians, Chinese, and Karen, would be sidelined if left to the ethnic majority Burmans. He accused the Burmans of blindly voting only for Buddhists and Burmans, instead of for the most qualified electoral candidates (such as himself). And he warned of "the suicidal plan" among some Burmese politicians "of kicking all non-Burmans on every occasion and at every opportunity."[83] Yet he immediately qualified this statement:

A Burman as a whole is friendly to non-Burmans. That is my experience from my visits in the districts. But there are a few educated Burmans who in season and out of season think it their duty to shout loudly that Burma is for Burmans only. Fortunately, it is a small section but at the same time it requires checking and the only way it can be checked is that communal representation must be preserved so that the rights of the minority are not easily trampled upon.[84]

The memorandum written by leading members of Indian communities in Burma (and discussed in chapter 5) similarly suggested that only a minority of the Burmese participated in anti-Indian agitation. The signatories clarified that "the fear of being swamped by Indians" was stoked "by the utterances of responsible high officials and others" and represented "the cry of the small but

vociferous section of the Burmese community against the Indian community."[85] Nevertheless, and as such memorandums reveal, the demand for
"Burma for Burmans" was increasingly "vociferous."

Or the reader might perceive the forgetting of violence as the failings of
the historian, that is, my failure to break the silence. Indeed, like many scholars before me who have written on violence, I have found unearthing the un-
spoken a complicated task that raises questions of care and respect for those
who have, unlike myself, had to continually redeem lives and reoccupy spaces
marked by destruction. What is accomplished by my asking Auntie Rosie and
her children to bespeak injury and loss? What am I asking in prevailing upon
them to evidence pain and suffering rather than strength and healing? Many
scholars have observed that evasions of memories of traumatic events such
as wars, mass murder, rape, slavery, and torture can serve as a process of self-
preservation—a refusal to relive physical, psychological, and emotional violence that gets in the way of overcoming the past.[86] Or, perhaps, Uncle Mohan,
as with Ma Galay, Ahmed, and Helen, had not forgotten at all. But they were
not going to define their lives and legacies in terms of their victimization.

"From the perspective of those who have suffered privations of various
sorts," Indrani Chatterjee remarks, "sanctuary, friendship, the restoration of
dignity were the key goals of political aspiration."[87] Reflecting on the "focused
remembering" of India's partition by her parents and grandparents, Chatterjee recalls:

> All that I was told as a child in the sixties and seventies was that suffer-
> ing was the one constant fact of all forms of life, and that it was neces-
> sary to work to alleviate others' pain and suffering rather than to dwell
> on one's own. . . . When stories were told of the remembered village,
> they invoked a world of friendships, a happy past. When stories of the
> departures from homelands were recounted, the persons mentioned
> were not the persecutors but those who helped them survive, those who
> gave them sanctuary.[88]

Spectacular acts of violence are hard to forget. They lend themselves to historical recording. They generate abundant press coverage and administrative
documentation. Quotidian acts of care, on the other hand, are hard to remember. They neither constitute news nor make the headlines nor enter archives.
They lend themselves to collective historical amnesia. Yet they can be more
memorable—and more important to commit to memory—than violence.

This was also the case of the New Burmas and Uncle Mohan. The only
memory of the 1938 riots that Ahmed and Helen shared with Auntie Rosie
was of their experience of distributing sacks of rice among the townspeople.

FIGURE 6.1.   Uncle Mohan with a fellow army medic. Photo taken in 1946. Courtesy of Dr. Hnin Yee and Mona Han.

Their memory coalesced around this prosaic work of living in and repairing a fractured community. As Veena Das points out, what is required in reinhabiting a world that has been devastated is not for ghostly pasts to be exorcized but for everyday life not to be expelled.[89] This delicate work of memory embodies the intimate effects and burdens of Burmese Buddhist exceptionalism. Perhaps so did Uncle Mohan's decision in 1939 to volunteer for the Burma Army Medical Corps, a colonial army of volunteers that would be deployed, imminently, during World War II (fig. 6.1). Rather than flee to India, as did Mya Sein and Raschid along with some nine hundred thousand Indians from Burma, including his own siblings, Uncle Mohan stayed to defend the country.

His wartime efforts and experiences, as with so many aspects of his life, represent a mystery. His wife and children know little about it, except that he was deployed as a medic in Kohima in northeast India. Fought between March and July 1944, the Battles of Kohima and neighboring Imphal between the Allied forces and the Japanese are regarded as among the most grueling—and in retrospect the most reckless—wartime military operations of the war and a turning point in the British campaign to retake Burma. Among his small collection of prized memorabilia were a *katana* (sword) he received from a Japanese army medic who had also been posted in Kohima, four medals that he was awarded for his gallantry and distinguished service during the war, and a page from a British government gazette listing his awards and his final rank: captain. We know that these material objects held particular significance for Uncle Mohan because they were among the personal possessions that he had taken with him when he and Auntie Rosie traveled in 1999 from Burma to Seattle, where two of their children lived, for what they expected would be a temporary visit. They still had a home in Rangoon to which they planned to return. Indeed, Uncle Mohan had been adamant that he would die in Burma, rebuffing his children's pleas to relocate to the United States so that they could look after their aging parents. The children eventually, and with great difficulty, managed to convince Uncle Mohan and Auntie Rosie to remain in the United States. But when he left Burma in 1999, he had no idea that he would never set foot in the country again. As such, the fact that he took with him the *katana*, war medals, and gazette clipping is instructive of what they meant to him. He viewed them as a testament to his life and achievements and an important legacy he wished for his children to inherit.

What the medals also tell us is that Uncle Mohan had risked his life and shown exceptional courage. Did he feel compelled to prove his fidelity to an amyo that viewed him as an interloper? To show that there were indeed kala men who would choose Burma over India and whose heart was as pure and genuine as the *seik* of the "real" Burmese? His explanation for joining the army, recounted by Auntie Rosie, was typically pithy: he owed his life to the country that had given him the chance to become something. He was repaying his debt, a *no bo* (milk price), so to speak. And through this filial act of reciprocation, he claimed his right to belong.

CHAPTER 7

War, Occupation, and Collaboration

The imperial Japanese army began its attack against the British colonial government in Burma in December 1941, triggering what historians describe as Asia's "unmixing of peoples" and the final blow against interAsian mobility and connections.[1] Europeans, Anglo-Burmans, and Anglo-Indians, numbering about three thousand in total, were the first to evacuate the country by plane and ship at the start of the war. Burmese elites like Mya Sein, who became an adviser to the British government in exile in Simla, also managed to escape to India by sea before ships ceased sailing. Some nine hundred thousand Indians left Burma for India, many, including Uncle Mohan's relatives, attempting a treacherous overland trek by foot. Only about five hundred thousand of these men, women, and children survived the arduous journey. An unknown number of Chinese people also fled to China for fear of persecution by the Japanese. Chinese in European colonies in the region were known for their support of the anti-Japanese resistance movement led by Chiang Kai-shek, the military leader of the Chinese nationalist forces, with the blessing of the Chinese Communist Party under the leadership of Mao Tse-tung. Many suspected that they would become the target of the Japanese military operations to "mop up" the fifth column in the civilian population. The Japanese Empire was, additionally, anticommunist, having signed an anti-Comintern pact with Nazi Germany in 1936. Known communist sympathizers like Thein Pe Myint joined the exodus to China.

Yet defining the Japanese occupation as "an unmixing" of Asians disregards the abrupt realignment of interAsian intimacies that Japanese colonialism and its ideology of pan-Asianism entailed. As critiques of the Eurocentrism of postcolonial studies have shown, Japanese imperialism diverged from its contemporary imperial formations, placing shared Asian heritage over colonial differences.[2] To meet the escalating demands of the Japanese total war effort after its invasion of Manchuria in 1931, the Japanese government sought to mobilize the cooperation of its subjects by promoting the ideal of "Asia for Asians": a logic of colonization through inclusion in which the Japanese claimed shared racial and religious heritage and, thereby, the right to possess "Asian" lands and bodies. Pan-Asianism provided the ideological bulwark for the Japanese military invasion of Southeast Asia—known euphemistically as *nanshin*, or "the southward advance"—and the grand imperial vision of an economically self-sufficient Dai tōa kyōei ken (Greater East Asia Co-Prosperity Sphere), which the Japanese touted as an alternative form of regionalism to the US-Eurocentric world order. In an era when imperialism was on the attack and nationalism was on the ascendancy the world over, pan-Asianism gained unprecedented popularity among Japanese political elites and intellectuals who used it to justify Japan's imperial aggrandizements.[3]

The impact of the Japanese imperial ideology of pan-Asianism exceeded the expectations of the Japanese Imperial General Headquarters (IGHQ) and the Southern Army General Command, who were alarmed by their soldiers' conviction that they were engaged in "a holy race war of liberation" of all Asians. Many Japanese soldiers in fact fought alongside Burmese and Indonesians against both Japanese and European reoccupation efforts.[4]

Even as the IGHQ and the Southern Command tried to contain what they perceived as overenthusiasm for pan-Asian sentiment among their ranks, they sought to indoctrinate the occupied peoples with the imperial idea of "Asia for Asians." Prior to the start of the war, some thirty Japanese professional writers and literary figures—novelists, scholars, and journalists—were recruited as *nanpō chōyō sakka* (southern propagandist writers) for the purpose of designing the military pacification campaigns. By 1944, over seventy were operating in situ. Those in Burma roamed the country promoting the idea that the Japanese, though belonging to the most powerful nation in the world, were fellow Asians and Buddhists just like the Burmese: "black haired, black eyed, and colored skin people" who recited Buddhist prayers every day.[5] In Burma as elsewhere in the Japanese Empire, *nihongo gakkō* (Japanese-language schools) helped implement Japan's twin imperial policies of *dōka* (assimilation) and *kōminka* (imperialization; lit. "the transformation into imperial subjects"). The former purported to aim at the eradication of all differences between its *naichi* (inner territory), or metropolitan, and *gaichi* (outer territory), or colonial, populations. The goal of the latter doctrine, associated with the Japanese imperial campaign in the 1930s to shore up the support of colonial subjects for its war effort, was the transformation of colonized populations into loyal subjects of the Japanese emperor.[6]

The Japanese military administration set up dozens of nihongo gakkō throughout the country with the intention of replacing English-language education with a learning that promoted Japan-centered Asianism.[7] It designed and published Japanese primers for the purpose of Japanese-language instruction that extolled the long history of the peaceful coexistence of Asian peoples (until the arrival of Europeans and the ensuing wars of colonization and domination) and tied the future of Asian nations such as Burma to the progress of Asia as a whole.[8]

The question of whether the Japanese wartime occupation of Southeast Asia signified a period of major transformation or relative continuity has long preoccupied historians of the region.[9] But they have failed to consider what effect such attempts at assimilation and imperialization had on interAsian intimacies. Defining the Japanese occupation as "an unmixing" of Asians also effaces such wartime intimacies as those recounted by Auntie Rosie that were forged between occupiers and the occupied.

"Best Years of My Life"

Auntie Rosie was ten years old and in the fourth grade at the outbreak of the war. As the bombings intensified, she and her family fled to a village a short distance from Pyinmana, though they returned to their home sooner than they had expected. It took the Japanese only a few months to occupy Rangoon and send the British fleeing to India to set up the government of Burma in exile in Simla. By May 1942, the Japanese had also captured Mandalay. The New Burmas returned to Pyinmana after the defeat of the British, relieved to find that the three houses they owned were still standing. Japanese soldiers had occupied two of them but allowed the family to move back into the remaining one. Ahmed returned to practicing medicine, becoming the go-to physician for the Japanese officers in the area.

During our discussion of the *japan khit*, as the Japanese wartime occupation is known in Burma, Auntie Rosie tells me that if asked when the best years of her life were, she replies: "During the war." Her life then was extraordinary, as she put it. She had spent much of her childhood in boarding schools, but during the war, she was with her family. All their relatives—from Ma Galay and Ahmed's siblings to Helen's sisters, including the youngest, Emma, and her adoptive siblings Freddie and Mary—had fled Rangoon and Insein once the bombings began, seeking refuge with Ahmed and Helen in Pyinmana. There were altogether about fifty people living together, at times in the one house that the Japanese had allotted them, at other times in small villages nearby. The expanded New Burma clan moved to fourteen different places during the war. They formed a large traveling caravan comprising the fifty or so family members; many bullock and horse carts carrying such supplies as rice, ghee, and marzipan; Ahmed's entire library; and, incredibly, a piano. He had bought it for Helen when she gave birth to Auntie Rosie. It was not the most sensible possession with which to wander around the countryside during a war. But along it went to the children's delight.

Auntie Rosie reveled in her newfound freedom and closeness to family. Both on the road and back in Japanese-occupied Pyinmana, she spent most of her days playing with her sisters, brothers, and cousins. Though Ahmed's mother and siblings returned to Rangoon after the final departure of the British, Helen's relatives lingered. Auntie Rosie played football and climbed trees, neither of which was an activity condoned by Catholic nuns at the boarding school. She read short stories of her choosing and studied what she wanted. Her aunt Cissie insisted on teaching her three sons math during the war, and Auntie Rosie joined them. She fell in love with a thick math textbook belonging to her older brother and raced through the exercises in it with the help of her brother and aunt. The war may very well have catalyzed her lifelong passion for math and science.

Auntie Rosie also attended a makeshift Japanese-language school that the Japanese soldiers had set up in one of the houses they occupied. There was only a dozen or so students, mostly Auntie Rosie's siblings and cousins. She was given a Japanese name: Mitsuko. She remembered that the few hours spent in school every day were mostly "play" and that the students were taught a smattering of colloquial Japanese.

"But, Auntie," I probed, "weren't your parents reluctant to let you and your siblings attend the Japanese school?" She insisted no, explaining that her parents made friends with everyone. They became particularly close with one Japanese officer, Captain Takahara, who was fluent in English and served as an interpreter. When the New Burmas relocated temporarily to Yezin, about fifteen kilometers northeast of Pyinmana, he came on his motorcycle to visit the family every week. Helen and Ahmed reciprocated the affection by preparing meals for his weekly visits. Looking back, Auntie Rosie wondered if he might have harbored romantic interest in Kitty or another of her older sisters, though the thought had not occurred to her at the time. She remembered Takahara as a fatherly person, kind and loving toward her and her siblings. In fact, he had expressed interest in adopting Auntie Rosie.

Not everyone among the New Burmas trusted Takahara and his comrades. Helen's sisters, both of whom had Anglo-Burman husbands, were scandalized. "You have young daughters—why are you friendly with them?" Auntie Rosie recalled her aunt Julie chiding her parents. Others warned Ahmed that given his tall stature and fair complexion, he might be mistaken for a *bo* and, therefore, a spy. The *bo* who remained in Burma during the occupation were presumed to be willing lingerers and, according to the Japanese, enemy agents.

Such concerns for the young daughters and the *bo*-appearing members of the family were not unfounded, as one incident revealed to Auntie Rosie. While the New Burmas were taking refuge in a remote village, she and her family encountered a group of Japanese soldiers. Ahmed and his two Anglo-Burman brothers-in-law hid while the soldiers inspected the remaining family members, asking if any were spies. Then, one of the soldiers pointed at Auntie Rosie's sister Angela and yelled, in Burmese, *"Meinma! Meinma!"* (Woman! Woman!). Alarmed, the family packed up their belongings and left the village that night. The next morning, the soldiers returned, looking for *"Biruma onna, Biruma meinma"* ("the Burmese woman": first in Japanese and then in Burmese).

As we wrapped up our conversation about her wartime experiences, Auntie Rosie observed that life during the japan khit for most, even for her family, could not have been as cheerful as her memory suggests. The period must have been a trying one for her parents, who had to manage the day-to-day life of the family. But they always had enough to eat. And her mother, who liked company, was elated to have her children and siblings with her. Auntie Rosie would not retract her memories of violence *and* intimacy under Japanese occupation.

Remembering Resistance

I was unprepared for her fond recollection of the japan khit, a period that has been memorialized as a reign of terror. Gruesome stories of rape, looting, torture, and purges of suspected anti-Japanese people have become abiding features of the collective memory of the occupation. The following passage from a biography of Aung San by his daughter Aung San Suu Kyi encapsulates the culturally shared, dominant narrative of the japan khit:

> Those who had believed they were about to gain freedom from the British were shattered to find themselves ground under the heels of their

fellow Asian instead. The soldiers of Nippon, whom many had welcomed as liberators, turned out to be worse oppressors than the unpopular British. Ugly incidents multiplied daily. *Kempei* [the Japanese military police] became a dreaded word, and people had to learn to live in a world where disappearances, torture, and forced labor conscription were part of everyday existence.[10]

Even Ba Maw, who became prime minister under Japanese occupation and is known as the most steadfast Burmese collaborator, acknowledged "the arrogance and brutality of the Japanese soldier." He described the Japanese, in general, as "domineering and blinded by delusions of their own racial grandeur and Asian destiny."[11]

Based on the recollections of well-known collaborators (e.g., Ba Maw), resisters (e.g., Thein Pe Myint), or collaborators-turned-resisters of the Japanese (e.g., Aung San, U Nu) published in ensuing years as memoirs, the japan khit has crystallized into a clear-cut story of Japanese oppression and Burmese resistance.[12] The lawyer, writer, and later attorney general and chief justice for postindependent governments of Burma, Maung Maung (1925–1994), who fought against the Japanese in the resistance force, described the japan khit in a talk broadcast in June 1946 as "those bitter days of difficulty, danger and death when Burma rose as one man against the Japanese to achieve that historic Resistance."[13] Upon realizing "their mistake in putting faith in Japanese promises," he remarked, the Burmese united behind the Burmese army as "the hope of the country":

> The Japanese found some excuses for disbanding the Burma Independence Army but were obliged to keep a skeleton force of a few battalions in order to please the outraged Burmese people. They called the force, "Burma Defense Army" or the BDA. The Japanese trained and controlled the BDA; Japanese instructors treated our boys brutally, slapped them, fed them poorly, worked them like slaves. They did everything to encourage the boys to desert but the boys stuck on. Our boys might be slapped hard but they would swallow the saltish blood that oozed out of their mouths and carry on. They might be starved and their strength grow feeble but their spirit and determine [sic] would be as strong as ever. They knew that a great and noble task was ahead: the battle for freedom was yet to be fought.[14]

As the first time since British colonization that Burman Buddhist men, rather than men of minoritized religions and races, were armed as soldiers, the occupation was a moment of profound remasculinization. It has been consecrated as a watershed in Burma's journey toward decolonization—an "ordeal by fire," in the words of one historian—out of which the Burmese, though brutalized, emerged stronger and more united and, thus, victorious over the Japanese and the British imperialists.[15]

As the scholarship on the Japanese wartime occupation of Southeast Asia (1941–1945) and, more broadly, the Japanese colonial empire has shown, the image of the savage Japanese colonizer is pronounced and pervasive.[16] The description by Aung San Suu Kyi is as applicable to British Malaya as to Indonesia; all one must do is replace "British" with "Dutch." There too memories of the occupation have become clichéd: bullying and plundering; shortages of food and employment; forced labor, detention, and torture by the *kempeitai*; "and the virtual guarantee that any attractive young woman would be raped by Japanese soldiers."[17]

Indeed, in narratives of the japan khit, women appear only as victims of Japanese aggression whose violation transforms Burmese men into heroes and patriots. It is as though women lived not only in constant fear of the Japanese but in perpetual hiding from them, never coming into contact with the occupiers unless abducted and conscripted as sexual labor. Or they came into view as the much maligned *japan gadaw* (the Japanese's mistress) who followed in the footsteps of the *kala gadaw*. A description of these "mistresses of the Japanese" by Hla Pe, who held the post of director of press and publicity during 1942–1945, is worth quoting at length:

Ex-prostitutes, by reason of their catches of husbands, and their ability to make use of these catches to make money earned for themselves the right to so-called polite society, and had cabinet ministers and leaders of learned professions at their table. When these women went out shopping, currency notes were carried along in packing cases. People who once upon a time, were so finicky and exclusive, took their children to elaborate social and charitable functions held by these nouveau riche. Wanton women, who showed off their Japanese husbands, did not mind the vulgar wisecracks to which they were subjected, because money could silence wagging tongues and Japanese husbands gave them all the money they wanted. . . . The morality of Burmese women sank to abject levels. Thousands of girls sold themselves for the love of jewelry and money to become mistresses of the Japanese. Besides these voluntary moral degenerates among Burmese, there were also young women who lost their chastity while they or their relatives were in the vice grip of the Japanese Police. . . . It is amazing how the very poorly paid Japanese N. C. O. could shower extravagant gifts on young ladies of easy virtue. It would have been an interesting study to trace backwards the original source of ownership of these gems and jewels, with which wartime Magdalenes were loaded.[18]

This scornful image of "the mistresses of the Japanese" as "wanton women," "voluntary moral degenerates," "ladies of easy virtue," and "wartime Magdalenes" circulated in postwar Burma in the form of an iconic song about the japan khit that chastised a woman by the name of Sein Kyi for marrying a Japanese soldier:

> Oh Sein Kyi . . . Sein Kyi
> so reckless in her spousal choice
> to Tokyo he has returned, your Japanese master
> left you, he has, rotund with child.[19]

In the aftermath of the war, the song gained popularity as a pithy allegory of the dangers of collaboration, one in which the pregnant and deserted *japan gadaw* symbolized the Japanese betrayal and humiliation of the Burmese. For the postwar generations in Burma, it is often their only reference point for remembering the japan khit.

The "impossible retroactive demands for unequivocal resistance" in nation-centered histories, to borrow Nayoung Aimee Kwon's words, has left formerly occupied women in Burma with the stark, binary subject positions of either unwilling, innocent victim (sex slave) or willing, guilty accomplice (*japan gadaw*).[20] It has deemed humiliation the only experience of women during the occupation worth remembering. It has portrayed all intimate relationships between Burmese women and the Japanese as shameful.

In contrast, Burmese men's wartime collaboration with the Japanese have been regarded as strategic, righteous, and necessary for Burma's national liberation. At the forefront of the Japanese forces that invaded and occupied Burma were Aung San and twenty-six other *thakins* (masters) who had escaped to the island of Hainan in the South China Sea to receive military training under the Japanese. Known as the "Thirty Comrades," they had returned to Burma with the imperial Japanese army. Aung San marched into Burma the head of the Burma Independence Army (BIA), which fought against the British and alongside the Japanese. And when the BIA was demobilized, he was made commander of the Burma Defense Army (BDA), consisting of three thousand men selected from among the fifteen thousand former BIA soldiers.

The Burma Civil Executive Administration, a puppet government that answered directly to the commander of the Japanese army and set up by the Japanese military administration in August 1942, was headed by Ba Maw. U Nu served as the foreign minister. Various other leading *thakins*, including Thakin

Than Tun, soon to become Aung San's brother-in-law, were appointed to other ministerial positions.[21] Well-known nationalist writers joined the Saye Saya Mya Athin (Writers' Association), established by the Japanese military administration as the local Burmese counterpart to the southern propagandist writers, and served as editors of the association's publication *Saye Saya* (Writers).[22]

One of the first Japanese-language schools established in Burma was the Ottama Japanese Language School for girls, named after Ottama (discussed in chapter 5). He had not lived to witness the war, having died in prison in 1939 while serving his sentence for sedition. His death prior to the occupation had allowed the Japanese to appropriate him as an icon of pan-Asian, Burmese-Japanese cooperation. The postwar Japanese prime minister Tanaka Kakuei (1918–1993) credited Ottama with sowing the seeds of Japanese-Burmese understanding, which, he proclaimed, came to fruition during the war in the institution of the Ottama Japanese Language School.[23] In death, the late Ottama could neither confirm nor rebut such attributions. But he had indeed made several visits to Japan after the Russo-Japanese War and published an account of his travels in Japan. And he had befriended Ito Jirozaemon Suketami (1897–1940), the scion of a wealthy family of textile merchants and an influential Buddhist, on whose estate Ottama made a habit of residing while in Nagoya.[24] In 1913, Ottama dispatched six young Burmese individuals, including his sister Ein Soe (1894–1978), who was eighteen years old at the time, to Japan for education with the expectation that Ito would look after them. Under his guidance, they became ardent anti-British Burmese nationalists, or so Ito is said to have claimed according to his official biography.[25] It was one of these "anti-British" Japanese-educated students, Ein Soe herself, who spent many years living in Nagoya, who founded and ran the Ottama Japanese Language School for girls.

The Japanese, who envisioned Indians as potential key allies and India as a major front in their war effort, also prioritized Burmese-Indian collaboration. Desperate to secure the labor force in Burma as well as the cooperation of the anti-British Indian National Army (INA) and its militant nationalist leader Subhas C. Bose, the Japanese military government deployed its soldiers to rein in anti-Indian violence by the BIA in the first year of the occupation. The India Independence League, an affiliate of the INA, was headquartered in Rangoon, and the Japanese granted it the authority to issue permits to Indians to travel and trade in Burma, and allowed the league to hold in trust the property of Indians in Burma who evacuated until their return.[26] Hla Pe recalled that Bose was enthusiastically welcomed in 1943 when he attended the official ceremony celebrating Burma's nominal independence, declared by the Japanese. "We were to fight together—India and Burma—and the other millions of Asians, forming a formidable army of a thousand million liberated Asians, destroying the evil forces of Anglo-American Imperialism." Reflecting upon the amicable relationship that developed between the Burmese and the INA soldiers, he mused that "the Indian problem seemed to have disappeared from the face of the earth," erasing "communal troubles between the Burmese and the Indians" that had existed prior to 1942.[27]

The formal cooperation of leading Burmese political figures with the Japanese—and allies of the Japanese—was not unique. Elites across Japanese occupied territories, from Burma to the Philippines, collaborated with the Japanese, lending their support to the rhetoric of pan-Asianism as well as to controversial policies, such as forced labor impressment.[28] One historian describes the likes of Aung San and Ba Maw as "patriotic collaborators" who maneuvered between the Japanese invaders and their former colonial masters in their struggle for decolonization and national independence. "This is why— unlike in Europe—many wartime collaborators in Southeast Asia are now considered national heroes," he concludes.[29] A long list of politicians in the region who held key military and political appointments under the Japanese—including Phibunsongkhram in Thailand; Sukarno and Muhammed Hatta in Indonesia; Jose P. Laurel and Claro M. Recto in the Philippines; and Aung San, U Nu, and Ne Win in Burma—went on to become leading statesmen in the postwar era. Their complicity with the Japanese has been rationalized as an act of fidelity to the nation. The same benefit of patriotism and political calculus has never been extended to Burmese women who have borne a disproportionate weight of the "impossible retroactive demands for unequivocal resistance."

This gendered narrative of "patriotic collaboration" has cast a long shadow over both popular and scholarly knowledge of the Japanese occupation. While acknowledging its elite bias, historians have continued to recycle it, re-citing the same corpus of memoirs of privileged men—and mostly Burman Buddhist in the case of Burma—in their analysis of the occupation, allowing the experiences and narrations of the same group of men to usurp the history and collective memory of the Japanese occupation. Women like Ein Soe, who established the Ottama Japanese Language School, and their experiences and memories of the japan khit have been consigned to the dustbin of history.

In an essay about Kim Hwallan (Anglicized name Helen Kim, 1899–1970), a pioneer in women's rights and education in Korea who was widely denounced as a collaborator in the 1990s, Insook Kwon pointedly warned that in the absence of alternative memories and interpretations, masculinist, nationalist narratives of colonialism and collaboration continue to monopolize truth and sweep away colonized women's realities.[30] More recently, Leo Ching has cautioned against judging expressions of intimacy toward the former Japanese colonizers as "the nostalgic yearnings of the formerly colonized or as the illusory fantasies of the feeble-minded" or construing them as evidence of a "pro-Japan" subjectivity.[31] "Pro-Japan" (*shin nichi*, lit. "intimate with Japan") and its constitutive other "anti-Japan" (*hi nichi* or *han nichi*) are politically charged designations. They signify, on the one hand, the categorization of Japan's former colonies and occupied territories into pro-Japan countries (such as Taiwan) that have established "friendly" diplomatic relations with Japan and anti-Japan ones (namely Korea and China) that remain critical of Japan's imperialist legacy and its deferral of responsibility, apology, and compensation for war crimes. When wielded by Japanese nationalists, "pro-Japan" refers to those perceived to have overcome antagonism and mistrust toward the Japanese rooted in the colonial past. Anti-Japanese nationalists, however, have used it as a term of incrimination and for the purpose of "condemning those who collaborated with Japanese rule and who, by definition, betrayed the nation."[32] Incidentally, and with the exception of Taiwan, there is arguably no country in Asia considered more "pro-Japan" than Burma, the first territory formerly under Japanese colonial rule or occupation to accept war reparations from the Japanese government in 1954.

While acknowledging "the necessary task of holding the Japanese state accountable for its colonial violence and war crimes," Ching insists on exploring how former subjects of the Japanese Empire come to terms with colonial memories and historical injustices when the geopolitics of patriarchal nation-states render redress insufficient and reconciliation impossible.[33] I join Ching and other scholars who have begun to assess the intimate relationships of marriage, family, and collaboration that have been overshadowed by the better-known violence of Japanese colonialism.[34] Rather than respond with incredulity as I initially did to Auntie Rosie's memories of the japan khit, I turn to such memories that defy the normative expectation of terror to reshape collective understandings of women's experiences of colonial violence and intimacy and explore changes in interAsian intimacies. I begin by attending to a potent site of memory—"lieux de mémoire" (places of memory), as Pierre Nora called them—of the japan khit for Auntie Rosie as for former Japanese occupiers: the nihongo gakkō.

Occupiers' Memories of Nihongo Gakkō

Japanese-language education was a defining instrument of Japanese imperialism.[35] The poet Jinbo Kotaro (1905–1990), who served as the principal of the Shōnan Nihon Gakuen, the most reputable of the many Japanese-language schools in Southeast Asia during the war, put it this way: the Japanese imperial army "scattered like flower petals" the Japanese language across Southeast

Asia.[36] The Japanese language was to function not only as the lingua franca but also as the foundation of *dōka* and *kōminka*—a means for fostering a sense of community among the ethnically diverse population of the Japanese Empire and way of transforming them into reliable imperial subjects.

With respect to Japanese migrants and settlers in *gaichi*, even those considered "pure blooded," Japanese government authorities were convinced that no amount of Japanese-language instruction in the colonies could prevent them from "going native." Japanese policymakers and education experts generally argued that Japanese children born or bred in the colonies, especially those with native mothers, needed to "return" to Japan for education if they were to become "real Japanese." This view applied even to those who attended the most well-regarded Japanese schools whose teachers came from the metropole.[37]

Japanese-language education was supposed to make "real" Japanese out of expatriate Japanese children living in the colonies. Nihongo gakkō were established throughout the Japanese Empire to indoctrinate colonial subjects and make Japanese their mother tongue.[38] The first Japanese-language school in Burma, the Gun Rangon Nihongo Gakkō (Army Japanese-Language School of Rangoon), opened its doors on 1 June 1942 with the grand vision of instilling an understanding of "Japanese spirit and culture."[39] The British government in exile observed that within a few months, the Japanese military administration operated no less than forty-four Japanese-language schools in Burma, and "thousands of Japanese language textbooks were translated into Burmese by the Nippon Language Decision Council and sent to Burma."[40] Between two hundred and three hundred Japanese teachers had reportedly arrived in Burma by January 1943, with the expectation that many more Japanese schools were to be set up all over the country. It added that "Japanese lessons were given on the Rangoon Radio every Tuesday, Thursday and Saturday" and that Japanese soldiers were encouraged to learn Burmese.[41]

The British government in exile was impressed by Japanese efforts at language instruction and its commitment "to eradicate all British and American influence and train the youth of the country to become good little Nipponese."[42] Yet nihongo gakkō were not set up in the country on the scale the British indicated. In addition to the two schools in Rangoon, one nihongo gakkō was set up by the Japanese army in Mandalay, Bassein, Pegu, Thaton, Moulmein, Maymyo, and Sagaing each and an additional twenty-five throughout the country that Japanese soldiers administered. Within their first year of operation, the nine schools run by the Japanese military administration graduated upward of three thousand students, the majority of whom worked as translators. As of February 1944, there were altogether thirty-nine nihongo gakkō in all of

Burma—a figure that may or may not have included the small makeshift schools such as the one that Auntie Rosie attended set up by Japanese soldiers.[43]

To put these figures into perspective: there were more than three hundred nihongo gakkō in Malaya (including the former Straits Settlements of Penang, Malacca, and Singapore). There were also 155 in the Philippines. The Shōnan Nihon Gakuen in Singapore alone graduated one thousand students in a span of six months (1942 May 1942–April 1943).[44] One estimate of Japanese-language schools on the island of Java in 1943 ran as high as 2,211 (with an enrolment of 1,221,988 students).[45] While some 270 Japanese-language instructors, many of whom were soldiers, were deployed in occupied Burma before the end of the war, only sixteen had been recruited as late as July 1943, and only eighty had arrived in Burma at the end of the year. The textbooks produced for use in the nihongo gakkō in Burma likewise were not printed until January 1944, making the use of textbooks in the classroom unlikely.[46]

The lofty goals of *dōka* and *kōminka* through Japanese-language education floundered. Japanese soldiers and teachers in Burma often expressed their frustration with communicative failure. Unlike in China, where they could achieve perfunctory communication via *kanji* (the "Chinese characters" ideographic system and one of the three scripts the Japanese used), their language was utterly incomprehensible to the Burmese. Japanese-language school teachers found themselves relying upon the English language as the medium of communication, as revealed in *Sekupan: Memories of Japanese Language Schools in Burma, 1942–1945* (hereafter, *Memories of Japanese Language Schools*): a collection of the memories of sixty-eight members of an association of former teachers who taught at the Japanese-language schools in wartime Burma. The contributors were all men except one woman who taught at the Ottama school and two widows of former Japanese teachers.[47]

Published in 1970, the commemorative volume was part of the Japanese postwar boom in literary and filmic representations of the Japanese experience in the *nanpō*.[48] During the second half of the twentieth century, the writings of the aforementioned southern propagandist writers were republished as multivolume compilations. Large numbers of diaries, letters, and memoirs of Japanese men who were deployed as military conscripts or army journalists were published alongside fictionalized accounts or "documentary novels" about their experiences. Some of these were turned into novels or films, such as Takeyama Michio's *Biruma no Tategoto* [Harp of Burma, 1946; film version, 1956] and Ōoka Shōhei's *Nobi* [Fires on the plain, 1951; film version, 1959] both of which were major international box office successes. *Memories of Japanese Language Schools* was a product of this cultural industry fueled by Japanese imperial nostalgia and government-sponsored historical revisionism—a systematic state effort to replace the discourse of Japanese wartime atrocity with one of Japanese victimhood and atomic trauma.

Kusanagi Masamichi, a soldier who taught at the army nihongo gakkō in Rangoon from October 1942 until November 1943, saw no alternative to conducting classes in English. Fellow teachers who had little knowledge of English, he recalled, worked hard to learn English rather than Burmese. He complained that with the instructors trying to teach Japanese in English, both students and teachers ended up focusing on the English language. Much to his chagrin, the Japanese teachers who struggled with English ended up "looking like fools."[49] Even at opening ceremonies of the nihongo gakkō, speeches by the Japanese teachers were first translated into English and only then into Burmese.[50] Unsurprisingly, many of the former teachers remembered the schools as precarious sites of Japanese-Burmese interaction that continually put Japanese imperial authority on trial. In their own assessment, the nihongo gakkō was a pitiful attempt at *dōka* or *kōminka*. "Teaching a few songs was all we could manage," rued one teacher.[51]

Despite their self-doubt, the schools quickly produced Japanese-speaking Burmese subjects. Some claimed that their students developed fluency in a matter of months, as a result of which the schools churned out interpreters for the army, Japanese corporations, and the nihongo gakkō themselves.[52] Many teachers credited the linguistic talent of their students, not their pedagogy or curriculum, for the speed and success with which they acquired Japanese. One teacher concluded that the Burmese must be natural polyglots; how else, he wondered, did they manage to learn the Japanese language so quickly and with so much nuance that they could discern various Japanese "dialects"?[53]

In this respect, Japanese imperial projects of assimilation and imperialization faced challenges akin to those experienced by early Christian missionary endeavors in Asia. Like Christian conversion, *dōka* and *kōminka* were predicated on translation, which determined the limits of colonial authority. Translation, which laid the basis for Spanish colonial and missionary incursions, is best understood, Vicente Rafael has shown, not as a straightforward transfer of meaning and intent between the ruler and the ruled but rather as "a near-chaotic exchange of signs" that "cast intentions adrift, now laying, now subverting the ideological grounds of colonial hegemony."[54] Similarly, the reliance on English and Burmese translators and translations to teach the original message of Japanese imperialism, pan-Asianism, and the Co-Prosperity Sphere—its ineluctable, multiple reformulations and recodings in English and Burmese—meant that imperial indoctrination and political submission were never assured.

Nevertheless, the contributors to *Memories of Japanese Language Schools* remembered the schools as special spaces where they realized Japanese-Burmese intimacy. The introduction to the volume stressed that only those who had been in Burma during the occupation could understand "the overwhelming feeling [among the Burmese] of affection and intimacy for the Japanese." Because the Burmese are brought up to respect their teachers no less than their parents, it explained, the Japanese teachers were treated kindly everywhere they went, allowing the teachers to forge "a true master-disciple relationship" and a natural, genuine bond with the Burmese without a care for the mandates of the military or propaganda campaigns.[55] The contributors imagined the nihongo gakkō as a sanctuary where they related to the Burmese not as occupiers and colonizers but as teachers and fellow humans, unencumbered by the violence of military occupation. For the former teachers, the nihongo gakkō was a lieu de mémoire that enabled them to forget the colonial relations of domination and inequality undergirding their very presence in Burma.

Emphatic declarations of Japanese-Burmese love and friendship reverberate through *Memories of Japanese Language Schools*. The intimate bond (*shin ai no kizuna*) of the Japanese teacher and Burmese student is memorialized as the single most cherished memory of Japanese-language education in wartime Burma. Several contributors had held on to letters they had received from their students during the war—the only mementos of their tender relationships—and reproduced them in a section of the volume titled "Letters from the Students" (*seito kara no tegami*). The last letter featured was a farewell note written in English by a young woman named May Kyi Shein to "her dearest teacher" Hashimoto when he was transferred from the nihongo gakkō in Taikkyi, just north of Rangoon. Like the other letters, it offered proof of the so-called pro-Japan feelings of the students and their reverence for their Japanese teachers. May Kyi indicates in the letter that she was giving Hashimoto "an East Asia Youth League badge" that she had herself embroidered as a token of her gratitude and love.[56]

The irony of *Memories of Japanese Language Schools*—and its professions of Burmese-Japanese intimacy—is that the former teachers rarely remembered their students with precision. The section "Letters from the Students" is the only slice of the nearly eight-hundred-page tome in which the students appear as central characters. In one of the longer entries in the volume, Oizumi Yukio, who was a superintendent of the military administration's Education Unit (*bunkyō han*), wrote nostalgically that by exchanging language, the teachers built a deep human connection that went above and beyond the immediate goals of the war and occupation.[57] Yet he does not offer a single description of such teacher-student relationships, and the Burmese students appear as nameless subjects.

Those who have names tend to be "beauties" (*bijin*). Observations on the beauty of Burmese women punctuate the volume, as do remarks upon the infatuation of the young female students with their Japanese teachers. If we are to believe *Memories of Japanese Language Schools*, the men welcomed the adulation. Kusanagi, for example, recorded with envy the way his comrades took pleasure in the attention and companionship of their female students, insisting that he never allowed himself to indulge his passions. When a student whom he secretly admired offered to become more than his student, he refused. Not because of a commitment to some professional or ethical high ground, he clarified; his sense of guilt for remaining alive while so many of his friends and comrades had perished kept him from enjoying life.[58]

Kusanagi's stint as a teacher might as well be summed up as one long and agonizing battle with his desire for his young female charges. Subsequent to his contribution to *Memories of Japanese Language Schools*, he wrote a memoir under the pseudonym Jikkoku Osamu in which he recounted his experience of being overwhelmed by what he characterized as the "determined advances" of his students.[59] Barely able to control his yearning for one student, he wrote a diary entry addressed to her. Referring to a "brown cake" that she had given him, he uttered how "sweet and delicious" the inside of the cake was and confessed: "I devoured it all, imagining that the cake was your body."[60] Having admitted his sexual desire for his student, he transmitted it to her in an act of sexual assault. Such erotic fantasies of seduction masked colonial power in the ambiguous guise of mutual desire. The nihongo gakkō was not, as the former teachers maintained, a space free of colonial relations of subjugation.

There are two moments in *Memories of Japanese Language Schools*—cracks in the narrative illusion—that confront, if only briefly and ambivalently, colonial violence lurking beneath its insistence on Japanese-Burmese intimacy. The first appears in an entry by Ishiwara (Ishihara?) Keizo, who taught at the Japanese-language school in Sagaing. He recalled an assistant teacher in her twenties by the name of Khin Mya, whom he described as a highly educated, "exceptional beauty" who was fluent in both English and Japanese. According to Ishiwara, she was quite the sensation among the Japanese soldiers based in the area. Her popularity among Japanese men, he perhaps recognized, must have been the reason for her so-called cool demeanor. As he explained, she might have felt the need to protect herself from the Japanese occupiers.[61]

It is unclear if Ishiwara drew a distinction between Japanese teachers and soldiers when he reflected on Khin Mya's fear of physical harm by Japanese men. In pointing out her popularity among Japanese soldiers, he may have intended to exempt civilian officers and teachers like himself from culpability in the predatory sexual behavior associated with the Japanese army. We can only imagine what Khin Mya thought of such attention, subjected as she must have been to the eroticizing, objectifying gaze of the Japanese teachers. She might have recognized the dangers of humoring, let alone courting, the interest of Japanese teachers and soldiers, who were potentially capable of sexual assault. Though Khin Mya may have had another threat in mind: castigation and reprisal from the Burmese. Their memories of the occupation fixed on the putatively fierce pro-Japanness of the Burmese, Japanese teachers like Ishiwara failed to recognize that women like Khin Mya were vulnerable to gossip about alleged moral degeneracy and "easy virtue" by the Burmese against women who became close with Japanese men.

Occupied Women's Memories of Nihongo Gakkō

For Auntie Rosie, the nihongo gakkō in Pyinmana was one memorable aspect of the carefree childhood she briefly enjoyed in the comfort of her home and in the company of all her siblings, not an institution fraught with anxiety as it apparently was for the Japanese teachers. Despite her comment that the nihongo gakkō was "mostly play," and more than seventy-five years after the war, she could recite the Japanese syllables, words, and phrases that she had learned: for example, *konichiwa* (hello), *arigatō* (thank you), *gohan o tabe nasai* (please eat/eat!), *oyasumi nasai* (good night), *ha ha* (mother), *chi chi* (father), *watashi wa nihonjin desu* (I am Japanese), and *watashi no namae wa Mitsuko desu* (my name is Mitsuko). She was still capable of reading the katakana syllabary, one of two Japanese phonetic scripts and the one taught most widely during the occupation. To my surprise, Auntie Rosie launched into a gleeful performance of a Japanese song that she had memorized:

> I am a sixteen-year-old Manchurian girl.
> Oh spring, when the snow melts in March
> And the ying chun hua [forsythias] bloom
> I will marry into a family in the neighboring village
> Mr. Wang, please wait for me, OK?[62]

She remembered the lyrics of the song but had no idea what they meant or what the song was about. The Japanese teacher had not bothered to explain to the students what he was teaching them.

I heard the song for the first time when Auntie Rosie sang it for me. As it turns out, it was one of the most popular Japanese songs of the late 1930s. Written by a Japanese colonial settler in Manchuria, it became a hit when Hattori Tomiko, a singer in the all-female Takarazuka revue, performed it in 1938. It was one in a string of cheerful *musume* (daughter or maiden) songs set in exotic colonial locations. The genre featured a female singer expressing the desires of a young girl who awaits longingly for the end of the frigid Manchurian winter when she would marry her lover.[63] Under the guise of learning the Japanese language, and without her knowledge, Auntie Rosie—and probably her sisters—had been made to perform the erotic role of the nubile, desiring female. The story left me disgusted and angry, a feeling incongruous with the lightheartedness of her singing.

At the same time, it brought back memories of conversations that I had in the early 2000s with women who had firsthand experience of the nihongo gakkō. One was with a close family friend Amy Po Sein (alias Myint Myint Sein). She was visiting my mother one day when, aware of my interest in the history of the japan khit, she began to recount her experience of learning Japanese. Like Auntie Rosie, Auntie Amy was about ten years old at the start of the war. And like Auntie Rosie, she recited Japanese lessons, phrases, and songs more than half a century after she had first learned them as a student at the Ottama Nihongo Gakkō.

The other conversation took place during a prearranged meeting with a famous Burmese author (to whom I will refer as Daw Nyein) who had written an authoritative book about the women she considered the most important in Burmese history. Her recollection of the japan khit was more sobering; it lacked the liveliness that characterized my conversations with Auntie Amy and Auntie Rosie. And yet it resonated with the stories that Auntie Rosie and Auntie Amy had shared with me. Daw Nyein had also been a student in a nihongo gakkō, but she was a decade older than Auntie Rosie and Auntie Amy. She was living in Lashio in northern Shan State when the Japanese army arrived. A Burmese monk opened a nihongo gakkō there, and four Japanese soldiers, all in their twenties, taught a group of fifty or so Burmese and Shan students. Like Auntie Rosie and Amy, Daw Nyein denigrated the educational value of the nihongo gakkō whose curriculum consisted, she joked, mostly of Japanese propaganda songs. Yet she too had retained some Japanese, as she demonstrated by pronouncing a list of Japanese vocabularies she still understood. She remembered the names of the four *heitai sensei* (soldier-teacher): Shibata, Fukai, Sawai, and Nagasaki. Prior to their conscription in the Japanese army, they had all been Buddhist monks in Japan. She described them as kind, unlike the lower-ranking soldiers who harassed the local people and robbed them of daily necessities; they shared their precious rations of gasoline. She approvingly pointed out that the former monks were educated and remembered that two were graduates of Oxford University.

Evidently, Daw Nyein had developed something of a friendship with the men who were, after all, more or less her age and class. They taught her Japanese, while she taught them Burmese, for which she received a salary of forty-five kyats per month. She had kept in touch with one of the men, whose address in Japan she shared with me. Perhaps it was one of these *heitai sensei* who gave the Japanese name "Hideo" to her oldest son, born on 8 December 1941—the day after Japan attacked Pearl Harbor.

It is possible to interpret these memories about Japanese-language instruction as assertions of Burmese-Japanese intimacy that support Hla Pe's accusations that the students of nihongo gakkō were "renegade Burmese who lost themselves in this new process of japonification which took them to the Kempetai or the Japanese firms."[64] These women, like the well-known collaborator Ba Maw, refused to condemn all Japanese as brutes. While Daw Nyein identified the violence and criminality of the Japanese imperial army with its lower-ranking members, rendering Japanese aggression a class-specific phenomenon, Ba Maw provided a race-based explanation. According to Ba Maw, the most vicious elements of the Japanese imperial army were "Korea men": Japanese settlers in Korea or government officials and soldiers who had been stationed in Korea prior to their arrival in Burma.[65] These "Koreanized" men were portrayed as degenerate Japanese expatriates and settlers who had been diminished by their experiences in the colony.

In redeeming the Japanese—or some among them—from the pervasive postwar image of them as aggressors, Ba Maw invoked a Japanese colonial discourse of "going native" that Todd Henry refers to as "yoboization." Once a derogatory label reserved for Koreans and used by the Japanese as "a pronoun synonymous with the inherent backwardness, weakness, and inferiority of Koreans," *yobo* became associated with Japanese colonial settlers who were perceived to have contracted the "deficiencies" of Koreans, including strong hierarchical sensibilities and lack of hygiene.[66] Auntie Rosie too referenced this racist theory of Koreanization in her recollection of the japan khit. She recalled that although her family did not suffer in the hands of Japanese soldiers while in Pyinmana, people in town experienced the routine looting and pillaging by Japanese soldiers who, she had been told, were "Korea men."

These stories seem to be as much about the virtue or vice of the Japanese as they are about the rectitude of the occupied subjects who deny associating or cooperating with "bad" Japanese occupiers. Even as Daw Nyein spoke fondly of her *heitai sensei*, portraying them as learned, considerate, "good" men, she demonstrated her disapproval of the lower-ranking Japanese soldiers. She did not idolize the Japanese, just as she did not demonize them. Her memories, like those of Auntie Rosie and Auntie Amy, were decidedly not about love or hatred for the Japanese occupiers. They were neither advocates nor antagonists of the Japanese.

What elicited these equivocal memories? The answer lies, I believe, in what their memories leave out. Auntie Amy neglected to mention that her father, Po Sein, a famous artist, had served in the official capacity of "Director of Entertainments" under the Japanese.[67] All three of his daughters attended the Ottama nihongo gakkō, as I learned from a picture of Auntie Amy with her two elder sisters featured in *Memories of Japanese Language Schools* (fig. 7.1).

Daw Nyein, on the other hand, was a member of the East Asia Youth League. A voluntary organization established and sponsored by the Japanese in all occupied territories, the league numbered some thirty-thousand members in Burma. It was the most popular youth organization in the country at the time and was known more for its nationalist and pro-*thakin* orientation than for its "pro-Japanness." Yet, as the British reconnaissance report noted, its members gave public speeches "containing pro-Japanese propaganda," and

FIGURE 7.1. Auntie Amy and elder sisters at the Ottama Japanese Language School. The caption reads: "Classroom scenery: Ottama Japanese Language School in Rangoon. The female students pictured in the photo are the three daughters of U Po Sein, the greatest Burmese dancer." Source: Sekupan Kai, ed., *Sekupan: Biruma Nihongo gakkō no kiroku, 1942–1945* (Tokyo: Shudōsha, 1970), front matter.

"in June 1944 it is said to have sent a message to the Youth of Japan reaffirming its vow to fight for the liberation of East Asia from the Anglo-Saxon yoke."[68]

And Auntie Rosie's parents were, as she suggested, "friendly" with the Japanese. The Japanese occupiers might have liked to construe as proof of "pro-Japaneseness" the consent of the New Burmas to the coercive actions of their new colonial masters—the requisition of their property, their provision of medical care for the Japanese stationed in Pyinmana, and the Japanese-language education of their children. That is to say, the Japanese occupiers may have regarded the New Burmas as with Daw Nyein, and Auntie Amy and her family, as collaborators. And for their perceived cooperation, they were spared the violence and dispossession inflicted upon the less privileged. While it is historically inaccurate to characterize the likes of the New Burmas, Daw Nyein, and Auntie Amy as "pro-Japan," it is also a historical error to overlook the concessions they won by working within the wartime patronage system.

After all, how did Helen and Ahmed manage to safeguard their large family from the ravages of the war and occupation? How was it that they always had enough food for everyone (and others such as Takahara)? While Auntie Rosie attributed her parents' relationship with the Japanese to their general friendliness, one has to wonder: To what extent did Helen and Ahmed actually reciprocate Takahara's affection? Was the relationship one of necessity, that is, of keeping their family safe with the protection of the Japanese? And protection from whom?

As Auntie Rosie's memory of the japan khit indicates, there were times when the New Burmas felt endangered by Japanese soldiers. But as a family made up of zerbadi, kabya, Karen, Christians, and Muslims—the very groups villainized as enemies of the Burmese Buddhist amyo—Helen and Ahmed had just as much reason to fear harm by fellow Burmese people, not least the BDA, which had set up its base and training center right in Pyinmana. Though feted in nationalist Burmese history as anticolonial resistance fighters, the BDA, like its predecessor the BIA, had a reputation for taking the law into their own hands, as Hla Pe recalled.[69] They robbed, assaulted, and massacred segments of the population, especially Indians and Karens.[70] In the most infamous of these acts, which took place in 1942 in the Myaungmya district, an estimated 1,800 Karens were killed and four hundred of their villages destroyed.[71]

In some villages, the civilian population turned to the Japanese army as the only force for law and order that could restrain the disorderly conduct of the BIA, BDA, and even of the village headmen, according to the wartime diary of the writer and ICS officer Theippan Maung Wa. What makes his account unique is that he died in June 1942. It is not affected by foibles of historical memory in the ways that memoirs often are. He never had the benefit of hindsight, the temporal distance to view the japan khit through the spectrum of national independence or postwar condemnation of Japanese imperialists. Conspicuously, there is not a single negative account of the Japanese in it. He describes Japanese soldiers as "friendly" with the Burmese, offering protection to those who had become victims of village headmen and *thakins* looking to extort "war levy." He also wrote that villagers sought help from the Japanese against dacoits.[72]

The nihongo gakkō functioned for Auntie Rosie, Auntie Amy, Daw Nyein, and the Japanese-language teachers as a site for forgetting the subtle expressions of power woven into the fabric of everyday life under occupation rule. These women and their families were confronted not just by the question of their complicity in the Japanese military regime, as in the case of the Japanese teachers, but also with the question of their blame for the modest privilege and security they enjoyed as subjects perceived to favor Japan. At the same time, the uncooperative and unfriendly among the occupied sustained an undue toll. And while the memories of Auntie Rosie, Amy, and Daw Nyein may only reveal some of the ways that occupied subjects accommodated or bargained with the Japanese, others are suggestive of how some instrumentalized their intimacy with the Japanese to promote their interests. As one entry in *Memories of Japanese Language Schools* shows, such covert exercise of power served to routinize coercion, especially against those regarded with disfavor by the Japanese.

Hata Kosuke, who served as the principal of the nihongo gakkō in Maubin in the delta region, recounted a dramatic incident triggered by the report of an abduction of a female student at the school, Khin Khin. Her frantic mother appeared at the school accompanied by her son, a fluent Japanese speaker and an employee of a Japanese trading company, pleading that Hata help them rescue Khin Khin, who had been kidnapped by "a wicked Chinese." Through her son, she implored Hata: "I am deathly worried about my daughter. As the principal of the nihongo gakkō, you must help your student. Khin Khin is your student. Please find her and bring her home. The Japanese are mightier than the English, so the Chinese will definitely listen to you."[73] When Hata asked about Khin Khin's age, the mother replied that her daughter was an innocent child only fourteen years old and that she had no relationship to the Chinese man who she claimed was eighteen or nineteen years old. The mother further alleged that the man would stand outside her house at night and call out to Khin Khin in an attempt to entice her. Having no success with seduction, he resorted to abducting her. She was deploying the tried and tested narrative of the lecherous amyo gya who entraps an unsuspecting Burmese girl.

Obliging the mother and son, Hata went to the Chinese quarter of Maubin, armed and in military uniform, to inquire about the whereabouts of Khin Khin and her captor. He was accompanied by a fellow Japanese teacher, likewise dressed in military garb and carrying a sword. Unsurprisingly, he drew the suspicion of the Chinese residents and relatives of the alleged kidnapper, who were all reluctant to speak. His investigation led to an unexpected discovery: Khin Khin was not fourteen, as her mother claimed, but sixteen years old; nor was she a captive as her mother and brother alleged but the architect of her own elopement with her Chinese lover. Hata concluded that had he been more culturally sensitive, he might have recognized from the start that the "kidnapping" was really just "marriage by other means."[74] His account closed with a snapshot of Khin Khin, her mother, brother, and captor-turned-husband living together happily under one roof.

Narrated as a tale of comical cultural misunderstanding, Hata's account of the "abduction" suppresses Khin Khin's mother's exploitation of her connection to Japanese authorities and the well-documented anti-Chinese hostility of the Japanese—and their presumption of Chinese lawlessness, savagery, and guilt—to frame and intimidate her daughter's lover. "The Chinese appear to have been much more ill-treated by the Japanese than any other community," the British reported, adding that the Japanese considered the Chinese "enemies to be killed out of hand."[75] This was no exaggeration. In the years leading up to World War II, the Japanese government surveilled the kakyō (overseas Chinese) population in Burma, as elsewhere in Southeast Asia, as a fifth column. The Japanese army in Burma, unlike those in Singapore or Malaya, did not carry out sweeping military operations aimed at purging anti-Japanese elements among the local Chinese communities. It nevertheless proved to be violently anti-Chinese. "Chinese," "communist," and "anti-Japan" were synonymous epithets for the Japanese soldiers who, almost without exception, described the Chinese in Burma as ruthless communist insurgents thirsty for Japanese blood and Burmese conversion to communism.[76] In the name of pacifying anticommunist, anti-Japanese insurgency and establishing law and order, the Japanese army detained, maimed, and massacred Chinese and Sino-Burmese people who crossed its path. In one egregious case, three hundred Chinese were murdered in Kayan to the north of Rangoon.[77] This explains why Hata felt compelled to take a Japanese colleague and arm himself when he went to the Chinese quarter of Maubin, an area of the city that he avoided. He had every reason to anticipate animosity from the Chinese and, though he did not admit it, must have feared that the situation might escalate into a skirmish.

Khin Khin's mother was taking advantage of this new sociopolitical dynamic that made the Chinese vulnerable. She did more than reimagine the trope of the amyo gya who violated the innocent Burmese Buddhist girl. She appealed to her family's close relationship with the Japanese and called on the Japanese master to protect his loyal subjects and punish the "wicked" Chinese. Her coercive tactic of managing her daughter's intimate transgressions ultimately failed. But she succeeded in applying pressure on Hata to act. And while Hata assigned a happy ending to the affair, the local Chinese and Sino-Burmese were no doubt affronted by her scheme to capitalize on the anti-Chinese sentiments of the Japanese. Such everyday forms of aggression predicated on a racialized hierarchy of more or less cooperative colonial subjects structured the micropolitics of intimacy under Japanese occupation.

CHAPTER 8

Ties That (Un)Bind Asians

I grew up hearing two stories of Japanese-Burmese wartime romance from my mother. One was about the Japanese obstetrician who attended my birth, whom I will call Sakai. He was stationed in the Arakan Mountains, the western limit of the Japanese Empire at the border of Burma and India and a major battlefront, where he fell in love with a young Arakanese woman. When the Japanese army began its retreat in 1944 and Sakai was ordered to make his way south to the port of Akyab, his lover, who was pregnant with his child, guided him through the Arakan mountain ranges. He boarded a boat back to Japan and promised her he would return to find her and their child as soon as possible. As promised, Sakai returned to Burma. But he was never able to find out what happened to his lover or their child. He eventually married a Japanese woman. But he insisted to my mother that the Arakanese woman was his first love and he had never loved another in the same way.

Though key details are missing (and more on this below), this is a story located in the broader arc of the collapse of the Japanese Empire with the British defeat of the Japanese army at Imphal and Kohima, where Uncle Mohan had been posted. According to the Japanese army's chief of logistics Lt. Colonel Kurahashi Takeo, only thirty-one thousand Japanese soldiers survived the battle and the ensuing retreat, ordered by the Japanese army on 2 July 1944.

If we are to believe him, 80 percent of the Japanese deployed to Imphal and Kohima perished.[1]

Sakai was among the fortunate minority who survived the war and the retreat, and he credited his Arakanese lover with his survival. Without her, he may have been captured by the Allied forces or the anti-Japanese Burmese soldiers of the Anti-Fascist People's Freedom League (AFPFL). And without her, he may have not survived the long trek through the treacherous hills of Arakan. The following excerpt from a British intelligence report that describes the passes at the Assam-Burma border and the local people, including women and children, who were pressed into corvée labor for the Allied forces during the war provides a sense of the arduous journey that Sakai's lover undertook while pregnant to ensure his safety: "The strain of persistent portering of 50lb loads over hilly country where stages are anything from 10–20 miles and where the path may descend 3000 feet or more to a stream and climb again to its original height inevitably begins to tell after two years and the coolie-potential itself is reduced by the resultant weakness and greater susceptibility to sickness, thereby increasing the burden on the other villagers."[2]

Though my mother never explained, it was clear that he had shared this story with her by way of explaining his tenderness for my mother, a Burmese woman in her twenties at the time. She has often spoken of his affection for her and how much it meant as she struggled to cope with the challenges of being a first-time mother far away from her own family and in a country (Japan) that only recognized her as a *gaijin* (outsider, foreigner). Sakai may have viewed my mother as an agent of redemption who provided an opportunity to atone for his decision to leave his own Arakanese lover and unborn child to save himself, a way to repay through proxy his debt to the one who helped him survive.

Sakai's story typifies both the motifs and tensions of Japanese postwar narratives of imperialism that displace violence, coercion, and domination with love, consent, and cooperation. One example that closely mirrors Sakai's story is the fabled tale of the seventeen-year-old aborigine woman (from the indigenous Atayal tribe) Sayon (or Sayun) set in Japanese Taiwan. In September 1938, Sayon and ten other Atayal women assisted a Japanese police officer cum schoolteacher who had been drafted by the Japanese forces in China to descend a precipitous mountain path, thirty-four kilometers long, during a torrential typhoon. Weighed down with three of his suitcases, Sayon fell into the river and drowned. "While many treatments of Sayon emphasize the hoopla generated by her supposed spirit of sacrifice," Paul D. Barclay notes, "she was essentially a porter."[3] The governor-general of Taiwan took the first step in representing Sayon the porter as Sayon the patriot when he presented Sayon with a commemorative bell inscribed with the phrase "The Bell of the Patriotic Maiden Sayon." Since then, songs and films have contributed to the memorialization of Sayon as the model colonial subject. Not unlike the colonial myth of Pocahontas and her intimate relationships with the British colonialists John Smith and John Rolfe, the legend of Sayon romanticized colonization by transposing the history of conquest with a tragic tale of love in which a noble savage and heroine rescued the colonizer.

The resemblance between the romantic tragedies of Sayon and Sakai is striking. It raises the question of Sakai's possible improvisation of his own memory. Perhaps his Arakanese lover-savior was not his lover after all. She may have been a porter or a guide, as in the case of Sayon. And she may not have chosen to accompany Sakai as he maintained.

Such sentimentalized master's narratives of wartime romances appeal to the mutual fidelity of the Japanese colonizer and the colonized female to justify Japanese imperialism, only to foreclose the possibility of the couple consummating their intimacy. The Japanese colonizer is forced to repatriate and abandon his native lover, as in the case of Sakai, or the native lover is killed off, as in the case of Sayon. In not a single case—none that I have come across—is there a happily ever after. Characteristic of colonial interracial love plots that culminate in the separation of the lovers, repatriation of the colonizer, and the early demise of the native, the colonial promise of pan-Asian union never materializes.[4]

The Pan-Asian Family Romance

Historians of imperial Japan have emphasized that after Japan annexed Korea in 1910, it embraced racial assimilation to promote "mixed-blood" imperialism. Only in the aftermath of World War II did the idea that the Japanese were a "pure-blood" race and nation become mainstream and *konketsuji* (mixed-blood children), once celebrated as offspring of imperial expansion, rejected.[5] In the lead-up to World War II, two different theories of the Japanese race gained adherents in Japanese circles. One posited that the Japanese were descendants of the Malay race, not the Indo-Aryan race, as had been theorized in the late 1800s and early 1900s. The other, known as *fukugō minzoku ron* (theory of a mixed nation), viewed the Japanese as a "mixed-blood" people with an exceptional gift for fusing the multiplicity of Asian races into a harmonious whole.[6] These ideas of Asians united by a primordial blood bond found advocates among those who had once insisted on Japanese racial purity and homogeneity.[7]

Accordingly, a country profile for Burma prepared by the Japanese military in anticipation of its "southward advance" emphasized the racial affinity of the Japanese and Burmese and their shared blood.[8] Its essay on Burmese culture emphasized that Burmese women, unlike their Chinese or Indian counterparts, shared not only the racial features (e.g., skin tone, "soft" or "kind" face) but also the "innocence" of Japanese women.[9] This closeness enabled the Japanese to appreciate the natives of the *nanpō* (southern regions) in ways that white imperialists never could, wrote the Southern propagandist writer Takami Jun (1907–1965) in his chronicle of wartime Burma.[10] Southern propagandist writers like Takami romanticized Japanese militarism as Japan's manifest destiny. Allegedly, conquest was a selfless labor of love by the Japanese to restore the Asian family torn asunder by Euro-American imperialists.

To take but one example, the semifictional travelogue *Biruma no asa* (Burma's dawn, 1943) by the writer Sakakiyama Jun (1900–1980) follows the evolving friendship between the Japanese soldier Shiki and his young Burmese charge U Thant, who continually refers to Shiki as "master."[11] Their relationship originates in a confession by U Thant that his wife, along with other young women from his village, was "taken" by the British—presumably for the purpose of sexual labor—only five months after the couple was married. Moved by this intimate revelation, Shiki returns U Thant's trust by taking on the role of confidante and mentor to the young man, who seeks Shiki's advice on whether to search for his wife or to avenge her violation by fighting the British. The two men part ways when U Thant joins the resistance army. They meet again and again throughout the course of the novel. In these reencounters, the reader learns of U Thant's bittersweet reunion with his wife, who manages to break free from the British only to fall fatally ill during her escape. Although rescued by a Japanese army doctor, she does not recover. She is on the verge of death when U Thant runs into Shiki, prompting Shiki to go see her as she lay dying. When the two men meet for the final time, U Thant informs Shiki that his wife took her last breath the day after Shiki visited her: "She was most grateful for your coming to see her," U Thant tells Shiki, declaring that "she died in peace because of your visit which, I believe, alone made bearable her unspeakable suffering."[12]

A melodramatic story of Asian brotherhood, the helpless native disciple (U Thant) becomes a real man under the tutelage of his loving Japanese master (Shiki), whose own imperial masculinity as warrior and savior is reaffirmed. The two male protagonists achieve both solidarity and a common Asian manhood over the dead body of "their" woman and against "their" common enemy (the white imperialists). The discourse of "Asia for Asians" disguised as Asian fraternity the coercive conditions that underwrote Japanese-Burmese "cooperation."[13]

Such self-serving narratives of the paternal Japanese master-comrade and the filial native, their shared experience of (British) colonial violence, and their mutual bond of affection were not artifacts of the officially appointed propagandists alone. They typify many postwar memoirs written by Japanese soldiers, such as *Tales of a Militarized Civilian in Burma* (1973) by Yoshiichi Shigemitsu.[14] Written by a civilian conscript of the Japanese imperial army in Burma, it centers around the author's relationship with Hla Maung, a young Burmese servant of the Japanese imperial army whom Yoshiichi describes endearingly as his brother. Halfway through the memoir, Hla Maung dies trying to save Yoshiichi during an airstrike by the Allied forces. This act of self-sacrifice is simultaneously—and ironically—an act of triumphant self-actualization in which the colonized native transforms himself into a full-fledged man and sovereign subject under the guidance of his Japanese master.

In the remainder of the memoir, Yoshiichi agonizes over the death of Hla Maung. While Yoshiichi loses other men, mostly fellow Japanese soldiers, it is Hla Maung's death that haunts him. According to Yoshiichi, Hla Maung, though initially his servant, became his "beloved brother" when Yoshiichi adopted him. In return, he himself was adopted by Hla Maung's mother and sisters as a member of their family. Fittingly, the memoir ends with moving descriptions of him grieving Hla Maung's death with his mother. Yoshiichi's feeling of kinship with Hla Maung, his family, and, more generally, the Burmese people is so strong that he considers himself Burmese. "The truth is," he proclaims, "I am Japanese and I am Burmese."[15] From the perspective of Japanese soldiers like Yoshiichi who shared the Asianist ideology of "one blood," this kinship was not metaphorical; it was literal. They were a brotherhood of men bound not only by cause but also by blood.

Though imbued with the language of kinship, love, and solidarity, pan-Asianism, like European and US imperial ideologies of assimilation, assumed the benevolence of the dominant power. Nevertheless, the Japanese idealization of the Asian family challenged the prewar political discourse of Burmese Buddhist exceptionalism and its attendant disavowal of interAsian intimacies. The Japanese occupiers called upon the Burmese, Indians, and Chinese, and Hindus, Muslims, Buddhists, and Confucians to imagine themselves as belonging to a family bound by blood and the goal of a pan-Asian revolution against white domination. InterAsian intimacy became a locus of a different sort of expressive, affective investment under Japanese occupation.

Japanese opinions on the desirability of *zakkon* (mixed marriage) and *konketsuji* and their potential as instruments of *dōka* (assimilation) and *kōminka* (imperialization) varied, however. Many scholars concluded that while the mixing of highly unrelated races—namely, Caucasians and Asians—produced unsatisfactory progeny, similar conclusions could not be drawn with respect to Asians who were "racially related"; most advocated further research about the health of mixed marriages and children among different groups of Asians.[16] According to the influential anthropologist Kiyono Kenji (1885–1955), it was neither possible nor practicable to prevent the mixing of blood in the southern regions. Though he also pointed out that available data indicated that *konketsuji* of Japanese descent found in the southern regions were inferior in their intellect and patriotism to pure-bred Japanese children (but superior to pure-bred native children). "It is true that if left entirely in the care of their native mothers, *konketsuji* become no different from natives," he concluded.[17] Views of *zakkon* and *konketsuji* were therefore ambivalent at best.

The policies and practices of the Japanese metropolitan government were much less equivocal. They did not encourage marriage between *naichi jin* (metropolitans) and *gaichi jin* (colonials). The government allocated its resources to recruiting young Japanese women to marry Japanese colonial settlers. And like British women who lost their status as British nationals upon marrying foreigners, Japanese women lost their status as Japanese nationals upon marrying a *gaichi jin*.[18] When the Japanese government finally legalized marriage between metropolitans and colonials—known as *nai gai jin kekkon*—in 1921, it did so to keep track of the empire's citizens.

The legalization of *nai gai jin kekkon*, moreover, did not resolve the problem created by Japan's bifurcated bureaucratic system of family registration that was divided into *naichi* and *gaichi* family registers (known as *koseki*). This dual system prohibited the transfer of one's family from one system to the other. A Taiwanese wife of a metropolitan, for instance, could not be registered in the latter's *koseki*; instead, a note would be added to his metropolitan *koseki* indicating that he took a Taiwanese woman as wife. Similarly, a metropolitan woman who married a Taiwanese colonial could not be removed from her *koseki* in the metropole.[19] In other words, family registration formed an unbreachable legal-institutional bulwark between metropole and colony that protected the Japanese nation and identity based on biologically determined race and jus sanguinis (the "right of blood") against Japan's own imperial doctrine of *dōka*.[20]

This imperial system of family registration posed a vexing problem for Japanese legislators, bureaucrats, and politicians especially as the Japanese military sought to mobilize colonized populations for its war efforts. The insistence on withholding from colonized subjects the "insider" status of *naichi jin* was not just a defect in the Japanese legal system but the main obstacle to mobilization efforts. Nevertheless, the separation of *naichi* and *gaichi* family registers remained intact, rendering impossible the full and unconditional assimilation of colonized subjects of the Japanese Empire.[21]

The legalization of *nai gai jin kekkon* did not result in the social acceptance of *nai gai jin* couples who continued to face censure from Japanese relatives. Nor did it resolve the question of *konketsuji*: What are the consequences of such blood mixing, and should it be condoned?[22] "On the question of Japanese-Burmese mixed blood," Yamada Hidezo, who resided in Burma for thirty-eight years, explained that he "cannot answer in the affirmative."[23] He arrived in Rangoon in 1904 with his Japanese wife in tow, and the couple went on to establish the first department store in Mandalay and Rangoon to specialize in Japanese import products. In a section entitled "the Japanese-Burmese mixed-blood question" in his autobiographical account of life in pre–World War II Burma, he explained that though Burmese women regarded marriage to Japanese men favorably, in all the years he spent in Burma, he had not met a single Japanese man who had benefited from taking a Burmese wife. According to Yamada, the problem was that in the company of their domineering Burmese spouses, the Japanese men lost their Japanese—and manly—pride, enterprise, and industriousness, becoming, essentially, a "lazy native." The trick, he proposed, was for Japanese men to marry Burmese women no younger than thirty years of age because at that age they became more matronly and submissive—in other words, more wife-like.[24]

The premature ending of intimate relations between Japanese colonizers and Burmese women enabled the idealization of the union of *naichi jin* and *gaichi jin*, while preserving the barrier between metropolitan and colonial subjects. It indulged the Japanese imperial romance of pan-Asianism, without acknowledging or resolving Japanese society's aversion toward mixed marriage and birth. Sakai's tragic separation from his Arakanese lover likewise spared him from confronting the ambivalence with which the Japanese apprehended intermarriage and miscegenation.

Marriage between Japanese subjects and Burmese women did occur during and immediately after the war. Takahara, the soldier who befriended the New Burmas, married a woman from Insein and had a child, instead of returning to Japan at the end of the war. Yoshioka Noriki and Kitamura Sanosuke also decided to remain in Burma. The former became a rice miller, and the latter joined the Burmese army; both married Burmese women and made Burma their home.[25]

Such anecdotes of wartime and postwar intermarriage find confirmation in oral interviews as well as British government records.[26] One reconnaissance report by the British stated that Japanese-Burmese marriages were widespread, and if rumors were to be believed, "the Japs have already produced 10,000 children with Burmese mothers."[27] A noncommissioned officer captured in

1944 had apparently testified that the marriage of Burmese women to Japanese soldiers was contributing to the low morale of the Burmese National Army (the successor to the BDA, which was renamed BNA when Burma declared its nominal independence from Japan in 1943), which objected to such marriages.

What concerned the British government in exile was the nature and extent of Burmese collaboration with the Japanese. Japanese-Burmese marriages and births served as one measure. There were others. Captain O. H. Molloy, an ICS officer reporting on the activities of Kachins in the "anti-Japanese campaign" in northeast Burma, extolled "the gallantry and loyalty of the ordinary villagers." Among those he praised were two Kachin women schoolteachers who "remained behind to act as a collecting post" for British agents and "sent very useful information up" to the British for six months.[28] A district commissioner of the Chin Hills, F. Franklin, was less impressed with the record of the Chins. The chief of the Tashon Chins, he complained, had given the Japanese "very active assistance," and one of his daughters was working as a stenographer for the senior Japanese official in the area.[29]

The "chieftain's daughter" featured centrally in the Japanese popular imagination of empire. She was, for instance, the subject of the 1930 hit song "Shūchō no musume" (The Chieftain's Daughter) about a love affair between a Japanese colonizer and an Indigenous woman much like the story of Sayon. Set in the Marshall Islands, then under Japanese rule, a Marshallese woman rescues a Japanese man who throws himself into the sea in an attempted suicide.[30] In colonial Taiwan, "political marriages" between low-ranking Japanese officers and Indigenous women of chiefly lineages were once instrumental in activating Japanese-native alliances and economic interdependence as well as gathering intelligence for both sides.[31] The "chieftain's daughter" was a stock figure in accounts of the Japanese occupation of Burma too. They appear as daughters "gifted" as wives, students, translators, assistant teachers, and stenographers by village chiefs to manage new relations of power and patronage. As the daughters of key collaborators with the Japanese, the women may have enjoyed a measure of security denied to the majority of women in Burma under the occupation. Though perhaps not. In her study of the Tokugawa government practice of encouraging—even mandating—Wajin migrants in Hokkaido to take Indigenous Ainu women as "local wives" (*genchi tsuma*) or "wife-mistresses" (*tsuma-mekake*), ann-elise lewallen argues that unlike the Japanese-native political marriage in Taiwan, the Wajin-Ainu unions were largely nonconsensual and failed to "convey social capital to Ainu women."[32] In her analysis, the practice represented a colonial system of sexual assault and reproductive exploitation of the Ainu women who were compelled to partner with Wajin men.

In the case of Burma, some women who partnered with the Japanese occupiers were spies for the British or the anti-Japanese resistance force who had knowingly contracted contrived conjugal relationships. Kyaw Win Maung (alias Wali Mohamed), a member of the BDA who served as liaison officer between the AFPFL and the US Army "Detachment 101" sent to assist the underground resistance force, recalled meeting many women trainees and operatives. In his memoir, he recounted the story of one such spy, Tin Tin Kyi, who married a Japanese soldier to spy for the resistance only to fall in love with him. The latter was apparently no less committed to the marriage and had entreated Tin Tin Kyi to accompany him back to Japan. But he died before the end of the war and just one week before she gave birth to their son.[33]

The relationships that occupied women developed with Japanese soldiers were not just effects of political expediency but also of economic necessity. Most were ordinary women who, to make a living for themselves and for their families, had little choice but to interact routinely with Japanese soldiers: as porters, food stall owners, cooks, sellers, laundresses, and so forth. In part this was due to the large number of men who had been drafted as soldiers and labor conscripts during the war. The aforementioned Kyaw Win Maung, for instance, lamented that over the course of the japan khit, he had relied upon his wife and her siblings to feed him (as well as a number of his comrades) because he had no salary or income as a member of the BDA.[34]

Lin Yone Thit Lwin, who worked as a propagandist during the war, recalled that although some laborers received a wage from the Japanese army, they had no means of remitting it to their families. He was tasked with promoting cooperation with the Japanese army among the one hundred seventy-seven thousand laborers, collectively known as the *chwe tat* (sweat army), recruited for the construction of the Thailand–Burma Railway.[35] As such, he lived for several years alongside the thousands of *chwe tat* troops, a significant number of whom perished along the railway that came to be known as the "death railway." While the sufferings of the approximately sixty-one thousand Allied prisoners of war who labored on the railway have defined the memory and history of the railway, many more Asians than POWs labored and died on the railway. Estimates of death among them have run as high as one hundred thousand or roughly one-half to one-third of Asian labor conscripts (compared with the estimated 12,568 deaths among POWs).[36] In Burma, it is estimated that anywhere between thirty thousand to eighty thousand *chwe tat* conscripts died.[37] Understandably, Lin Yone Thit Lwin's memoir concentrates on the horrifying living and working conditions for the undernourished, tortured, and diseased *chwe tat* soldiers who were left to die. But what kept many members of the *chwe tat* up at night was the anxiety over the fate of their wives and children—and how were they feeding themselves when the men were never allowed to return home and give their wages to their families.[38]

The absence of adult men turned many women into sole providers of their family. Women also bore the responsibility of freeing their kinsmen from labor conscription, arrest, or detention. This development formed the backbone of the main plot of the acclaimed Burmese satirical-historical novel *Nga Ba* (1947), written by Maung Htin. Told from the vantage point of rural people in the 1930s and 1940s, it follows the life of the eponymous protagonist and his tenant farmer family, increasingly caught among turbulent events they do not fully understand: the war, Japanese occupation, antifascist resistance movements, and insurrections. Nga Ba is imprisoned by village authorities for refusing to "donate" some of his crops as protection money to Burmese soldiers and then dragooned to work on the Thailand–Burma Railway. This leaves his wife, Mi Po, and their children to take on the work of farming and harvesting rice. All the while, Mi Po pleads with village elders for Nga Ba's safe return.[39] Mi Po spends what time and energy she has beseeching her relatives and friends to lend her money to save her family from starvation. Since the majority of *chwe tat* troops were tenant farmers, there were doubtless many women like Mi Po who assumed the full range of daily chores once divided among family members, kept their family alive and together, and struggled to repay large amounts of debt they incurred in the process.

I mentioned at the beginning of chapter 7 that it is the specter of young nubile women ravished by Japanese colonizers or abducted for comfort stations that haunts Burmese narratives of the japan khit. *Nga Ba* is no exception. Mi Po and Nga Ba's daughter Mi Ni is raped by a Japanese soldier and becomes pregnant. With Mi Po's help, Mi Ni delivers and kills the baby.[40] As the novel suggests, however, there is another visceral fear that permeates stories of the japan khit: women's fear of their men being taken and disappearing. It was this fear that resulted in my own family story of wartime Japanese-Burmese romance, though that is not how my mother tells it.

Ghosts of War and Romance

At the start of the war, Thein Yin and Albert Maitland Hood, my mother's Shan mother and Anglo-Burmese father, lived in Maymyo, a hilltop city that had become a garrison town, British enclave, holiday destination, and summer headquarters of the British administration in Burma. It was home to scores of retired Europeans, Anglo-Indians, and Anglo-Burmans. Given its large population of Europeans and Eurasians, the Japanese army may have viewed Maymyo with both suspicion and fascination: a hotbed of pro-British, anti-Japanese activity, on the one hand, and an exotic location populated by "mixed-blood" women, on the other. Japanese soldiers were reputed to be avid admirers of Eurasian women in particular—a reputation they shared with the British and American soldiers who, upon reoccupying Maymyo in 1944–1945, competed to court Eurasian women.[41]

Like the New Burmas, Thein Yin and Albert enrolled all their children—Rita, Phylomena, Mary, Albert, and, my mother, Teresa, who was their only child born after the war—in Catholic boarding schools far away from home. And as with the New Burmas, the war occasioned a rare reunion for the family, which periodically fled to nearby villages to escape the air raids.

The oldest, Rita, who must have been about fourteen or fifteen years old at the time, earned income for the family mending clothes, especially the uniforms of Japanese soldiers. The war had led to an acute shortage of clothing and textiles. British intelligence even reported that some families shared "one presentable longyi" between its many members and were able to "venture out in public in turns and only one at a time." Women in one district were found wearing longyi "made of gunny bags and jackets of mosquito-netting."[42] The war had made cloth mending and sewing indispensable and thus provided women with reliable jobs during the war. For Rita it was an important livelihood. Her siblings were young, and her father, who had worked as an electrical engineer prior to the war, had no job. The family worried that he might be forced into the labor corps for the Thailand–Burma Railway or arrested by the Japanese under suspicion of spying for the British, as had been the case for P. D. Patel, the Parsi resident of Insein mentioned in chapter 6.

Patel had moved to Kalaw, another hilltop station a stone's throw from Maymyo, during the war, where life for Patel was at first untroubled, perhaps owing to the fact that he had an Indian acquaintance who was persona grata with the Japanese commander in town. But he too came under suspicion and was "classed as a British spy" and spent twenty-one days in detention, where he was tortured in 1943. As it turned out, a kempeitai chief and his Japanese interpreter had moved into Patel's house during his imprisonment, and upon his release, all three men began living together. "Every day I provided dinner and so became friendly with the Chief," Patel recalled in a published biographical essay. The "friendship" apparently came with the expectation on the part of the military police chief that Patel serves as an informer; he asked Patel "to prepare a list of all Anglo-Indians, Anglo-Burmans and Europeans" and "to report as to their antecedents and whether they could be trusted." In return, Patel faced "no more trouble": "As a matter of fact, Indians who had any difficulty came to me for help owing to my friendship with the Kempeitai Chief."[43]

"Anglo-" families such as my mother's and the New Burmas thus faced the possibility of suspicion and incrimination not only from the Japanese occupiers but also neighbors and acquaintances. In recounting his experience as a member of the BDA, Kyaw Win Maung lamented that kabya men like him—he was of Indian, British, and Shan descent—faced discrimination from Bamar officers. Many were prevented from enlisting in the BDA.[44] The British reported that *thakins* made Anglo-Burmans and Anglo-Indians "declare themselves to be 'Dobamas.'"[45] So, like Auntie Rosie's Anglo-Burmese uncles, Albert spent much of the japan khit in hiding.

Rita did not live long enough to tell her story of the occupation. Although she died of illness during the war, she became close to one of her Japanese customers before her death. Had she not died when she did, the relationship between Rita and the Japanese soldier may have blossomed into something more, my mother thinks.

I do not present Rita's story (as my mother recounted it) as some form of indubitable evidence that such romance "really" occurred. Nor do I suggest that because it is narrated by a Burmese woman, it must be less mediated than the memories of Japanese men such as Sakai. After all, my mother had her own motivations for telling the story. She was, as she has often insisted, Rita's reincarnation, which explains her own marriage to a Japanese man. Far from a banal tale of wartime romance, the tragic story of Rita served to legitimize my mother's relationship with my father, who was a Japanese consular officer in Rangoon in the 1960s. He was also one of the first foreigners in the postwar period to be permitted to matriculate at Rangoon University, where he met my mother, who, like him, majored in Burmese language and literature.

Their relationship had been roundly condemned by my mother's siblings, one of whom warned that it would ruin her; rather than marry her, he would abandon her, probably with child and with no prospect of a future marriage. In casting such aspersions on the couple, my aunt was invoking the specter of the *japan gadaw*. Rare was a Burmese person who did not view their relationship through the allegory of the *japan gadaw*, according to my mother. No one expected their relationship to result in marriage. In return, she summoned the ghost of Rita and her chaste wartime romance to justify her relationship to the man whom she subsequently married. The relationship had been destined, a predetermined fate over which my mother had little control and for which she could not be blamed. She was not being reckless. She was accepting her karma as a good Buddhist should.

There are other reasons for approaching my mother's narrative with the proverbial grain of salt. As a Burmese woman who had moved to Japan as a young bride and lived there continuously for almost two decades, she had heard nostalgic tales of Japanese-Burmese love affairs from men like Sakai, who must have presumed that she would lend them a sympathetic ear. It was not enough that men like Sakai had once been saved by a Burmese woman. They wanted to be saved again by my mother, who could offer them redemption by forgiving or legitimizing their actions. Both parties were invested in memories of occupation romance, though in different ways.

Intimacies of Colonialisms

No aspect of Japanese colonialism has been more emblematic of its atrocities than the military institution of *ian fu*, or "comfort women," the official and euphemistic coinage of imperial Japan to refer to the women conscripted to provide their bodies to Japanese soldiers before and during World War II. Debates about comfort women and whether they represented a state-sanctioned or regulated institution, to what extent it can be accurately described as sexual slavery versus prostitution, and what are just and equitable forms of reparation have proved exceptionally contentious and intractable.[46] The danger in arguing that not all comfort women were sexual slaves is clear: the nuance and complexity of personal stories can be misappropriated as denial of or apology for Japanese wartime aggression.

At the same time, the fixation with comfort women as a uniquely Japanese colonial atrocity has helped whitewash coeval and overlapping colonial structures and cultures of sexual violence, including crimes committed by the Allied forces. In 1944 in the northern Arakanese town of Paletwa, one British force alone reportedly committed more than fifty rapes.[47] In the case of Korea and Japan, Katherine Moon, Sarah C. Soh, and Lisa Yoneyama have emphasized how the discussion of comfort women has turned a blind eye to the intersections and collusions of Korean, Japanese, and US patriarchal regimes across colonial divides, resulting in a neglect of the sexual crimes committed by US soldiers as the Japanese colonial system of comfort women evolved into new military sexual operations catering to American troops in the two countries under US occupation (1945–1948 in Korea, 1945–1952 in Japan) and the Korean War (1950–1953).[48] Indeed, state licensed brothels and lock hospitals were among the first colonial government institutions to be established under every European and US imperial flag in Asia.[49] Enslaved, indentured, and colonized women in colonial households, as well as plantations, were denied protection from sexual assault and control over their own reproductive capacity.⁵⁰ In rare cases where European men in the colonies were accused of rape, they were exonerated despite overwhelming evidence to the contrary.⁵¹ While colonization and military occupation in general are equated with the conquest of women, the focus on comfort women has rendered Japanese colonialism anomalous and sadistic.

In addition, redress movements in the name of comfort women have too often reduced the issue to a matter of national humiliation or the model victim story of sexual slavery. Nationalist politicians and activists have turned former comfort women into symbols of national shame—a reminder of the failure of colonized men to protect "their" women, female chastity, and therefore national purity and honor—while international women's and human rights advocates have cast them in the single, fixed mold of the innocent young girl taken from her family by the Japanese military to be imprisoned in "rape centers."⁵² In what amounts to institutionalized forgetting, they have suppressed memories of wartime embodied labor that diverge from these scripts.

I have endeavored to repopulate the archive and history of Japanese colonialism with the marginalized memories and stigmatized subjectivities of occupied women that upset collective memories that deem militarized sexual violence the only—albeit deeply shameful—experience of occupied women worth remembering. The stories I examine do not resonate with the triumphalist nationalist narrative of Burmese antifascist, anticolonialist resistance. They do not coordinate with wartime and postwar Japanese romances of the occupation either, troubling the assumption that stories of intimacy under Japanese rule affirm imperial nostalgia and redeem Japanese colonialism. They reveal instead that new dynamics of power and patronage were enacted, routed, and managed through everyday relations of intimacy between Japanese occupiers and occupied women that had uncertain ramifications for the women. The ubiquity of such intimate relationships index neither Japanese colonial benevolence nor Burmese women's naivety. Reducing wartime intimacies to matters of personal sentiment only obscures the political and economic exigencies that produced and governed the relationships. It conceals the complicity of the Burmese elites in routinizing gender and sexual exploitation and violence, especially against amyo gya and kabya populations, under the Japanese.

Here as in the previous chapters, I deemphasize historical rupture. The veneer of abrupt and radical change (war, exodus, "unmixing," pan-Asianism, etc.) notwithstanding, interAsian intimacies remained perilous sites through which distinctions between colonizer and colonized—and among the colonized—

were reconstituted and made to matter. Mixed marriage, sex, and birth remained the focus of colonial bureaucratic anxiety and regulation under the Japanese and sites of Burmese collaboration and tension with the Japanese. Even in the Japanese imperial romance of pan-Asianism, intermarriage and miscegenation occupied an ambiguous position. That the discourse and imaginary of the suffering captive of the amyo gya was reinscribed during the Japanese interregnum and its immediate aftermath with the *japan gadaw* betrays the commensurability of the politics of interAsian intimacies under British colonial and Japanese occupation rule.

The history of intimacy and violence in Japanese-occupied Burma thus unsettles assumptions about the incomparability of Japanese imperialism to European and US imperial formations. The othering of Japanese colonizers as abnormally atrocious has enabled other former imperial powers to normalize their own history of colonial violence and claim intimacy as the privilege and property of European and US colonial enterprises. Historians of Japan and its empire have critiqued this Eurocentric paradigm of incomparability, though through an East Asia–centric framework that marginalizes the Japanese wartime colonization of Southeast Asia and reproduces the artificial subregional divisions that have traditionally characterized the field of Asian studies. As a multiply colonized space, Southeast Asia represents an unparalleled temporal and geographical field in which to interrogate changes and continuities, and differences and similarities, across European, US, and Japanese colonialisms and within the Japanese colonial empire itself.

Despite the brevity of the Japanese occupation compared to such colonies as Taiwan and Korea, the logics and legacies of Japanese colonialism are more comparable across the East-Southeast Asia divide than acknowledged. Memories of intimate contact through which the Japanese metropolitan and colonial governments pursued the imperial visions of *dōka, kōminka,* and the pan-Asian family, such as Japanese-language schools, intermarriage, miscegenation, and collaboration, have proved more controversial and contested in Burma—and therefore more akin to memories of Japanese colonialism elsewhere—than popular and scholarly narratives have suggested. The story of interAsian intimacies in Burma unravels these unlikely intimacies and interwoven histories of colonization across chronologies and territories.

Epilogue

16 NOVEMBER 2015 (SEATTLE, WASHINGTON).

Ma Mona and I are sitting in the dining room of the apartment that she shares with her mother. We have just finished feasting on an elaborate meal that Ma Mona has prepared to celebrate our reunion. Auntie Rosie has retired to her bedroom. It is getting late but Ma Mona and I have much to catch up on. Our conversation turns to the persecution of the Rohingya since 2012, which has since been declared a genocide, and the ascendancy of the monastic nationalist movement Ma Ba Tha (Association to Protect Nation and Buddhism) and their "Buy Buddhist" and "Marry Buddhist" campaigns targeting Muslims and more generally those labeled kala. Just two months before my trip to Seattle, Ma Ba Tha had won its most notable victory to date: the passing of four controversial laws euphemistically known as "National Race and Religion Protection Laws," including a revised version of the Buddhist Women's Special Marriage and Succession Act (1954), first debated in the legislature in 1927 and finally enacted seven years after Burma declared independence from Britain in 1948. The laws collectively restrict interfaith marriages by requiring non-Buddhist men to obtain permission from the Buddhist woman's parents and local authorities.

In response, Ma Mona recounts the "religious fluidity" (her description) that characterized her family and upbringing in Burma. This is when I learn that

Uncle Mohan was baptized at the age of forty and became a devoted member of the Immanuel Baptist Church in Rangoon. All his brothers converted from Hinduism, as it turned out. Sundram, who joined the army at a young age and spent much of his life in the company of Burmese soldiers, became Buddhist. Like Uncle Mohan, Bodi joined the Baptist church, while Seena converted to Catholicism even as he shared a life-long companionship with a Hindu widow.

After her marriage to Uncle Mohan in June 1961, Auntie Rosie began reading the bible and reciting Christian prayers, though she did not get baptized until she was fifty-two years of age. "Good, he is a famous cardiologist!" Ahmed Meah reportedly remarked upon hearing news of the marriage. At the time,

FIGURE E.1.   Uncle Mohan. Photo taken in the 1960s. Courtesy of Dr. Hnin Yee and Mona Han.

Uncle Mohan was a professor and Auntie Rosie an assistant surgeon at the Institute of Medicine 1, the premier medical school in Burma (fig. E.1).

Helen May did not share the enthusiasm—not on account of his religion nor his Indian descent but rather his age. He was forty-five years old, fifteen years Auntie Rosie's senior. But Helen May relented, just as she had with many of her children. Few followed her wishes or expectations for marriage. The eldest, Kitty, returned from Delhi, where she was a medical school student, to Pyinmana without her degree but with a husband and with child—Helen and Ahmed's first grandchild, whom Helen helped deliver in 1947. When the eldest son, Hardy, was posted to Mandalay as a civil assistant surgeon, he had a Muslim girlfriend, a medical student and Auntie Rosie's classmate, whom his family believed would soon become his wife. Instead, he fell in love with a Karen Christian doctor eight years his senior and married her. Helen May and Ahmed heard about the marriage only after the fact from a servant they had sent with Hardy to Mandalay who dutifully reported the news to the parents via telegram. Hardy remained Muslim until the eve of his death when he converted to Christianity. But he and his wife Priscilla raised their two children Christian.

The marriage of the youngest child, Nyi Ma Lay ("little sister" in Burmese), also shocked Helen May. An ophthalmologist, she had been posted to Taunggyi. A family acquaintance in Pyinmana knew of a relative traveling to Taunggyi and asked Helen May if she wished to send something along to Nyi Ma Lay. Helen May sent her daughter a house for her cat with a young man, Maung Maung. Not long after, she received news that Nyi Ma Lay had married Maung Maung. "For a measly pet house, I gave away my dear daughter," Helen May bemoaned. Nyi Ma Lay became Buddhist, like her husband.

The history of intermarriage and conversion thus persisted among the Meah-Mohan family. "We celebrated every single religion in Burma," Ma Mona recalled ever so wistfully. For *waso*, the month marking the beginning of the Buddhist lent, they would perform *sun kywe* and *thin gan kat*—the ceremonial offering of food and robes to monks—at Nyi Ma Lay's house. For Christmas, everyone gathered at Auntie Rosie and Uncle Mohan's, while Mummy-gyi and Papa-gyi held grand celebrations for Eid at their home. Everyone attended the baptisms of the children, Ma Mona points out. She can still visualize all her relatives sitting in the pew.

Ma Mona's memories of interfaith attachments in postcolonial Burma, like Auntie Rosie's recollections of the anti-Indian riots and the Japanese occupation, refused to naturalize antagonism or disavow intimacies in the face of violence and incitement to estrangement. A subtle but clear gesture of refusal, she insisted that mixed families and individuals formed through migration, conversion, and intermarriage such as hers have never been strangers in Burma. She rejected the circumscribed meaning of Burmese kinship propagated by the likes of Ma Ba Tha that conflate Burma with Buddhism.

Such stories of belonging across boundaries illuminate the unruly ties and complex subjectivities that constitute reality for so many and yet are so hard to capture in studies. They confound neat historical narratives and periodizations that proclaim the demise of precolonial cultures of pluralism, localization, and hybrid identities with the onslaught of colonialism, World War II, and finally postcolonial nationalism, which sealed the process of the "unmixing" of people already underway. The stories of the Meah-Mohans highlight instead the discontinuous yet persistent record of interAsian intimacies across the long twentieth century, which I have explored in the book.

They also serve as powerful reminders of the normative nature of ideas of the Burmese Buddhist amyo that have become taken-for-granted truths: that Burma is fundamentally a Buddhist country and the Burmese Buddhist an exceptional *and* endangered species of uniquely just, tolerant, and liberal people who have no history of sex, caste, racial, and religious discrimination; that the Burmese Buddhists are therefore worthy of universal admiration and protection from intermarriage, conversion, and "degeneration." This logic, which I have termed Burmese Buddhist exceptionalism, rationalizes fears and suspicions of the so-called amyo gya and the "impure" Burmese, such as the zerbadi and kabya. It furthermore normalizes the conjugal mandate that Burmese Buddhist women repudiate intermarriage and conversion and marry Burmese Buddhist men to preserve and regenerate their unique lineage and heritage.

As is often the case with national mythologies—of Japanese racial homogeneity or US exceptionalism, for example—no amount of evidence of the fallacies of such assertions diminishes their power. Proponents of Burmese Buddhist exceptionalism neither hide nor deny the persistent history of migration, intermarriage, and conversion in Burma, as the book has shown. They willingly admit that most Burmese are in one way or another mixed. This has not lessened the appeal of the Manichean myth of a *sin sit* (pure, genuine) Burmese community whose survival demands vigilant regulation and segregation of the "impure," "other" Burmese.

The Meah-Mohan family are all too familiar with such forbidding imaginations of the Burmese body politic and their material, embodied effects. The year after Auntie Rosie and Uncle Mohan married, General Ne Win ousted the democratically elected prime minister U Nu to take power in a military coup, remaining the country's socialist dictator until 1988. His revolutionary ideology of "Burmese Way to Socialism," which justified the nationalization of industry, agriculture, and foreign trade, resulted in the forced "repatriation" of an estimated three hundred thousand people of "Indian origin" between 1962 and 1965. Their properties and businesses in Burma were seized. Families such as Uncle Mohan's were partitioned. Sundram and Mohan became citizens of Burma, while their brothers Seena and Bodi became Indian citizens.

Uncle Mohan could have left Burma. He had earned enough from his service in the Burma Army Medical Corp to finance his postgraduate studies in London, where he trained with Paul Hamilton Wood, a leading scholar in the emerging field of cardiology. He turned down a position as a consultant physician in England and returned to Burma to establish the practice of cardiology in the country—only to find himself transferred to Mandalay University, a move that amounted to a demotion. Uncle Mohan believed that he would not have been transferred back to Rangoon in 1965 if not for the intervention of Ne Win's wife, Khin May Than (better known as Kitty Ba Than), who, requiring heart care, became his patron. Yet, even as the personal physician to the favorite wife of the country's dictator, Uncle Mohan faced professional discrimination from the Burmese medical establishment that refused to promote him—respected as the top cardiologist in the country but penalized as kala. It was a bitter experience his children too endured as they became distinguished students and scholars in their own right in a society that alternately embraced them as exemplary Burmese citizens and denigrated them as kala kabya.

The twin remembrance of interAsian belonging and alienation is crucial for documenting the resilience of interAsian intimacies in the face of repeated injunctions and threats of violence, and for other reasons as well. As the book has demonstrated, interAsian intimacies have represented a major locus for the production of difference. They are therefore key to elucidating how colonized subjects theorized difference and improvised new regimes of knowledge, power, and desire spawned through but not determined by colonial agendas. Only by interrogating the intimate grounds and routes of social reproduction that have made difference matter can we effectively comprehend interAsian violence and its gendered dynamics and ramifications.

The study of interAsian intimacies also reclaims intimacy from the continued Anglo- and Euro-centrism of postcolonial studies in which the intimate lives and lifeworld of Asians merit analysis only when they interact with white subjects. Colonial political economies mobilized people across far-flung spaces, bringing into close contact Asian migrants and Indigenous populations. In Burma, as elsewhere, such connections among colonized subjects have been negatively referenced in public records and archives: as offenses under the law and sources of social ill, moral panic, and political turmoil that require prohibition and suppression, all implying fears and fantasies of mobility and mixing across categories. In scholarship, theories of communalism and the so-called plural society—in which people of different races and religions exist as proximate yet separate communities without ever forging a common sense of belonging—have dominated interpretations of interAsian relations in colonial and postcolonial Asia.

In the foregoing pages, I have endeavored to chart the history of interAsian relations beyond such "negative references" of anxieties and apprehensions. This work has compelled me to reconsider the possibilities and limitations of archival excavation, family history, and multigenerational storytelling and explore unchronicled struggles and experiments in self-fashioning and world making across boundaries of belonging. Little known figures at the margins of history, such as Ma Galay, Di Di, Helen May, Auntie Rosie, and Uncle Mohan, have much to teach historians about the ingenious ways that people have confronted shifting bodies of knowledge, relationships of power, and terms of social existence to sustain intimacies many find unthinkable. With the help of their knowledge of existing and relating otherwise, we too may reimagine and remake intimacies—past, present, and future.

NOTES

Introduction

1. A historically pejorative label, "coolie" is thought to have derived from the Tamil word *kuli* (meaning "wages" or "hire"). It was appropriated by the British, who, like other imperial powers, introduced a new system of coercive yet ostensibly free labor from Asia in the aftermath of the official abolition of slavery in the 1830s in most parts of the British Empire. See the discussion of the term "coolie" and its significance in Gaiutra Bahadur, *Coolie Woman: The Odyssey of Indenture* (Chicago: University of Chicago Press, 2014), xix–xxi; and Lisa Lowe, *The Intimacies of Four Continents* (Durham, NC: Duke University Press, 2015), 21–28.

2. Lower Burma, *Report on the Census of British Burma Taken in August 1872, Part I, Report* (Rangoon: Government Press, 1875), lv–lvii; F. S. Copleston, *Report on the Census of British Burma, Taken on the 17th February 1881, Part I, Report* (Rangoon: Government Press, 1881), 70; Government of India, *Census of 1891, Imperial Tables, X, Burma Report, Volume II* (Rangoon: Superintendent, Government Printing, 1892), 184; C. C. Lowis, *Census of India, 1901, XIIA, Burma, Part II, Imperial Tables* (Rangoon: Office of the Superintendent, Government Printing, 1902), 206; Government of India, *Census of India, 1911, IX, Burma, Part I, Report* (Rangoon: Office of the Superintendent, Government Printing and Stationery, 1912), 81–82; Government of India, *Census of India, 1911, IX, Burma, Part II, Tables* (Rangoon: Office of the Superintendent, Government Printing and Stationery, 1912), 124; Government of India, *Census of India, 1921, X, Burma, Part II, Tables* (Rangoon: Office of the Superintendent, Government Printing and Stationery, 1923), 150; Government of India, *Census of India, 1931, XI, Burma, Part II, Tables* (Rangoon: Office of the Superintendent, Government Printing and Stationery, 1933), 27.

3. G. William Skinner, "Creolized Chinese Societies in Southeast Asia," in *Sojourners and Settlers: Histories of Southeast Asia and the Chinese*, ed. Anthony Reid (Honolulu: University of Hawai'i Press, 1996), 86.

4. For example, see Amarjit Kaur, "Indian Labour, Labour Standards, and Workers' Health in Burma and Malaya, 1900–1940," *Modern Asian Studies* 40, no. 2 (2006): 425–427.

5. For examples of this growing body of scholarship, see Renisa Mawani, *Colonial Proximities: Crossracial Encounters and Juridical Truths in British Columbia, 1871–1921* (Vancouver: University of British Columbia Press, 2009); Bahadur, *Coolie Women*; Ana Paulina Lee, *Mandarin Brazil: Race, Representation, and Memory* (Stanford, CA: Stanford University Press, 2018); and Juliana Hu Pegues, *Space-Time Colonialism: Alaska's Indigenous and Asian Entanglements* (Chapel Hill: University of North Carolina Press, 2021).

6. On this pivot to Asian interactions and interconnections, see Tim Harper and Sunil S. Amrith, eds., *Sites of Asian Interaction: Ideas, Networks and Mobility* (Delhi: Cambridge University Press, 2014); and the forums "Asia Redux: Conceptualizing a Region for Our Times," *Journal of Asian Studies* 69, no. 4 (November 2010): 963–1029, and "The Flow of Migration beyond the Nation," *Journal of Asian Studies* 76, no. 4 (November 2017): 907–962.

7. For a critical assessment of this conceptualization of Asia and the Indian Ocean world and its tendency to stress connectivity and conviviality at the expense of divisions and disaffections, see Nile Green, "The Waves of Heterotopia: Toward a Vernacular Intellectual History of the Indian Ocean," *American Historical Review* 123, no. 3 (June 2018): 846–874; Michael Laffan, "Introduction: Dhows, Steamers, Lifeboats," in *Belonging across the Bay of Bengal: Religious Rites, Colonial Migrations, National Rights*, ed. Michael Laffan (London: Bloomsbury Academic, 2017), 1–14. For a critique of the gender assumptions about mobility in interAsian studies, see Nicole Constable, "Revisiting Distant Divides and Intimate Connections in Asia: Comments on Engseng Ho's 'Inter-Asian Concepts for Mobile Societies,'" *Journal of Asian Studies* 76, no. 4 (November 2017): 953–959; and Samia Khatun, "The Book of Marriage: Histories of Muslim Women in Twentieth-Century Australia," *Gender and History* 29, no. 1 (2017): 8–30.

8. The first half of the phrase, buddha batha, is a compound of the word Buddha and batha. The Burmese word batha is derived from Pali *bhāsā*, meaning "speech" or "language." Starting in the mid- to late nineteenth century, batha came to gloss the European Christian concept of "religion," for which no comparable term existed in Burmese, even as the term continued to refer to language. No vernacular word for "Buddhism" existed either, so it was translated as buddha batha. The second half of the phrase, bama amyo, combines the term for Burman/Burmese with the polysemic word amyo, which denotes "roots, origin, and descent" and is defined variously as "breed," "family," "relatives," "lineage," "kind," and "group." While retaining these meanings, amyo also came to dub the European notion of "race" in the nineteenth century. See *A Burmese-English Dictionary*, compiled by J. A. Stewart and C. W. Dunn (Rangoon: University of Rangoon, 1940), 282–283; and Alexey Kirichenko, "From *Thathanadaw* to Theravāda Buddhism: Construction of Religion and Religious Identity in Nineteenth- and Early Twentieth-Century Myanmar," in *Casting Faiths: Imperialism and the Transformation of Religion in East and Southeast Asia*, ed. Thomas David Dubois (Basingstoke: Palgrave Macmillan, 2009), 23–45.

9. Judith Surkis, *Sex, Law, and Sovereignty in Algeria, 1830–1930* (Ithaca, NY: Cornell University Press, 2019), 182–184.

10. The works I have in mind include but are not limited to Jean G. Taylor, *The Social World of Batavia: European and Eurasian in Dutch Asia* (Madison: University of Wisconsin Press, 1983; rev. ed. 2009); Ann L. Stoler, "Making Empire Respectable: The Politics of Race and Sexual Morality in 20th-Century Colonial Cultures," *American Ethnologist* 16, no. 4 (November 1989): 634–660; Anne McClintock, *Imperial Leather: Race, Gender and Sexuality in the Colonial Conquest* (New York: Routledge, 1995); and Julia Clancy-Smith and Frances Gouda, eds., *Domesticating the Empire: Race, Gender, and Family Life in French and Dutch Colonialism* (Charlottesville: University of Virginia Press, 1998).

11. For a review of this rich and voluminous literature, see Durba Ghosh, "Gender and Colonialism: Expansion or Marginalization?," *Historical Journal* 47, no. 3 (September 2004): 737–755.

12. Barbara Andaya, "From Temporary Wife to Prostitute: Sexuality and Economic Change in Early Modern Southeast Asia," *Journal of Women's History* 9, no. 4 (Winter 1998), 12, 28.

13. M. Page Baldwin, "Subject to Empire: Married Women and the British Nationality and Status of Aliens Act," *Journal of British Studies* 40, no. 4 (October 2001): 522–556.

14. On this (neo)colonial "sexual double standard," see Joane Nagel, *Race, Ethnicity, and Sexuality: Intimate Intersections, Forbidden Frontiers* (New York: Oxford University Press, 2003).

15. Anna Davin, "Imperialism and Motherhood," *History Workshop Journal* 5, no. 1 (Spring 1978): 9–65; and Lucy Bland, "White Women and Men of Colour: Miscegenation Fears in Britain after the Great War," *Gender and History* 17, no. 2 (April 2005): 29–61.

16. Ann L. Stoler, *Carnal Knowledge and Imperial Power: Race and the Intimate in Colonial Rule* (Berkeley: University of California Press, 2002), 19.

17. Indrani Chatterjee, "Colouring Subalternity: Slaves, Concubines and Social Orphans under the East India Company," in *Subaltern Studies*, vol. 10, ed. Gautam Bhadra, Gyan Prakash, and Susie Tharu (New Delhi: Oxford University Press, 1999), 49–97; and Christina Firpo, *The Uprooted: Race, Children, and Imperialism in French Indochina, 1890–1980* (Honolulu: University of Hawai'i Press, 2016).

18. In formulating this critique of the possessive, imperialistic calculus of intimacies, I draw in particular on Tamara Loos, *Subject Siam: Family, Law, and Colonial Modernity in Thailand* (Ithaca, NY: Cornell University Press, 2006); Tamara Loos, "A History of Sex and the State in Southeast Asia: Class, Intimacy and Invisibility," *Citizenship Studies* 12, no. 1 (January 2008): 27–43; Nayan Shah, *Stranger Intimacy: Contesting Race, Sexuality, and the Law in the North American West* (Berkeley: University of California Press, 2011); Lowe, *Intimacies of Four Continents*; and Jennifer L. Morgan, *Reckoning with Slavery: Gender, Kinship, and Capitalism in the Early Black Atlantic* (Durham, NC: Duke University Press, 2021).

19. See Frederick Cooper and Ann L. Stoler, eds., *Tensions of Empire: Colonial Cultures in a Bourgeois World* (Berkeley: University of California Press, 1997); Clancy-Smith and Gouda, *Domesticating the Empire*; Antoinette Burton, ed., *Gender, Sexuality and Colonial Modernities* (London: Routledge, 1999); Ann L. Stoler, ed., *Haunted by Empire: Geographies of Intimacy in North American History* (Durham, NC: Duke University Press, 2006); and Tony Ballantyne and Antoinette Burton, *Bodies in Contact: Rethinking Colonial Encounters in World History* (Durham, NC: Duke University Press, 2005).

20. For a critique of the systemic disavowal of the comparability of Japanese imperialism, see Leo T. S. Ching, *Becoming "Japanese": Colonial Taiwan and the Politics of Identity Formation* (Berkeley: University of California Press, 2001); Robert Thomas Tierney, *Tropics of Savagery: The Culture of Japanese Empire in Comparative Frame* (Berkeley: University of California Press, 2010); Takashi Fujitani, *Race for Empire: Koreans as Japanese and Japanese as Americans during World War II* (Berkeley: University of California Press, 2011); and Nayoung Aimee Kwon, *Intimate Empire: Collaboration and Colonial Modernity in Korea and Japan* (Durham, NC: Duke University Press, 2015).

21. Satoshi Nakano, *Japan's Colonial Moment in Southeast Asia, 1942–1945: The Occupiers' Experience* (London: Routledge, 2018), 2, 16, 23. In addition, nearly three hundred thousand Javanese laborers (called *rōmusha*, or "drifters," in Japanese) were sent to colonies under Japanese occupation as "economic soldiers." One of the largest construction projects carried out by the imperial army during the Japanese occupation, the Thailand-Burma railway, which stretched four hundred kilometers from Bampong in Thailand to Thanbyuzayat in Burma, alone levied an estimated two hundred thousand to three hundred thousand Asian laborers recruited from Thailand, Burma, Malaya, French Indochina, and the Indonesian archipelago. An unknown number of women from across Asia accompanied all of these deployments as "auxiliary forces": nurses, teachers, porters, and sexual laborers. See Paul H. Kratoska, ed., *Asian Labor in the Wartime Japanese History: Unknown Histories* (Armonk, NY: M. E. Sharpe, 2005).

22. Jun Uchida, *Brokers of Empire: Japanese Settler Colonialism in Korea, 1876–1945* (Cambridge, MA: Harvard University Asia Center, 2011); Kwon, *Intimate Empire*; Christopher P. Hanscom and Dennis Washburn, *The Affect of Difference: Representations of Race in East Asian Empire* (Honolulu: University of Hawai'i Press, 2016); Paul D. Barclay, *Outcasts of Empire: Japan's Rule on Taiwan's "Savage Border," 1874–1945* (Oakland: University of California Press, 2018); David Ambaras, *Japan's Imperial Underworlds: Intimate Encounters at the Borders of the Sinosphere* (Cambridge: Cambridge University Press, 2018); Eiichiro Azuma, *In Search of Our Frontier: Japanese America and Settler Colonialism in the Construction of Japan's Borderless Empire* (Berkeley: University of California Press, 2019); Sidney Xu Lu, *The Making of Japanese Settler Colonialism: Malthusianism and Trans-Pacific Migration, 1868–1961* (Cambridge: Cambridge University Press, 2019); and Su Yun Kim, *Imperial Romance: Fictions of Colonial Intimacy in Korea, 1905–1945* (Ithaca, NY: Cornell University Press, 2020). There are two notable exceptions: Keith L. Camacho's *Cultures of Commemoration: The Politics of War, Memory, and History in the Mariana Islands* (Honolulu: University of Hawai'i Press, 2011) and Greg Dvorak's *Coral and Concrete: Remembering Kwajalein Atoll between Japan, America, and the Marshall Islands* (Honolulu: University of Hawai'i Press, 2018) which examine the overlaps and parallels between US and Japanese imperialism in Guam, the Northern Mariana Islands, and the Marshall Islands before, during, and after World War II.

23. Urvashi Butalia, *The Other Side of Silence: Voices from the Partition of India* (Durham, NC: Duke University Press, 2000); Charu Gupta, *Sexuality, Obscenity, Community: Women, Muslims, and the Hindu Public in Colonial India* (New York: Palgrave, 2002); and Veena Das, *Life and Words: Violence and the Descent into the Ordinary* (Berkeley: University of California Press, 2006).

24. On "inter-Asia," see Sunil S. Amrith, *Crossing the Bay of Bengal: The Furies of Nature and the Fortunes of Migrants* (Cambridge, MA: Harvard University Press, 2013); Harper and Amrith, *Sites of Asian Interaction*; Eric Tagliacozzo, Helen F. Siu, and Peter C. Perdue, eds., *Asia Inside Out: Changing Times* (Cambridge, MA: Harvard University Press, 2015); and Engseng Ho, "Inter-Asian Concepts for Mobile Societies," *Journal of Asian Studies* 76, no. 4 (November 2017): 907–928.

25. Prasenjit Duara, "The Discourse of Civilization and Pan-Asianism," *Journal of World History* 12, no. 1 (Spring 2001): 99–130.

26. Prasenjit Duara, "Asia Redux: Conceptualizing a Region for Our Times," *Journal of Asian Studies* 69, no. 4 (November 2010): 982–983.

27. For a classic study of the ready incorporation of migrants and amicable "localization" of the foreign into indigenous state and society, see G. William Skinner, *Chinese Society in Thailand: An Analytical History* (Ithaca, NY: Cornell University Press, 1957).

28. María Lugones, "Heterosexualism and the Colonial/Modern Gender System," *Hypatia* 22, no. 1 (2007): 186–209.

29. See, for example, Helen Fujimoto, *The South Indian Muslim Community and the Evolution of the Jawi Peranakan in Penang up to 1948: A Comparative Study on the Modes of Inter-Action in Multi-Ethnic Societies*, monograph series no. 1 (Tokyo: Tokyo Gaikokugo Daigaku, 1988); Anthony Reid, ed., *Sojourners and Settlers: Histories of Southeast Asia and the Chinese* (Honolulu: University of Hawai'i Press, 1996); Engseng Ho, *The Graves of Tarim: Genealogy and Mobility across the Indian Ocean* (Berkeley: University of California Press, 2006), 184–187; and Natasha Pairaudeau, *Mobile Citizens: French Indians in Indochina, 1858–1954* (Copenhagen: NIAS Press, 2016), 222–224.

30. Barbara Andaya, *The Flaming Womb: Repositioning Women in Early Modern Southeast Asia* (Honolulu: University of Hawai'i Press, 2006), 147.

31. Karen M. Teoh, *Schooling Diaspora: Women, Education, and the Overseas Chinese in British Malaya and Singapore, 1850s–1960s* (New York: Oxford University Press, 2018); Sumita Mukherjee, *Indian Suffragettes: Female Identities and Transnational Networks* (New Delhi: Oxford University Press, 2018): 167–170; Arunima Datta, *Fleeting Agencies: A Social History of Indian Coolie Women in British Malaya* (Cambridge: Cambridge University Press, 2021); Sandy F. Chang, "Intimate Itinerancy: Sex, Work, and Chinese Women in Colonial Malaya's Brothel Economy, 1870s–1930s," *Journal of Women's History* 33, no. 4 (Winter 2021): 92–117; and Eri Kitada, "Intimately Intertwined: Settler and Indigenous Communities, Filipino Women, and U.S.-Japanese Imperial Formations in the Philippines, 1903–1956" (PhD diss., Rutgers University, 2023).

32. Ho, "Inter-Asian Concepts," 916.

33. Tony Ballantyne and Antoinette Burton, "Introduction," in *Moving Subjects: Gender, Mobility, and Intimacy in an Age of Global Empire*, ed. Tony Ballantyne and Antoinette Burton (Urbana: University of Illinois Press, 2009), 6.

34. On the challenges of locating women, especially non-European women, in colonial archives, see Durba Ghosh, *Sex and the Family in Colonial India: The Making of Empire* (Cambridge: Cambridge University Press, 2005); Antoinette M. Burton, "Archive Stories: Gender in the Making of Imperial and Colonial Histories," in *Gender and Empire*, ed. Philippa Levine (Oxford: Oxford University Press, 2004), 281–293; and Marisa Fuentes, *Dispossessed Lives: Enslaved Women, Violence and the Archive* (Philadelphia: University of Pennsylvania Press, 2016).

35. Saidiya Hartman, *Scenes of Subjection: Terror and Self-Making in Nineteenth Century America* (New York: Oxford University Press, 1997); Saidiya Hartman, *Wayward Lives, Beautiful Experiments: Intimate Social Histories of Social Upheaval* (New York: W. W. Norton, 2019).

36. Insook Kwon, "Feminists Navigating the Shoals of Nationalism and Collaboration: The Post-Colonial Korean Debate over How to Remember Kim Hwallan," *Frontiers: A Journal of Women Studies* 27, no. 1 (2006): 39–66.

37. Camilla Townsend, *Malintzin's Choices: An Indian Woman in the Conquest of Mexico* (Albuquerque: University of New Mexico Press, 2006), 7.

1. Making Kin and Remaking Worlds

1. Record of burials at the Town Cemetery Rangoon of Europeans or Eurasians for the Quarter commencing from the 1 October to 31 December 1908, dated 26 January 1909. British India Office deaths and burials, N-1-353, fol. 342.

2. Record of baptisms at Christ Church, Mandalay, of Europeans or Eurasians for the quarter commencing from July 1, 1910, to September 30, 1910, dated 7 October 1910. British India Office births and baptisms, N-1-366, fol. 240.

3. *Long Ago, Far Away: The Burma Diaries of Doris Sarah Easton*, compiled by M. Sylvia Morris (London: Minerva Press, 1994), 61.

4. F. E. Penny, *On the Coromandel Coast* (London: Smith, Elder, 1908), 127.

5. Ghosh, *Sex and the Family*, 19.

6. Taylor, *Social World*; Ghosh, *Sex and the Family*; Carmen Nocentelli, *Empires of Love: Europe, Asia, and the Making of Early Modern Identity* (Philadelphia: University of Pennsylvania Press, 2013). In the Dutch East Indies, Indo-Europeans, the equivalent of Eurasians, were eligible for European legal status but only with the recognition of a European father; that of a European mother could not confer European status upon an Indo-European child.

7. Ronald Hyam, *Empire and Sexuality: The British Experience* (Manchester: Manchester University Press, 1990), 116.

8. Chatterjee, "Colouring Subalternity"; Ghosh, *Sex and the Family*.

9. Adrian Carton, "'Faire and Well-Formed': Portuguese Eurasian Women and Symbolic Whiteness in Early Colonial India," in Ballantyne and Burton, *Moving Subjects*, 231–251.

10. Holden Furber, *Private Fortunes and Company Profits in the India Trade in the 18th Century*, ed. Rosane Rocher (Aldershot, UK: Variorum, 1997), 267. Furber does not provide any details or evidence for this attribution.

11. Stephen Sulivan, letter to Sir Robert Palk, dated 5 February 1780, Fort St. George, reproduced in Great Britain, *Report on the Palk manuscripts in the possession of Mrs. Bannatyne, of Haldon, Devon* (London: H. M. Stationery, 1922), 331–332. Sir Robert Palk was a former officer of the British East India Company and governor of the Madras Presidency (1755–1763). Stephen Sulivan was the son of Laurence Sulivan, former director and chairman of the company and longtime friend of Palk.

12. Henry Davison Love, *Vestiges of Old Madras, 1640–1800* (London: J. Murray, 1913), 491.

13. Elizabeth Buettner "Problematic Spaces, Problematic Races: Defining 'Europeans' in Late Colonial India," *Women's History Review* 9, no. 2 (2000): 277–298.

14. David Arnold, "European Orphans and Vagrants in India in the Nineteenth Century," *Journal of Imperial and Commonwealth History* 7, no. 2 (1979): 104–127; Charles Hawes, *Poor Relations: The Making of a Eurasian Community in British India 1730–1833* (Surrey, UK: Curzon, 1996); P. J. Marshall, "British Society in India under the East India Company," *Modern Asian Studies* 31, no. 1 (1997): 89–108.

15. R. E. Culley, *The "Euro-Asian" or "Anglo-Indian": A Burma Brochure by One of the Community* (Rangoon: Mayles Standish & Co. Ltd. Electric Press, 1910), 1, 3, 5, 8, 16–18, 21.

16. Sebouh David Aslanian, *From the Indian Ocean to the Mediterranean: The Global Trade Networks of Armenian Merchants from New Julfa* (Berkeley: University of California Press, 2011), 54–56.

17. Hitomi Fujimura, "A View of the Karen Baptists in Burma of the Mid-Nineteenth Century, from the Standpoint of the American Baptist Mission," *Journal of Sophia Asian Studies* 32, (2014), 132; W. C. B. Purser, *Christian Missions in Burma* (Westminster: Society for the Propagation of the Gospel in Foreign Parts, 1911), 103–104.

18. Kazuto Ikeda, "Two Versions of Buddhist Karen History of the Late British Colonial Period in Burma: Kayin Chronicle (1929) and Kuyin Great Chronicle (1931)," *Southeast Asian Studies* 1, no. 3 (December 2012), 434–435. Sgaw and Pwo represent the two Karen languages with the largest populations of speakers in Burma. As Kato Atsuhiko observes, however, "the range of people who consider themselves to be ethnic 'Karen' can vary according to various contexts, including political, ethnic, and linguistic." Atsuhiko Kato, "Karen and Surrounding Languages," in *Topics in Middle Mekong Linguistics*, ed. Norihiko Hayashi (Kobe: Kobe City University of Foreign Studies, 2019), 123.

19. William Womack, "Contesting Indigenous and Female Authority in the Burma Baptist Mission: The Case of Ellen Mason," *Women's History Review* 17, no. 4 (September 2008): 543–559.

20. On the interrelated history of Christian missions, female education, and nursing, see Atsuko Naono, "Educating Lady Doctors in Colonial Burma: American Baptist Missionaries, the Lady Dufferin Hospital, and the Local Government in the Making of Burmese Medical Women," in *Contesting Colonial Authority: Medicine and Indigenous Responses in 19th- and 20th-Century India*, ed. Poonam Bala (Lanham, MD: Lexington Books, 2012), 97–114.

21. The other, the Eurasian school and "home for destitute Eurasian girls" in Moulmein and run by American Baptist missionaries, is reported to have predated the British annexation of the province of Tenasserim in 1826. "Eighty-fifth Annual Report," *Baptist Missionary Magazine* 79, no. 1 (January 1899), 285.

22. Chatterjee, "Colouring Subalternity"; Firpo, *Uprooted*.

23. J. E. Marks, *Forty Years in Burma, with a foreword by the Archbishop of Canterbury* (New York: E. P. Dutton, 1917), 137.

24. Christina Firpo and Margaret D. Jacobs, "Taking Children, Ruling Colonies: Child Removal and Colonial Subjugation in Australia, Canada, French Indochina, and the United States, 1870–1950s," *Journal of World History* 29, no. 4 (December 2018), 542, 551–552.

25. Marks, *Forty Years*, 139.

26. *Long Ago, Far Away*, 63, 152. Archived in the India Office Records collection at the British Library (mss. Eur C399), Easton's diaries and letters of her experience in Burma as the headmistress of St. Mary's School (1916–1917) and then wife of a longtime government officer and headmaster of a government school were compiled by her daughter and published as *Long Ago, Far Away*.

27. Penny Edwards, "Mixed Metaphors: Other Mothers, Dangerous Daughters, and the Rhetoric of Child Removal in Burma, Australia, and Indochina," *Balayi: Culture, Law and Colonialism* 3, no. 6 (January 2004): 41–61.

28. C. Bennett, *The Third Annual Report of the Eurasian Ladies' Society, 1877–78* (Rangoon: American Mission, 1878), 10.

29. Marks, *Forty Years*, 134; Purser, *Christian Missions*, 156–158, 239.

30. Henry Yule and Arthur Coke Burnell, *Hobson-Jobson: A Glossary of Colloquial Anglo-Indian Words and Phrases, and of Kindred Terms, Etymological, Historical, Geographical*

and Discursive, new ed., ed. William Crooke (London: John Murray, 1903), 669; Pu Galay, *Kabya pyatthana* (Mandalay: Kyi pwa ye, 1939), 8.

31. See, for example, H. L. Eales, *Census of 1891, Imperial Series (Burma Report)*, vol. 9 (Rangoon: Government Printing, 1892), 212–214.

32. For an insightful analysis of how the word kala became a derogatory term to index foreignness and to refer particularly to Muslims, see Alexandra de Mersan's study of the shifting usage of kala in Arakan. Alexandra de Mersan, "How Muslims in Arakan Became Arakan's Foreigners," in *Current Myanmar Studies, Aung San Suu Kyi, Muslims in Arakan, and Economic Insecurity*, ed. Georg Winterberger and Esther Tenberg (Newcastle: Cambridge Scholars, 2019), 59–98.

33. Aurore Candier, "Mapping Ethnicity in Nineteenth Century Burma: When 'Categories of People' (*lumyo*) Became 'Nations,'" *Journal of Southeast Asian Studies* 50, no. 3 (September 2019), 354–356; Eales, *Census of 1891*, 213n ; John Crawfurd, *Journal of an Embassy from the Governor General of India to the Court of Ava in the Year 1827* (London: Henry Colburn, 1829), 70.

34. Henry Yule, *Narrative of Mission to the Court of Ava in 1855* (London: Smith, Elder, 1858), 142.

35. Albert Fytche, *Burma Past and Present; with Personal Reminiscences of the Country, Volume 1* (London: C. K. Paul, 1878), 325n.

36. According to Yule, his "Bengalee" servants constantly referred to themselves as "kala admi" (black/dark kala) (*Narrative of Mission*, 37), suggesting that a distinction between "black" and "white" kala had been established, at least in the minds of some segments of the kala population in Burma, by the mid-nineteenth century. Yet I am aware of only one nineteenth-century usage of the Burmese terms *kala byu* vs. *kala amè*, the first Anglo-Burmese treaty of Yandabo (1826), for which the main interpreter was the US-born missionary Adoniram Judson.

37. Yule, *Narrative of Mission*, 150–151.

38. Yule, 150.

39. *The Royal Administration of Burma*, compiled by U Tin, translated by Euan Bagshawe, foreword by Michael Aung-Thwin (Bangkok: Ava, 2001), 439–440.

40. Sayyid (male) and sayyida (female) are the Arabic terms used throughout the Muslim world for the descendants of the Prophet Muhammad through his cousin and son-in-law Ali, the husband of Fatima, and their younger son Husayn. The descendants through the elder grandson, Hasan, are known as sharif and sharifa.

41. Cenap Cakmak, "Sayyid (Master)," in Cenap Cakmak, ed., *Islam: A Worldwide Encyclopedia*, vol. 1, A–E (Santa Barbara, CA: ABC-CLIO, 2017), 1403.

42. Thibaut D'Hubert, *In the Shade of the Golden Palace: Alaol and Middle Bengali Poetics in Arakan* (New York: Oxford University Press, 2018), 87. On "Persianization," also see Nile Green, ed., *The Persianate World: The Frontiers of a Eurasian Lingua Franca* (Oakland: University of California Press, 2019).

43. Ulrike Freitag and William G. Clarence-Smith, eds., *Hadhrami Traders, Scholars, and Statemen in the Indian Ocean, 1750s to 1960s* (Leiden, Netherlands: Brill, 1997); Ho, *Graves of Tarim*.

44. R. Michael Feener, "Hybridity and the 'Hadhrami Diaspora' in the Indian Ocean Muslim Networks," *Asian Journal of Social Science* 32, no. 3 (2004), 358; William Gervase Clarence-Smith, "Entrepreneurial Strategies of Hadhrami Arabs in Southeast Asia,

c. 1750s–1950s," in *The Hadhrami Diaspora in Southeast Asia: Identity Maintenance or Assimilation?*, ed. Hassan Ahmed Ibrahim and Ahmed Ibrahim Abushouk (Leiden, Netherlands: Brill, 2009), 136.

45. For biographies of these and other influential pathi, see Shwe Bo U Bo U, *Shwe man a hnit taya pyi bama mutsalin to e atôk patti* (Mandalay: Kyi pwa ye pôn hneik taik, 1959); U Maung Maung Gyi (Mann), *Myanma islam gantha win sa so to gyi*, vol. 1 (Mandalay: Academy of Islamic Historical Research Foundation, 1972); and Aung Zaw, *Taing yin mutslim sa pyu sa so pôggo kyaw mya* (Yangon: Pan we we sa pe, 2013); and D'Hubert, *In the Shade*.

46. Yule, *Narratives*, 151–152.

47. Victor B. Lieberman, "Reinterpreting Burmese History," *Comparative Studies in Society and History* 29, no. 1 (January 1987), 167. Also see Jos Gommans and Jacques Leider, eds., *The Maritime of Burma: Exploring Political, Cultural and Commercial Interaction in the Indian Ocean World, 1200–1800* (Leiden, Netherlands: Koninklijke Nederlandse Akademie van Wetenschappen, 2002).

48. On the concept of bureaucratic capitalists, see Craig J. Reynolds's "Editor's Foreword," in Jennifer W. Cushman, *Family and State: The Formation of a Sino-Thai Tin-mining Dynasty, 1797–1932*, ed. Craig J. Reynolds (Singapore: Oxford University Press, 1991), vii–xvi.

49. Yi Li, *Chinese in Colonial Burma: A Migrant Community in a Multiethnic State* (New York: Palgrave Macmillan, 2017), 27–28.

50. Jörg Armin Schendel, "The Mandalay Economy: Upper Burma's External Trade, c. 1850–90" (PhD diss., University of Heidelberg, 2003).

51. Li, *Chinese in Colonial Burma*, 46–49.

52. Government of Burma, *Report of an Enquiry into the Standard and Cost of Living of the Working Classes in Rangoon* (Rangoon: Labor Statistics Bureau, 1928), 3–12.

53. Lowis, *Census of India 1901*, 111.

54. John Nisbet, *Burma Under British Rule and Before*, vol. 1 (Westminster: Archibald Constable, 1901), 451n1; R. Grant Brown, "The Kadus of Burma," *Bulletin of the School of Oriental Studies, University of London* 1, no. 3 (1920), 2.

55. This interdiction was based on the principle of *kafa'ah* ("sufficiency" or "equivalence"), which stated that a woman's partner should be no less than her social equivalent. The long-standing Hadrami interpretation of this principle was that a sayyida could only marry a sayyid or sharif. See Ho, *Graves of Tarim*, 152–187; Natalie Mobini-Kesheh, *The Hadrami Awakening: Community and Identity in the Netherlands East Indies, 1900–1942* (Ithaca, NY: Cornell University Press, Southeast Asia Publications Program, 1999), 93–98.

56. Jane F. Collier and Sylvia J. Yanagisako, eds., *Gender and Kinship: Essays toward a Unified Analysis* (Stanford, CA: Stanford University Press, 1987); Rubie S. Watson and Patricia Ebrey, eds., *Marriage and Inequality in Chinese Society* (Berkeley: University of California Press, 1991).

57. Ian Brown, *A Colonial Economy in Crisis: Burma's Rice Cultivators and the World Depression of the 1930s* (London: Routledge Curzon, 2005), 15–17, 22, 37.

58. Government of Burma, *Report on the Administration of Burma for the Year 1911–12* (Rangoon: Office of the Superintendent, Government Printing, 1913), 15.

59. John S. Furnivall, *Colonial Policy and Practice: A Comparative Study of Burma and Netherlands India* (New York: New York University Press, 1956), 116.

60. Though much of the scholarship on "milk debt" has been produced in the context of Buddhist Asia, breastfeeding and mother's milk function as symbols of the unrepayable love and sacrifice of the mother in a wide range of contexts. See Alan Cole, *Mothers and Sons in Chinese Buddhism* (Stanford, CA: Stanford University Press, 1998); Jenny B. White, *Money Makes Us Relatives: Women's Labor in Urban Turkey* (London: Routledge, 2004); Reiko Ohnuma, "Debt to the Mother: A Neglected Aspect of the Founding of the Buddhist Nuns' Order," *Journal of the American Academy of Religion* 74, no. 4 (December 2006): 861–901; Andaya, *Flaming Womb*, 129, 214.

61. Clarence-Smith, "Entrepreneurial Strategies," 154.

62. On the eve of the Great Depression of the 1930s, *chettiars* owned roughly one-fifth of land in Lower Burma in the possession of nonagriculturists; later in the decade, the figure shot up to almost one-half. Furnivall, *Colonial Policy*, 111. On *chettiars* in Burma, see I. Brown, *Colonial Economy*, 14–15.

63. George Orwell, *Burmese Days* (New York: Penguin Books, 2001), 126, 285.

2. Mobility and Marital Assimilation

1. Arnold Wright, *Twentieth Century Impressions of British Burma* (London: Lloyd's Greater Britain, 1910), 309–312; Jayde Lin Roberts, *Mapping Chinese Rangoon: Place and Nation among the Sino-Burmese* (Seattle: University of Washington Press, 2016), 64–65; Li, *Chinese in Colonial Burma*, 66–71.

2. See Wright, *Twentieth Century Impressions*, 307–326.

3. "Death of Mr. Choa Chuan Ghiock," *Straits Times* (25 January 1900); Song Ong Siang, *One Hundred Years' History of the Chinese in Singapore*, annotated ed. (Singapore: National Library Board, 2020): 422; Choa Eng Wan v. Choa Giant Tee (1923) in *The Privy Council Cases: Malaysia, Singapore, Brunei, 1875–1990*, ed. Visu Sinnadurai, vol. 1 (London: Sweet & Maxwell, 1990), 197–201.

4. Choa Eng Wan v. Choa Giant Tee (1923), 198–199.

5. Captain Abdul Rahman Khan Laudie, by his agent, Fazal Rahman Khan vs. Ma Kye (1914), 8 BLT, 87, 88.

6. Augustin Bergeron, "The Distribution of Top Incomes in British India: An Exploration of Income Tax Records, 1885–1922" (master's thesis, Paris School of Economics, 2014), 10.

7. S. Anamalay Pillay v. Po La (1906), 3 LBR, 228.

8. S. Anamalay Pillay v. Po La.

9. S. Anamalay Pillay v. Po La, 229.

10. Abdul Razack v. Aga Mahomed Jaffer Bindaneem (1893–1894), 21 Indian Appeals, 56–70, 63, 70.

11. Abdul Razack v. Aga Mahomed Jaffer Bindaneem, 57.

12. Abdul Razack v. Aga Mahomed Jaffer Bindaneem, 57.

13. Abdul Razack v. Aga Mahomed Jaffer Bindaneem, 66–67.

14. Azam Khan v. Daw Khin and Others, BLR 1950, 23 March, 189.

15. Ma Me Gale v. Ma Sa Yi, IA 1904–1905, 72; *Privy Council Judgments on Appeals from India*, vol. 8 (1901–1905), ed. Pandit Upendranath Mukhopadhyay and Babu Priya Sankar Majumdar, (Phowanipore: Sreenath Banerjee, 1908), 743.

16. Andaya, *Flaming Womb*, 146–147; Li Minghuan, "'Sons of the Yellow Emperor' to 'Children of Indonesian Soil': Studying Peranakan Chinese Based on the Batavia Kong Koan Archives," *Journal of Southeast Asian Studies* 34, no. 2 (June 2002): 215–230; Ho, *Graves of Tarim*.

17. Skinner, *Chinese Society*; Skinner, "Creolized Chinese Societies"; Cushman, *Family and State*, 16–26.

18. Alexander Hamilton, *A new account of the East Indies, being the observations and remarks of Capt. Alexander Hamilton*, vol. 2 (Edinburgh: printed by John Mosman, 1727), 51–52.

19. Michael Symes, *An Account of an Embassy to the Kingdom of Ava: Sent by the Governor-General of India in the Year 1795* (London: W. Bulmer, 1800), 72–73.

20. Symes, *Account of an Embassy*, 217, 328–329.

21. Fitz William Thomas Pollok, *Fifty Years' Reminiscences of India: A Retrospect of Travel, Adventure and Shikar* (London: Edward Arnold, 1896), 103–104.

22. Nisbet, *Burma under British Rule*, 250, 253.

23. Kumal Sheriff v. Mi Shwe Ywet (1875), SJLB, 49, 50.

24. Kumal Sheriff v. Mi Shwe Ywet, 50.

25. Government of India, *Census of India, 1911, Report*, 82, 146, 149, 281.

26. For detailed analyses of representations of the allegedly unfettered sexuality of Burmese women by British scholar officials and how they served to rationalize Burmese otherness and British colonial rule, see Jonathan Saha, "The Male State: Colonialism, Corruption and Rape Investigations in the Irrawaddy Delta c.1900," *Indian Economic and Social History Review* 47, no. 3 (July/September 2010): 343–376; and Lucy Delap, "Uneven Orientalisms: Burmese Women and the Feminist Imagination," *Gender and History* 24, no. 2 (August 2012): 389–410.

27. Malek Alloula, *The Colonial Harem* (Minneapolis: University of Minnesota Press, 1986); Marilyn Booth, ed., *Harem Histories: Lived Spaces and Imagined Places* (Durham, NC: Duke University Press, 2010).

28. Chamion Caballero and Peter J. Aspinall, "'Disharmony of Physical, Mental and Temperamental Qualities': Race Crossing, Miscegenation and the Eugenics Movement," in *Mixed Race Britain in The Twentieth Century*, ed. Chamion Caballero and Peter J. Aspinall (London: Palgrave, 2018), 21–52.

29. Great Britain, *Minutes of Evidence Taken before the Royal Commission upon Decentralization in Burma*, vol. 3 (London: H. M. Stationery Office, 1908), 16.

30. Copleston, *Report on the Census*, 71.

31. Reid, *Age of Commerce*; Peletz, *Gender Pluralism: Southeast Asia since Early Modern Times* (New York: Routledge, 2009).

32. On Buddhism and law in Burma generally and the *dhammasat* in particular, see D. Christian Lammerts, *Buddhist Law in Burma: A History of Dhammasattha Texts and Jurisprudence, 1250–1850* (Honolulu: University of Hawai'i Press, 2018).

33. On liberalism and the British Empire, see Sudipta Sen's review essay, "Liberalism and the British Empire in India," *Journal of Asian Studies* 74, no. 3 (August 2015): 711–722.

34. For an outline of nineteenth-century legal reforms and judicial administration in India, see Bernard S. Cohn, "Law and the Colonial State in India," in *Colonialism*

and Its Forms of Knowledge: The British in India (Princeton, NJ: Princeton University Press, 1996); Robert Travers, *Ideology and Empire in Eighteenth Century India: The British Bengal* (Cambridge: Cambridge University Press, 2007), 100–140; Julia Stephens, *Governing Islam: Law, Empire, and Secularism in South Asia* (Cambridge: Cambridge University Press, 2018), 22–56.

35. Furnivall, *Colonial Policy*, 29–33, 62–64, 71–77, 131–37.

36. Lammerts, *Buddhist Law*, 9. See Lammerts's discussion of the colonial production of "Buddhist law" (4–11).

37. For comparison, see Daniel S. Lev, "Colonial Law and the Genesis of the Indonesian State," *Indonesia* 40 (October 1985): 57–74; Susan L. Burns and Barbara J. Brooks, eds., *Gender and Law in the Japanese Imperium* (Honolulu: University of Hawai'i Press, 2014); Surkis, *Sex, Law, and Sovereignty*; and Nurfadzilah Yahaya, *Fluid Jurisdictions: Colonial Law and Arabs in Southeast Asia* (Ithaca, NY: Cornell University Press, 2020).

38. U Gaung, *A Digest of the Burmese Buddhist Law concerning Inheritance and Marriage; being a collection of texts from thirty-six Dhammathats, composed and arranged under the supervision of the Hon'ble U Gaung, C.S.I. ex-Kinwun Mingyi*, 2 vols. (Rangoon: Superintendent, Government Printing, 1899).

39. Government of India, *Census of India, 1911, Report*, 149.

40. U Gaung, *Digest*, 270, 313, 316. On the *Ketujā*, *Vinicchayarāsi*, and *Manugyè dhammasat*, see Lammerts, *Buddhist Law*.

41. Kirichenko, "From Thathanadaw," 37. Uposatha days are Buddhist equivalents of Lent or the Sabbath and are determined by the waxing and waning of the moon.

42. Kirichenko, "From Thathanadaw," 31.

43. Thant Myint-U, *The Making of Modern Burma* (Cambridge: Cambridge University Press, 2001), 244; Eric Tagliacozzo, *The Longest Journey: Southeast Asians and the Pilgrimage to Mecca* (New York: Oxford University Press, 2013), 230.

44. *Ponna* here refers to the Manipuri Brahmin ritualists in Mandalay in the employ mainly of the royal family. However, *ponna* were not always or necessarily Brahmin, and the term has other meanings. See Thant Myint-U, *Making of Modern Burma*, 95.

45. *The Royal Orders of Burma, AD 1598–1855*, 10 vols. [henceforth ROB], ed. Than Tun (Kyoto, 1983–1990), 17 November 1807, 6:535–536; U Hla Tin (compiled), *Myanmar min ôk kyut pôn sa dan nhit Bodaw paya e yaza thit khaw thaw amein daw tan kyi*, vol. 4 (Yangon: She haung sa pe hnit yin kye hmu tana su, 1970), 252–254; Thant Myint-U, 51.

46. Scott Alan Kugle, "Framed, Blamed, and Renamed: The Recasting of Islamic Jurisprudence in Colonial South Asia," *Modern Asian Studies* 35, no. 2 (May 2001): 263.

47. ROB, 11 November 1878, 9:914; Htun Yee, *Yadana bôn kit upade mya / Collection of Upade (Laws and Regulations of Myanmar Last Two of Kings, AD 1853–1885)*, vol. 4 (Toyohashi, Japan: Aichi University, 1999), 69. The *amein daw* read: "Cases concerning the department of joint court: cases concerning pathi, tayoke, and kala lu myo gya residing in Mandalay are to go to the Wun Dauk Min Gyi Maha Min Htin Yaza, Myoza of Pathanago."

48. Candier, "Mapping Ethnicity," 4–5.

49. Victor B. Lieberman, "Ethnic Politics in Eighteenth-Century Burma," *Modern Asian Studies* 12, no. 3 (July 1978), 459–460.

50. Victor B. Lieberman, "Ethnic Hatred and Universal Benevolence: Ethnicity and Loyalty in Precolonial Myanmar, and Britain," *Comparative Studies in Society and History* 63, no. 2 (April 2021): 313.

51. Lieberman, "Ethnic Hatred," 326–327.

52. Victor B. Lieberman, *Strange Parallels*, vol. 1, *Southeast Asia in Global Context, c. 800–1830* (Cambridge: Cambridge University Press, 2003), 40–43, 50, 200.

53. Duara, "Asia Redux," 982.

54. Candier, "Mapping Ethnicity," 11–12.

55. Yoshinari Watanabe, "Ethnic Policy towards Various 'Peoples' in the Early Konbaung Dynasty: Ethnic Awareness in Eighteenth- to Nineteenth-Century Burma," in *The Changing Self-Image of Southeast Asian Society during the 19th and 20th Centuries*, ed. Yoneo Ishii (Tokyo: Toyo Bunko, 2009), 27–53.

56. Lieberman, *Strange Parallels*, 182.

57. ROB, 10:31; Htun Yee, *Collection of Hpyat-sa*, vol. 2 (Yangon: Myanmar Affairs Bureau, Literature Bank, 2006), 2–3, 32–35, 42–45; Lieberman, *Strange Parallels*.

58. Andaya, *Flaming Womb*, 145.

59. Lieberman, *Strange Parallels*, 195.

60. James C. Scott, *Weapons of the Weak: Everyday Forms of Peasant Resistance* (New Haven, CT: Yale University Press, 1987).

61. Li, "Sons."

62. Skinner, "Creolized Chinese Societies," 74–76; Andaya, *Flaming Womb*, 100.

63. Andaya, 97–103.

3. Religion, Race, and Personal Law

1. The judge in this case had followed a precedent set in 1895 in another case, Ahmed and another v. Ma Pwa (1895), concerning a zerbadi family. For a discussion of Ahmed and another v. Ma Pwa (1895), see Chie Ikeya, "The Body of the Burmese Muslim," in *Bodies Beyond Binaries in Colonial and Postcolonial Asia*, ed. Kate Imy, Teresa Segura-Garcia, Elena Valdameri, and Erica Wald (Leiden, Netherlands: Leiden University Press, forthcoming).

2. Ma Le and Ma Me v. Maung Hlaing and Ma Mi (1905), 2 UBR, 1, 1–2.

3. Ma Le and Ma Me v. Maung Hlaing and Ma Mi, 3–4.

4. Mitra Sharafi, "The Marital Patchwork of Colonial South Asia: Forum Shopping from Britain to Baroda," *Law and History Review* 28 (2010): 979–1009.

5. Ma Le and Ma Me v. Maung Hlaing and Ma Mi, 1, 6.

6. Candier, "Mapping Ethnicity," 9.

7. Andrew Huxley, "The Anglo-Buddhist War (1875–1905): The Circumstances under Which Christians Developed Their Theory of Buddhism," *Journal of Comparative Law* 7, no. 2 (2012): 23.

8. William H. Morley, *The Administration of Justice in British India: Its Past History and Present State* (1858), quoted in Kugle, "Framed, Blamed, and Renamed," 300.

9. Kugle, 270.

10. Cohn, *Colonialism*; and James C. Scott, *Seeing Like a State: How Certain Schemes to Improve the Human Condition Have Failed* (New Haven, CT: Yale University Press, 1998).

11. Eales, *Census of 1891*, 4, 193–194.

12. Eales, 197, 203–204.

13. Copleston, *Report on the Census*, 46.

14. Eales, *Census of 1891*, 65, 196.

15. Eales, 72–73, 196.

16. Eales, 55.

17. Hla Aung, "Sino-Burmese Marriages and Conflict of Laws," *Burma Law Institute Journal* 1 no. 1 (Autumn 1958): 25–55; M. B. Hooker, "The 'Chinese Confucian' and the 'Chinese Buddhist' in British Burma, 1881–1947," *Journal of Southeast Asian Studies* 21, no. 2 (September 1990): 384–401.

18. See major race/blood, language, and states/countries divisions in the report of the census of 1891. Eales, *Census of 1891*, 75, 146, 178, 189.

19. Gyanendra Pandey, *The Construction of Communalism in Colonial North India* (Oxford: Oxford University Press 2006), 6, 10.

20. Benedict Anderson, *The Spectre of Comparisons: Nationalism, Southeast Asia, and the World* (New York: Verso, 1998), 318–330.

21. Though census instructions did not explicitly rule out female heads of household, the sample register appended in the report only listed men. The ten houses and one monastery it enumerated were all headed by men. Eales, *Census of 1891*, lvii.

22. Benedict Anderson, *Imagined Communities: Reflections on the Origin and Spread of Nationalism*, rev. ed. (London: Verso, 1991), 166, 184.

23. Lower Burma, *Report on the Census*, 33; Copleston, *Census of British Burma*, 70.

24. Copleston, 71.

25. India, *Census of 1891, Imperial Tables*, 189, 276.

26. Lowis, *Census of India, 1901*, 228, 236, 260; India, *Census of India, 1911, Tables*.

27. Lowis, 111; India, *Census of India, 1931, Report*, 230–232.

28. India, *Census of India, 1931, Report*, 210–211, 231.

29. Lowis, *Census of India*, 95–96.

30. Lowis, 96.

31. India, *Census 1891, Report*, 212; Lowis, 131; India, *Census of India, 1921, Report*, 90–91; India, *Census of 1931, Report*, 60–63.

32. India, *Census of India, 1911, Report*, 82, 281.

33. Eales, *Census of 1891*, 212.

34. Skinner, "Creolized Chinese Societies," 68–70.

35. The descriptive "Straits-born" or "Straits Chinese" were used to differentiate Chinese who were born in the Straits Settlements from the so-called *sinkeh* (literally "new guest").

36. Hugh Clifford and Frank A. Swettenham, *A Dictionary of the Malay Language, Part I* (Taiping: Government Printing Office, 1894), 57.

37. C. A. Vlieland, *British Malaya: A Report on the 1931 Census and Certain Problems of Vital Statistics* (London: Crown Agents for the Colonies, 1932), cited in Charles Hirschman, "The Meaning and Measurement of Ethnicity in Malaysia: An Analysis of Census Classifications," *Journal of Asian Studies* 46, no. 3 (August 1987): 565.

38. The classification sino mestizo was used thereafter in Spanish and American Philippines as a legal category inclusive of mixed nonwhites. See Caroline S. Hau, *The Chinese Question: Ethnicity, Nation, and Region in and beyond the Philippines*, Kyoto CSEAS Series on Asian Studies (Singapore: NUS Press, 2014), esp. 7–25; Richard T. Chu,

Chinese and Chinese Mestizos of Manila: Family, Identity, and Culture, 1860s–1930s (Leiden, Netherlands: Brill, 2010), 240, 265.

39. Yahaya, *Fluid Jurisdictions*, 19. While I have come across unconfirmed references to the use of the category Peranakan in Dutch colonial censuses prior to 1930, thereafter, if a child was a recognized child of, say, a Chinese or Indian father, she or he was by legal definition a "foreign Asiatic." If unrecognized or if the father was native, the child would have been classified as native. See Nederlandsch-Indië, Departement van Economische Zaken, *Volkstelling 1930, Deel VII, Chineezen en andere vreemde oosterlingen in Nederlandsch-Indië* (Batavia: Landsdrukkerij, 1935); Guo-Quan Seng, *Strangers in the Family: Gender, Patriliny, and the Chinese in Colonial Indonesia* (Ithaca, NY: Cornell University Press, 2023).

40. Gouvernement général de l'Indochine, *Annuaire Statistique de L'Indochine*, vol. 1, Recueil de Statistiques relatives aux années 1913 à 1922 (Hanoi: Imprimerie D'Extrême–Orient, 1927), 33; Gouvernement général de l'Indochine, *Annuaire Statistique De L'Indochine*, vol. 7, *1936–1937* (Hanoi: Imprimerie D'Extrême–Orient, 1938), 21–24.

41. For an example of census discussion of "hybrid races," see the entry on "Kachin-Burma Hybrids" in the 1911 census. India, *Census of 1911, Report*, 261.

42. India, 248, 250.

43. India, *Census of India 1931, Report*, 245.

44. India, 207.

45. Jonathan Silk, "The Victorian Creation of Buddhism: Review of Philip C. Almond, 'The British Discovery of Buddhism,'" *Journal of Indian Philosophy* 22, no. 2 (June 1994): 174–195; and Charles Hallisey, "Roads Taken and Not Taken in the Study of Theravada Buddhism," in *Curators of the Buddha: The Study of Buddhism under Colonialism*, ed. Donald Lopez (Chicago: University of Chicago Press, 1995), 31–62.

46. Peter van der Veer, *Imperial Encounters: Religion and Modernity in India and Britain* (Princeton, NJ: Princeton University Press, 2001).

47. For a discussion of a movement, in the 1930s, that rejected the use of zerbadi and advocated for the recognition of "Bamar Muslims," i.e., as native or Indigenous Muslims, see Ayako Saito, "The Formation of the Concept of Myanmar Muslims as Indigenous Citizens: Their History and Current Situation," *Journal of Sophia Asian Studies* 32 (2014): 25–40.

48. Edmund Burke, *The Annual Register: A Review of Public Events at Home and Abroad for the Year 1919* (London: Longmans, Green, 1920), 258.

49. Mersan, "Muslims in Arakan," 85–86.

50. India, *Census of 1931, Report*, 230–231.

51. Khan Bahadur Munshi Ghulam Ahmed Khan, *Census of India 1901, Vol. 23, Kashmir, Part 1: Report* (Lahore: Civil and Military Gazette Press, 1902), 84.

52. Sonia Nishat Amin, *The World of Muslim Women in Colonial Bengal, 1876–1939* (Leiden, Netherlands: Brill, 1996), 6–7.

53. Government of Burma, *Notes and Statistics on Hospitals and Dispensaries in Burma for the Year 1920* (Rangoon: Office of the Superintendent, Government Printing, Burma, 1921), 5.

54. Naono, "Educating Lady Doctors."

55. Government of Burma, *Notes and Statistics on Hospitals and Dispensaries in Burma for the Year 1903* (Rangoon: Office of the Superintendent, Government Printing, Burma,

1904), 9; Government of Burma, *Notes and Statistics on Hospitals and Dispensaries in Burma for the Year 1912* (Rangoon: Office of the Superintendent, Government Printing, Burma, 1913), 14; and Burma, *Notes and Statistics on Hospitals and Dispensaries in Burma for the Year 1921* (Rangoon: Office of the Superintendent, Government Printing, Burma, 1922), 7, 14.

56. Eales, *Census of 1891*, 14–15.

57. J. George Scott and J. P. Hardiman, "Gazetteer of Upper Burma and the Shan States," *Compiled from Official Papers by J. G. Scott, Assisted by J. P. Hardiman, Part 2*, vol. 2 (Rangoon: Superintendent, Government Printing, 1901), 800; J. George Scott and J. P. Hardiman, "Gazetteer of Upper Burma and the Shan States," *Compiled from Official Papers by J. G. Scott, Assisted by J. P. Hardiman, Part 2*, vol. 3 (Rangoon: Superintendent, Government Printing, 1901), 368.

58. Scott and Hardiman, "Gazetteer," *Part 2*, vol. 3, 368; Eales, *Census of 1891*, 20–21; Government of Burma, *Burma Gazetteer, Yamethin District*, vol. B, no. 37 (Rangoon: Office of the Superintendent, Government Printing, 1913), 44.

59. Eales, *Census of 1891*; Government of Burma, *Reports on Public Instruction in Burma for the Year 1891–92* (Rangoon: Superintendent, Government Printing, Burma, 1892), 52.

60. Case, whose parents were in charge of the American Baptist Mission in Myingyan—a town situated about ninety miles southwest of Mandalay—since the early 1880s, lived most of his sixty years in the country. See P. H. J. Lerrigo, ed., *All Kindreds and Tongues: An Illustrated Survey of the Foreign Mission Enterprise of Northern Baptists*, 4th issue (New York: American Baptist Foreign Mission Society, 1940), 28–29.

61. To some leading African American intellectuals, such as Booker T. Washington, who founded the Tuskegee Institute in Tuskegee, Alabama, this model of industrial education was the means to self-supporting trades and businesses. To others, such as W. E. B. du Bois, the model's "denigration of academic subjects" represented a second-class education to keep Black people in low-skilled jobs and preserve the racial caste system. See Andrew E. Barnes, *Global Christianity and the Black Atlantic: Tuskegee, Colonialism, and the Shaping of African Industrial Education* (Waco, Texas: Baylor University Press, 2017).

62. Brayton C. Case, "Christianity in Action on the Village Fields of Burma, or Agriculture in Mission Work," *Missions: A Baptist Monthly Magazine*, January 1921, 139.

63. Legislative Council of Burma, *Proceedings of the Legislative Council of the Governor of Burma*, vol. 17 (Rangoon: Office of the Superintendent, Government Printing, Burma, 1932), 65.

64. Government of India, *Burma Gazetteer, Yamethin District*, vol. A (Rangoon: Superintendent of Government Printing and Stationery, 1934), 43.

65. Firpo and Jacobs, "Taking Children"; Firpo, *Uprooted*.

66. Institutionalized under Sir Arthur Phayre, the first chief commissioner of Burma, the "grant-in-aid" system of education aimed at sidestepping an expensive duplication of schools throughout Burma. U Kaung, "A Survey of the History of Education in Burma before the British Conquest and After," *Journal of Burma Research Society* 46, no. 2 (December 1963): 73, 79–81.

67. The vast majority of these boarding facilities were for primary and secondary schools and were privately run (with government aid).

68. *Anicca* (impermanence), *dukkha* (suffering), and *anattā* (nonself, substancelessness) are the three basic principles of Buddhism, thought to characterize all phenomena.

69. The majority view is that the initial interdiction against the visitation of graves by men and women was replaced by support for the permissibility of visiting graves by men and women. See Obdřej Beránek and Pavel Ťupek, *From Visiting Graves to Their Destruction: The Question of Ziyara through the Eyes of Salafis* (Waltham, MA: Brandeis University, Crown Center for Middle East Studies, 2009).

4. The Alienable Rights of Women

1. WR Vanoogopaul v. R Kristnasawmy Muduliar alias Maung (1905), 3 LBR, 25.

2. WR Vanoogopaul v. Muduliar.

3. Ma Yait v. Maung Chit Maung; and Maung Chit Maung v. Ma Yait and Another (1921), 11 LBR, 155.

4. Taw Sein Ko, "Correspondence on Buddhist Wills," *Journal of Burma Research Society* 7, no. 1 (April 1917): 56–57; Tha Gywe, "Burman Buddhist Wills," *Journal of Burma Research Society* 7, no. 1 (April 1917): 57–69; Taw Sein Ko, "Buddhist Wills," *Journal of Burma Research Society* 7, no. 3 (December 1917): 274–277; Than Tun, "The Legal System in Burma, 1000–1300," *Burma Law Institute Journal* 1, no. 2 (June 1959): 171–184; Andrew Huxley, "Wills in Theravada Buddhist S. E. Asia," *Recueils de la société Jean Bodin pour l'histoire comparative des institutions* 62, no. 4 (1994): 53–92.

5. Great Britain, *Minutes of Evidence*, 50.

6. Ma Yait v. Maung Chit Maung, 158, 160; Chit Maung v. Ma Yait and Ma Noo (1913), 7 LBR, 362, 363.

7. On the Maha Bodhi Society, see Alan Trevithick, *The Revival of Buddhist Pilgrimage at Bodh Gaya (1811–1949): Anagarika Dharmapala and the Mahabodhi Temple* (Delhi: Motilal Banarsidass, 2007). On the International Buddhist Society, see Elizabeth J. Harris, "Ananda Metteyya: Controversial Networker, Passionate Critic," in *A Buddhist Crossroads: Pioneer Western Buddhists and Asian Networks 1860–1960*, ed. Brian Bocking, Phibul Choompolpaisal, Laurence Cox, and Alicia Turner (London: Routledge, 2015), 77–92.

8. Ma Yait v. Maung Chit Maung, 158–159.

9. Ma Yait v. Maung Chit Maung, 158, 160.

10. Eales, *Census of 1891*, 73.

11. Nisbet, *Burma under British*, 2:195.

12. Ma Yait v. Maung Chit Maung, 157–159, 162.

13. Maung Man v. Doramo (1906), 3 LBR, 244, 244–45.

14. Pillay v. Firm, AIR 1914, 63, 64.

15. Saw Maung Gyi v. Ma Thu Kha (1915), 8 BLT, 198.

16. Maung Kyi and others v. Ma Shwe Baw (1929), 7 ILR Ran, 777.

17. Kumal Sheriff v. Mi Shwe Ywet, 50.

18. Sona Ullah v. Ma Kin, AIR 1919, also in 12 BLT 1919, 61.

19. For other examples, see Hussain Unwar v. Fatima Bee (1885), SJLB, 368; Ma Saing v. Kader Moideen (1901) in Aviet Agabeg, ed., *The Burma Law Reports*, vol. 8, pt. 1 (Rangoon: British Burma Press, 1902), 16–18; Ali Asghar v. Mi Kra Hla U (1916), 8 LBR, 461.

20. Queen-Empress v. Nga Pale (1892), *Printed Judgments, Lower Burma, 1893–1900*, 608.

21. See Kugle, "Framed, Blamed, and Renamed," 265–281.

22. Esoof Mahomed Baroocha v. Hayatoonnisa, AIR 1918, also 9 BLT (1918), 120.

23. Kyin Wet v. Ma Gyok, Sabyapo, Seikwan, Saing Thein, Khin Myo (1918), 9 LBR, 179. Also see Hong Ku and Hock Kung v. Ma Thin, *Selected judgements and Ruling of the Court of the Judicial Commissioner and of the Special Court, Lower Burma, 1872–1892* (Rangoon: Office of the Superintendent, Government Printing, 1907), 135; Lee Lim Ma Hock v. Saw Mah Hone & three (1923), 2 ILR Ran, 4; and Phan Tiyok v. Lim Kyin Kauk (1930), 8 ILR Ran, 57. The last case, which entailed a discussion of no less than nineteen precedent cases on Sino-Burmese marriages over almost one hundred pages, is particularly illuminating.

24. In Re Ma Yin Mya and one v. Tan Yauk Pu and two (1927), 5 ILR Ran, 406, 419.

25. Ma Sein v. Ma Pan Nyun and Two (1924), 2 ILR Ran, 94, 97.

26. Ma Sein v. Ma Pan Nyun, 97–98.

27. Tim Stretton and Kirsta J. Kesselring, eds., *Married Women and the Law: Coverture in England and the Common Law World* (New York: Hill & Wang, 1998); Ghosh, *Sex and the Family*, 111.

28. Rachel Sturman, *The Government of Social Life in Colonial India: Liberalism, Religious Law, and Women's Rights* (Cambridge: Cambridge University Press, 2012); Stephens, *Governing Islam*.

29. Ma Pwa v. Yu Lwai & another, AIR 1916, 12, 13. The legality of Ma Yin's adoption was further adjudicated in Ma Pwa v. Ma Yin & another, AIR 1919, 4.

30. Ma Pwa v. Yu Lwai, 13–14.

31. Chan Eu Ghee v. Mrs. Iris Maung Sein alias Lim Gai Po and Two Others, BLR 1953, 294, 299–300.

32. Chan Eu Ghee v. Mrs. Iris Maung Sein, 302.

33. Khoo Sain Ban v. Tan Guat Tean and others, ILR Ran 7 (1929), 234; Li, *Chinese in Colonial Burma*, 95.

34. Chan Eu Ghee v. Mrs. Iris Maung Sein, 300.

35. For select examples of this vast literature, see Lev, "Colonial Law"; Indrani Chatterjee, *Gender, Slavery and Law in Colonial India* (Delhi: Oxford University Press, 1999); Loos, *Subject Siam*; Sturman, *Government of Social Life*; Burns and Brooks, *Gender and Law*; Surkis, *Sex, Law, and Sovereignty*; Yesenia Barragan, *Freedom's Captives: Slavery and Gradual Emancipation on the Colombian Black Pacific* (Cambridge: Cambridge University Press, 2021); Yahaya, *Fluid Jurisdictions*; Seng, *Strangers in the Family*.

36. Peggy Pascoe, *What Comes Naturally: Miscegenation Law and the Making of Race in America* (Oxford: Oxford University Press, 2010); Shah, *Stranger Intimacy*.

37. Gayatri Spivak, "Can the Subaltern Speak?," in *Marxism and the Interpretation of Culture*, ed. Cary Nelson and Lawrence Grossberg (Urbana: University of Illinois Press, 1988), 271–314.

38. Lata Mani, *Contentious Traditions: The Debate on Sati in Colonial India* (Berkeley: University of California Press, 1998); Tanika Sarkar, *Hindu Wife, Hindu Nation: Community, Religion, and Cultural Nationalism* (Bloomington: Indiana University Press, 2001); Patricia Buckley Ebrey, *Women and the Family in Chinese History* (London: Routledge, 2003); Mrinalini Sinha, *Specters of Mother India: The Global Restructuring of an Empire* (Durham, NC: Duke University Press, 2007); Surkis, *Sex, Law, and Sovereignty*.

39. Patriarchal authority, dubbed "traditional," was bolstered and entrenched not just throughout European colonial empires but also in Siam and the Japanese Empire. See Loos, *Subject Siam*; and Burns and Brooks, *Gender and Law*.

40. John Jardine, "Marriage—Its Incidents" (21 July 1882), in *Notes on Buddhist Law* I, 2nd reprint (Rangoon: Office of the Superintendent of Government Printing and Stationery, 1953), 1, 5.

41. Harold Fielding Hall, *The Soul of a People* (Bangkok: White Orchid, 1995; originally published in 1898), 171–172, 189.

42. R. Grant Brown, "Burmese Women," in *Shades of Gold and Green: Anecdotes of Colonial Burmah (1886–1948), Comp. N. Greenwood* (New Delhi: Asian Educational Services, 1995), 216–217.

43. James G. Scott, *Burma: A Handbook of Practical Information*, rev. ed. (London: A. Morning, 1911), 77.

44. Lammerts, *Buddhist Law*.

45. Ma Wun Di and another v. Ma Kin and others, BLR 1908, 14:3, 6.

46. Yahaya, *Fluid Jurisdictions*.

47. Surkis, *Sex, Law, and Sovereignty*, 185.

48. See Lauren Benton, *Law and Colonial Cultures: Legal Regimes in World History, 1400–1900* (Cambridge: Cambridge University Press, 2004); Sharafi, "Marital Patchwork"; Elizabeth Kolsky, *Colonial Justice in British India: White Violence and the Rule of Law* (Cambridge: Cambridge University Press, 2010); and Stephens, *Governing Islam*.

49. Ma E Khin & ors v. Maung Sein & ors (1924), 2 ILR Ran, 495.

50. Ma E Khin & ors v. Maung Sein & ors, 500.

51. Ma E Khin & ors v. Maung Sein & ors, 512.

52. Benton, *Law and Colonial Cultures*, 10.

53. Feener, "Hybridity," 367.

5. Burmese Buddhist Exceptionalism

1. Taw Sein Ko, *Burmese Sketches*. The commission was appointed in response to the growing demand in India for the recruitment and training of Indians to the ICS.

2. Penny Edwards, "Relocating the Interlocutor: Taw Sein Ko (1864–1930) and the Itinerancy of Knowledge in British Burma," *South East Asia Research* 12, no. 3 (November 2004): 309.

3. Gandhi went to Burma in 1902, 1915, and 1929 for the purpose of raising funds from the Indian communities in Burma for the All-India Spinners' Association, which he had founded.

4. Mahatma Gandhi, "Speech at Indians' Meeting, Rangoon," in *The Collected Works of Mahatma Gandhi*, vol. 45, 4 February 1929–11 May 1929 (New Delhi: Publications Division Government of India, 1999), 207–209.

5. Mahatma Gandhi, "Report on Burma P. C. C. Affairs," in *Collected Works of Mahatma Gandhi*, 276–277, 277.

6. Mahatma Gandhi, "To Gujaratis Resident in Burma," in *Collected Works of Mahatma Gandhi*, 286–289, 287.

7. "Bagyi metta tôn e adata mukha dipani,'" *Thuriya Magazine*, September 1926, 100.

8. Known as the "Simon Commission" after its chairman Sir John Simon, the commission's visit to Burma came on the heels of its visit, first, to India in 1927 for the similar purpose of evaluating constitutional reforms.

9. Burma for Burmans League, *Memorandum Submitted to the Indian Statutory Commission by the Burma for Burmans League, Parts I to III* (Rangoon: Impress Press, 1929), IOR/Q/13/1/7, item 22, E-Bur-987: The Burma for Burmans League (31 Jan 1929), 4.

10. *Memorandum Submitted to the Indian Statutory Commission by the Separation League* (Rangoon: National Printing Works, 1929), IOR/Q/13/1/7, item 23, E-Bur-988: The League for the Separation of Burma, iv; Mya U, *Plea for Separation of Burma from India* (Rangoon: Rangoon Times, 1929), 3.

11. Burma for Burmans League, *Memorandum*, 9, 31.

12. "National Deterioration: Myanmar amyo tha mya nyi pa sôk yôk kyin a kyaung," *Myanmar Alin Magazine* 1, no. 2 (February 1912): 133.

13. "Myanmar amyo tha mya nyi pa sôk yôk kyin a kyaung," 134.

14. "Myanmar pyi thi myanmar lu myo tho a bo pyit taik kyaung" (Burma for the Burmans), *Myanmar Alin Magazine* 3, no. 8 (April 1914): 649.

15. Aye Kyaw, *The Voice of Young Burma* (Ithaca, NY: Southeast Asia Program, Cornell University, 1993), 64–65. Niklas Foxeus, "The Buddha Was a Devoted Nationalist: Buddhist Nationalism, *Ressentiment*, and Defending Buddhism in Myanmar," *Religion* 49, no. 4 (May 2019): 661–690.

16. "Reception to U Ottama: Speech at Jubilee Hall," *Supplement to New Burma* (5 July 1922), cited in Donald Eugene Smith, *Religion and Politics in Burma* (Princeton, NJ: Princeton University Press, 1965), 96.

17. Robert H. Taylor, *The State in Myanmar*, rev. and expanded (London: Hurst, 2008; originally published in 1987), 192–195. *Wunthanu* (Pali: *vaṃsānu*) is derived from the Pali words *vaṃsa* and *anurakkhita*, meaning "lineage" and "protected," respectively, or a "protected lineage."

18. Few scholars have probed the parallels and links between Hindu and Buddhist revivalist movements in India and Burma at the turn of the twentieth century. See Emanuel Sarkisyanz, *Buddhist Backgrounds of the Burmese Revolution* (The Hague: Martinus Nijhoff, 1965), 126–127; Foxeus, "Buddha"; and Sana Aiyar, "Revolutionaries, Maulvis, Swamis, and Monks: Burma's Khilafat Moment," in *Oceanic Islam: Muslim Universalism and European Imperialism*, ed. Sugata Bose and Ayesha Jalal (New Delhi: Bloomsbury, 2020), chap. 5.

19. Anne M. Blackburn, *Locations of Buddhism: Colonialism and Modernity in Sri Lanka* (Chicago: University of Chicago Press, 2010), 104–142; Padma Anagol, "Gender, Religion, and Anti-Feminism in Hindu Right Wing Writings: Notes from a Nineteenth Century Indian Woman-Patriot's Text 'Essays in the Service of a Nation,'" *Women's Studies International Forum* 37 (2013): 104–113.

20. Maung Kan Baw, *Proceedings of the Burma Reforms Committee*, vol. 2 (1921), 58.

21. Chie Ikeya, *Refiguring Women, Colonialism, and Modernity in Burma* (Honolulu: University of Hawai'i Press, 2011), 86–88.

22. Joseph Alter, *Gandhi's Body: Sex, Diet, and the Politics of Nationalism* (Philadelphia: University of Pennsylvania Press, 2000); Srirupa Prasad, *Cultural Politics of Hygiene in India, 1890–1940: Contagions of Feeling* (London: Palgrave Macmillan, 2015).

23. Po Hla, *Burma Legislative Council Proceedings* (henceforth BLCP) (31 January 1927), 146.

24. U Pu, BLCP (31 January 1927), 148–149.

25. Kya Gaing, BLCP (1 February 1927), 155–156.

26. U Pu, BLCP, 149.

27. Kyaw Dun, BLCP (1 February 1927), 157.

28. Tun Win, BLCP (1 February 1927), 159.

29. Alison Bashford and Philippa Levine, eds., *The Oxford Handbook of the History of Eugenics* (New York: Oxford University Press, 2010).

30. Tani E. Barlow, *The Question of Women in Chinese Feminism* (Durham, NC: Duke University Press Books, 2004); Asha Nadkarni, *Eugenic Feminism: Reproductive Nationalism in the United States and India* (Minneapolis: University of Minnesota Press, 2014).

31. Tun Win, BLCP, 159.

32. Mabel Mary Agnes Chan-Toon, *A Marriage in Burmah: A Novel* (London: Greening, 1905), 22–23, 25.

33. May Oung and John S. Furnivall, "The Dawn of Nationalism in Burma: The Modern Burman," *Journal of the Burma Research Society* 33, no. 1 (1950): 4.

34. May Oung and Furnivall, "Dawn of Nationalism in Burma." On May Oung, see Alicia M. Turner, *Saving Buddhism: The Impermanence of Religion in Colonial Burma* (Honolulu: University of Hawai'i Press, 2014).

35. Also known as Mrs. M. M. Hla Oung, Mya May was married to the acting controller of Indian treasuries Hla Oung, the first Burmese to serve in such a high position in the Treasury Department. She was the patron and treasurer of the International Buddhist Society. See Turner, *Saving Buddhism*, 66–67.

36. All-Asian Women's Conference, *Report of the All-Asian Women's Conference, First Session, Lahore, 19th to 25th January 1931* (Bombay: Times of India, 1931), 2.

37. I. Brown, *Colonial Economy in Crisis*.

38. The series of peasant uprisings that began on 22 December 1930 came to be known as the Saya San rebellion after Saya San, the prime mover behind them. See Maitrii Aung-Thwin, *The Return of the Galon King: History, Law, and Rebellion in Colonial Burma* (Athens: Ohio University Press, 2011).

39. Burma Government, "Minute Paper, Burma Office," file B3932/38(i), "Burma Riots: Situation Reports," M/3/513, IOR, 1938; E. J. L. Andrew, *Indian Labour in Rangoon* (Oxford: Oxford University Press, 1933), 279–292.

40. Li, *Chinese in Colonial Burma*, 206.

41. Khin Yi, *The Dobama Movement in Burma, 1930–1938* (Ithaca, NY: Southeast Asia Program, Cornell University, 1988), 5; Dobama Asi Ayone, "Nainggan pyu sar zu ahmat 1" (National/Country Reform Series No. 1), reproduced in Khin Yi, *The Dobama Movement in Burma, Appendix* (Ithaca, NY: Southeast Asia Program, Cornell University, 1988), 1–9, 5–6.

42. Khin Yi, *Appendix*, 3.

43. Khin Yi, 8.

44. Margaret Cousins, *The Awakening of Asian Womanhood* (Madras: Ganesh, 1922), 9.

45. Margaret Cousins, "Notes and Comments," *Stri Dharma* 6, no. 2 (December 1922): 17–18.

46. Nehru, *Stri Darpan*, February 1920, quoted in Shobna Nijhawan, "At the Margins of Empire: Feminist-Nationalist Configurations of Burmese Society in the Hindi Public (1917–1920)," *Journal of Asian Studies* 71, no. 4 (November 2012): 8.

47. Mya May, "Burmese Women," *Buddhism* 1, no. 1 (15 September 1903): 62.

48. Mya May, "Burmese Women," 62, 64.

49. Maung Thaw, "Buddhist Activities," *Buddhism* 1, no. 1 (15 September 1903): 174.

50. Lowis, *Census of India, Report*, 68; India, *Census of India, 1911, Report*, 170.

51. All-Asian Women's Conference, *Report*, 38.

52. All-Asian Women's Conference, 45.

53. See, for example, Mi Kin Gale et al v. Mi Kin Gyi, et al (1910), 1 UBR, 1910–13, 42; Maung Shwe Sa v. Ma Mo, AIR (1914) and AIR (1922); Maung Hme v. Ma Sein, AIR (1918); Po Nyein v. Ma Shwe Kin, AIR (1918); San Paw v. Ma Yin, AIR (1920); Maung Tha Dun & 10 v. Ma Thein Yin, 2 ILR Ran (1923), 1; Ma Thein Yin v. Maung Tha Dun & Ten, 2 ILR Ran (1923), 62; Ma Shwe Yin v. Maung Ba Tin, 1 ILR Ran (1923), 343; Maung Po Nyun v. Ma Saw Tin (1925), 3 ILR Ran; Maung Po An v. Ma Dwe (1926), 4 ILR Ran; Ma Paing v. Maung Shwe Hpaw & 8 others (1927), 5 ILR Ran, 296.

54. All-Asian Women's Conference, *Report*, 67–68.

55. All-Asian Women's Conference, 110, 138.

56. All-Asian Women's Conference, 138.

57. Mukherjee, *Indian Suffragettes*, 167–170.

58. *Burma Round Table Conference, 27 November 1931–12 January 1932, Proceedings of the Committee of the Whole Conference* (Rangoon: Superintendent of Government Printing and Stationery, 1932), 39.

59. Mya Sein, "Land of Happy Marriage," *Daily Herald*, 7 December 1931; Mya Sein, "Myanmar amyo thami mya hnit ein daung hmu," *Thuriya*, 1 January 1932.

60. Mya Sein, "Land of Happy Marriage," 8.

61. Mya Sein.

62. Ikeya, *Refiguring Women*.

63. Ann McClintock, "Family Feuds: Gender, Nationalism, and the Family," *Feminist Review*, no. 44 (Summer 1993): 61–80; Sarkar, *Hindu Wife, Hindu Nation*.

64. Kathleen Blee, *Women of the Klan* (Berkeley: University of California Press, 1991); Paola Bachetta and Margaret Power, eds., *Right Wing Women: From Conservatives to Extremists around the World* (London: Routledge 2002); Devaki Menon, *Everyday Nationalism: Women of the Hindu Right in India* (Philadelphia: University of Pennsylvania Press, 2010).

65. The prefixing of the title of newspapers and periodicals to the names of editors and columnists is a practice that remains common to this day. The practice appears to have sprung from the absence of surnames in Burma. To distinguish famous or public figures, who often possess matching names, an identifier of some sort is prefixed to their names.

66. Mya Sein, "The Women of Burma: A Tradition of Hard Work and Independence," *Atlantic Monthly* (February 1958), 123; Mya Sein, "Myanmar amyo thami," in *Myanmar amyo thami kye moun* (Yangon: Myanmar nainggan sape hnik sanezin apwe, 1998; originally published in 1958), 19.

67. Mya Sein, "Towards Independence in Burma: The Role of Women," *Asian Affairs* 3, no. 3 (1972): 297.

68. BLCP (3 February 1927), 214.

69. Quoted in Yin Yin Htun, *Independent Daw San* (Yangon: Pinnya than saung poun hneik taik, 2009), 25.

70. Buddha batha myanmar ma, "Khin aye kyi," *Thuriya Magazine*, August 1918.

71. For an in-depth examination of the life and writings of Daw San, see Chie Ikeya, "The Life and Writing of a Patriotic Feminist: Independent Daw San of Burma," in *Women in Southeast Asian Nationalist Movements*, ed. Susan Blackburn and Helen Ting (Singapore: National University of Singapore Press, 2013), 23–47.

72. Draft Bill, Buddhists Marriage and Divorce Bill, 20 July 1927, IOR/L/PJ 6.1944.2398, 3.

73. Jardine, "Marriage," 6.

74. Quoted in Trudy Jacobsen, *Sex Trafficking in Southeast Asia: A History of Desire, Duty, and Debt* (New York: Routledge, 2017), 65.

75. See the lawsuits cited above in note 53.

76. "Chief and Lesser Wives," *Burma Law Times* 6, no. 4 (April 1913): i–x.

77. Draft Bill, Buddhists Marriage and Divorce Bill, 20 July 1927, IOR/L/PJ 6.1944.2398, 3.

78. Letter from Brahmasree Pandit Suryanarayana Sarma, Bharatasimha, Esquire, B. A., Member of the League of Nations Union (London), President, Burma Buddhist Mission, RGN, to the Secretary to the Government of Burma, Judicial Dept., 24th September 1927, in file Buddhist Marriage and Divorce Bill, Protest Against, L/PJ/6/1944 (P&J 2398, 1927).

6. The Conditions of Belonging

1. House of Commons Parliamentary Papers, *Proceedings of the Burma Round Table Conference*, 27 November 1931 to 12 January 1932 (London: His Majesty's Stationery Office, 1932), 178, 182.

2. Ba Than, BLCP (29 April 1933), 205.

3. Jacques P. Leider, "The Chittagonians in Colonial Arakan: Seasonal and Settlement Migrations," in *Colonial Wrongs and Access to International Law*, ed. Morten Bergsmo, Wolfgang Kaleck, and Kyaw Yin Hlaing (TOAEP, 2020), 177–227.

4. Hnin Mya, BLCP (22 December 1932), 1–3.

5. Kya Gaing, BLCP (2 May 1933), 303.

6. Kya Gaing, 304.

7. Ba Maw and Ba Pe, BLCP (5 May 1933), 412.

8. For examples, see issues of *Thuriya* from September 1931.

9. Shwe Mann Thi, "Amyo anwe ma pyek si yan saung shauk kya gôn," *Mandalay Thuriya*, 21 July 1932, 1–2.

10. Lammerts, *Buddhist Law*.

11. The Nītimañjarī contains about 166 verses, divided into eight chapters. The author, Dyā Dviveda, defines *Nīti* as "that law which bids us to act in a right way and forbids us to act in a wrong way. It consists of both injunctions and prohibitions." See *Niti Manjari of Dya Dviveda*, edited with an introduction, notes, and appendixes by Sitaram Jayaram Joshi (Benares: Saligram Sharma, 1933), xxvi.

12. Ledi Pandita U Maung Gyi, *Nīti manjari kyan*, 1st print (Yangon: Hanthawaddy, 1956).

13. Maung Gyi, *Nīti manjari kyan*, 1–11.

14. On Ledi Pandita U Maung Gyi, see Ikeya, *Refiguring Women*, 60–70.

15. Shwe Mann Thi, "Amyo anwe ma pyek si yan saung shauk kya gôn," 1. *Dhamma* (Burmese *taya*; Sanskrit *dharma*), which is often translated as "law of nature" or "universal law," is a complex concept that has multiple meanings. In general, it refers to the Buddha's teachings, laws, or rules of conduct that express the true nature of reality, lead to the cultivation of virtuous and meritorious conduct, and sustain universal cosmic order and justice. See Lammerts, *Buddhist Law*.

16. Shwe Mann Thi, "Amyo anwe ma pyek si yan saung shauk kya gôn," 1.

17. See Chie Ikeya, "Talking Sex, Making Love: P. Moe Nin and Intimate Modernity in Colonial Burma," in *Modern Times in Southeast Asia, 1920s–1970s*, ed. Susie Protschky and Tom van den Berge (Leiden, Netherlands: Brill, 2018), 136–165.

18. For comparisons, see Stephanie Coontz, *Marriage, a History: From Obedience to Intimacy, or How Love Conquered Marriage* (New York: Penguin Books, 2006); Mytheli Sreenivas, *Wives, Widows, Concubines: The Conjugal Family Ideal in Colonial India* (Bloomington: Indiana University Press, 2008); Barlow, *Question of Women*.

19. Leerom Medovoi, "Dogma-Line Racism: Islamophobia and the Second Axis of Race," *Social Text 111* 30, no. 2 (Summer 2012): 43–74; Stoler, *Carnal Knowledge*; Hanscom and Washburn, *Affect of Difference*.

20. Thein Pe Myint, "Khin Myo Chit," reprinted in *Thein Pe Myint wutthu do baung gyôk thit* (Yangon: Ya pyi sa ôk taik, 1998), 34.

21. Lawyer U Ba Bwa, "Amyo thami mya ko hlit hlyu pyu ta kya myi law," *Kyi Pwa Ye Magazine*, March 1935, 25–27.

22. Ba Bwa, "Amyo thami mya," 25–26.

23. Mani, *Contentious Traditions*; Sarkar, *Hindu Wife, Hindu Nation*; Mrinalini Sinha, *Colonial Masculinity: The "Manly Englishman" and the "Effeminate Bengali" in the Late Nineteenth Century* (Manchester: Manchester University Press, 1995); Chen Chao Ju, "Simpua under the Colonial Gaze: Gender, 'Old Customs,' and the Law in Taiwan under Japanese Imperialism," in Burns and Brooks, *Gender and Law*, 189–218.

24. Po Kyar, "Kala gadaw," *Yôp Shin Lan Hnyun*, May 1934, 26. On Po Kyar, see Khin Maung Nyunt, "U Po Kya's Writings: His Rejoinder to Mr. Noyce," *Texts and Contexts in Southeast Asia: Proceedings of the Texts and Contexts in Southeast Asia Conference, 12–14 December 2001*, part 2 (Yangon: Universities Historical Research Centre, 2003), 137–144.

25. Po Kyar, "Kala gadaw," 31.

26. Mi Nafizunissa alias Ma Enda v. Bodi Rahiman (1913), 6.3 BLT June 1913, 125.

27. Mi Nafizunissa v. Bodi Rahiman, 125, 126.

28. Mi Nafizunissa v. Bodi Rahiman, 128.

29. Riot Inquiry Committee, *Interim Report of the Riot Inquiry Committee* (Rangoon: Office of the Superintendent, Government Printing and Stationery, 1939), 13; Riot Inquiry Committee, *Final Report of the Riot Inquiry Committee* (Rangoon: Office of the Superintendent, Government Printing and Stationery, 1939), 1–2, 6–7.

30. Riot Inquiry Committee, *Final Report*, 11.

31. Riot Inquiry Committee, 13.

32. The Buddhist Women's Special Marriage and Succession Act (Burma Act XXIV 1939), NAD 1/1 (B) Acc 877, 15–24.

33. Riot Inquiry Committee, *Final Report*, 319.

34. Riot Inquiry Committee, 19. The translation is my own.

35. Riot Inquiry Committee, 281, 284–285.

36. Riot Inquiry Committee, xxxii–xxxix.

37. IOR/M/5/12, B(P) "Memorandum of the Burma Association to the President and Members of the Riot Inquiry Committee," 26 October 1938, 3.

38. Hans-Bernd Zoellner, ed., *Myanmar Literature Project Working Paper No. 10:12, Material on Thein Pe: Indo-Burman Conflict* (University Passau, 2006).

39. Ikeya, *Refiguring Women*, 88–89.

40. Thein Pe Myint, *Kala-bama taik pwe* (Yangon: Nagani 1938), 12.

41. Thein Pe Myint, *Kala-bama taik pwe*, 14, 17.

42. Riot Inquiry Committee, *Interim Report*, 28.

43. Riot Inquiry Committee, *Final Report*, 287, 289–290.

44. Riot Inquiry Committee, 273.

45. Riot Inquiry Committee, 3–4.

46. Bama amyo thami me me, "Amyo thami ta u," *Kyi Pwa Ye*, July 1939, 24.

47. Ikeya, *Refiguring Women*, 76–80.

48. Bama amyo thami me me, "Amyo thami ta u," 24.

49. *Khoda* or *khuda*, meaning "god" in Urdu.

50. Bama amyo thami me me, "Amyo thami ta u," 25.

51. Bama amyo thami me me, 25.

52. On the press and the famous husband-wife partnership, see Ludu Daw Amar, *Kyun ma ye te thu bawa Ludu U Hla* (Yangon: Kyi pwa ye sa pe, 2009), 326–329.

53. Hla, "Meik set," in Pu Galay, *Kabya pyatthana*, 6.

54. Pu Galay, *Kabya pyatthana*, 39, 57–58.

55. Hla, "Meik set," 6.

56. Pu Galay, *Kabya pyatthana*, 11–12.

57. Pu Galay, 89.

58. Pu Galay, 100–105.

59. Pu Galay, 90–91, 95–98, 116–117.

60. Buddhist Women's Special Marriage and Succession Act, 15–19. The permissible objections had to be made on the grounds that one (or both) of the parties were underage, of unsound mind, or, for the female party, already married.

61. Pu Galay, *Kabya pyatthana*, 132.

62. Gupta, *Sexuality, Obscenity, Community*, 298. Also see Kumari Jayawardena and Malathi de Alwis, eds., *Embodied Violence: Communalising Women's Sexuality in South Asia* (New Delhi: Kali for Women, 1996).

63. Micheline R. Lessard, "'Organisons-nous! Racial Antagonism and Vietnamese Economic Nationalism in the Early Twentieth Century," *French Colonial History* 8 (2007): 184–188; Pairaudeau, *Mobile Citizens*, 222–227.

64. Pascoe, *What Comes Naturally*; Shah, *Stranger Intimacy*.

65. Naoki Sakai, "Introduction: Nationality and the Politics of the 'Mother Tongue,'" in *Deconstructing Nationality*, ed. Naoki Sakai, Brett de Bary, and Iyotani Toshio (Ithaca, NY: East Asia Program, Cornell University, 2005), 33.

66. Though the question of how the nation and its citizens were imagined has preoccupied historians of Southeast Asia, few have interrogated the centrality of gender and sexuality to this process. On the feminist rejoinder to probe the embodied, inter-

sectional dynamics of nationalism and state-formation in Southeast Asia, see Aihwa Ong and Michael Peletz, eds., *Bewitching Women, Pious Men: Gender and Body Politics in Southeast Asia* (Berkeley: University of California Press, 1995); Raquel A. G. Reyes, *Love, Passion, and Patriotism: Sexuality and the Philippine Propaganda Movement, 1882–1892* (Seattle: University of Washington Press, 2008); and Michael G. Peletz, "Gender, Sexuality, and the State in Southeast Asia," *Journal of Asian Studies* 71, no. 4 (2012): 895–917.

67. Furnivall, *Colonial Policies and Practices*, 157. See Ikeya's discussion of the concept of the "plural society" in *Refiguring Women*, 5–8.

68. Anderson, *Imagined Communities*; Anderson, *Spectre of Comparisons*.

69. Historians of Thailand have made significant inroads in dismantling the long-held view of nationalism as necessarily anticolonial, highlighting how nationalists deployed, under the banner of anticolonialism, the very tools of colonial governance for political and territorial aggrandizement. See Thongchai Winitchakul, *Siam Mapped: A History of the Geo-Body of a Nation* (Honolulu: University of Hawai'i Press, 1994); Loos, *Subject Siam*.

70. Barlow, *Question of Women*, 4.

71. Barlow, 114.

72. Pandey, *Construction of Communalism*; Nikhil Pal Singh, "On Race, Violence, and So-Called Primitive Accumulation," *Social Text* 34, no. 3 (September 2016): 27–50.

73. Riot Inquiry Committee, *Final Report*, 218–219.

74. Swami Jagadiswarananda, *Hinduism Outside India* (Rajkot: Kathiawar, 1945), 77.

75. Though born in India and brought to Burma by his Burma-born parents only at the age of three, Raschid belonged to a zerbadi family with deep roots in the country. On Raschid, see Bilal M. Raschid, *The Invisible Patriot: Reminiscences of Burma's Freedom Movement* (Bethesda, MD: Raschid, 2015); Maung Maung, "M. A. Raschid," *Guardian* 3, no. 4 (December 1956), reproduced in *Maung Maung: Gentleman, Scholar, Patriot*, ed. Robert H. Taylor (Singapore: ISEAS, 2008), 229–242, 237.

76. Josef Silverstein and Julian Wohl, "University Students and Politics in Burma," *Pacific Affairs* 37, no. 1 (Spring 1964): 52; Aye Kyaw, *Voice of Young Burma*, 63.

77. Raschid, *Invisible Patriot*, 26–28.

78. Patricia Hill Collins, "The Tie That Binds: Race, Gender, and US Violence," *Ethnic and Racial Studies* 21, no. 5 (September 1998): 932, 924.

79. Parsis are an ethnic group that traces itself back to Persian followers of the prophet Zoroaster (or Zarathustra), who emigrated to India to avoid religious persecution by Muslims.

80. According to Mitra Sharafi's list of Parsi tombstones from Burma, the inscription on his tombstone reads: "Mr. P. D. Patel. Born 14.10.1874. Died 26.11.1961." See Mitra Sharafi, "Parsi Tombstones from Burma," https://hosted.law.wisc.edu/wordpress/sharafi/files/2013/04/Burmese-Tombstones-as-of-8-Dec-2014.pdf.

81. IOR/Q/13/1/7, item 18, E-Bur-979: P. D. Patel, Barrister-at-law, Rangoon (1929?), 9.

82. P. D. Patel, 3.

83. P. D. Patel, 10.

84. P. D. Patel, 10

85. *Memorandum Submitted to the Indian Statutory Commission*, 11.

86. Liisa H. Malkki, *Purity and Exile: Violence, Memory, and National Cosmology among Hutu Refugees in Tanzania* (Chicago: University of Chicago Press, 1995); David P. Chandler,

Voices from S-21: Terror and History in Pol Pot's Secret Prison (Berkeley: University of California Press, 1999); Butalia, *Other Side of Violence*; Gail Hershatter, *The Gender of Memory: Rural Women and China's Collective Past* (Berkeley: University of California Press, 2011).

87. Indrani Chatterjee, *Forgotten Friends: Monks, Marriages, and Memories of Northeast India* (New Delhi: Oxford University Press, 2013), 365.

88. Chatterjee, *Forgotten Friends*, 366–367.

89. Das, *Life and Words*, 215–216.

7. War, Occupation, and Collaboration

1. Sunil Amrith, "Reconstructing the 'Plural Society': Asian Migration between Empire and Nation, 1940–1948," *Past and Present*, supplement 6 (2011): 255; Kratoska, *Asian Labor*; Christopher Bayly and Tim Harper, *Forgotten Armies: The Fall of British Asia, 1941–1945* (Cambridge: Belknap Press of the Harvard University Press, 2006); Gregg Huff, *World War II and Southeast Asia: Economy and Society under Japanese Occupation* (Cambridge: Cambridge University Press, 2020).

2. Tani Barlow, "Colonialism's Career in Postwar China Studies," *Positions: East Asia Critique* 2, no. 1 (Spring 1993): 224–267.

3. Duara, "Discourse of Civilization."

4. Nakano, *Japan's Colonial Moment*, 19.

5. Bunka hōkōkai, *Dai tōa sensō rikugun hōdō han in shuki: Biruma kanteisen* (Tokyo: Kōdansha, 1942), 148.

6. Much scholarship exists on Japan's imperial policies of *dōka* and *kōminka*. For recent examples, see Ching, *Becoming "Japanese"*; N. A. Kwon, *Intimate Empire*; Kawanishi, *Teikoku nihon*; Fujitani, *Race for Empire*; Hanscom and Washburn, *Affect of Difference*.

7. Ota Tsunozo, *Biruma ni okeru nihon gunseishi no kenkyū* (Tokyo: Yoshigawa Kobunkan, 1967), 189; Ishii Hitoshi, "Nihon gunseika ni okeru nanpō senryōchi no kyōiku seisaku ni kansuru kisoteki kenkyū," *Bulletin of Okayama Prefectural Junior College* 1 (1994): 68; Seki Masaaki, *Nihongo kyōikushi kenkyū josetsu* (Tokyo: Suri E Network, 2004; originally published in 1997), 60.

8. Biruma nihongo kyōkasho hensan iinkai, *Nippon go tokuhon II* (Rangoon: Biruma koku kyōiku eisei shō, 1944), 58; Biruma nihongo kyōkasho hensan iinkai, *Nippon go tokuhon III* (Rangoon: Biruma koku kyōiku eisei shō, 1944), 85.

9. Willard Elsbree, *Japan's Role in Southeast Asian Nationalist Movements, 1940–1945* (Cambridge, MA: Harvard University Press, 1953); Josef Silverstein, ed., *Southeast Asia in World War II: Four Essays* (New Haven, CT: Yale University Southeast Asian Studies, 1966); Alfred McCoy, ed., *Southeast Asia under Japanese Occupation* (New Haven, CT: Yale University Southeast Asia Studies, 1985); Paul H. Kratoska, *The Japanese Occupation of Malaya, 1941–1945: A Social and Economic History* (Honolulu: University of Hawai'i Press, 1997); Nicholas Tarling, *The Japanese Occupation of Southeast Asia, 1941–1945* (Honolulu: University of Hawai'i Press, 2001).

10. Aung San Suu Kyi, *Aung San of Burma: A Biographical Portrait by His Daughter* (Edinburgh: Kiscadale, 1991), 21.

11. Ba Maw, *Breakthrough in Burma: Memoirs of a Revolution, 1939–1946* (New Haven, CT: Yale University Press, 1968), 274, 276.

12. Ba Maw, *Breakthrough*; Thein Pe Myint, *What Happened in Burma: The Frank Revelations of a Young Burmese Revolutionary Leader Who Has Recently Escaped from Burma to India* (Allahabad: Kitabistan, 1943); Aung San, *Burma's Challenge* (Rangoon: New Light of Burma, 1946); Thakin Nu, *Nga hnit yadi bama pyi* (Yangon: Myanmar Alin, 1946); Thakin U Thein Pe Myint, *Ko twe hmattan* (Yangon: Taing Chit, 1950); Thein Pe Myint, *Sit atwin kayi the* (Rangoon: Shumawa sa ôk taik, 1952); Thakin Nu, *Burma under the Japanese: Pictures and Portraits*, ed. and trans. with an introduction by J. S. Furnivall (London: Macmillan, 1954).

13. Maung Maung, "The Resistance Movement," *The Guardian* 2, no. 5 (March 1954): 9.

14. Maung Maung, "Resistance Movement," 10.

15. Htin Aung, *The Stricken Peacock: Anglo-Burmese Relations, 1752–1948* (The Hague: Martinus Nijhoff, 1965), 112.

16. Peter Post and Elly Touwen-Bouwsma, eds., *Japan, Indonesia, and the War: Myths and Realities* (Leiden, Netherlands: KITLV, 1997); Remco Raben, ed., *Representing the Japanese Occupation of Indonesia: Personal Testimonies and Public Images in Indonesia, Japan, and the Netherlands* (Amsterdam: Waanders, 1999); and Ronald D. Klein, *The Other Empire: Literary Views of Japan from the Philippines, Singapore, and Malaysia* (Quezon City: University of Philippines Press, 2008).

17. William Bradley Horton, "Sexual Exploitation and Resistance: Indonesian Language Representations since the Early 1990s of the Japanese Occupation History," *Asia-Pacific Forum* 28 (2005/6): 71.

18. Hla Pe, *Narrative of the Japanese Occupation of Burma*, recorded by U Khin, foreword by Hugh Tinker (Ithaca, NY: Southeast Asia Program, Cornell University, 1961), 77.

19. "Sein Kyi nau . . . Sein Kyi / lin yu pek sek the / master-gyi Tokyo pyan / baik ta lon ne kyan." Sein Kyi, the main character of a popular book by Thu Kha, is an archetypical *japan gadaw* who marries a Japanese soldier during the occupation out of opportunism, not love. Tharaphi Than, *Women in Modern Burma* (New York: Routledge, 2013), 144–145.

20. N. A. Kwon, *Intimate Empire*, 200.

21. Won Zoon Yoon, "Japan's Occupation of Burma, 1941–1945" (PhD diss., New York University, 1971), 195–204.

22. Minamida Midori, "Nihon senryō ni okeru Biruma sakka kyōkai kikanshi 'sakka' no yakuwari ni tsui te," *Ōsaka Daigaku Sekai Gengo Kenkyū Sentā ronshū* 5 (2011): 143–171; Minamida Midori, "Biruma sakka tachi no 'nihon jidai,'" *Ōsaka Daigaku Sekai Gengo Kenkyū Sentā ronshū* 7 (2012): 285–311.

23. Tanaka Kakuei, "Biruma gawa shusai utage ni okeru Tanaka naikakusōri daijin aisatsu, 1974 nen 11 gatsu 7 nichi," *Tanaka naikakusōri daijin enzetsu shū* (Tokyo: Nihon kōhō kyōkai, 1975), 569–571.

24. On the relationship between Ottama and Ito, see Takano Ikuro, *Jūgodai Itō Jirōzaemon Suketami tsuisōroku* (Nagoya: Matsuzakaya 1977); Ito Toshikatsu, "Ottama sōjō to Nagai Gyōji Shōnin," in *Bukkyō o meguru Nihon to Tōnan Ajia Chiiki*, ed. Osawa Koji (Tokyo: Bensei Shuppan, 2016), 127–142; and Zaw Linn Aung, "Ito Jirozaemon Suketami."

25. Ito Jirozaemon Suketami, "Indo Biruma shisatsu dan," lecture given at Tōa Kenkyū Jo, 20 December 1938, published in Ito Jirozaemon Suketami, *Indo Biruma shisatsu dan* (Tokyo: Tōa Kenkyū Jo, 1938), 11.

26. Burma Intelligence Bureau, *Burma during the Japanese Occupation*, vol. 2 (Simla, India: Government of India, 1944), 145.

27. Hla Pe, *Narrative*, 37, 39.

28. McCoy, *Southeast Asia*; and Jeremy Yellen, *The Greater East Asia Co-Prosperity Sphere: When Total Empire Met Total War* (Ithaca, NY: Cornell University Press, 2019).

29. Yellen, *Greater East Asia*, 21.

30. I. Kwon, "Feminists Navigating."

31. Leo T. S. Ching, *Anti-Japan: The Politics of Sentiment in Postcolonial East Asia* (Durham, NC: Duke University Press, 2019), 120.

32. Ching, *Anti-Japan*, 6.

33. Ching, 129.

34. See, for example, N. A. Kwon, *Intimate Empire*; Ambaras, *Japan's Imperial Underworlds*; Ai Baba, "Policies, Promoters, and Patterns of Japanese-Korean and Japanese-Taiwanese Marriages in Imperial Japan: Making a Case for Inclusive History" (PhD diss., Cornell University, 2019); Kim, *Imperial Romance*; and Ching, *Anti-Japan*.

35. E. Patricia Tsurumi, *Japanese Colonial Education in Taiwan, 1895–1945* (Cambridge, MA: Harvard University Press, 1977); Tani Yasuyo, *Nihongo kyōiku to kindai nihon* (Tokyo: Iwata Shoin, 2006), 200–221; Kate McDonald, "Speaking Japanese: Language and the Expectation of Empire," in Hanscom and Washburn, *Affect of Difference*, 159–179; Furukawa Noriko, "Kyōiku no seido to kōzō," in *Nihon shokuminchi kenkyū no ronten*, ed. Nihon Shokuminchi Kenkyūkai (Tokyo: Iwanami Shoten, 2018), 132–142.

36. Quoted in Kawamura Minato, *Umi wo watatta nihongo: Shokuminchi no "kokugo" no kikan* (Tokyo: Seidōsha, 2004), 108.

37. "Nanpō kyōeiken no kyōiku zadan kai," *Kōa Kyōiku* 1, no. 3 (1942): 78–81; Kojima Masaru, "Nanyō ni okeru nihonjin gakko to dōtai," *Tōnan Ajia Kenkyū* 18, no. 3 (December 1980): 460–475; Kojima Masaru, *Dainiji sekai taisenzen no zaigai shitei no kyōikuron no keifu* (Kyoto: Ryūkoku Gakkai, 1993), esp. 153–184.

38. Nihongo kyōiku shinkō kai, "Nanpō kensetsu to nihongo fukyū," *Nihongo* 2, no. 5 (May 1942): 86–104.

39. Sekupan Kai, ed., *Sekupan: Biruma nihongo gakkō no kiroku, 1942–1945* (Tokyo: Shudōsha, 1970), 10.

40. Burma Intelligence Bureau, *Burma during the Japanese Occupation*, vol. 1 (Simla, India: Government of Burma, 1943), 42.

41. Burma Intelligence Bureau, *Japanese Occupation*, 2:48.

42. Burma Intelligence Bureau, 2:46.

43. Ishii, "Nihon gunseika," 69, 72.

44. Matsunaga Noriko, *Nihon gunseika no maraya ni okeru nihongo kyōiku* (Tokyo: Kazama Shobō, 2002), 30, 60; Seki, *Nihongo kyōikushi*, 61.

45. Tani, *Nihongo kyōiku*, 200.

46. T. Ota, *Biruma ni okeru*, 190–191; Ishii, "Nihon gunseika," 69–77.

47. Sekupan Kai, *Sekupan*, 23.

48. See Saya Shiraishi, introduction to Takao Fusayama, *A Japanese Memoir of Sumatra 1945–1946: Love and Hatred in the Liberation War* (Ithaca, NY: Cornell Modern Indonesia Project, 1993); Ota Atsushi, "Kioku sareru Indoneshia: 1945–70 nen no Nihon shōsetsu ni egakareru senji senryō," *Journal of Asia Pacific Studies*, no. 20 (February 2013): 121–136.

49. Sekupan Kai, *Sekupan*, 23.

50. Sekupan Kai, 242.

51. Sekupan Kai, 282.

52. Sekupan Kai, 163.

53. Sekupan Kai, 86.

54. Vicente L. Rafael, *Contracting Colonialism: Translation and Christian Conversion in Tagalog Society under Early Spanish Rule* (Ithaca, NY: Cornell University Press, 1988), 8, 21.

55. Sekupan Kai, *Sekupan*, 2.

56. Sekupan Kai, 429.

57. Sekupan Kai, 73.

58. Sekupan Kai, 24.

59. Jikkoku Osamu, *Myanmā monogatari: Hitowa naze sensō o surunoka* (Tokyo: Sanseidō, 1995), 171.

60. Jikkoku, *Myanmā monogatari*, 168

61. Sekupan Kai, *Sekupan*, 232–233.

62. "Watashi jūroku manshū musume / haruyo san gatsu yukidoke ni / in shun hwa ga saitanara / o yome ni ikimasu tonarimura / Wan san mattete chōdai ne."

63. Michael K. Bourdaghs, "Japan's Orient in Song and Dance," in *Sino-Japanese Transculturation: From the Late Nineteenth Century to the End of the Pacific War*, ed. Richard King, Cody Poulton, and Katsuhiko Endo (Lanham, MD: Lexington Books, 2012), 178.

64. Hla Pe, *Narrative*, 78.

65. Ba Maw, *Breakthrough*, 283.

66. Todd A. Henry, "Assimilation's Racializing Sensibilities: Colonized Koreans ad *Yobos* and the '*Yobo*-ization' of Expatriate Japanese," in Hanscom and Washburn, *Affect of Difference*, 85.

67. Burma Intelligence Bureau, *Japanese Occupation*, 2:152.

68. Burma Intelligence Bureau, 2:139.

69. Hla Pe, *Narrative*, 40.

70. Burma Intelligence Bureau, *Japanese Occupation*, 1:23–25.

71. Ba Maw, *Breakthrough*, 186–192.

72. Theippan Maung Wa, *Wartime in Burma: A Diary, January to June 1942*, ed. and trans. from Burmese by L. E. Bagshawe and Anna J. Allott (Athens: Ohio University Press, 2009), 179–180.

73. Sekupan Kai, *Sekupan*, 560.

74. Sekupan Kai, 566.

75. Burma Intelligence Bureau, *Japanese Occupation*, 1:26.

76. On the Japanese army's persecution of Chinese people in Southeast Asia, see Hayashi Hirofumi, *Kakyō gyakusatsu: Nihongun shihaika no marē hantō* (Tokyo: Suzusawa Shoten, 1992).

77. IOR M/4/2964, B/F& FA 14/46(26), China: Kayan murder case, 1947.

8. Ties That Un(Bind) Asians

1. Nakano, *Japan's Colonial Moment*, 208.

2. Burma Frontier Service, "The War Effort of the Naga Hills District of Burma," 5 February 1944, Scheduled Areas, 1943, NAD.

3. Barclay, *Outcasts of Empire*, 156. For an analysis of the tale of Sayon, also see Ching, *Anti-Japan*, 120–123.

4. Mary Louise Pratt, *Imperial Eyes: Travel Writing and Transculturation* (London: Routledge, 1992), 95–98.

5. Kristin Roebuck, "Science without Borders? The Contested Science of 'Race Mixing' circa World War II in Japan, East Asia, and the West," in *Who Is the Asianist? The Politics of Representation in Asian Studies*, ed. Will Bridges, Nitasha Tamar Sharma, and Marvin D. Sterling (Columbia University Press, 2022), 109–124.

6. Roebuck, "Science without Borders," 112.

7. Oguma Eiji, *Tan itsu minzoku shinwa no kigen—"Nihonjin" no jigazō no keifu* (Tokyo: Shinyosha, 1995); Kawanishi, *Teikoku nihon*, 235–236, 244–245.

8. Naosuke Warabe, *Biruma kō* (Tokyo: Tōfūkaku 1938), 90.

9. Warabe, *Biruma kō*, 116–122.

10. Takami Jun, *Biruma no inshō* (1943), in *Nanpō chōyō sakka sōsho, Biruma hen*, vol. 2, edited by Kimura Kazuaki and Takematsu Yoshiaki (Tokyo: Ryūkei Shosha, 2010), 37.

11. Sakakiyama Jun, *Biruma no asa* (Tokyo: Nambokusha, 1963; originally published in 1943); also republished in *Nanpō chōyō sakka sōsho, Biruma hen*, vol. 5, edited by Kimura Kazuki and Takematsu Yoshiaki (Tokyo: Ryūkei Shosha, 2010).

12. Sakakiyama, *Biruma no asa*, 289.

13. N. A. Kwon, *Intimate Empire*, 200.

14. Yoshiichi Shigemitsu, *Gunzoku Biruma monogatari* (Tokyo: Ōshisha, 1973).

15. Yoshiichi, *Gunzoku Biruma monogatari*, 10.

16. See, for example, Itai Takeo, *Kekkon kokusaku no teishō* (Tokyo: Taiyōdō Shobō, 1939), 13–16; Matsuoka Juhachi, *Dai tōa minzoku mondai* (Tokyo: Showa Shobō, 1942), 357–363. For scholarship on the history of *konketsuji*, see the special issue "Rekishi no naka no ikokujin/nihonjin no kodomo," *Rekishi Hyōron* 815 (March 2018), esp. Lee Jeong-Seon, "Naisen kekkon no kodomo tachi: naichi jin to chosen jin no hazama de," 42–55; and Roebuck, "Science without Borders."

17. Kiyono Kenji, "Dai nanyō ni okeru konketsu no mondai," *Nanyō Keizai Kenkyū* 1, no. 7 (July 1942): 69.

18. Kamoto Itsuko, *Kokusai kekkon no tanjō: "Bunmei koku nihon" e no michi* (Tokyo: Shiyōsha, 2001).

19. Huang Chia-chi, "Nihon tōchi jidai ni okeru 'uchidai-domo kon' no kōzō to tenkai," *Hikaku kazokushi kenkyū* 27 (March 2013): 129.

20. Endo Masataka, *Kindai nihon no shokuminchi tōchi ni okeru kokuseki to koseki: Manshū, Chōsen, Taiwan* (Tokyo: Akashi Shoten, 2010), 124.

21. See Endo, *Kindai nihon*; David Chapman and Karl Jakob Krogness, eds., *Japan's Household Registration System and Citizenship: Koseki, Identification, and Documentation* (London: Routledge, 2014), 79–92; J.-S. Lee, "Naisen kekkon."

22. Baba, "Policies, Promoters, and Patterns."

23. Yamada Hidezo, *Biruma no seikatsu* (Tokyo: Hōun sha, 1944), 55–56.

24. Yamada, *Biruma no seikatsu*, 55–57.

25. Thet Tun, *Than to amyin: Bilingual Essays of Retired Ambassador U Thet Tun* (Yangon: Meik Kaung, 2000), 155–165.

26. See, for example, the story of Ma E in Nemoto Yuriko, *Sokoku wo senjou ni sarete: Biruma no sasayaki* (Fukuoka: Sekifusha, 2000), 13–29.

27. Burma Intelligence Bureau, *Japanese Occupation*, 2:164.

28. Government of Burma, Reconstruction Department, Simla, Letter from D. O. Leyden to T. L. Hughes, Public Adviser, Simla, dated 2 December 1944, forwarding a copy of Father D. McAlindon and Capt. O. H. Molloy's joint note on the activities of the Kachins in the anti-Japanese campaign, Scheduled Areas, 1943, NAD.

29. DC CAO, IV Corps, Sd/J. F. Franklin, Reports from the Chin Hills, dated 3 January 1944 and 21 February 1944, Chief Civil Affairs Office (B), NAD.

30. Greg Dvorak, "Who Closed the Sea? Archipelagoes of Amnesia between the United States and Japan," in ed. Lon Kurashige, *Pacific America: Histories of Transoceanic Crossings* (Honolulu: University of Hawai'i Press, 2017), 229–246.

31. Barclay, *Outcasts of Empire*.

32. ann-elise lewallen, "Intimate Frontiers": Disciplining Ethnicity and Ainu Women's Sexual Subjectivity in Early Colonial Hokkaido," in Hanscom and Washburn, *Affect of Difference*, 24.

33. Kyaw Win Maung, *Japan pet sit taw hlan ye ledi thama mya* (Yangon: Thiha Yadana, 2008, originally published in 1967), chap. 33.

34. Kyaw Win Maung, *Japan pet sit*, chap. 12

35. At the behest of the Japanese, the Ba Maw administration organized a corps of laborers known as "the Great Sweat Army" (*chwe tat gyi*) to supplement the prisoners of war.

36. E. Bruce Reynolds, "History, Memory, Compensation, and Reconciliation: The Abuse of Labor along the Thailand-Burma Railway," in Kratoska, *Asian Labor*, 329.

37. Lin Yone Thit Lwin, *Yodayar myanmar mi yatha lan ko twe chwe tat hmattan* (Yangon: Sape Beikman Apwe, 1991), 10.

38. Lin Yone Thit Lwin, *Yodayar myanmar mi yatha*, 478.

39. Maung Htin, *Nga Ba* (Yangon: Pyi Thu Sa Pe, 1957), 68, 85–87.

40. Maung Htin, *Nga Ba*, 146–157.

41. Jikkoku, *Myanmā monogatari*, 79; Kyaw Win Maung, *Japan pet sit*, chap. 31.

42. Burma Intelligence Bureau, *Japanese Occupation*, 1:67, 2:198.

43. P. D. Patel, "Just Fifty Years Ago," *The Guardian* 5, no. 7 (July 1958): 15.

44. Kyaw Win Maung, *Japan pet sit*, 30–32.

45. Burma Intelligence Bureau, *Japanese Occupation*, 1:26.

46. For a review of these debates, see Edward Vickers and Mark R. Frost, "Introduction: The 'Comfort Women' as Public History—Scholarship, Advocacy, and the Commemorative Impulse," in "The 'Comfort Women' as Public History," ed. Edward Vickers and Mark R. Frost, special issue, *Japan Focus: The Asia-Pacific Journal* 19, no. 5 (March 2021). On a recent dispute over whether comfort women should be analyzed as contract labor, see J. Mark Ramseyer, "Contracting for Sex in the Pacific War," *International Review of Law and Economics* 65 (2021): 1–8; and the rejoinders in "Academic Integrity at Stake: The Ramseyer Article—Four Letters," ed. Alexis Dudden, supplement to the special issue, *Japan Focus: The Asia-Pacific Journal* 19, no. 5 (March 2021).

47. Bayly and Harper, *Forgotten Armies*, 383.

48. Katherine Moon, *Sex among Allies: Military Prostitution in U.S.-Korea Relations* (New York: Columbia University Press, 1997); Sarah C. Soh, *The Comfort Women: Sexual Violence and Postcolonial Memory in Korea and Japan* (Chicago: University of Chicago

Press, 2008); and Lisa Yoneyama, *Cold War Ruins: Transpacific Critique of American Justice and Japanese War Crimes* (Durham, NC: Duke University Press, 2016).

49. For regional overviews of prostitution in colonial Southeast Asia, see Eric Tagliacozzo, "Morphological Shifts in Southeast Asian Prostitution: The Long Twentieth Century," *Journal of Global History* 3, no. 2 (July 2008): 251–273; Philippa Levine, *Prostitution, Race, and Politics: Policing Venereal Disease in the British Empire* (New York: Routledge, 2003).

50. For a recent summary of the voluminous literature on this gendered, sexualized, and racialized history of the colonial regulation of women's sexuality and reproduction, see Françoise Vergès, *The Wombs of Women: Race, Capital, Feminism* (Durham, NC: Duke University Press, 2020).

51. Kolsky, *Colonial Justice*; Saha, "Male State."

52. Elaine H. Kim and Chungmoo Choi, eds., *Dangerous Women: Gender and Korean Nationalism* (New York: Routledge, 1998); Hyunah Yang, "Finding the 'Map of Memory': Testimony of the Japanese Military Sexual Slavery Survivors," *Positions: East Asia Cultures critique* 16, no. 1 (Spring 2008): 79–107; Soh, *Comfort Women*; Chungmoo Choi, "The Politics of War Memories toward Healing," in *Perilous Memories: The Asia Pacific War(s)*, ed. Takashi Fujitani, Geoffrey M. White, and Lisa Yoneyama (Durham, NC: Duke University Press, 2001), 395–409; Katharine McGregor, "Emotions and Activism for Former So-Called 'Comfort Women' of the Japanese Occupation of the Netherlands East Indies," *Women's Studies International Forum* 54 (2016): 67–78.

BIBLIOGRAPHY

Archives

Diplomatic Archives, Ministry of Foreign Affairs of Japan, Tokyo
India Office Records and Private Papers, British Library, London (IOR)
Japan Center for Asian Historical Records (https://www.jacar.go.jp)
Ludu Library, Mandalay Myanmar
Myanmar National Archives, Yangon (NAD)
National Archives of Japan, Tokyo
Universities Central Library, Yangon University, Myanmar
Universities Historical Research Centre, Yangon University, Myanmar

Law Reports Consulted

All India Reporter (AIR)
Burma Law Reports (BLR)
Burma Law Times (BLT)
Indian Appeals
Indian Law Reports, Rangoon Series (ILR Ran)
Law Reports, Indian Appeals (IA)
Lower Burma Rulings (LBR)
Printed Judgments of the Court of the Judicial Commissioner, Lower Burma, and
    the Special Court, Lower Burma, 1893–1900
Privy Council Cases: Malaysia, Singapore, Brunei, 1875–1990
Privy Council Judgments on Appeals from India
Rangoon Law Reports (RLR)
Selected judgements and ruling of the Court of the Judicial Commissioner and of
    the Special Court, Lower Burma, 1872–1892 (SJLB)
Upper Burma Rulings (UBR)

Newspapers and Periodicals

Asian Affairs
Atlantic Monthly
Buddhism
Burma Law Times
Daily Herald

Guardian
Journal of Burma Research Society
Kōa Kyōiku
Kyi Pwa Ye
Kyi Pwa Ye Magazine
Mandalay Thuriya
Missions: A Baptist Monthly Magazine
Myanmar Alin
Myanmar Alin Magazine
Nihongo
Stri Dharma
Thuriya
Thuriya Magazine
Yôp Shin Lan Hnyun

Published and Unpublished Sources

Aiyar, Sana. "Revolutionaries, Maulvis, Swamis, and Monks: Burma's Khilafat Moment." In *Oceanic Islam: Muslim Universalism and European Imperialism*, edited by Sugata Bose and Ayesha Jalal, chapter 5. New Delhi: Bloomsbury, 2020.

All-Asian Women's Conference. *Report of the All-Asian Women's Conference, First Session, Lahore, 19th to 25th January 1931*. Bombay: Times of India, 1931.

Allott, Anna. "Half a Century of Publishing in Mandalay: The Ludu Kyi-Bwa-Yay Press." *Journal of Burma Studies* 1 (1997): 107–124.

Alloula, Malek. *The Colonial Harem*. Minneapolis: University of Minnesota Press, 1986.

Alter, Joseph. *Gandhi's Body: Sex, Diet, and the Politics of Nationalism*. Philadelphia: University of Pennsylvania Press, 2000.

Amar, Ludu Daw. *Kyun ma ye te thu bawa Ludu U Hla*. Yangon: Kyi pwa ye sa pe, 2009.

Ambaras, David. *Japan's Imperial Underworlds: Intimate Encounters at the Borders of the Sinosphere*. Cambridge: Cambridge University Press, 2018.

Amin, Sonia Nishat. *The World of Muslim Women in Colonial Bengal, 1876–1939*. Leiden, Netherlands: Brill, 1996.

Amrith, Sunil S. *Crossing the Bay of Bengal: The Furies of Nature and the Fortunes of Migrants*. Cambridge, MA: Harvard University Press, 2013.

Amrith, Sunil S. "Reconstructing the 'Plural Society': Asian Migration between Empire and Nation, 1940–1948." *Past and Present*, supplement 6 (2011): 237–257.

Anagol, Padma. "Gender, Religion, and Anti-Feminism in Hindu Right-Wing Writings: Notes from a Nineteenth Century Indian Woman-Patriot's Text 'Essays in the Service of a Nation.'" *Women's Studies International Forum* 37 (2013): 104–113.

Andaya, Barbara. *The Flaming Womb: Repositioning Women in Early Modern Southeast Asia*. Honolulu: University of Hawai'i Press, 2006.

Andaya, Barbara. "From Temporary Wife to Prostitute: Sexuality and Economic Change in Early Modern Southeast Asia." *Journal of Women's History* 9, no. 4 (1998): 11–34.

Anderson, Benedict. *Imagined Communities: Reflections on the Origin and Spread of Nationalism*. Rev. ed. London: Verso, 1991.

Anderson, Benedict. *The Spectre of Comparisons: Nationalism, Southeast Asia, and the World.* London: Verso, 1998.

Andrew, E. J. L. *Indian Labour in Rangoon.* Oxford: Oxford University Press, 1933.

Arnold, David. "European Orphans and Vagrants in India in the Nineteenth Century." *Journal of Imperial and Commonwealth History* 7, no. 2 (1979): 104–127.

Aslanian, Sebouh David. *From the Indian Ocean to the Mediterranean: The Global Trade Networks of Armenian Merchants from New Julfa.* Berkeley: University of California Press, 2011.

Aung San. *Burma's Challenge.* Rangoon: New Light of Burma, 1946.

Aung San Suu Kyi. *Aung San of Burma: A Biographical Portrait by His Daughter.* Edinburgh: Kiscadale, 1991.

Aung-Thwin, Maitrii. *The Return of the Galon King: History, Law, and Rebellion in Colonial Burma.* Athens: Ohio University Press, 2011.

Aung Zaw. *Taing yin mutsalin sa pyu sa so pôggo kyaw mya.* Yangon: Pan we we sa pe, 2013.

Aye Kyaw. *The Voice of Young Burma.* Ithaca, NY: Southeast Asia Program, Cornell University, 1993.

Azuma, Eiichiro. *In Search of Our Frontier: Japanese America and Settler Colonialism in the Construction of Japan's Borderless Empire.* Berkeley: University of California Press, 2019.

Ba Bwa, Lawyer U. "Amyo thami mya ko hlit hlyu pyu ta kya mi law." *Kyi Pwa Ye Magazine,* March 1935, 25–27.

Ba Maw. *Breakthrough in Burma: Memoirs of a Revolution, 1939–1946.* New Haven, CT: Yale University Press, 1968.

Baba, Ai. "Policies, Promoters, and Patterns of Japanese-Korean and Japanese-Taiwanese Marriages in Imperial Japan: Making a Case for Inclusive History." PhD diss., Cornell University, 2019.

Bachetta, Paola, and Margaret Power, eds. *Right Wing Women: From Conservatives to Extremists around the World.* London: Routledge, 2002.

Bahadur, Gaiutra. *Coolie Woman: The Odyssey of Indenture.* Chicago: University of Chicago Press, 2014.

Baldwin, M. Page. "Subject to Empire: Married Women and the British Nationality and Status of Aliens Act." *Journal of British Studies* 40, no. 4 (October 2001): 522–556.

Ballantyne, Tony, and Antoinette Burton. *Bodies in Contact: Rethinking Colonial Encounters in World History.* Durham, NC: Duke University Press, 2005.

Ballantyne, Tony, and Antoinette Burton. "Introduction." In *Moving Subjects: Gender, Mobility, and Intimacy in an Age of Global Empire,* edited by Tony Ballantyne and Antoinette Burton, 1–16. Urbana: University of Illinois Press, 2009.

Ballantyne, Tony, and Antoinette Burton, eds. *Moving Subjects: Gender, Mobility, and Intimacy in An Age of Global Empire.* Urbana: University of Illinois Press, 2009.

Bama amyo thami me me. "Amyo thami ta u e haw pyaw kyek." *Kyi Pwa Ye,* July 1939, 24–25.

Barclay, Paul D. *Outcasts of Empire: Japan's Rule on Taiwan's "Savage Border," 1874–1945.* Oakland: University of California Press, 2018.

Barlow, Tani E. "Colonialism's Career in Postwar China Studies." *Positions: East Asia Critique* 2, no. 1 (1993): 224–267.

Barlow, Tani E. *The Question of Women in Chinese Feminism*. Durham, NC: Duke University Press, 2004.

Barnes, Andrew E. *Global Christianity and the Black Atlantic: Tuskegee, Colonialism, and the Shaping of African Industrial Education*. Waco, Texas: Baylor University Press, 2017.

Barragan, Yesenia. *Freedom's Captives: Slavery and Gradual Emancipation on the Colombian Black Pacific*. Cambridge: Cambridge University Press, 2021.

Bashford, Alison, and Philippa Levine, eds. *The Oxford Handbook of the History of Eugenics*. New York: Oxford University Press, 2010.

Bayly, Christopher, and Tim Harper. *Forgotten Armies: The Fall of British Asia, 1941–1945*. Cambridge, MA: Belknap; Harvard University Press, 2005.

Bennett, C. *The Third Annual Report of the Eurasian Ladies' Society, 1877–78*. Rangoon: American Mission, 1878.

Benton, Lauren. *Law and Colonial Cultures: Legal Regimes in World History, 1400–1900*. Cambridge: Cambridge University Press, 2004.

Beránek, Obdřej, and Pavel Ťupek. *From Visiting Graves to Their Destruction: The Question of Ziyara through the Eyes of Salafis*. Waltham, MA: Brandeis University, Crown Center for Middle East Studies, 2009.

Bergeron, Augustin. *The Distribution of Top Incomes in British India: An Exploration of Income Tax Records, 1885–1922*. Master's thesis, Paris School of Economics, 2014.

Biruma nihongo kyōkasho hensan iinkai. *Nippon go tokuhon II*. Rangoon: Biruma koku kyōiku eisei shō, 1944.

Biruma nihongo kyōkasho hensan iinkai. *Nippon go tokuhon III*. Rangoon: Biruma koku kyōiku eisei shō, 1944.

Blackburn, Anne M. *Locations of Buddhism: Colonialism and Modernity in Sri Lanka*. Chicago: University of Chicago Press, 2010.

Blackburn, Susan, and Helen Ting, eds. *Women in Southeast Asian Nationalist Movements*. Singapore: National University of Singapore Press, 2013.

Bland, Lucy. "White Women and Men of Colour: Miscegenation Fears in Britain after the Great War." *Gender and History* 17, no. 2 (April 2005): 29–61.

Blee, Kathleen. *Women of the Klan*. Berkeley: University of California Press, 1991.

Bo U, Shwe Bo U. *Shwe man a hnit taya pyi bama mutsalin to e atôk patti*. Mandalay: Kyi pwa ye pôn hneik taik, 1959.

Booth, Marilyn, ed. *Harem Histories: Lived Spaces and Imagined Places*. Durham, NC: Duke University Press, 2010.

Bourdaghs, Michael K. "Japan's Orient in Song and Dance." In *Sino-Japanese Transculturation: From the Late Nineteenth Century to the End of the Pacific War*, edited by Richard King, Cody Poulton, and Katsuhiko Endo, 167–188. Lanham, MD: Lexington Books, 2012.

Brown, Ian. *A Colonial Economy in Crisis: Burma's Rice Cultivators and the World Depression of the 1930s*. London: Routledge Curzon, 2005.

Brown, R. Grant. "Burmese Women." In *Shades of Gold and Green: Anecdotes of Colonial Burmah (1886–1948), Comp. N. Greenwood*. New Delhi: Asian Educational Services, 1995.

Brown, R. Grant. "The Kadus of Burma." *Bulletin of the School of Oriental Studies, University of London* 1, no. 3 (1920): 1–28.

Budda batha myanmar ma. "Khin Aye Kyi." *Thuriya Magazine*, August 1918, 52–67.

Buettner, Elizabeth. "Problematic Spaces, Problematic Races: Defining 'Europeans' in Late Colonial India." *Women's History Review* 9, no. 2 (2000): 277–298.

Bunka hōkōkai. *Dai tōa sensō rikugun hōdō han in shuki: Biruma kanteisen*. Tokyo: Kōdansha, 1942.

Burke, Edmund. *The Annual Register: A Review of Public Events at Home and Abroad for the Year 1919*. London: Longmans, Green, 1920.

Burma Intelligence Bureau. *Burma During the Japanese Occupation, Volume I*. Simla, India: Government of Burma, 1943.

Burma Intelligence Bureau. *Burma During the Japanese Occupation, Volume II*. Simla, India: Government of India Press, 1944.

Burma Round Table Conference. *Proceedings of the Committee of the Whole Conference*. Rangoon: Superintendent of Government Printing and Stationery, 1931.

Burns, Susan L., and Barbara J. Brooks, eds. *Gender and Law in the Japanese Imperium*. Honolulu: University of Hawai'i Press, 2014.

Burton, Antoinette M. "Archive Stories: Gender in the Making of Imperial and Colonial Histories'." In *Gender and Empire*, edited by Philippa Levine, 281–293. Oxford: Oxford University Press, 2004.

Burton, Antoinette M., ed. *Gender, Sexuality, and Colonial Modernities*. New York: Routledge, 1999.

Butalia, Urvashi. *The Other Side of Silence: Voices from the Partition of India*. Durham, NC: Duke University Press, 2000.

Caballero, Chamion, and Peter J. Aspinall. "'Disharmony of Physical, Mental, and Temperamental Qualities': Race Crossing, Miscegenation, and the Eugenics Movement." In *Mixed Race Britain in the Twentieth Century*, edited by Chamion Caballero and Peter J. Aspinall, 21–52. London: Palgrave, 2018.

Cakmak, Cenap. "Sayyid (Master)." In *Islam: A Worldwide Encyclopedia*, vol. 1, A–E, edited by Cenap Cakmak, 1401–1404. Santa Barbara, CA: ABC-CLIO, 2017.

Candier, Aurore. "Mapping Ethnicity in Nineteenth Century Burma: When 'Categories of People' (*Lumyo*) Became 'Nations.'" *Journal of Southeast Asian Studies* 50, no. 3 (September 2019): 347–364.

Carton, Adrian. "'Faire and Well-Formed': Portuguese Eurasian Women and Symbolic Whiteness in Early Colonial India." In Ballantyne and Burton, *Moving Subjects*, 231–251.

Case, Brayton C. "Christianity in Action on the Village Fields of Burma, or Agriculture in Mission Work." *Missions: A Baptist Monthly Magazine*, January 1921, 132–141.

Chan-Toon. *Leading Cases on Buddhist Law*. Rangoon: Hanthawaddy, 1899.

Chan-Toon, Mabel Mary Agnes. *A Marriage in Burmah, a Novel*. London: Greening, 1905.

Chandler, David P. *Voices from S-21: Terror and History in Pol Pot's Secret Prison*. Berkeley: University of California Press, 1999.

Chang, Sandy F. "Intimate Itinerancy: Sex, Work, and Chinese Women in Colonial Malaya's Brothel Economy, 1870s–1930s." *Journal of Women's History* 33, no. 4 (2021): 92–117.

Chapman, David, and Karl Jakob Krogness, eds. *Japan's Household Registration System and Citizenship: Koseki, Identification, and Documentation.* London: Routledge, 2014.

Chatterjee, Indrani. "Colouring Subalternity: Slaves, Concubines, and Social Orphans under the East India Company." In *Subaltern Studies X*, edited by Gautam Bhadra, Gyan Prakash, and Susie Tharu, 49–97. Delhi: Oxford University Press, 1999.

Chatterjee, Indrani. *Forgotten Friends: Monks, Marriages, and Memories of Northeast India.* New Delhi: Oxford University Press, 2013.

Chatterjee, Indrani. *Gender, Slavery, and Law in Colonial India.* Delhi: Oxford University Press, 1999.

"Chief and Lesser Wives." *Burma Law Times* 6, no. 4 (April 1913): i–x.

Ching, Leo T. S. *Anti-Japan: The Politics of Sentiment in Postcolonial East Asia.* Durham, NC: Duke University Press, 2019.

Ching, Leo T. S. *Becoming "Japanese": Colonial Taiwan and the Politics of Identity Formation.* Berkeley: University of California Press, 2001.

Choi, Chungmoo. "The Politics of War Memories toward Healing." In *Perilous Memories: The Asia Pacific War(s)*, edited by Takashi Fujitani, Geoffrey M. White, and Lisa Yoneyama, 395–409. Durham, NC: Duke University Press, 2001.

Chu, Richard T. *Chinese and Chinese Mestizos of Manila: Family, Identity, and Culture, 1860s–1930s.* Leiden, Netherlands: Brill, 2010.

Clancy-Smith, Julia, and Frances Gouda, eds. *Domesticating the Empire: Race, Gender, and Family Life in French and Dutch Colonialism.* Charlottesville: University of Virginia Press, 1998.

Clarence-Smith, William Gervase. "Entrepreneurial Strategies of Hadhrami Arabs in Southeast Asia, c. 1750s–1950s." In *The Hadhrami Diaspora in Southeast Asia: Identity Maintenance or Assimilation?*, edited by Hassan Ahmed Ibrahim and Ahmed Ibrahim Abushouk, 135–158. Leiden, Netherlands: Brill, 2009.

Clifford, Hugh, and Frank A. Swettenham. *A Dictionary of the Malay Language, Part I.* Taiping: Government Printing Office, 1894.

Cohn, Bernard S. *Colonialism and Its Forms of Knowledge: The British in India.* Princeton, NJ: Princeton University Press, 1996.

Cole, Alan. *Mothers and Sons in Chinese Buddhism.* Stanford, CA: Stanford University Press, 1998.

Collier, Jane F., and Sylvia J. Yanagisako, eds. *Gender and Kinship: Essays toward a Unified Analysis.* Stanford, CA: Stanford University Press, 1987.

Collins, Patricia Hill. "The Tie That Binds: Race, Gender, and US Violence." *Ethnic and Racial Studies* 21, no. 5 (September 1998): 917–938.

Constable, Nicole. "Revisiting Distant Divides and Intimate Connections in Asia: Comments on Engseng Ho's 'Inter-Asian Concepts for Mobile Societies.'" *Journal of Asian Studies* 76, no. 4 (November 2017): 953–959.

Coontz, Stephanie. *Marriage, a History: From Obedience to Intimacy, or How Love Conquered Marriage.* New York: Penguin Books, 2006.

Cooper, Frederick, and Ann L. Stoler, eds. *Tensions of Empire: Colonial Cultures in a Bourgeois World.* Berkeley: University of California Press, 1997.

Copleston, F. S. *Report on the Census of British Burma, Taken on the 17th February 1881, Part I, Report.* Rangoon: Government Press, 1881.

Cousins, Margaret. *The Awakening of Asian Womanhood.* Madras: Ganesh, 1922.

Cousins, Margaret. "Notes and Comments." *Stri Dharma* 6, no. 2 (December 1922): 17–18.

Crawfurd, John. *Journal of an Embassy from the Governor General of India to the Court of Ava in the Year 1827.* London: Henry Colburn, 1829.

Culley, R. E. *The "Euro-Asian" or "Anglo-Indian": A Burma Brochure by One of the Community.* Rangoon: Mayles Standish, 1910.

Cushman, Jennifer W. *Family and State: The Formation of a Sino-Thai Tin-Mining Dynasty, 1797–1932.* Edited by Craig J. Reynolds. Singapore: Oxford University Press, 1991.

Das, Veena. *Life and Words: Violence and the Descent into the Ordinary.* Berkeley: University of California Press, 2006.

Datta, Arunima. *Fleeting Agencies: A Social History of Indian Coolie Women in British Malaya.* Cambridge: Cambridge University Press, 2021.

Datta, Pradip Kumar. *Carving Blocs: Communal Ideology in Early Twentieth-Century Bengal.* New Delhi: Oxford University Press, 1999.

Davin, Anna. "Imperialism and Motherhood." *History Workshop Journal* 5, no. 1 (1978): 9–65.

Delap, Lucy. "Uneven Orientalisms: Burmese Women and the Feminist Imagination." *Gender and History* 24 (2012): 389–410.

D'Hubert, Thibaut. *In the Shade of the Golden Palace: Alaol and Middle Bengali Poetics in Arakan.* New York: Oxford University Press, 2018.

Duara, Prasenjit. "Asia Redux: Conceptualizing a Region for Our Times." *Journal of Asian Studies* 69, no. 4 (November 2010): 963–983.

Duara, Prasenjit. "The Discourse of Civilization and Pan-Asianism." *Journal of World History* 12, no. 1 (2001): 99–130.

Dudden, Alexis, ed. "Academic Integrity at Stake: The Ramseyer Article—Four Letters." Supplement to the special issue, *Japan Focus: The Asia-Pacific Journal* 19, no. 5 (March 2021). https://apjjf.org/2021/5/ToC2.html.

Dvorak, Greg. *Coral and Concrete: Remembering Kwajalein Atoll between Japan, America, and the Marshall Islands.* Honolulu: University of Hawai'i Press, 2018.

Dvorak, Greg. "Who Closed the Sea? Archipelagoes of Amnesia between the United States and Japan." In *Pacific America: Histories of Transoceanic Crossings*, edited by Lon Kurashige, 229–246. Honolulu: University of Hawai'i Press, 2017.

Eales, H. L. *Census of 1891, Imperial Series (Burma Report).* Vol. 9. Rangoon: Government Printing, 1892.

Easton, Doris Sarah. *Long Ago, Far Away: The Burma Diaries of Doris Sarah Easton.* Compiled by M. Sylvia Morris. London: Minerva, 1994.

Ebrey, Patricia Buckley. *Women and the Family in Chinese History.* London: Routledge, 2003.

Edwards, Penny. "Mixed Metaphors: Other Mothers, Dangerous Daughters, and the Rhetoric of Child Removal in Burma, Australia, and Indochina." *Balayi: Culture, Law, and Colonialism* 3, no. 6 (January 2004): 41–61.

Edwards, Penny. "Relocating the Interlocutor: Taw Sein Ko (1864–1930) and the Itinerancy of Knowledge in British Burma." *South East Asia Research* 12, no. 3 (November 2004): 277–335.

Elsbree, Willard. *Japan's Role in Southeast Asian Nationalist Movements, 1940–1945*. Cambridge, MA: Harvard University Press, 1953.

Endo, Masataka. *Kindai nihon no shokuminchi tōchi ni okeru kokuseki to koseki: Manshū, Chōsen, Taiwan*. Tokyo: Akashi Shoten, 2010.

Feener, R. Michael. "Hybridity and the 'Hadhrami Diaspora' in the Indian Ocean Muslim Networks." *Asian Journal of Social Science* 32, no. 3 (2004): 353–372.

Firpo, Christina. *The Uprooted: Race, Children, and Imperialism in French Indochina, 1890–1980*. Honolulu: University of Hawai'i Press, 2016.

Firpo, Christina, and Margaret D. Jacobs. "Taking Children, Ruling Colonies: Child Removal and Colonial Subjugation in Australia, Canada, French Indochina, and the United States, 1870–1950s." *Journal of World History* 29, no. 4 (December 2018): 529–562.

Foxeus, Niklas. "The Buddha Was a Devoted Nationalist: Buddhist Nationalism, Ressentiment, and Defending Buddhism in Myanmar." *Religion* 49, no. 4 (May 2019): 661–690.

Freitag, Ulrike, and William G. Clarence-Smith, eds. *Hadhrami Traders, Scholars, and Statesmen in the Indian Ocean, 1750s to 1960s*. Leiden, Netherlands: Brill, 1997.

Fuentes, Marisa. *Dispossessed Lives: Enslaved Women, Violence, and the Archive*. Philadelphia: University of Pennsylvania Press, 2016.

Fujimoto, Helen. *The South Indian Muslim Community and the Evolution of the Jawi Peranakan in Penang up to 1948: A Comparative Study on the Modes of Inter-Action in Multi-Ethnic Societies*. Tokyo: Tokyo Gaikokugo Daigaku, 1988.

Fujimura, Hitomi. "A View of the Karen Baptists in Burma of the Mid-Nineteenth Century, from the Standpoint of the American Baptist Mission." *Journal of Sophia Asian Studies* 32 (2014): 129–145.

Fujitani, Takashi. *Race for Empire: Koreans as Japanese and Japanese as Americans during World War II*. Berkeley: University of California Press, 2011.

Furber, Holden. *Private Fortunes and Company Profits in the India Trade in the 18th Century*. Aldershot, UK: Variorum, 1997.

Furnivall, John S. *Colonial Policy and Practice: A Comparative Study of Burma and Netherlands India*. New York: New York University Press, 1956.

Furukawa, Noriko. "Kyōiku no seido to kōzō." In *Nihon shokuminchi kenkyū no ronten*, edited by Nihon Shokuminchi Kenkyūkai, 132–142. Tokyo: Iwanami Shoten, 2018.

Fytche, Albert. *Burma Past and Present; with Personal Reminiscences of the Country*. Vol. 1. London: C. K. Paul, 1878.

Gandhi, Mohandas Karamchand. *The Collected Works of Mahatma Gandhi*. Vol. 45, 4 February 1929–11 May 1929. New Delhi: Publications Division Government of India, 1999.

Gandhi, Mohandas Karamchand. *The Collected Works of Mahatma Gandhi*. Vol. 67, 1 April–14 October 1938. Ahmedabad: Navajivan Trust, 1938.

Gaung, U. *A Digest of the Burmese Buddhist Law concerning Inheritance and Marriage; being a collection of texts from thirty-six Dhammathats, composed and arranged under the supervision of the Hon'ble U Gaung, C. S. I. ex-Kinwun Mingyi*. 2 vols. Rangoon: Superintendent, Government Printing, 1899.

Ghosh, Durba. "Gender and Colonialism: Expansion or Marginalization?" *Historical Journal* 47, no. 3 (September 2004): 737–755.

Ghosh, Durba. *Sex and the Family in Colonial India: The Making of Empire*. Cambridge: Cambridge University Press, 2005.

Gommans, Jos, and Jacques Leider, eds. *The Maritime of Burma: Exploring Political, Cultural, and Commercial Interaction in the Indian Ocean World, 1200–1800*. Leiden, Netherlands: Koninklijke Nederlandse Akademie van Wetenschappen, 2002.

Gouvernement général de L'Indochine. *Annuaire Statistique de L'Indochine, Premier Volume, Recueil de statistiques relatives aux années 1913 à 1922*. Hanoi: Imprimerie D'Extrême-Orient, 1927.

Gouvernement général de L'Indochine. *Annuaire Statistique de L'Indochine, Septieme Volume, 1936–1937*. Hanoi: Imprimerie D'Extrême-Orient, 1938.

Government of Burma. *Burma Gazetteer, Yamethin District*. Rangoon: Office of the Superintendent, Government Printing, 1913.

Government of Burma. *Burma Gazetteer, Yamethin District, Volume A*. Rangoon: Superintendent of Government Printing and Stationery, 1934.

Government of Burma. *Notes and Statistics on Hospitals and Dispensaries in Burma for the Year 1903*. Rangoon: Office of the Superintendent, Government Printing, 1904.

Government of Burma. *Notes and Statistics on Hospitals and Dispensaries in Burma for the Year 1912*. Rangoon: Office of the Superintendent, Government Printing, 1913.

Government of Burma. *Notes and Statistics on Hospitals and Dispensaries in Burma for the Year 1920*. Rangoon: Office of the Superintendent, Government Printing, 1921.

Government of Burma. *Proceedings of the Legislative Council of the Governor of Burma*. Vol. 17. Rangoon: Office of the Superintendent, Government Printing, 1932.

Government of Burma. *Report of an Enquiry into the Standard and Cost of Living of the Working Classes in Rangoon*. Rangoon: Labour Statistics Bureau, 1928.

Government of Burma. *Report on the Administration of Burma for the Year 1911–12*. Rangoon: Office of the Superintendent, Government Printing, 1913.

Government of Burma. *Reports on Public Instruction in Burma for the Year 1891–92*. Rangoon: Office of the Superintendent, Government Printing, 1892.

Government of India. *Census of 1891, Imperial Tables, X, Burma Report, Volume II*. Rangoon: Superintendent, Government Printing, 1892.

Government of India. *Census of India, 1911, IX*. Rangoon: Office of the Superintendent, Government Printing and Stationery, 1912.

Government of India. *Census of India, 1911, IX, Burma, Part II, Tables*. Rangoon: Office of the Superintendent, Government Printing and Stationery, 1912.

Government of India. *Census of India, 1921*. Vol. 10, *Burma and Part I, Report*. Rangoon: Office of the Superintendent, Government Printing and Stationery, 1923.

Government of India. *Census of India, 1921*. Vol. 10. *Burma and Part II, Tables*. Rangoon: Office of the Superintendent, Government Printing and Stationery, 1923.

Government of India. *Census of India, 1931, XI, Burma, Part I, Report*. Rangoon: Office of the Superintendent, Government Printing and Stationery, 1933.

Government of India. *Census of India, 1931, XI, Burma, Part II, Tables*. Rangoon: Office of the Superintendent, Government Printing and Stationery, 1933.

Great Britain. *Minutes of Evidence Taken Before the Royal Commission Upon Decentralization in Burma, Presented to Both Houses Parliament by Command of His Majesty*. Vol. III. London: His Majesty's Stationery Office, Darling & Son, 1908.

Green, Nile, ed. *The Persianate World: The Frontiers of a Eurasian Lingua Franca*. Oakland: University of California Press, 2019.

Green, Nile, ed. "The Waves of Heterotopia: Toward a Vernacular Intellectual History of the Indian Ocean." *American Historical Review* 123, no. 3 (June 2018): 846–874.

Gupta, Charu. *Sexuality, Obscenity, Community: Women, Muslims, and the Hindu Public in Colonial India.* New York: Palgrave, 2002; first published, Delhi: Permanent Black, 2001.

Hall, Harold Fielding. *The Soul of a People.* Bangkok: White Orchid, 1995.

Hallisey, Charles. "Roads Taken and Not Taken in the Study of Theravada Buddhism." In *Curators of the Buddha: The Study of Buddhism under Colonialism,* edited by Donald Lopez, 31–62. Chicago: University of Chicago Press, 1995.

Hamilton, Alexander. *A new account of the East Indies, being the observations and remarks of Capt. Alexander Hamilton.* Vol. 2. Edinburgh: printed by John Mosman, 1727.

Hanscom, Christopher P., and Dennis Washburn, eds. *The Affect of Difference: Representations of Race in East Asian Empire.* Honolulu: University of Hawai'i Press, 2016.

Harper, Tim, and Sunil S. Amrith, eds. *Sites of Asian Interaction: Ideas, Networks, and Mobility.* Delhi: Cambridge University Press, 2014.

Harris, Elizabeth J. "Ananda Metteyya: Controversial Networker, Passionate Critic." In *A Buddhist Crossroads: Pioneer Western Buddhists and Asian Networks 1860–1960,* edited by Brian Bocking, Phibul Choompolpaisal, Laurence Cox, and Alicia Turner, 77–92. London: Routledge, 2015.

Hartman, Saidiya. *Scenes of Subjection: Terror and Self-Making in Nineteenth-Century America.* New York: Oxford University Press, 1997.

Hartman, Saidiya. *Wayward Lives, Beautiful Experiments: Intimate Social Histories of Social Upheaval.* New York: W. W. Norton, 2019.

Hau, Caroline S. *The Chinese Question: Ethnicity, Nation, and Region in and beyond the Philippines.* Kyoto CSEAS Series on Asian Studies. Singapore: NUS Press, 2014.

Hawes, Charles. *Poor Relations: The Making of a Eurasian Community in British India 1730–1833.* Surrey, UK: Curzon, 1996.

Hayashi, Hirofumi. *Kakyō gyakusatsu: Nihongun shihaika no marē hantō.* Tokyo: Suzusawa Shoten, 1992.

Henry, Todd A. "Assimilation's Racializing Sensibilities: Colonized Koreans ad *Yobos* and the '*Yobo*-ization' of Expatriate Japanese." In Hanscom and Washburn, *Affect of Difference,* 81–107.

Hershatter, Gail. *The Gender of Memory: Rural Women and China's Collective Past.* Berkeley: University of California Press, 2011.

Hirschman, Charles. "The Meaning and Measurement of Ethnicity in Malaysia: An Analysis of Census Classifications." *Journal of Asian Studies* 46, no. 3 (August 1987): 555–582.

Hla. "Meik set." In *Kabya pyatthana* by Pu Galay, 6. Mandalay: Kyi pwa yay, 1939.

Hla Aung. "Sino-Burmese Marriages and Conflict of Laws." *Burma Law Institute Journal* 1, no. 1 (1958): 25–55.

Hla Pe. *Narrative of the Japanese Occupation of Burma, Recorded by U Khin, Foreword by Hugh Tinker.* Ithaca, NY: Southeast Asia Program, Cornell University, 1961.

Hla Tin, U, ed. *Myanmar min ôk kyut pôn sa dan nhit Bodaw paya e yaza thit khaw thaw amein daw tan kyi.* Vol. 4. Yangon: She haung sa pe hnit yin kye hmu tana su, 1970.

Ho, Engseng. *The Graves of Tarim: Genealogy and Mobility across the Indian Ocean.* Berkeley: University of California Press, 2006.

Ho, Engseng. "Inter-Asian Concepts for Mobile Societies." *Journal of Asian Studies* 76, no. 4 (November 2017): 907–928.

Hooker, M. B. "The 'Chinese Confucian' and the 'Chinese Buddhist' in British Burma, 1881–1947." *Journal of Southeast Asian Studies* 21, no. 2 (September 1990): 384–401.

Horton, William Bradley. "Sexual Exploitation and Resistance: Indonesian Language Representations since the Early 1990s of the Japanese Occupation History." *Asia-Pacific Forum* 28 (June 2005): 54–77.

House of Commons Parliamentary Papers. *Proceedings of the Burma Round Table Conference.* London: His Majesty's Stationery Office, 1931.

Htin Aung. *The Stricken Peacock: Anglo-Burmese Relations, 1752–1948.* The Hague: Martinus Nijhoff, 1965.

Htun Yee. *Collection of Hpyat-sa.* Vol. 2. Yangon: Myanmar Affairs Bureau, Literature Bank, 2006.

Htun Yee. *Yadana bôn kit upade mya / Collection of Upade (Laws and Regulations of Myanmar Last Two of Kings, A. D. 1853–1885).* Vol. 4. Toyohashi, Japan: Aichi University, 1999.

Huang, Chia-chi. "Nihon tōchi jidai ni okeru 'uchidai-domo kon' no kōzō to tenkai." *Hikaku Kazokushi Kenkyū* 27 (March 2013): 128–155.

Huff, Gregg. *World War II and Southeast Asia: Economy and Society under Japanese Occupation.* Cambridge: Cambridge University Press, 2020.

Huxley, Andrew. "The Anglo-Buddhist War (1875–1905): The Circumstances under which Christians Developed Their Theory of Buddhism." *Journal of Comparative Law* 7, no. 2 (2012): 18–38.

Huxley, Andrew. "Wills in Theravada Buddhist S. E. Asia." *Recueils de la société Jean Bodin pour l'histoire comparative des institutions* 62, no. 4 (1994): 53–92.

Hyam, Ronald. *Empire and Sexuality: The British Experience.* Manchester: Manchester University Press, 1990.

Ishii, Hitoshi. "Nihon gunseika ni okeru nanpō senryōchi no kyōiku seisaku ni kansuru kisoteki kenkyū." *Bulletin of Okayama Prefectural Junior College* 1 (1994): 67–79.

Ikeda, Kazuto. "Two Versions of Buddhist Karen History of the Late British Colonial Period in Burma: Kayin Chronicle (1929) and Kuyin Great Chronicle (1931)." *Southeast Asian Studies* 1, no. 3 (December 2012): 431–460.

Ikeya, Chie. "The Body of the Burmese Muslim." In *Bodies Beyond Binaries in Colonial and Postcolonial Asia*, edited by Elena Valdameri, Kate Imy, Teresa Segura-Garcia, and Erica Wald. Leiden, Netherlands: Leiden University Press, forthcoming.

Ikeya, Chie. "The Life and Writing of a Patriotic Feminist: Independent Daw San of Burma." In *Women in Southeast Asian Nationalist Movements*, edited by Susan Blackburn and Helen Ting, 23–47. Singapore: National University of Singapore Press, 2013.

Ikeya, Chie. *Refiguring Women, Colonialism, and Modernity in Burma.* Honolulu: University of Hawai'i Press, 2011.

Ikeya, Chie. "Talking Sex, Making Love: P. Moe Nin and Intimate Modernity in Colonial Burma." In *Modern Times in Southeast Asia, 1920s–1970s*, edited by Susie Protschky and Tom Berge, 136–165. Leiden, Netherlands: Brill, 2018.

Itai, Takeo. *Kekkon kokusaku no teishō*. Taiyōdō Shobō, 1939.

Ito, Jirozaemon Suketami. *Indo biruma shisatsu dan*. Tokyo: Tōa Kenkyū Jo, 1938.

Ito, Toshikatsu. "Ottama sōjō to nagai gyōji shōnin." In *Bukkyō o meguru nihon to tōnan ajia chiiki*, edited by Koji Osawa, 127–142. Tokyo: Bensei Shuppan, 2016.

Jacobsen, Trudy. *Sex Trafficking in Southeast Asia: A History of Desire, Duty, and Debt*. New York: Routledge, 2017.

Jagadiswarananda, Swami. *Hinduism outside India*. Rajkot: Kathiawar, 1945.

Jardine, John. "Marriage—Its Incidents" (21 July 1882). In *Notes on Buddhist Law I*, 2nd reprint, 1–12. Rangoon: Office of the Superintendent of Government Printing and Stationery. 1953.

Jayawardena, Kumari, and Malathi Alwis, eds. *Embodied Violence: Communalising Women's Sexuality in South Asia*. New Delhi: Kali for Women, 1996.

Jikkoku, Osamu. *Myanmā monogatari: Hitowa naze sensō o surunoka*. Tokyo: Sanseidō, 1995.

Jinbo, Kotaro. *Shōnan nippon gakuen*. Tokyo: Aino Jigyōsha, 1943.

Ju, Chen Chao. "Sim-pua under the Colonial Gaze: Gender, 'Old Customs,' and the Law in Taiwan under Japanese Imperialism." In *Gender and Law in the Japanese Imperium*, edited by Susan L. Burns and Barbara J. Brooks, 189–218. Honolulu: University of Hawai'i Press, 2014.

Kamoto, Itsuko. *Kokusai kekkon no tanjō: "Bunmei koku nihon" e no michi*. Tokyo: Shiyōsha, 2001.

Kato, Atsuhiko. "Karen and Surrounding Languages." In *Topics in Middle Mekong Linguistics*, edited by Norihiko Hayashi, 123–150. Kobe: Kobe City University of Foreign Studies, 2019.

Kaung, U. "A Survey of the History of Education in Burma before the British Conquest and After." *Journal of Burma Research Society* 46, no. 2 (December 1963): 1–129.

Kaur, Amarjit. "Indian Labour, Labour Standards, and Workers' Health in Burma and Malaya, 1900–1940." *Modern Asian Studies* 40, no. 2 (2006): 425–475.

Kawamura, Minato. *Umi wo watatta nihongo: Shokuminchi no "kokugo" no kikan*. Tokyo: Seidōsha, 2004.

Kawanishi, Kosuke. *Teikoku nihon no kakuchō to hōkai: "Daitōa kyōeiken" eno rekishi-teki tenkai*. Tokyo: Hōseidaigaku Shuppan Kyoku, 2012.

Khan, Khan Bahadur Munshi Ghulam Ahmed. *Census of India*. Vol. 23. *Kashmir, Part I: Report*. Lahore: Civil and Military Gazette Press, 1901.

Khatun, Samia. "The Book of Marriage: Histories of Muslim Women in Twentieth-Century Australia." *Gender and History* 29, no. 1 (2017): 8–30.

Khin Maung Nyunt. "U Po Kya's Writings: His Rejoinder to Mr. Noyce." In *Texts and Contexts in Southeast Asia: Proceedings of the Texts and Contexts in Southeast Asia Conference*, part 2, 137–144. Yangon: Universities Historical Research Centre, 2001.

Khin Yi. *The Dobama Movement in Burma, 1930–1938*. Ithaca, NY: Southeast Asia Program, Cornell University, 1988.

Khin Yi. *The Dobama Movement in Burma, Appendix*. Ithaca, NY: Southeast Asia Program, Cornell University, 1988.

Kim, Elaine H., and Chungmoo Choi, eds. *Dangerous Women: Gender and Korean Nationalism*. New York: Routledge, 1998.

Kim, Su Yun. *Imperial Romance: Fictions of Colonial Intimacy in Korea, 1905–1945.* Ithaca, NY: Cornell University Press, 2020.

Kirichenko, Alexey. "From Thathanadaw to Theravāda Buddhism: Construction of Religion and Religious Identity in Nineteenth- and Early Twentieth-Century Myanmar." In *Casting Faiths: Imperialism and the Transformation of Religion in East and Southeast Asia,* edited by Thomas David Dubois, 23–45. New York: Palgrave Macmillan, 2009.

Kitada, Eri. "Intimately Intertwined: Settler and Indigenous Communities, Filipino Women, and U.S.-Japanese Imperial Formations in the Philippines, 1903– 1956." PhD diss., Rutgers University, 2023.

Kiyono, Kenji. "Dai nanyō ni okeru konketsu no mondai." *Nanyō Keizai Kenkyū* 1, no. 7 (July 1942): 64–73.

Klein, Ronald D. *The Other Empire: Literary Views of Japan from the Philippines, Singapore, and Malaysia.* Quezon City: University of the Philippines Press, 2008.

Kojima, Masaru. *Dainiji sekai taisenzen no zaigai shitei no kyōikuron no keifu.* Kyoto, Ryūkoku Gakkai, 1993.

Kojima, Masaru. "Nanyō ni okeru nihonjin gakko to dōtai." *Tōnan Ajia Kenkyū* 18, no. 3 (December 1980): 460–475.

Kolsky, Elizabeth. *Colonial Justice in British India: White Violence and the Rule of Law.* Cambridge: Cambridge University Press, 2010.

Kratoska, Paul H., ed. *Asian Labor in the Wartime Japanese History: Unknown Histories.* Armonk, NY: M. E. Sharpe, 2005.

Kratoska, Paul H., ed. *The Japanese Occupation of Malaya, 1941–1945: A Social and Economic History.* Honolulu: University of Hawai'i Press, 1997.

Kugle, Scott Alan. "Framed, Blamed, and Renamed: The Recasting of Islamic Jurisprudence in Colonial South Asia." *Modern Asian Studies* 35, no. 2 (May 2001): 257–313.

Kwon, Insook. "Feminists Navigating the Shoals of Nationalism and Collaboration: The Post-Colonial Korean Debate over How to Remember Kim Hwallan." *Frontiers: A Journal of Women Studies* 27, no. 1 (2006): 39–66.

Kwon, Nayoung Aimee. *Intimate Empire: Collaboration and Colonial Modernity in Korea and Japan.* Durham, NC: Duke University Press, 2015.

Kyaw Win Maung. *Japan pet sit taw hlan ye ledi thama mya.* Yangon: Thiha Yadana, 2008.

Laffan, Michael, ed. *Belonging across the Bay of Bengal: Religious Rites, Colonial Migrations, National Rights.* London: Bloomsbury Academic, 2017.

Laffan, Michael, ed. "Introduction: Dhows, Steamers, Lifeboats." In *Belonging across the Bay of Bengal: Religious Rites, Colonial Migrations, National Rights,* edited by Michael Laffan, 1–14. London: Bloomsbury Academic, 2017.

Lammerts, D. Christian. *Buddhist Law in Burma: A History of Dhammasattha Texts and Jurisprudence, 1250–1850.* Honolulu: University of Hawai'i Press, 2018.

Lee, Ana Paulina. *Mandarin Brazil: Race, Representation, and Memory.* Stanford, CA: Stanford University Press, 2018.

Lee, Jeong-Seon. "Naisen kekkon no kodomo tachi: Naichi jin to chosen jin no hazama de." *Rekishi Hyōron* 815 (March 2018): 42–55.

Leider, Jacques P. "The Chittagonians in Colonial Arakan: Seasonal and Settlement Migrations." In *Colonial Wrongs and Access to International Law*, edited by Morten Bergsmo, Wolfgang Kaleck, and Kyaw Yin Hlaing, 177–227. TOAEP, 2020.

Lerrigo, P. H. J., ed., with the collaboration of Doris M. Amidon. *All Kindreds and Tongues: An Illustrated Survey of the Foreign Mission Enterprise of Northern Baptists*, 4th issue. New York: American Baptist Foreign Mission Society, 1940.

Lessard, Micheline R. "*Organisons-Nous!* Racial Antagonism and Vietnamese Economic Nationalism in the Early Twentieth Century." *French Colonial History* 8 (2007): 171–201.

Lev, Daniel S. "Colonial Law and the Genesis of the Indonesian State." *Indonesia* 40 (October 1985): 57–74.

Levine, Philippa. *Prostitution, Race, and Politics: Policing Venereal Disease in the British Empire*. New York: Routledge, 2003.

lewallen, ann-elise. "Intimate Frontiers: Disciplining Ethnicity and Ainu Women's Sexual Subjectivity in Early Colonial Hokkaido." In Hanscom and Washburn, *Affect of Difference*, 20–37.

Li, Minghuan. "'Sons of the Yellow Emperor' to 'Children of Indonesian Soil': Studying Peranakan Chinese Based on the Batavia Kong Koan Archives." *Journal of Southeast Asian Studies* 34, no. 2 (June 2002): 215–230.

Li, Yi. *Chinese in Colonial Burma: A Migrant Community in a Multiethnic State*. New York: Palgrave Macmillan, 2017.

Lieberman, Victor B. "Ethnic Hatred and Universal Benevolence: Ethnicity and Loyalty in Precolonial Myanmar, and Britain." *Comparative Studies in Society and History* 63, no. 2 (April 2021): 310–338.

Lieberman, Victor B. "Ethnic Politics in Eighteenth-Century Burma." *Modern Asian Studies* 12, no. 3 (July 1978): 455–482.

Lieberman, Victor B. "Reinterpreting Burmese History." *Comparative Studies in Society and History* 29, no. 1 (January 1987): 162–194.

Lieberman, Victor B. *Strange Parallels*. Vol. 1, *Southeast Asia in Global Context, c. 800–1830*. Cambridge: Cambridge University Press, 2003.

Lin Yone Thit Lwin. *Yodayar myanmar mi yatha lan ko twe chwe tat hmattan*. Yangon: Sape Beikman Apwe, 1991.

Loos, Tamara. "A History of Sex and the State in Southeast Asia: Class, Intimacy, and Invisibility." *Citizenship Studies* 12, no. 1 (January 2008): 27–43.

Loos, Tamara. *Subject Siam: Family, Law, and Colonial Modernity in Thailand*. Ithaca, NY: Cornell University Press, 2006.

Love, Henry Davison. *Vestiges of Old Madras, 1640–1800*. London: J. Murray, 1913.

Lowe, Lisa. *The Intimacies of Four Continents*. Durham, NC: Duke University Press, 2015.

Lower Burma. *Report on the Census of British Burma Taken in August 1872, Part I, Report*. Rangoon: Government Press, 1875.

Lowis, C. C. *Census of India, XIIA, Burma, Part II, Imperial Tables*. Rangoon: Office of the Superintendent, Government Printing, 1901.

Lu, Sidney Xu. *The Making of Japanese Settler Colonialism: Malthusianism and Trans-Pacific Migration, 1868–1961*. Cambridge: Cambridge University Press, 2019.

Lugones, María. "Heterosexualism and the Colonial/Modern Gender System." *Hypatia* 22, no. 1 (2007): 186–209.

Malkki, Liisa H. *Purity and Exile: Violence, Memory, and National Cosmology among Hutu Refugees in Tanzania*. Chicago: University of Chicago Press, 1995.

Mani, Lata. *Contentious Traditions: The Debate on Sati in Colonial India*. Berkeley: University of California Press, 1998.

Marks, J. E. *Forty Years in Burma, with a Foreword by the Archbishop of Canterbury*. New York: E. P. Dutton, 1917.

Marshall, P. J. "British Society in India under the East India Company." *Modern Asian Studies* 31, no. 1 (1997): 89–108.

Matsunaga, Noriko. *Nihon gunseika no maraya ni okeru nihongo kyōiku*. Tokyo: Kazama Shobō, 2002.

Matsuoka, Juhachi. *Dai tōa minzoku mondai*. Tokyo: Showa Shobō, 1942.

Maung Gyi, Ledi Pandita U. *Nīti Manjari Kyan*. Yangon: Hanthawaddy, 1956.

Maung Htin. *Nga Ba*. Yangon: Pyi Thu Sa Pe, 1957.

Maung Maung. "M. A. Raschid," *The Guardian* 3, no. 4 (December 1956), reproduced in *Maung Maung: Gentleman, Scholar, Patriot*, edited by Robert H. Taylor, 229–242. Singapore: ISEAS, 2008.

Maung Maung. "The Resistance Movement." *The Guardian* 1, no. 5 (March 1954): 9–11.

Maung Maung Gyi, U. *Myanma islam gantha win sa so do gyi*. Vol. 1. Mandalay: Academy of Islamic Historical Research Foundation, 1972.

Maung Thaw. "Buddhist Activities." *Buddhism* 1, no. 1 (15 September 1903): 174.

Mawani, Renisa. *Colonial Proximities: Crossracial Encounters and Juridical Truths in British Columbia, 1871–1921*. Vancouver: University of British Columbia Press, 2009.

May Oung, and John S. Furnivall. "The Dawn of Nationalism in Burma: The Modern Burman." *Journal of the Burma Research Society* 33, no. 1 (1950): 1–7.

McClintock, Anne. "Family Feuds: Gender, Nationalism, and the Family." *Feminist Review*, no. 44 (1993): 61–80.

McClintock, Anne. *Imperial Leather: Race, Gender, and Sexuality in the Colonial Conquest*. New York: Routledge, 1995.

McCoy, Alfred, ed. *Southeast Asia under Japanese Occupation*. New Haven, CT: Yale University Southeast Asia Studies, 1985.

McDonald, Kate. "Speaking Japanese: Language and the Expectation of Empire." In Hanscom and Washburn, *Affect of Difference*, 159–179.

McGregor, Katharine. "Emotions and Activism for Former So-Called 'Comfort Women' of the Japanese Occupation of the Netherlands East Indies." *Women's Studies International Forum* 54 (2016): 67–78.

Medovoi, Leerom. "Dogma-Line Racism: Islamophobia and the Second Axis of Race." *Social Text* 30, no. 2 (2012): 43–74.

Menon, Devaki. *Everyday Nationalism: Women of the Hindu Right in India*. Philadelphia: University of Pennsylvania Press, 2010.

Mersan, Alexandra de. "How Muslims in Arakan Became Arakan's Foreigners." In *Current Myanmar Studies, Aung San Suu Kyi, Muslims in Arakan, and Economic Insecurity*, edited by Georg Winterberger and Esther Tenberg, 59–98. Newcastle, UK: Cambridge Scholars, 2019.

Minamida, Midori. "Biruma sakka tachi no 'Nihon jidai.'" *Osaka Daigaku Sekai Gengo Kenkyū Sentā Ronshū* 7 (2012): 285–311.

Minamida, Midori. "Nihon senryō ni okeru Biruma sakka kyōkai kikanshi 'Sakka' no yakuwari ni tsui te." *Osaka Daigaku Sekai Gengo Kenkyū Sentā Ronshū* 5 (2011): 143–171.

Mobini-Kesheh, Natalie. *The Hadrami Awakening: Community and Identity in the Netherlands East Indies, 1900–1942.* Ithaca, NY: Cornell University Press, Southeast Asia Publications Program, 1999.

Moon, Katherine. *Sex among Allies: Military Prostitution in U.S.-Korea Relations.* New York: Columbia University Press, 1997.

Morgan, Jennifer L. *Reckoning with Slavery: Gender, Kinship, and Capitalism in the Early Black Atlantic.* Durham, NC: Duke University Press, 2021.

Mukherjee, Sumita. *Indian Suffragettes: Female Identities and Transnational Networks.* New Delhi: Oxford University Press, 2018.

Mya May. "Burmese Women." *Buddhism* 1, no. 1 (15 September 1903): 61–82.

Mya Sein. "Land of Happy Marriage." *Daily Herald,* 7 December 1931.

Mya Sein. "Myanmar amyo thami." In *Myanmar amyo thami kye môn,* 18. Yangon: Myanmar nainggan sa pe hnik sanezin apwe, 1998. Originally published in 1958.

Mya Sein. "Myanmar amyo thami mya hnit ein daung hmu." *Thuriya,* 1 January 1932, kha–ga.

Mya Sein. "Towards Independence in Burma: The Role of Women." *Asian Affairs* 3, no. 3 (1972): 288–299.

Mya Sein. "The Women of Burma: A Tradition of Hard Work and Independence." *Atlantic Monthly,* February 1958, 123.

Mya U. *Plea for Separation of Burma from India.* Rangoon: Rangoon Times, 1929.

"Myanmar mutsalin amyo thami hnit wut sa sin yin hmu." *Thuriya,* 22 February 1932, 9.

"Myanmar pyi thi Myanmar lu myo tho a bo pyit taik kyaung." *Myanmar Alin Magazine,* April 1914, 644–652.

Nadkarni, Asha. *Eugenic Feminism: Reproductive Nationalism in the United States and India.* Minneapolis: University of Minnesota Press, 2014.

Nagel, Joane. *Race, Ethnicity, and Sexuality: Intimate Intersections, Forbidden Frontiers.* New York: Oxford University Press, 2003.

Nakano, Satoshi. *Japan's Colonial Moment in Southeast Asia, 1942–1945: The Occupiers' Experience.* London: Routledge, 2018.

Nanpō chōyō sakka sōsho, Biruma hen. Vols. 1–5. Tokyo: Ryūkei Shosha, 2010.

"Nanpō kyōeiken no kyōiku zadan kai." *Kōa Kyōiku* 1, no. 3 (1942): 74–88.

Naono, Atsuko. "Educating Lady Doctors in Colonial Burma: American Baptist Missionaries, the Lady Dufferin Hospital, and the Local Government in the Making of Burmese Medical Women.'" In *Contesting Colonial Authority: Medicine and Indigenous Responses in 19th and 20th-Century India,* edited by Poonam Bala, 97–114. Lanham, MD: Lexington Books, Rowman and Littlefield, 2012.

"National Deterioration: Myanmar amyo tha mya nyi pa sut yut kyin a kyaung." *Myanmar Alin Magazine,* February 1912, 129–146.

Nederlandsch-Indië. *Departement van Economische Zaken, Volkstelling 1930, Deel VII, Chineezen en andere vreemde oosterlingen in Nederlandsch-Indië.* Batavia: Lands-drukkerij, 1935.

Nemoto, Yuriko. *Sokoku wo senjō ni sarete: Biruma no sasayaki.* Fukuoka: Sekifusha, 2000.

Nihongo kyōiku shinkō kai. "Nanpō kensetsu to nihongo fukyū." *Nihongo* 2, no. 5 (May 1942): 86–104.

Nijhawan, Shobna. "At the Margins of Empire: Feminist-Nationalist Configurations of Burmese Society in the Hindi Public (1917–1920)." *Journal of Asian Studies* 71, no. 4 (November 2012): 1–21.

Nisbet, John. *Burma under British Rule and Before.* Vols. 1–2. Westminster: Archibald Constable, 1901.

Niti Manjari of Dya Dviveda. Edited with an introduction, notes, and appendices by Sitaram Jayaram Joshi. Benares: Saligram Sharma, 1933.

Nocentelli, Carmen. *Empires of Love: Europe, Asia, and the Making of Early Modern Identity.* Philadelphia: University of Pennsylvania Press, 2013.

Nu, Thakin. *Burma under the Japanese: Pictures and Portraits.* Edited, translated, and with an introduction by J. S. Furnivall. London: Macmillan, 1954.

Nu, Thakin. *Nga hnit yadi Bama pyi.* Yangon: Myanmar Alin, 1946.

Oguma, Eiji. *Tan itsu minzoku shinwa no kigen—"Nihonjin" no jigazō no keifu.* Tokyo: Shinyōsha, 1995.

Ohnuma, Reiko. "Debt to the Mother: A Neglected Aspect of the Founding of the Buddhist Nuns' Order." *Journal of the American Academy of Religion* 74, no. 4 (December 2006): 861–901.

Ong, Aihwa, and Michael Peletz, eds. *Bewitching Women, Pious Men: Gender and Body Politics in Southeast Asia.* Berkeley: University of California Press, 1995.

Orwell, George. *Burmese Days.* New York: Penguin Books, 2001. Originally published by Harper & Brothers, 1934.

Ota, Atsushi. "Kioku sareru Indoneshia: 1945–70 nen no Nihon shōsetsu ni egakareru senji senryō." *Journal of Asia Pacific Studies* 20 (February 2013): 121–136.

Ota, Tsunozo. *Biruma ni okeru nihon gunseishi no kenkyū.* Tokyo: Yoshigawa Kōbunkan, 1967.

Pairaudeau, Natasha. *Mobile Citizens: French Indians in Indochina, 1858–1954.* Copenhagen: NIAS Press, 2016.

Pandey, Gyanendra. *The Construction of Communalism in Colonial North India.* Oxford: Oxford University Press, 2006.

Pascoe, Peggy. *What Comes Naturally: Miscegenation Law and the Making of Race in America.* Oxford: Oxford University Press, 2010.

Patel, P. D. "Just Fifty Years Ago." *The Guardian* 5, no. 7 (July 1958): 13–15.

Pegues, Juliana Hu. *Space-Time Colonialism: Alaska's Indigenous and Asian Entanglements.* Chapel Hill: University of North Carolina Press, 2021.

Peletz, Michael G. *Gender Pluralism: Southeast Asia Since Early Modern Times.* New York: Routledge, 2009.

Peletz, Michael G. "Gender, Sexuality, and the State in Southeast Asia." *Journal of Asian Studies* 71, no. 4 (2012): 895–917.

Penny, F. E. *On the Coromandel Coast.* London: Smith, Elder, 1908.

Po Kyar. "Kala Gadaw." *Yôp Shin Lan Hnyun,* May 1934, 26–32.

Pollok, Fitz William Thomas. *Fifty Years' Reminiscences of India: A Retrospect of Travel, Adventure and Shikar.* London: Edward Arnold, 1896.

Post, Peter, and Elly Touwen-Bouwsma, eds. *Japan, Indonesia, and the War: Myths and Realities.* Leiden: KITLV Press, 1997.

Prasad, Srirupa. *Cultural Politics of Hygiene in India, 1890–1940: Contagions of Feeling.* London: Palgrave Macmillan, 2015.

Pratt, Mary Louise. *Imperial Eyes: Travel Writing and Transculturation*. London: Routledge, 1992.

Pu Galay. *Kabya pyatthana*. Mandalay: Kyi pwa ye, 1939.

Purser, W. C. B. *Christian Missions in Burma*. Westminster: Society for the Propagation of the Gospel in Foreign Parts, 1911.

Raben, Remco, ed. *Representing the Japanese Occupation of Indonesia: Personal Testimonies and Public Images in Indonesia, Japan, and the Netherlands*. Amsterdam: Waanders, 1999.

Rafael, Vicente L. *Contracting Colonialism: Translation and Christian Conversion in Tagalog Society under Early Spanish Rule*. Ithaca, NY: Cornell University Press, 1988.

Ramseyer, J. Mark. "Contracting for Sex in the Pacific War." *International Review of Law and Economics* 65 (2021): 1–8.

Raschid, Bilal M. *The Invisible Patriot: Reminiscences of Burma's Freedom Movement*. Bethesda, MD: Raschid, 2015.

Reid, Anthony, ed. *Sojourners and Settlers: Histories of Southeast Asia and the Chinese*. Honolulu: University of Hawai'i Press, 1996.

Reid, Anthony, ed. *Southeast Asia in the Age of Commerce, 1450–1680: The Lands below the Winds*. New Haven, CT: Yale University Press, 1988.

Reyes, Raquel A. G. *Love, Passion, and Patriotism: Sexuality and the Philippine Propaganda Movement, 1882–1892*. Seattle: University of Washington Press, 2008.

Reynolds, E. Bruce. "History, Memory, Compensation, and Reconciliation: The Abuse of Labor along the Thailand-Burma Railway." In Kratoska, *Asian Labor*, 326–347.

Riot Inquiry Committee. *Final Report of the Riot Inquiry Committee*. Rangoon: Office of the Superintendent, Government Printing and Stationery, 1939.

Riot Inquiry Committee. *Interim Report of the Riot Inquiry Committee*. Rangoon: Office of the Superintendent, Government Printing and Stationery, 1939.

Roberts, Jayde Lin. *Mapping Chinese Rangoon: Place and Nation among the Sino-Burmese*. Seattle: University of Washington Press, 2016.

Roebuck, Kristin. "Science without Borders? The Contested Science of 'Race Mixing' circa World War II in Japan, East Asia, and the West." In *Who Is the Asianist? The Politics of Representation in Asian Studies*, edited by Will Bridges, Nitasha Tamar Sharma, and Marvin D. Sterling, 109–124. New York: Columbia University Press, 2022.

Rubin, Gayle. "The Traffic in Women: Notes on the 'Political Economy' of Sex." In *Toward an Anthropology of Women*, edited by Rayna Rapp Reiter, 157–210. New York: Monthly Review, 1975.

Saha, Jonathan. "The Male State: Colonialism, Corruption, and Rape Investigations in the Irrawaddy Delta c. 1900." *Indian Economic and Social History Review* 47, no. 3 (July/September 2010): 343–376.

Saito, Ayako. "The Formation of the Concept of Myanmar Muslims as Indigenous Citizens: Their History and Current Situation." *Journal of Sophia Asian Studies* 32 (2014): 25–40.

Sakai, Naoki. "Introduction: Nationality and the Politics of the 'Mother Tongue.'" In *Deconstructing Nationality*, edited by Naoki Sakai, Brett de Bary, and Iyotani Toshio, 1–38. Ithaca, NY: East Asia Program, Cornell University, 2005.

Sakakiyama, Jun. *Biruma no asa*. Tokyo: Nambokusha, 1963. Originally published in 1943.

Sarkar, Tanika. *Hindu Wife, Hindu Nation: Community, Religion, and Cultural Nationalism*. Bloomington: Indiana University Press, 2001.

Sarkissian, Margaret. "Armenians in South-East Asia." *Crossroads: An Interdisciplinary Journal of Southeast Asian Studies* 2, no. 3 (1987): 1–33.

Sarkisyanz, Emanuel. *Buddhist Backgrounds of the Burmese Revolution*. The Hague: Martinus Nijhoff, 1965.

Schendel, Jörg Armin. "The Mandalay Economy: Upper Burma's External Trade, c. 1850–90." PhD diss., University of Heidelberg, 2003.

Scott, James C. *Seeing Like a State: How Certain Schemes to Improve the Human Condition Have Failed*. New Haven, CT: Yale University Press, 1998.

Scott, James C. *Weapons of the Weak: Everyday Forms of Peasant Resistance*. New Haven, CT: Yale University Press, 1987.

Scott, James G. *Burma: A Handbook of Practical Information*. Rev. ed. London: A. Morning, 1911.

Scott, James George, and J. P. Hardiman. *Gazetteer of Upper Burma and the Shan States, Compiled from Official Papers by J. G. Scott, Assisted by J. P. Hardiman, Part 2*. Vols. 2–3. Rangoon: Superintendent of Government Printing, 1901.

Seki, Masaaki. *Nihongo kyōikushi kenkyū josetsu*. Tokyo: Suri E Network, 2004.

Sekupan Kai, ed. *Sekupan: Biruma nihongo gakkō no kiroku, 1942–1945*. Tokyo: Shudōsha, 1970.

Sen, Sudipta. "Liberalism and the British Empire in India." *Journal of Asian Studies* 74, no. 3 (August 2015): 711–722.

Seng, Guo-Quan. *Strangers in the Family: Gender, Patriliny, and the Chinese in Colonial Indonesia*. Ithaca, NY: Cornell University Press, 2023.

Shah, Nayan. *Stranger Intimacy: Contesting Race, Sexuality, and the Law in the North American West*. Berkeley: University of California Press, 2011.

Sharafi, Mitra. "The Marital Patchwork of Colonial South Asia: Forum Shopping from Britain to Baroda." *Law and History Review* 28 (2010): 979–1009.

Shiraishi, Saya. Introduction to Takao Fusayama, *A Japanese Memoir of Sumatra 1945–1946: Love and Hatred in the Liberation War*, 9–14. Ithaca, NY: Cornell Modern Indonesia Project, 1993.

Shwe Mann Thi. "Amyo anwe ma pyek si yan saung shauk kya gôn." *Mandalay Thuriya*, 21 July 1932, 1–2.

Siang, Song Ong. *One Hundred Years' History of the Chinese in Singapore*. Annotated ed. Singapore: National Library Board, 2020.

Silk, Jonathan. "The Victorian Creation of Buddhism: Review of Philip C. Almond, *The British Discovery of Buddhism*." *Journal of Indian Philosophy* 22, no. 2 (June 1994): 174–195.

Silverstein, Josef, ed. *Southeast Asia in World War II: Four Essays*. New Haven, CT: Yale University Southeast Asian Studies, 1966.

Silverstein, Josef, and Julian Wohl. "University Students and Politics in Burma." *Pacific Affairs* 37, no. 1 (1964): 50–65.

Singh, Nikhil Pal. "On Race, Violence, and So-Called Primitive Accumulation." *Social Text* 34, no. 3 (September 2016): 27–50.

Sinha, Mrinalini. *Colonial Masculinity: The "Manly Englishman" and the "Effeminate Bengali" in the Late Nineteenth Century*. Manchester: Manchester University Press, 1995.

Sinha, Mrinalini. *Specters of Mother India: The Global Restructuring of an Empire*. Durham, NC: Duke University Press, 2007.

Skinner, G. William. *Chinese Society in Thailand: An Analytical History*. Ithaca, NY: Cornell University Press, 1957.

Skinner, G. William. "Creolized Chinese Societies in Southeast Asia." In Reid, *Sojourners and Settlers*, 51–93.

Smith, Donald Eugene. *Religion and Politics in Burma*. Princeton, NJ: Princeton University Press, 1965.

Soh, Sarah C. *The Comfort Women: Sexual Violence and Postcolonial Memory in Korea and Japan*. Chicago: University of Chicago Press, 2008.

Spivak, Gayatri. "Can the Subaltern Speak?" In *Marxism and the Interpretation of Culture*, edited by Cary Nelson and Lawrence Grossberg, 271–314. Urbana: University of Illinois Press, 1988.

Sreenivas, Mytheli. *Wives, Widows, Concubines: The Conjugal Family Ideal in Colonial India*. Bloomington: Indiana University Press, 2008.

Stephens, Julia. *Governing Islam: Law, Empire, and Secularism in South Asia*. Cambridge: Cambridge University Press, 2018.

Stewart, A., and C. W. Dunn. *A Burmese-English Dictionary*. Rangoon: University of Rangoon, 1940.

Stoler, Ann L. *Carnal Knowledge and Imperial Power: Race and the Intimate in Colonial Rule*. Berkeley: University of California Press, 2002.

Stoler, Ann L., ed. *Haunted by Empire: Geographies of Intimacy in North American History*. Durham, NC: Duke University Press, 2006.

Stoler, Ann L. "Making Empire Respectable: The Politics of Race and Sexual Morality in 20th-Century Colonial Cultures." *American Ethnologist* 16, no. 4 (November 1989): 634–660.

Stretton, Tim, and Kirsta J. Kesselring, eds. *Married Women and the Law: Coverture in England and the Common Law World*. New York: Hill & Wang, 1998.

Sturman, Rachel. *The Government of Social Life in Colonial India: Liberalism, Religious Law, and Women's Rights*. Cambridge: Cambridge University Press, 2012.

Surkis, Judith. *Sex, Law, and Sovereignty in Algeria, 1830–1930*. Ithaca, NY: Cornell University Press, 2019.

Symes, Michael. *An Account of an Embassy to the Kingdom of Ava: Sent by the Governor-General of India in the Year 1795*. London: W. Bulmer, 1800.

Tagliacozzo, Eric. *The Longest Journey: Southeast Asians and the Pilgrimage to Mecca*. New York: Oxford University Press, 2013.

Tagliacozzo, Eric. "Morphological Shifts in Southeast Asian Prostitution: The Long Twentieth Century." *Journal of Global History* 3, no. 2 (July 2008): 251–273.

Tagliacozzo, Eric, Helen F. Siu, and Peter C. Perdue, eds. *Asia Inside Out: Changing Times*. Cambridge, MA: Harvard University Press, 2015.

Tagliacozzo, Eric, Helen F. Siu, and Peter C. Perdue, eds. *Asia Inside Out: Itinerant People*. Cambridge, MA: Harvard University Press, 2019.

Takami, Jun. *Biruma no inshō* (1943). In *Nanpō chōyō sakka sōsho, Biruma hen*, vol. 2, edited by Kimura Kazuaki and Takematsu Yoshiaki, 31–133. Tokyo: Ryūkei Shōsha, 2010.

Takano, Ikuro. *Jūgodai itō jirōzaemon suketami tsuisōroku*. Nagoya: Matsuzakaya, 1977.

Tanaka, Kakuei. "Biruma gawa shusai utage ni okeru Tanaka naikakusōri daijin aisatsu, 1974 nen 11 gatsu 7 nichi." In *Tanaka naikakusōri daijin enzetsu shū*, 569–571. Tokyo: Nihon kōhō kyōkai, 1975.

Tani, Yasuyo. *Nihongo kyōiku to kindai nihon*. Tokyo: Iwata Shoin, 2006.

Tarling, Nicholas. *The Japanese Occupation of Southeast Asia, 1941–1945*. Honolulu: University of Hawai'i Press, 2001.

Taw Sein Ko. "Buddhist Wills." *Journal of Burma Research Society* 7, no. 3 (December 1917): 274–277.

Taw Sein Ko. *Burmese Sketches*. Rangoon: British Burma Press, 1913.

Taw Sein Ko. "Correspondence on Buddhist Wills." *Journal of Burma Research Society* 7, no. 1 (April 1917): 56–57.

Taylor, Jean G. *The Social World of Batavia: European and Eurasian in Dutch Asia*. Rev. ed. Madison: University of Wisconsin Press, 2009. Originally published in 1983.

Taylor, Robert H. *The State in Myanmar*. Rev. and expanded ed. London: Hurst, 2008. Originally published in 1987.

Teng, Emma Jinhua. *Eurasian: Mixed Identities in the United States, China, and Hong Kong, 1842–1943*. Berkeley: University of California Press, 2013.

Teoh, Karen M. *Schooling Diaspora: Women, Education, and the Overseas Chinese in British Malaya and Singapore, 1850s–1960s*. New York: Oxford University Press, 2018.

Tha Gywe. "Burman Buddhist Wills." *Journal of Burma Research Society* 7, no. 1 (April 1917): 57–69.

Than Tun. "The Legal System in Burma, 1000–1300." *Burma Law Institute Journal* 1, no. 2 (June 1959): 171–184.

Than Tun, ed. *The Royal Orders of Burma, AD 1598–1855*. 10 vols. Kyoto: Center for Southeast Asian Studies, 1983–1990.

Thant Myint-U. *The Making of Modern Burma*. Cambridge: Cambridge University Press, 2001.

Thein Pe Myint. *Kala-Bama taik pwe*. Yangon: Nagani, 1938.

Thein Pe Myint. "Khin Myo Chit." Reprinted in *Thein Pe Myint wutthu do baung gyôk thit*, 19–40. Yangon: Ya pyi sa ôk taik, 1998.

Thein Pe Myint. *Sit atwin kayi the*. Rangoon: Shumawa sa ôk taik, 1952.

Thein Pe Myint. *What Happened in Burma: The Frank Revelations of a Young Burmese Revolutionary Leader Who Has Recently Escaped from Burma to India*. Allahabad: Kitabistan, 1943.

Thein Pe Myint, Thakin U. *Ko twe hmattan*. Yangon: Taing Chit, 1950.

Theippan Maung Wa. *Wartime in Burma: A Diary, January to June 1942*. Edited by L. E. Bagshawe and Anna J. Allott. Athens: Ohio University Press, 2009.

Thet Tun. *Than taw amyin: Bilingual Essays of Retired Ambassador U Thet Tun*. Yangon: Meik Kaung, 2000.

Tierney, Robert Thomas. *Tropics of Savagery: The Culture of Japanese Empire in Comparative Frame*. Berkeley: University of California Press, 2010.

Townsend, Camilla. *Malintzin's Choices: An Indian Woman in the Conquest of Mexico*. Albuquerque: University of New Mexico Press, 2006.

Travers, Robert. *Ideology and Empire in Eighteenth-Century India: The British Bengal*. Cambridge: Cambridge University Press, 2007.

Trevithick, Alan. *The Revival of Buddhist Pilgrimage at Bodh Gaya (1811–1949): Anagarika Dharmapala and the Mahabodhi Temple*. Delhi: Motilal Banarsidass, 2007.

Tsurumi, E. Patricia. *Japanese Colonial Education in Taiwan, 1895–1945*. Cambridge, MA: Harvard University Press, 1977.

Turner, Alicia M. *Saving Buddhism: The Impermanence of Religion in Colonial Burma*. Honolulu: University of Hawai'i Press, 2014.

U Tin, comp. *The Royal Administration of Burma*. Translated by Euan Bagshawe, foreword by Michael Aung-Thwin. Bangkok: Ava, 2001.

Uchida, Jun. *Brokers of Empire: Japanese Settler Colonialism in Korea, 1876–1945*. Cambridge, MA: Harvard University Asia Center, 2011.

Veer, Peter van de. *Imperial Encounters: Religion and Modernity in India and Britain*. Princeton, NJ: Princeton University Press, 2001.

Vergès, Françoise. *The Wombs of Women: Race, Capital, Feminism*. Durham, NC: Duke University Press, 2020.

Vickers, Edward, and Mark R. Frost. "Introduction: The 'Comfort Women' as Public History—Scholarship, Advocacy, and the Commemorative Impulse." In "The 'Comfort Women' as Public History," edited by Edward Vickers and Mark R. Frost, special issue, *Japan Focus: The Asia-Pacific Journal* 19, no. 5 (March 2021). https://apjjf.org/2021/5/Frost-Vickers.html.

Warabe, Naosuke. *Biruma kō*. Tokyo: Tōfūkaku, 1938.

Watanabe, Yoshinari. "Ethnic Policy towards Various 'Peoples' in the Early Konbaung Dynasty: Ethnic Awareness in Eighteenth to Nineteenth Century Burma." In *The Changing Self Image of Southeast Asian Society during the 19th and 20th Centuries*, edited by Ishii Yoneo, 27–53. Tokyo: Toyo Bunko, 2009.

Watson, Rubie S., and Patricia Ebrey, eds. *Marriage and Inequality in Chinese Society*. Berkeley: University of California Press, 1991.

White, Jenny B. *Money Makes Us Relatives: Women's Labor in Urban Turkey*. London: Routledge, 2004.

Winitchakul, Thongchai. *Siam Mapped: A History of the Geo-body of a Nation*. Honolulu: University of Hawai'i Press, 1994.

Wolters, O. W. *History, Culture, and Region in Southeast Asian Perspectives*. Ithaca, NY: Southeast Asian Program, Cornell University, 1999.

Wolters, O. W. *A Theory of Indigenous Southeast Asian Urbanism*. Singapore: Institute of Southeast Asian Studies, 1983.

Womack, William. "Contesting Indigenous and Female Authority in the Burma Baptist Mission: The Case of Ellen Mason." *Women's History Review* 17, no. 4 (September 2008): 543–559.

Wright, Arnold. *Twentieth Century Impressions of British Burma*. London: Lloyd's Greater Britain, 1910.

Yahaya, Nurfadzilah. *Fluid Jurisdictions: Colonial Law and Arabs in Southeast Asia*. Ithaca, NY: Cornell University Press, 2020.

Yamada, Hidezo. *Biruma no seikatsu*. Tokyo: Hōun sha, 1944.

Yang, Hyunah. "Finding the 'Map of Memory': Testimony of the Japanese Military Sexual Slavery Survivors." *Positions: East Asia Cultures Critique* 16, no. 1 (2008): 79–107.

Yegar, Moshe. *The Muslims of Burma*. Wiesbaden: O. Harrassowitz, 1972.

Yellen, Jeremy. *The Greater East Asia Co-Prosperity Sphere: When Total Empire Met Total War*. Ithaca, NY: Cornell University Press, 2019.

Yin Yin Htun. *Independent Daw San*. Yangon: Pinnya than saung pôn hneik taik, 2009.

Yoneyama, Lisa. *Cold War Ruins: Transpacific Critique of American Justice and Japanese War Crimes*. Durham, NC: Duke University Press, 2016.

Yoon, Won Zoon. "Japan's Occupation of Burma, 1941–1945." PhD diss., Columbia University, 1971.

Yoshiichi, Shigemitsu. *Gunzoku biruma monogatari*. Tokyo: Ōshisha, 1973.

Yule, Henry. *Narrative of Mission to the Court of Ava in 1855*. London: Smith, Elder, 1858.

Yule, Henry, and Arthur Coke Burnell. *Hobson-Jobson: A Glossary of Colloquial Anglo-Indian Words and Phrases, and of Kindred Terms, Etymological, Historical, Geographical and Discursive*. New ed., edited by William Crooke. London: John Murray, 1903.

Zaw Linn Aung. "Ito Jirozaemon Suketami and Sayadaw U Ottama: Refiguring the Japan-Myanmar Relations before World War II." *Journal of the Myanmar Academy of Arts and Sciences* 18, no. 7 (2020): 59–72.

Zaw Linn Aung. *Taing yin mutslim sa pyu sa so pôggo kyaw mya*. Yangon: Pan we we sa pe, 2013.

Zoellner, Hans-Bernd, ed. *Myanmar Literature Project Working Paper No. 10:12, Material on Thein Pe: Indo-Burman Conflict*. University of Passau, 2006.

Index

Figures and tables are indicated by *f* and *t* following the page number.

www.ingramcontent.com/pod-product-compliance
Lightning Source LLC
Chambersburg PA
CBHW030348270326
41926CB00009B/1001